INTELLECTUAL VIRTU

Out of the ferment of recent debates about the intellectual virtues, Roberts and Wood have developed an approach they call 'regulative epistemology'. This is partly a return to classical and medieval traditions, partly in the spirit of Locke's and Descartes's concern for intellectual formation, partly an exploration of connections between epistemology and ethics, and partly an approach that has never been tried before.

Standing on the shoulders of recent epistemologists—including William Alston, Alvin Plantinga, Ernest Sosa, and Linda Zagzebski—Roberts and Wood pursue epistemological questions by looking closely and deeply at particular traits of intellectual character such as love of knowledge, intellectual autonomy, intellectual generosity, and intellectual humility. Central to their vision is an account of intellectual goods that includes not just knowledge as properly grounded belief, but understanding and personal acquaintance, acquired and shared through the many social practices of actual intellectual life.

This approach to intellectual virtue infuses the discipline of epistemology with new life, and makes it interesting to people outside the small circle of professional epistemologists. It is epistemology for the whole intellectual community, as Roberts and Wood carefully sketch the ways in which virtues that would have been categorized earlier as moral make for agents who can better acquire, refine, and communicate important kinds of knowledge.

Robert C. Roberts is Distinguished Professor of Ethics at Baylor University.

W. Jay Wood is Professor of Philosophy at Wheaton College, Illinois.

INTELLECTUAL VIRTUES

An Essay in Regulative Epistemology

Robert C. Roberts

and

W. Jay Wood

CLARENDON PRESS · OXFORD

OXFORD
UNIVERSITY PRESS

Great Clarendon Street, Oxford OX2 6DP

Oxford University Press is a department of the University of Oxford.
It furthers the University's objective of excellence in research, scholarship,
and education by publishing worldwide in

Oxford New York

Auckland Cape Town Dar es Salaam Hong Kong Karachi
Kuala Lumpur Madrid Melbourne Mexico City Nairobi
New Delhi Shanghai Taipei Toronto

With offices in

Argentina Austria Brazil Chile Czech Republic France Greece
Guatemala Hungary Italy Japan Poland Portugal Singapore
South Korea Switzerland Thailand Turkey Ukraine Vietnam

Oxford is a registered trade mark of Oxford University Press
in the UK and in certain other countries

Published in the United States
by Oxford University Press Inc., New York

© Robert C. Roberts and W. Jay Wood 2007

The moral rights of the authors have been asserted
Database right Oxford University Press (maker)

First published 2007
First published in paperback 2009

All rights reserved. No part of this publication may be reproduced,
stored in a retrieval system, or transmitted, in any form or by any means,
without the prior permission in writing of Oxford University Press,
or as expressly permitted by law, or under terms agreed with the appropriate
reprographics rights organization. Enquiries concerning reproduction
outside the scope of the above should be sent to the Rights Department,
Oxford University Press, at the address above

You must not circulate this book in any other binding or cover
and you must impose the same condition on any acquirer

British Library Cataloguing in Publication Data

Data available

Library of Congress Cataloging in Publication Data

Data available

Typeset by Laserwords Private Limited, Chennai, India
Printed in Great Britain
by
The MPG Book Group

ISBN 978–0–19–928367–5 (Hbk.); 978–0–19–957570–1 (Pbk.)

10 9 8 7 6 5 4 3 2 1

With Gratitude, we Dedicate this Book to Alvin Plantinga

Acknowledgments

This book, which resulted from the collaboration of an epistemologist (Wood) and a moral psychologist (Roberts), began during the academic year 2002–3 when Wood was the recipient of a generous fellowship from Baylor University's Institute for Faith and Learning, under the leadership of Michael Beaty. That fellowship would not have existed apart from a program of improvement in the university more generally, a program called "Baylor 2012", whose chief architects were Robert Sloan and Don Schmeltekopf, with high-energy implementation a little later by David Jeffrey. These men also deserve our special thanks for the wonders they worked at Baylor during the first five years of the new millennium. Wood was also supported by a sabbatical leave and an Aldeen Grant from Wheaton College, and Baylor granted Roberts a teaching load reduction. For these forms of support, without which the book could not be appearing, we are grateful to Baylor and Wheaton. The early beginnings of our collaboration were supported in 1998–9 when Roberts had a Distinguished Scholar Fellowship at the Center for Philosophy of Religion at the University of Notre Dame, a Fellowship for College Teachers from the National Endowment for the Humanities, and a sabbatical leave from Wheaton College. We are grateful to Alvin Plantinga and Thomas Flint and the philosophy of religion seminar that gathered that year at Notre Dame, for three weeks of critical discussion of some of our initial efforts. In the summer of 2003 some chapters received critical discussion from a seminar sponsored by the Baptist Association of Philosophy Teachers, which met at Notre Dame. Several chapters also received useful discussion from philosophy department colloquia at Baylor and Wheaton, and at various meetings of the American Philosophical Association.

Individuals who deserve special thanks for their comments on earlier drafts of chapters are Robert Audi, Jason Baehr, Bob Baird, Mike Beaty, Sarah Borden, Todd Buras, David Cook, Steve Evans, John Greco, John Hare, Josh Hochschild, David Holley, Tom Kennedy, Bob Kruschwitz, Alasdair MacIntyre, Zach Manis, Michael Rea, Wayne Riggs, David Solomon, Margaret Watkins Tate, Linda Zagzebski, and an anonymous reviewer for Oxford University Press. Jason Baehr read especially widely in the manuscript and gave us many hours of fruitful discussion. Jim Marcum, Susan Bratton, and Gerry Cleaver each gave several hours of their time, sharing insights about the relevance of virtues and vices to the conduct of their own fields of scientific research, and a conversation with Ernan McMullen provided help with Chapter 9. Years ago (about 1985), Nick Wolterstorff encouraged Roberts to apply his thinking about the virtues to the problems of epistemology. We thank David O'Hara for showing us the passage from Charles Sanders Peirce that forms the epigraph, and Bruce Benson for advice concerning Continental thinkers. Alan Jacobs has been a constant companion in conversation about virtues, and he recommended readings that would not otherwise have come to our attention. We thank Steve Green for showing us the paper by Glenn Loury that is discussed in Chapter 5, and for discussion of it.

Earlier versions of two of the chapters have previously appeared in print: Chapter 9 as "Humility and Epistemic Goods", in Michael DePaul and Linda Zagzebski (eds), *Intellectual Virtue: Perspectives from Ethics and Epistemology* (Oxford: Oxford University Press, 2003), and Chapter 11 as "Generosity as an Intellectual Virtue", *The Cresset* 67 (2003): 10–22. A few passages were also pirated (and then modified) from our "Proper Function, Emotion, and Virtues of the Intellect", *Faith and Philosophy* 21 (2004): 3–24. Bible quotations are from the Revised Standard Version or the New Revised Standard Version, sometimes with modifications.

Contents

Were there nothing in reasoning more than the old traditional treatises set forth, then a rogue might be as good a reasoner as a man of honor; although a coward could not, even under such an idea of reasoning. But in induction a habit of probity is needed for success: a trickster is sure to play the confidence game upon himself. And in addition to probity, industry is essential. In the presumptive choice of hypotheses, still higher virtues are needed—a true elevation of soul. At the very lowest, a man must prefer the truth to his own interest and well-being and not merely to his bread and butter, and to his own vanity, too, if he is to do much in science. This ... is thoroughly borne out by examining the characters of scientific men and of great heuretic students of all kinds. ... we can perceive that good reasoning and good morals are closely allied; and I suspect that with the further development of ethics this relation will be found to be even more intimate than we can, as yet, prove it to be.

C. S. Peirce, "Minute Logic"

PART I
Contexts

1

Epistemology

Introduction

Human knowledge, understanding, and experience are as distinctive of our life as anything, including even the opposed thumb and erect posture, and the varieties of them are among the deepest distinguishers of human beings from one another. Virtually every people across the world are concerned to educate their children in what they take to be knowledge, understanding, and powers of recognition. The human tribe form universities for finding and transmitting knowledge, and many of us think a university education to be far more than equipment for survival and financial prosperity. We think that knowing what the sciences and history can teach, and understanding what great literature and philosophy can help us to understand, are themselves a kind of prosperity, indeed a necessary and central component of the highest human flourishing. In some societies, and in some corners even of our own society, some of the elderly are held in special esteem because of their wisdom, which is taken to be a rare achievement and legacy of great value.

The ancient discipline that philosophers call epistemology is the study of human knowledge and related epistemic goods. Every university discipline is, of course, a study of human knowledge (chemistry studying chemical knowledge, history historical knowledge, and so forth), but epistemology is a study of the *concept* of knowledge. It turns reflective about this ubiquitous concern, this central and distinctive human good, and asks critical and normative questions about it: What is knowledge and what are its limits? Can we know anything? How do we know what we know? Can we know something without knowing that we know it? What is the proper basis of knowledge? What are the faculties by which we know? What are the proper objects of knowledge? Is genuine knowledge immune from error, or is fallible knowledge a coherent concept?

Philosophers have offered various and conflicting answers to such questions, but since knowledge, like ethics, is everybody's practical business, epistemology's aims have seldom been merely descriptive. Accounts of the nature and reach of our faculties typically come bundled with prescriptions concerning how we ought to regulate our intellectual lives. "Don't look to the senses for knowledge" (Plato); "Don't look beyond the senses for knowledge" (David Hume); "Accept testimony only from sources whose reliability is known to you" (John Locke); "Accept testimony from any source you do not have good reason to question" (Thomas Reid); "It is wrong always, everywhere, for anyone, to believe anything on insufficient evidence" (William Clifford); "It is not wrong to accept some beliefs in the absence of evidence" (Alvin Plantinga).

Epistemological debates in the twentieth century were especially tumultuous. Early twentieth-century rationalisms and idealisms gave way to an empiricism that, as if unaware of what Kant had written, thought that everything we know about the world must arise out of sensory experience (tautologies are also an important sort of truth, but not about the world). The nature of sensation and perception and debates about sense data figured prominently in epistemological controversies of the first half of the twentieth century. Some empiricists noted that although one may be mistaken in claims about material objects and states of affairs, no such errors attach to immediate sensory deliverances: I may err in thinking I'm seeing a tree, but I can hardly be mistaken in seeming to be seeing a tree. Thus Rudolph Carnap, a logical positivist, believed that an incorrigible science could be constructed from the invincible reports of sensation and the connectives of first-order predicate logic. If this were possible, it would show that empirical science could deliver knowledge that satisfied the ancient Greek gold standard for knowledge, viz., indefeasible certainty.

Empiricists tended to think science the premier knowledge-generating enterprise. If any practice can confer irrefragable epistemic goods, it is science, not metaphysics or religion. And the success of science is due to its methods. Given sufficient background information and skill, one need only ply the right technique or follow the right rules to achieve knowledge and justified belief. Looking longingly on the success of modern science, epistemologists have devised methods of their own: the Baconian method, Descartes's *Rules for the Direction of the Mind*, Locke's Historical Plain Method, Mill's methods, Husserl's phenomenological method, and so forth. So the concerns of epistemology were bound up with the concerns of science. Does scientific knowledge form a hierarchical or foundationalist structure? Are the observations on which scientific claims are based free of theoretical content? Must scientific standards of evidence and confirmation be met before we are justified in believing something? Linked to these questions are the familiar epistemological controversies over foundationalism, the theory-ladenness of observation statements, and the standards for epistemic justification.

Starting in the 1950s, the association of science with foundationalism and its aspirations to certainty came under heavy attack from philosophers of science such as N. R. Hanson, Stephen Toulmin, Michael Polanyi, and Thomas Kuhn, whose personal acquaintance with science and scientific methods suggested to them that science falls far short of the foundationalist ideal of an edifice consisting of a groundwork of unshakeable basic statements fastened firmly to a rich superstructure of knowledge by the well-tempered bolts of modern logic. The problems with this picture are legion. Our empirical observations are theory-laden and susceptible to error, our reasoning depends on unprovable assumptions, our criteria for dividing justifier and justified are unclear, and our standards of evidence and argumentation contested, to cite just a few of the problems. The reigning epistemological paradigm of the first half of the century came under withering fire, from which, some say, it has not recovered.

Whatever difficulties epistemologists may have faced in describing the sources and structure of knowledge, at least they shared a common concept of knowledge as justified true belief—until 1963, when Edmund Gettier's famous three-pager appeared,[1] offering a small array of cases of justified true belief that seemed pretty clearly not to be cases of knowledge. The rough consensus about the definition of knowledge that had held for over 2,000 years unraveled. A cottage industry sprang up in response, as scores of epistemologists wove thousands of pages to repair the damage done when Gettier tugged on that loose thread. Notions of truth, certainty, belief, justification, and other epistemological concepts were also judged inadequate or unworkable after similar deconstructive analysis. Epistemologists

---

[1] Edmund Gettier, "Is Justified True Belief Knowledge?", *Analysis* 23 (1963): 121–3.

appeared to think that salvation from Gettier lay in fastidiousness and technical finery, so that epistemology became increasingly ingrown, epicyclical, and irrelevant to broader philosophical and human concerns. The fortunes of the guild were in steep decline from the halcyon days when discussions about the right use of reason were supposed to lay the groundwork of lasting epistemological happiness.

The last thirty years have seen radical departures from old ways of doing business. Epistemological naturalists, such as W. V. O. Quine, think that the time-honored task of describing the nature and limits of reason should be handed over to cognitive scientists. Anti-theorists like Richard Rorty urge us to look to literature and poetry for guidance about the right use of reason. Epistemologists of a more traditional vein, like William Alston and Alvin Plantinga, nevertheless break ranks with long-standing views about justification and warrant. Others have simply despaired. Articles with titles such as "The False Hopes of Traditional Epistemology"[2] and "Recent Obituaries of Epistemology"[3] have appeared. In an article entitled "Overcoming Epistemology", Charles Taylor writes: "it seems to be rapidly becoming a new orthodoxy that the whole enterprise from Descartes, through Locke and Kant, and pursued by various nineteenth and twentieth century succession movements, was a mistake."[4] No neo-orthodoxy has emerged concerning the proper projects of epistemology. Contemporary epistemology's disarray has nevertheless yielded this positive result: the discipline is more receptive than ever to new ideas.

Virtue Epistemologies

A most promising development is epistemologists' recent attention to the human virtues. Philosophical reflection about the intellectual virtues is still in its infancy, but we think it holds enormous promise for the recovery of epistemology as a philosophical discipline with broad human importance.

---

[2] Bas van Fraasen, "The False Hopes of Traditional Epistemology", *Philosophy and Phenomenological Research* 60 (2000): 253–80.

[3] Susan Haack, "Recent Obituaries of Epistemology", *American Philosophical Quarterly* 27 (1990): 199–212.

[4] "Overcoming Epistemology", in Kenneth Baynes, James Bohman, and Thomas McCarthy (eds), *After Philosophy, End or Transformation*, (Cambridge, MA: MIT Press, 1987), p. 465.

The first stirrings of this recovery were Ernest Sosa's early essays,[5] the first of which is now more than twenty years old. Sosa and some of his disciples tended to think of the intellectual virtues as faculties (eyesight, hearing, introspection, memory, inferential reason, a priori intuition, etc.),[6] but more recently Linda Zagzebski,[7] with some inspiration from Lorraine Code[8] and James Montmarquet,[9] has focused on virtues like intellectual courage, generosity, tenacity, openness, and humility—dispositions that are not faculties, but character traits. Thus her notion of virtue is much closer to that of the philosophical tradition and our contemporary ordinary language. Focusing on virtues in this sense also seems to offer a better prospect of humanizing and deepening epistemology.

Another important philosopher in this development is Alvin Plantinga. Although Plantinga, like Sosa, focuses his epistemology on the performances of faculties, but, unlike Sosa, does not use the language of virtue, we think that his epistemology is an incipient virtues epistemology[10]—indeed, more so than Sosa's, for two reasons. First, he defines knowledge as warranted true belief and defines warrant in terms of the proper functioning of epistemic faculties in a congenial environment.[11] The notion of proper function is reminiscent of the classical and medieval understanding of virtues: virtues are bases of excellent human functioning, and epistemic virtues are bases of excellent epistemic functioning. Second, Plantinga's thought stretches in the direction of virtues that are not merely properly functioning faculties, because his religious commitment draws him away from the trivial examples of belief formation that are so characteristic of recent epistemology (believing that one's wife is home or that the lawn in one's backyard is green). In the third volume of his epistemology Plantinga focuses on the deep and character-involving knowledge of God, and follows Jonathan Edwards in giving the emotions an important role in

---

[5] See the essays collected in Ernest Sosa, *Knowledge in Perspective* (Cambridge: Cambridge University Press, 1991).

[6] See Ch. 4 below for refinement of this statement.

[7] Linda Zagzebski, *Virtues of the Mind: An Inquiry into the Nature of Virtue and the Ethical Foundations of Knowledge* (Cambridge: Cambridge University Press, 1996).

[8] Loraine Code, *Epistemic Responsibility* (Hanover, NH: University Press of New England, 1987).

[9] James Montmarquet, *Epistemic Virtue and Doxastic Responsibility* (Lanham, MD: Rowman and Littlefield, 1993).

[10] We will pursue this thesis further in Ch. 4; we developed it in a somewhat different direction in R. C. Roberts and W. J. Wood, "Proper Function, Emotion, and Virtues of the Intellect", *Faith and Philosophy* 21 (2004): 3–24.

[11] Alvin Plantinga, *Warrant and Proper Function* (New York: Oxford University Press, 1993).

the formation of this kind of knowledge. In attending to the involvement of emotions in the knowledge of God, Plantinga is striking a theme that has been nearly constant across the ages in philosophical discussions of the moral virtues. The life of virtue is composed of appetitive dispositions, and emotions are consequences of caring about things, of taking some things to be important, of having steady, long-term desires for things of value.

The triviality of standard epistemology's examples is due in part to the historical preoccupation with skepticism. If one cannot secure so simple a claim as "I have two hands" or "The world has existed for quite a while" against the mischief of evil demons and manipulative brain scientists, it makes little sense to worry about how we know difficult truths about the causes of the Second World War or the structure of DNA. Anti-skeptical maneuvers are a strong motif in the history of philosophy: Plato opposes the Sophists, Augustine the academic skeptics, Descartes Montaigne, Reid Hume, and Moore and Wittgenstein set themselves against skepticism inspired by Russell. However dominant anti-skepticism may be historically, some of epistemology's most productive moments—in Aquinas, Kant, Plantinga—arose because philosophers were willing to set aside skeptical worries and look into what ordinary practitioners of science, religion, politics, and humanistic inquiry were willing to call knowledge. Intellectual virtues of the kind that interest Zagzebski and us seem likely to have relevance to high-end kinds of knowledge like scientific discoveries, the subtle understanding of difficult texts, moral self-knowledge, and knowledge of God, while being marginal to knowing, upon taking a look, that a bird is outside my window, or that what is in front of me is white paper.

Given the central place of knowledge and understanding in human life, one would expect epistemology to be one of the most fascinating and enriching fields of philosophy and itself an important part of an education for life. We might expect that any bright university student who got all the way to her junior year without dipping her mind in an epistemology course would have to hang her head in shame of her cultural poverty. But the character and preoccupations of much of the epistemology of the twentieth century disappoint this expectation. We think that the new emphasis on the virtues and their relation to epistemic goods has the potential to put epistemology in its rightful place. And we hope that the present book, whatever its many shortcomings in detail, will suggest the rich ways in which epistemology—the study of knowledge and related human goods—connects with ethical and political issues, with the practice of science and other forms of inquiry, with religion and spirituality, with appreciation of the arts, and with the enterprise of education.

Defining Knowledge

The concern to broaden and humanize the discipline is at best a peripheral concern of the contemporary epistemologists we have mentioned. The concepts of the virtues and proper function interest them chiefly as providing new strategies for achieving old epistemological goals, prominent among them that of defining knowledge in the traditional style. Zagzebski, for example, says, that "the most critical concern of epistemology ... [is] the analysis of knowledge" (*Virtues of the Mind*, p. 259). All these philosophers accept the general model of knowledge as adequately grounded (warranted, justified) true belief and seek a conception of such grounding, or some supplement to that grounding, that enables them to specify the logically necessary and sufficient conditions for any belief's being a case of knowledge. Let us call this kind of knowledge "propositional knowledge", to distinguish it from the broader and richer concept of knowledge that we will outline in Chapter 2. And we call a definition of propositional knowledge an "e-definition" when it is in the style that has dominated recent epistemology—namely, a formula proposing logically necessary and sufficient conditions. Consider some proposed definitions of knowledge in this style.

Sosa distinguishes "animal knowledge" from "reflective knowledge" and defines animal knowledge as any true belief produced by an intellectual virtue (that is, an epistemic faculty) in an environment that is appropriate for that virtue; reflective (that is, distinctively human) knowledge is animal knowledge about which the epistemic subject has another ("reflective") belief: namely, the belief that his animal knowledge in question was produced by a virtuous belief-producing process, and this reflective belief too is true and produced by a virtue. Plantinga defines knowledge, roughly, as any true belief produced by a faculty or faculties that are aimed at truth and are functioning properly in an appropriate environment according to a good design plan. We say "roughly" because in the second chapter of *Warrant and Proper Function* Plantinga considers a number of needed qualifications of his already complex formula and gives up the effort to produce a precise definition with the words, "What we need to fill out the account is not an ever-increasing set of additional conditions and subconditions; that way lies paralysis" (p. 47). Earlier he had said, "Maybe there isn't any neat formula, any short and snappy list of conditions (at once informative and precise) that are severally necessary and jointly sufficient for warrant; if so, we won't make much progress by grimly pursuing them" (p. 20). And he goes on to fill out the account by looking in some detail at several particular faculties, to show how the proper function approach to knowledge solves problems that stymie other approaches. We have said already that the kind of virtue that Zagzebski makes central has potential for deepening and humanizing epistemology, but little potential for the routine epistemological goal of e-defining knowledge. The reason is that an e-definition has to specify conditions that are necessary for all the cases, including very simple ones, such as the following: I am sitting in a room at night with the lights blazing, and suddenly all the lights go out. Automatically, without reflection or any other kind of effort, I form the belief that the lights have gone out. Clearly, I *know* that the lights went out, and it didn't take any act of intellectual courage, humility, attentiveness, perseverance, or any other virtue to do so.[12] Despite the apparent awkwardness of making the concept of an intellectual virtue the key to an e-definition of knowledge, Zagzebski defines knowledge as any true belief produced by an act of intellectual virtue, and she struggles to accommodate the low-end cases of knowledge to her definition (see *Virtues of the Mind*, pp. 277–83).

We see here a dilemma for the virtue epistemologist. Plantinga's and Sosa's definitions of knowledge are pretty good at specifying conditions that are necessary for the whole range of cases, because they aim *very low*. They are particularly well-designed to accommodate cases like the lights-out case, because really, all you need in such simple cases is well-functioning faculties in an appropriate environment. But faculty-oriented definitions are poor at specifying conditions that are sufficient for the whole range of cases. It is implausible to think that all you need, to make great scientific discoveries or gain a deep understanding of your own moral

---

[12] We owe the example to Jason Baehr. See his article "Virtue Epistemology" in the Internet Encyclopedia of Philosophy.

nature, is well-functioning faculties like eyesight, hearing, logical powers, and the like. It seems that you do need traits like courage, perseverance, humility, and love of truth. So definitions like Zagzebski's are pretty good at specifying sufficient conditions: a person with trait virtues will be able, in all likelihood, to get knowledge from the highest to the lowest. The trouble for her definition is that it's implausible to think you need such virtues to know that the lights have just gone out. It seems that neither kind of virtue epistemologist will succeed in e-defining knowledge. So we might think that we need a disjunctive definition that says something like the following: A true belief is knowledge just in case it is produced either by a faculty virtue in a congenial environment or by acts or an act of an intellectual trait virtue, but not necessarily both. Toward the end of this section we will see why such a definition will not succeed.

Let us take a closer look at Zagzebski's definition of knowledge. She argues that Gettier cases (see pp. 283–99) all have a common structure in which the subject gets a true belief, and does so in a way that is canonical (that is, justifying, warranting) by some definition of knowledge, but in which the connection between the way the belief is justified or warranted and the truth of the belief is somehow accidental. Accordingly, she offers a recipe for concocting Gettier cases that works no matter whether you make the canonical grounding internalist justification, externalist justification, or warrant.[13] Here is Zagzebski's recipe: Start with a case of well-grounded (justified, warranted) belief (by well-grounded, we mean well-grounded enough that, if the belief is true, it will ordinarily be knowledge). Make the belief epistemically unlucky (that is, such that, despite being well-grounded, the belief would not be true except in very lucky circumstances).[14] You

---

[13] Internalist justification is justification by some factor, such as evidence, to which the subject has reflective access, at least potentially. Thus a person might be justified in believing that he is famous by seeing himself often discussed in newspapers. This is an internalist justification because the subject has reflective access to the justifying factor, as well as, in all likelihood, the *way* in which such a factor justifies. Externalist justification (warrant) is justification by some factor to which the subject does not necessarily have access. A person might be justified in his belief that there is white paper in front of him by the fact that white paper is appearing to him visually, without his having reflective access to how such an appearance justifies his belief.

[14] Zagzebski says, "Start with a case of justified (or warranted) false belief. ... Now amend the case by adding another element of luck, only this time an element that makes the belief true after all" (*Virtues of the Mind*, pp. 288–9f). But obviously, the false belief cannot be the main belief of the Gettier example, since that is a justified true belief. The Gettier examples do not involve any belief's changing truth-value. Thus we have slightly reformulated Zagzebski's recipe.

can do this only because well-grounding does not entail truth. Add another element of luck to the case, which makes the unlucky belief true. And *voilà!* You have whipped up a Gettier case. Consider some.

An internalist case. In the original Gettier case of *Smith owns a Ford or Brown is in Barcelona* you are justified in believing the proposition because you have excellent evidence that Smith owns a Ford, though you have no idea where Brown is. However, Smith has been pulling your leg; but improbably enough, Brown happens to be in Barcelona. Thus you have a justified true belief, but not knowledge. You are unlucky enough to be plausibly lied to by Smith, but your mischance is reversed by the luck that Brown is in Barcelona.

A reliabilist case. You're driving in rural Wisconsin, where the inhabitants, eager to appear prosperous, have erected three fake barn façades for every real barn. You are a reliable barn-spotter and, happening to look at one of the real ones, you form the belief *there's a barn*. Your belief is true and justified, but not knowledge. In this case you're unlucky enough to be driving through a neighborhood beset by deceptive appearances, but this misluck is corrected by your just happening to fix on a real barn.

A proper function case. Mary has properly functioning but not infallible eyes; she looks at her husband's usual chair in normal lighting from about fifteen feet away and forms the belief that her husband *Herb is sitting in the living room*. So the environment is normal, and her faculties are functioning properly. But the man sitting in the chair is her husband's brother, who looks very much like Herb. But, as it turns out, Herb is sitting in the living room, out of her sight. So she has a warranted true belief that is not knowledge.

But can't we construct, following Zagzebski's recipe, a counterexample to her own definition of knowledge? Consider

A virtues case. Sam is a forensic pathologist well known for his care, creativity, and persistence in solving difficult cases. A case of poisoning has stumped him because at the current state of the art the poison involved is undetectable. Sam wracks his brain for a compound that will detect the suspected poison, and after several days of agonizing research and a few sleepless nights he hits on a formula. He goes to the lab in the middle of the night and combines three substances according to a formula that calls for particular amounts in a particular sequence. Unknown to him, a jar from which he got one of the substances was mislabeled by his lab assistant and in fact contains something completely inert. He goes home satisfied that in the morning he will have a solution to the case. During the night the janitor inadvertently spills a bit of the needed third substance on the slide that Sam will use the following morning to conduct his test. When Sam runs the test the next day, he gets the result he wanted, and declares that *the murder poison was X*, as indeed it was. Thus Sam has a true belief, acquired by the performance of acts of intellectual virtue, which is not knowledge. The assistant's mislabeling the jar is Sam's bad luck, and the janitor's spilling the right substance on the slide in just the night amount, is his good luck.

Zagzebski does not apply her recipe to a virtues case. In fact, she offers it as a prelude to showing that her e-definition succeeds where all the others fail. She thinks it succeeds because grounding in intellectual virtues, unlike grounding in all the other ways, *entails truth*. She holds that acts of virtue necessarily succeed in their goals, and so acts of intellectual virtue always succeed in securing the truth. She argues as follows. Suppose a jury judges a case as virtuously as possible. All the jury members deliberate with consummate skill and desire with the purest hearts that justice be done in the case before them. But the result of their verdict is that an innocent man is sent to prison for twenty years. In that case we do not call their action an *act of justice*. An act of justice is by definition one that succeeds in bringing about justice. The jury may well have acted justly, but it has not performed an act of justice. And similarly for all other cases of virtues, we can distinguish *acting V-ly* from *performing an act of V*. Since intellectual virtues are virtues that aim at the truth, we can make the same distinction there, with the result that no act of intellectual virtue can fail to secure the truth.

Zagzebski errs in extrapolating from the case of an act of justice to all other acts of virtue. We think that her intuition about the English phrases "act justly" and "perform an act of justice" has some merit, but most of the other virtues do not follow suit. From the fact that I performed an act of generosity, it does not follow that I actually helped anybody. From the fact that I performed an act of perseverance toward some goal, it does not follow that I achieved the goal. The same is true of intellectual virtues. A person can perform acts of open-mindedness, of diligence in investigations, of charity in his interpretations of others' views, of honesty with himself and with others, and still not hit on the truth. For example, had it not been for the clumsy janitor, Sam would not have got the truth about the poisoning case, despite an impeccable sequence of acts of intellectual virtue.

The requirement, in Zagzebski's definition, that the act of intellectual virtue guarantee the truth of the belief that it generates, trades on so artificial a conception of an act of intellectual virtue as to make the definition *ad hoc* and insufficiently informative, thus violating her own stated standards for a good definition. In her discussion of desiderata in definitions, Zagzebski says that while a definition needs to be Gettier-proof, it must not be artificially tailored to guarantee this result.[15] For example, it would not be legitimate to avoid Gettier examples by defining knowledge as *"justified true belief that is not a Gettier case"* (ibid., p. 102). The concepts of a virtue and of an act of virtue have the merit of being uncontrived: they are widespread in the history of philosophy and in ordinary discourse about both ethics and knowledge (see ibid., p. 106). But the infallibility of acts of virtues presupposed by her definition of knowledge is not a noticeable part of that history, or of ordinary people's use of 'virtue'; her particular twist on the concept of an act of virtue seems specially tailored for closing the gap between justification and truth. Besides avoiding *ad hoc* stipulation, the definition should be informative, giving us insight into the nature of knowledge that we would not have without it. In particular, her definition should allow us to identify cases of knowledge if only we know whether the beliefs in question were produced by acts of intellectual virtue. But on her understanding of "act of intellectual virtue", we cannot tell whether an intellectual act is an act of intellectual virtue unless we know *independently* whether the belief that it generated was true.

We might wonder whether the same strategy of avoiding Gettier examples by defining the justifier so as to guarantee its achieving truth is not available to advocates of other epistemological theories. What if a reliabilist were to distinguish beliefs produced by a reliable belief-producing process from beliefs produced reliably by such a process? Couldn't the reliabilist then claim that any false beliefs produced by a reliable belief-producing process were not *produced reliably* by such a process, and therefore could not be used in constructing Gettier examples? Or perhaps Plantinga could close

---

[15] Linda Zagzebski, "What is Knowledge?", in John Greco (ed.), *The Blackwell Guide to Epistemology* (Oxford: Blackwell, 1992), pp. 92–116, p. 104.

the gap between properly functioning faculties and truth by distinguishing beliefs produced by properly functioning faculties from beliefs *produced properly* by such faculties.

We earlier offered a simple counterexample to Plantinga's proper function account. We expect that Plantinga will regard our "counterexample" as anything but such. Following the drift of his discussion of Gettier cases in *Warrant and Proper Function* (pp. 31–7), no doubt he will say that we haven't made the environment normal or paradigmatic. There is something "tricky" about this environment, and consequently Mary is *not* warranted in believing that Herb is sitting in the living room. Such an answer as this raises the question: Exactly *how* normal or paradigmatic must the environment be for a belief produced by properly functioning faculties in that environment to be warranted for the subject? If the concept of *normal* here is such that for any Gettier case, necessarily, the environment (or the functioning of the faculty) is not normal, then of course the proper function construal of warrant avoids Gettier problems. But this solution seems as artificial as Zagzebski's redefinition of *act of intellectual virtue*, because surely, in normal everyday discourse and thought, a person might well think that Mary is warranted in her belief, despite the trickiness of the environment. And if such an ordinary epistemological thinker were asked why he thinks she is warranted in her belief, he might (if articulate enough) cite Plantingian criteria for warrant: she has good eyesight, the lighting was decent, her distance from the object was in the range prescribed for good viewing, etc. So we might think that for the Plantingian criteria to be realistic, there must be the normal flexibility in the concept of *normal* and thus some room for warranted beliefs that are not true (or that are, as in Gettier cases, true only by a stroke of good luck). Otherwise there is something fishy about the concept of warrant.

It might be thought that our counterexample fails to meet the conditions of Zagzebski's definition of knowledge because the *truth* of Sam's belief that the poison was X does not derive from his acts of intellectual virtue. Admittedly, his acts of intellectual virtue had something to do with his getting the truth, but the clumsy janitor seems to be causally crucial too. So it is hard to tell what to say about the case. As Zagzebski admits, it is unclear what *because of* means in her requirement that the believing of the truth be *because of* the agent's acts of virtue (see ibid., pp. 108, 111).

John Greco[16] uses a strategy similar to Zagzebski's in defining knowledge, but seems to avoid the pitfalls of Zagzebski's definition. In particular, he does not try to make justification entail truth, and he gives us a clear enough account of what 'because of' means when he says that the agent believes the truth because of his intellectual virtue. Like Zagzebski's project, Greco's definition is largely driven by the desire to avoid counterexamples in which the subject's justified true belief fails to be knowledge because of something accidental in the way the belief turns out to be true. The lottery problem is such a case: Nate buys a lottery ticket and then, on the basis of information about the odds against winning, forms the true belief that he will lose. His inductive evidence is excellent, much better than for many cases of inductively based knowledge; yet we do not think he knows he will lose. The Gettier cases are other examples. Greco's solution is to develop a concept of responsibility for getting the truth, and then to say that an epistemic agent knows a truth p only if he is responsible, in that sense, for getting the truth in believing p. He says, "The key idea here is not that knowledge requires responsibility *in* one's conduct, although that might also be the case, but that knowledge requires responsibility *for* true belief" (p. 111).

We can explain Greco's concept of responsibility by comparing it with a couple of other concepts.

A) Responsibility *in* one's conduct:
   One does what it canonically takes to get X right.
B) A common concept of being responsible *for* getting X right:
   One does what it canonically takes to get X right.
   One gets X right.
C) Greco's concept of being responsible *for* getting X right:
   One does what it canonically takes to get X right.
   One gets X right.
   What one does *in* getting X right is the most salient causal explanation *of* one's getting X right.

His explanation of why Nate in the lottery case, and the subjects in the Gettier cases, do not have knowledge, is that the epistemically virtuous behavior by which they form their true belief is not the *most salient*

[16] John Greco, "Knowledge as Credit for True Belief", in Michael DePaul and Linda Zagzebski (eds), *Intellectual Virtue: Perspectives from Ethics and Epistemology* (Oxford: Oxford University Press, 2003), pp. 111–34.

explanation of how they came to have the right belief; instead, something accidental is *more* explanatorily prominent. By contrast, in cases of knowledge by induction the act of induction is salient in the causal story, and in cases of justified true belief that are knowledge the justifier is salient in the explanation of how the agent got the true belief.

> Greco's definition of knowledge has three clauses: S knows *p iff*
>
> S's believing *p* is *subjectively* justified in the following sense: S's believing *p* is the result of dispositions that S manifests when S is trying to believe the truth,
>
> and
>
> S's believing *p* is *objectively* justified in the following sense: the dispositions that result in S's believing *p* make S reliable in believing *p*. Alternatively, the dispositions that result in S's believing *p* constitute intellectual abilities, or powers, or virtues,
>
> and
>
> S believes the truth regarding *p because* S is reliable in believing *p*. Alternatively: the intellectual abilities (i.e., powers or virtues) that result in S's believing the truth regarding *p* are an important necessary part of the total set of causal factors that give rise to S's believing the truth regarding *p*. (pp. 127, 128)

The structure of this definition makes clear that the causal condition is *added to* the two justification conditions; justification does not *entail* getting the truth. In particular, it specifies how the objective justifier—the traits that make S a reliable producer of true beliefs—must cause S's believing the truth in believing *p*, if believing *p* is to amount to knowledge. And Greco's concept of being responsible *for* getting X right (see above), in which the notion of salience or importance or prominence plays a key role, seems to us to be an ordinary and natural concept, not one that is contrived simply for avoiding counterexamples. The concept of salience or importance that is crucial to Greco's explanation of believing the truth because of S's intellectual virtues is vague (just *how* important or salient must S's intellectual virtues be in the explanation of how S gets the truth of *p*? and what is salience, after all?), but this vagueness may not prevent its being informative.

However, once the causal condition is made informative, the definition becomes vulnerable to both Gettier examples and straightforward counterexamples. Our case of Sam the forensic pathologist is a Gettier-type case. Sam's virtuous epistemic behavior is very salient in his getting the truth that the poison was X; the accidental intervention of the clumsy janitor seems a minor contribution by comparison, though it is admittedly crucial. Greco might defend his definition by saying that Sam's virtuous behavior is not salient *enough*. But this would be exactly the kind of special pleading that everybody admits we need to avoid. However, even if we allow the definition to escape the counterexample on the grounds that Sam's virtuous behavior is not a salient enough cause of his getting the truth, the definition falls prey to straightforward counterexamples.

In Charles Dickens's *A Christmas Carol* Ebenezer Scrooge lacks the knowledge that he is a mean old miser. With rationalizations such as "I've worked hard for every penny I've got" and "if those shiftless poor would only bestir themselves, they wouldn't be so wretched", he explains away every challenge to his picture of himself as a frugal hard-working businessman. Then comes the epistemic pressure. First Jacob Marley's ghost appears to Scrooge, doomed to carry the symbols of his greed chained to his body. He comes to warn Scrooge that he is indeed a mean old miser and will suffer a similar fate unless he changes his ways. Scrooge explains away the apparition by attributing it to undigested beef, then he goes to bed and promptly falls asleep. The ghost of Christmas Past appears next, taking Scrooge back to a kinder and gentler time of his life, to convince him that he once embraced a different understanding of himself. He still resists. Then the ghost of Christmas Present shows Scrooge the family of Bob Cratchit and the suffering Tiny Tim. Scrooge is softened, but still not to the level of assent. Finally, the ghost of Christmas Future pulls out all the stops, and shows Scrooge his own lonely, unmourned, pathetic death, and the hell that awaits him. The cumulative effect of these cognitive onslaughts is to disarm his ability to resist assent; Scrooge's will-to-ignorance is overwhelmed. The knowledge comes to him unbidden. Of course Scrooge's epistemic capacities make some contribution to his getting knowledge; he hears and understands the words of the various ghosts, and there is a limit to his powers of rationalization. But Nate in the lottery case, and the subject in the case of Smith owns a Ford or Brown is in Barcelona, also display a modicum of virtuous behavior. Greco's point is that the primary or salient explanation of how they got their true beliefs is something other than their virtuous behavior, and this is true of Scrooge as well. We say that Scrooge has genuine knowledge of himself, and in the causal story of this knowledge Scrooge's intellectual virtues play a relatively minor role.

We have seen that recent virtue epistemologists have tried to use the concept of a virtue to answer routine[17] questions of late twentieth-century epistemology, especially in formulating definitions of justification, warrant, and knowledge. We have given our reasons for thinking that the latest efforts have not succeeded. It appears to us that the reason why simple definitions fail is the complexity and diversity within the concept of knowledge. The concept may be held together by a set of overlapping resemblances between kinds of cases, as Wittgenstein argued that the concept of *game* is, rather than by a single set of properties that are both individually necessary and jointly sufficient for any case to belong to the class.[18] To take Greco's definition as an example, he is surely right about *many* cases of knowledge, that it is a necessary condition of their being knowledge that the agent's epistemic excellences have a prominent place in the explanation of the agent's being in possession of the truth. But to claim that this is a necessary condition for *all* cases seems to be going too far.

In the anxiety to get a definition of knowledge, philosophers have sometimes lost sight of the basic purpose of definitions: namely, to facilitate *understanding of the concept* in question. The real goal is not just to get a formula that "works", by triumphing over all its enemies armed with the latest precision anti-Gettier weapons. The great purpose of philosophical epistemology is to sharpen our understanding of knowledge and related epistemic goods. Somewhere in Plato's *Republic* Socrates remarks that the point of the dialectic about justice is not the formulas in which the concept of justice may be more or less successfully defined; its point is the cultivation of the minds of those who participate in it. The process of thinking in the context of a rigorous conceptual debate does clarify

---

[17] David Solomon has shown a similar tendency among recent virtue ethicists. In "routine" virtue ethics the concept of a virtue is exploited to answer the central question of modern moral theory—what is the foundation of morality?—while in "radical" virtue ethics it is put to purposes less traditional, or at least less *modernly* traditional. See his "Virtue Ethics: Radical or Routine?", in DePaul and Zagzebski (eds), *Intellectual Virtue*; pp. 57–80.

[18] For an illuminating exposition of Wittgenstein's notion of family resemblances, see Renford Bambrough, "Universals and Family Resemblances", in George Pitcher (ed.), *Wittgenstein: The Philosophical Investigations* (Garden City, NY: Doubleday, 1966), pp. 186–204. While it may not be a new orthodoxy among epistemologists, a growing segment of its practitioners are sympathetic to Timothy Williamson's judgment that "the upshot of [the debate over the definition of knowledge] is that no currently available analysis of knowledge in terms of belief is adequate" (*Knowledge and its Limits* (Oxford: Oxford University Press, 2000), p. 4).

and deepen the participants' understanding of the concepts discussed, even if no "conclusion" is reached. (In the next chapter we will point out that understanding is a kind of knowledge that is subject to degrees.) The definition may elude us, as Plantinga seems to admit that the strict definition of knowledge eludes him in *Warrant and Proper Function*, but still, all the hard head work involved does result in (some, or a better) knowledge of what knowledge is. Which shows that the wise course is to use formulas for their heuristic value, which is very great, but to have good sense for when paralysis has begun to set in, and to be supple enough in our imagination and adventuresome enough to try a new approach. The concept of an intellectual virtue invites us to a new way of thinking about epistemology, but one that has, up to now, not been far pursued. The practitioners of "virtue epistemology" have been trammeled by the character of late twentieth-century debates about the nature of knowledge.[19]

Finally, let us offer a brief comment on a way in which our enterprise resembles the definition project. If we think of a definition not as a single formula that captures without remainder the essential characteristics of every instance of some kind, but rather as an expedient for making a concept more "definite" for some person or group of persons, then we too are offering "definitions" of various concepts—in Chapter 2 of the concept of knowledge, in Chapter 5 of the concept of an intellectual practice, in Chapters 7–12 of the concepts of various virtues.

Analytic and Regulative Epistemology

Nicholas Wolterstorff[20] distinguishes two kinds of epistemology, which he calls "analytic" and "regulative". Analytic epistemology aims to produce theories of knowledge, rationality, warrant, justification, and so forth, and proceeds by attempting to define these terms. The English-speaking epistemology of the twentieth century is chiefly of this kind, and all of the virtue epistemologies of the last twenty-five years have been attempts

---

[19] Several years ago Jonathan Kvanvig said something similar. See *The Intellectual Virtues and the Life of the Mind: On the Place of the Virtues in Contemporary Epistemology* (Savage, MD: Rowman and Littlefield Publishers, 1992), p. 187.

[20] Nicholas Wolterstorff, *John Locke and the Ethics of Belief* (Cambridge: Cambridge University Press, 1996).

to turn the intellectual virtues to the purposes of analytic epistemology. Regulative epistemology, which is the kind mostly practiced by Locke and Descartes and others of their period, does not aim to produce a theory of knowledge (though something like classical foundationalism does get produced as a by-product by Locke and Descartes). Instead, it tries to generate guidance for epistemic practice, "how we ought to conduct our understandings, what we ought to do by way of forming beliefs" (p. xvi). Regulative epistemology is a response to perceived deficiencies in people's epistemic conduct, and thus is strongly practical and social, rather than just an interesting theoretical challenge for philosophy professors and smart students. This kind of epistemology aims to change the (social) world. According to Wolterstorff, Locke's regulative epistemology was a response to the social and intellectual crisis created by the breakup of medieval Christendom's intellectual consensus. As Locke and others saw it, people's intellectual lives needed to be reformed—based on reason, rather than tradition or passions—because only thus could disagreements about the most fundamental issues, along with the resulting social conflicts, be resolved. But Locke also saw the need for reformation as perennial and generically human: "I think there are a great many natural defects in the understanding capable of amendment." Since "we are all short sighted", seeing things from our own particular angle and not possessing comprehensive faculties, we need to learn the habit and inclination to consult others whose opinions differ from our own and read outside our discipline.[21]

In effect, Wolterstorff distinguishes two kinds of regulative epistemology, a rule-oriented kind and a habit-oriented kind (see pp. 152–4). Rule-oriented epistemology, exemplified by Descartes's *Discourse on Method* and *Rules for the Direction of the Mind*, provides procedural directions for acquiring knowledge, avoiding error, and conducting oneself rationally.[22] By contrast, Locke's regulative epistemology, as exemplified in Book IV of his *Essay Concerning Human Understanding* and *Of the Conduct of the Understanding*, aims less at the direct regulation of epistemic conduct than

---

[21] John Locke, *Some Thoughts Concerning Education* and *Of the Conduct of the Understanding*, ed. Ruth W. Grant and Nathan Tarcov (Indianapolis: Hackett, 1996). See *Conduct*, §§2, 3, pp. 168, 169.

[22] But notice that Descartes writes of "practicing the method I had prescribed for myself so as to *strengthen myself* more and more in its use" (*Discourse On Method*, trans. Donald A. Cress (Indianapolis: Hackett Publishing Company, 1998), Part 2, p. 13; italics added).

at the description of the habits of mind of the epistemically rational person. As Locke comments,

Nobody is made anything by hearing of rules, or laying them up in his memory…and you may as well hope to make a good painter or musician, extempore, by a lecture and instruction in the arts of music and painting, as a coherent thinker, or a strict reasoner, by a set of rules, showing him wherein right reasoning consists. (*Conduct*, §4, p. 175)

We need not rule-books, but a *training* that nurtures *people* in the right intellectual *dispositions*.

Wolterstorff emphasizes that Locke focuses not on the belief-producing mechanisms or faculties that are native to the human mind, but instead on the ways in which such natural faculties are employed in more complex intellectual practices, which have a social dimension and are culturally shaped. Locke aims to reform that culture, to reshape the practices, and thus to foster in his contemporaries habits that support the reshaped practices. It is implicit in Locke's discussions, and often explicit as well, that the habits in question are not mere habits, but virtues. Many habits are nothing more than skills—expertise in plying methods and techniques—but the habits that Locke describes are in many cases "habits of the heart", determinate dispositional states of concern, desire, and pleasure and pain, rather than mere habituated aptitudes. We will return to Locke when we take up the topic of intellectual practices in Chapter 5.

The virtues epistemology of this book is a return to this tradition of the seventeenth century, to a regulative epistemology which, like Locke's, describes the personal dispositions of the agent rather than providing direct rules of epistemic action. It focuses on forming the practitioner's character and is strongly education-oriented. The stress on intellectual virtues that has arisen among us is a start that can be felicitously developed in the regulative direction. Like Locke's, our book is a response to a perception of deficiency in the epistemic agents of our time. But it is not a response to any particular historical upheaval or social crisis. We see a perennial set of deficiencies which in every generation need to be corrected, and a perennial positive need for formation in dispositions of intellectual excellence. Our response to pluralism of belief systems differs from that of Locke and his fellow promoters of the life of "reason". Our regulative epistemology does not aim at quieting fundamental disagreement. Virtues presuppose one or another particular metaphysical or world-view background, and the prospect of securing universal agreement about that is dim. However, several of the virtues that we will discuss in Part II broaden minds and civilize intellectual exchange.

The formation of excellent intellectual agents is clearly the business of schools and parents. They are the chief educators of character. But Locke and Descartes think that philosophers have a role as well, and we agree. What is that role, and how does it work? How do philosophers contribute to the regulation of intellectual character? The role that we picture for ourselves both resembles and diverges from the one that epistemologists in the twentieth century implicitly accepted for themselves.

Concept Exploration versus System Creation

The preoccupation with e-definitions of knowledge is often part of a larger project of theory building. Many in the modern period assume, almost without reflection, that a philosopher's business is to regiment the concepts in a domain (say, moral concepts, or epistemic concepts, or ontological concepts) in a monistic, reductive, hierarchical, or derivational style. In epistemology, the debate between rationalists and empiricists has this character, with the empiricists thinking that knowledge about the world ought really to be derivable from sensory experience alone, so that knowledge is somehow "ultimately" a product of experience; while the rationalists think that knowledge is essentially theoretical or conceptual, and experience is, at best, just a kind of material of, or stimulus to, the production of a conceptual system. In metaphysics, physicalism would be an example, with Berkeleyan idealism the mirror opposite. The theory of meaning in Wittgenstein's *Tractatus* is another example: every sentence that *has* meaning has it by picturing a possible state of affairs. In his later writings Wittgenstein rejects this monistic view for a rich pluralism about how language works. No doubt there are dualists in metaphysics and Kantians in epistemology; but philosophers with the mind-set we are describing feel that such "mixed" theories are a sort of unfortunate compromise, a concession to "impure" thinking or "weak" theorizing. The real goal of philosophy, perhaps unachievable but still ideal, is reduction, the derivation of all the concepts in a given field from some single, key concept.

We find the same monistic presumption in recent virtue epistemology. Simon Blackburn,[23] supposing virtue epistemology to be modeled on modern ethical theories, considers what it would take for an epistemology to be "anything worth calling virtue epistemology" (p. 24). The question, he says, is about conceptual priority: in particular, whether it can be made out that the concept of an epistemic virtue is prior to other crucial concepts like justification (of beliefs), knowledge, and truth (see p. 17). He considers various ways of conceptualizing truth and looks for a way to avoid the conclusion that the intellectual virtues are "handmaidens to the truth" (p. 24). To admit that truth is "prior" to intellectual virtue would be to "throw in the towel" for virtue epistemology. To avoid this defeating conclusion, he suggests adopting an expressivist theory of truth. On this view, truth is a property of propositions, but "propositions are a kind of abstraction from the nature of judgment", and "judgment is an activity somehow constituted by what counts as exercising virtue in doing it" (p. 25). Thus truth, as a product of human activities, might derive from human virtues, in which case we might be able to satisfy the formal requirements for any account to be legitimately called a virtue epistemology. Blackburn does not thoroughly develop this theory, or even advocate it. His purpose is just to determine what it would take for an epistemology to be a virtue epistemology. Any "virtue epistemology" according to which virtues are conceived as dispositions to get the truth by "adjusting our confidences to probabilities", and in which "knowledge arises when we accept propositions in circumstances that require their acceptance", is so weak as to be "only a fig leaf for reliabilism" (p. 18).

All philosophy consists in proposals about the relations among concepts, in proposed orderings of concepts, and the arguments for those orderings. This is clearly what Blackburn is doing in his paper. In philosophy we ask why-questions that are usually not causal. Thus we might ask, Why is intellectual courage a virtue? or Why is it essential to acts of intellectual charity that they be motivated by goodwill for the interlocutor rather than a concern to crush him in argument? or Why is this one belief a case of knowledge and that other one not? or Why does this belief require evidential support and that one not? Why is it good to be motivated in this

---

[23] Simon Blackburn, "Reason, Virtue, and Knowledge", in Abrol Fairweather and Linda Zagzebski (eds), *Virtue Epistemology: Essays on Epistemic Virtue and Responsibility* (New York: Oxford University Press, 2001), pp. 15–29.

particular way and not that? We might call these *conceptual* why-questions, because answers to them show how one concept can be explained in terms of another, or "derived" (at least partially) from another. Explanation or derivation of this sort is the central activity of philosophers, and not just of philosophers promoting reductive, monistic, hierarchizing theories.

But a philosophical theory, on the hierarchical understanding of it that we have been considering, is not just a pattern of answers to a set of why-questions of this sort, but one that is constrained by special rules concerning what counts as a theory.

> Rule 1: If "A" is an answer to "why B?", then "B" cannot be an answer to "why A?"
>
> Rule 2: There must be one and only one ultimate answer to the string of why-questions: that is, one and only one answer about which further why-questions cannot be asked. (This answer provides the name of the theory.)

So, on the hierarchizing view of philosophy, if we ask, "Why is intellectual honesty a virtue?", and the answer is, "Its motivational component is the desire for truth *and* it is a disposition to be reliably successful in the pursuit of truth", only one of these answers will be ultimate. So if you ask, "Why does being reliably successful in the pursuit of truth make honesty a virtue?", the answer can be given, "Because this kind of success is what the motivational component aims at", but if that is the answer, then you can't answer the question, "why does being motivated by the desire for truth make intellectual honesty a virtue?" by saying, "The desire for truth aims at reliable success in the pursuit of truth". You have three options. You can derive the value of the success component from the value of the motivational component (in which case you have what Linda Zagzebski calls a "pure virtue theory"[24]). Or you can derive the motivational component from the success component (in which case you have a consequentialist theory, "reliabilism"). Or, finally, you can derive both components from a concept of human well-being: the answer to "Why A?" and to "Why B?" is "C": both of the components are virtuous because dispositions with these characteristics are constitutive of human flourishing (in which case we have a "happiness theory"). But the thing you can't do is both or all at the same time—e.g., say "The motivation

---

[24] Zagzebski, *Virtues of the Mind*, pp. 77–80 and *passim*.

component is virtuous because it aims at knowledge, and knowledge is good because it satisfies the motivational component, and both are good because they contribute to human happiness, and they contribute to human happiness because they are good." In that case you wouldn't have a theory at all, and would simply be a bad philosopher, since Rules 1 and 2 say what a theory is, and conceptual theories are the proper business of philosophers. If you violate these rules, then if the result can be called a theory at all, it is neither pure nor strong.

In this book we follow a different standard. In fact, in light of what mostly counts as theory among philosophers today, we prefer to say that we are offering no theory, and would say this, except that when we do, our friends start quibbling about what counts as a "theory". We will make many conceptual proposals—proposals about how epistemic and epistemic-moral concepts relate to one another, how virtues interact with and depend on one another, the varieties of intellectual goods and how they are connected with one another and with the various virtues, the relations that virtues bear to human faculties and various epistemic practices. In Part II we will offer extended analyses of particular virtues. These analyses will constitute something like "definitions"; at any rate we aim, by way of our discussions, to make the concepts more definite in our minds. If *such* definition and conceptual clarification is theory, then we are doing theory; but our "definitions" will not be formulas that aspire to specify the logically necessary and sufficient conditions for anything's falling under whatever concept is in question; nor will we have any qualms about multi-directional "derivations" of concepts. It seems to us that in fact this messy, non-hierarchical logic is actually the logic of the concepts that govern the intellectual life, and that attempts to regiment them into hierarchical orderings satisfying the strictures of typical philosophical theorizing result only in confusing and pedantic analyses that are ill fit to regulate anybody's epistemic life.

We hope that the philosophical work presented in this book will bear out the metaphor of cartography. A map is a schematic representation with a bent toward some particular aspect of the mapped territory. In these two ways, a map is a little bit like a theory, since a theory too is a *schematic* representation pitched toward *certain* questions and not towards others. Thus any map of West Virginia will be an abstraction in these two ways. It is never as big and detailed as West Virginia itself, and it can be a road map or a topographical map or an economic map of one sort or another, in which case it can ignore many other aspects of the territory. But while cartographers are abstracters with particular interests, they are quite far from being hierarchical derivers. Maps generally have an empirical and messy look. Philosophers, by contrast, are often done in by a neatness compulsion. They like to make crooked lines straight and differences the same. If a philosopher goes to a conference and proposes to some other philosophers that justice is really utility maximization, or that minds are just brains, or that knowledge is always the product of acts of intellectual virtue, or that knowledge is nothing but beliefs produced by properly functioning faculties, she may meet with a lot of disagreement from her colleagues, but she will not be hooted out of the profession. But if a cartographer went to a professional conference and proposed a kind of map showing that swamps are nothing but very wet and low-lying mountains, or that rivers are a deceptively fluid and meandering sort of forest, he would fall on hard times professionally.

Maps are pictures that are typically meant as guides to something or other. The present book means to represent the intellectual life in some of its conceptual messiness, and by virtue of this "realism" to function as a guide. We are particularly attentive to the character traits of the excellent epistemic agent. Our "map" is pitched in that special way, and it is toward the virtues that it is especially designed to guide. Our sketches of the other, related things are subordinated to that primary object of interest. Just as the cartographer can draw a map that highlights the railway system of a country, without any pretension that the railway system is somehow the foundation or source of derivation of everything else in the country, so in this book we want to map the intellectual virtues, without any pretension that they are the key or the foundation or the wellspring of everything intellectual.

How Regulative Epistemology Regulates

We have distinguished regulative epistemology from analytic epistemology. But to say that our virtue epistemology is regulative is not to deny that it's analytic. In fact, what we call analysis is our chief expedient of regulation. By the conceptual work that is distinctive of philosophical discourse, we propose to facilitate the improvement of intellectual character. If conceptual analysis is done right, it clarifies the character of the intellectual life in a way that can actually help people live that life. Conceptual clarification is an important part of education, and the improvement of intellectual character is a kind of education. It is a truism that greater understanding of a practice or way of life can facilitate that practice. Conceptual clarification is not the whole of education; a person can be quite adept at explaining the relevant concepts without being very serious about the intellectual life, just as a philosopher of ethics may be good at explaining ethical concepts without being very ethical herself. But if conceptual clarification is not the whole of character education, it is at least something, and it is what the philosopher is well suited to contribute.

A few pages ago we noted that all the virtue epistemologists who have written in the recent past are "analytic" or theoretical epistemologists, still focused primarily on the twentieth-century problems of defining knowledge, justification, warrant, and so forth. It is noteworthy and a symptom of this aim that they write almost nothing by way of sustained analysis of particular virtues.[25] If one's purpose is to formulate a definition of knowledge or an account of justification, it might seem an extravagant expenditure of analytic energy to explore in detail the individual virtues. A general conception of intellectual virtue, with a bit of attention to one or two virtues by way of illustration, should suffice.

But if one aims to provide guidance, the focus shifts to a fairly detailed exploration of the particular dimensions or territories of the life of knowledge—in the present study, the intellectual virtues themselves. The descriptions we offer of the virtue we call love of knowledge and the virtues of epistemic humility, caution, courage, tenacity, openness, charity, and generosity *are* the chief regulators, insofar as philosophers can provide such. The concrete description of particular virtues is central and essential to what we are doing here, and distinguishes it from everything else in the field. Thus the chapters of Part II, which are devoted to exploring particular virtues, are the heart of our study. Even someone who denies that the particular virtues ought to be the central focus of virtue epistemology may

---

[25] The central core of Plantinga's *Warrant and Proper Function* does offer fairly sustained analyses of several of the epistemic faculties insofar as they function properly in the kind of environment to which they are suited, which are Plantinga's counterparts of the intellectual virtues. In Ch. 4 we hope to show that his chapters invite completion in an account of the virtues.

find it useful to have an extended discussion of a few of them. After all, if one is going to base a theory of knowledge on the concept of a virtue, it might be helpful to start with the kind of clarity about virtues that comes from detailed knowledge.

As our brief discussion of Locke indicates, regulative epistemology is nothing new. But regulative philosophical ethics is perhaps easier to recognize. Indeed, before the modern period, in which it seems to be an invisible, compelling, and unquestioned assumption that any philosopher who "does ethics", including "virtue ethics", will be found doing moral theory in the hierarchizing sense, philosophical ethics was often and probably mostly a regulative enterprise. Early in his *Nicomachean Ethics*, Aristotle comments that "the present inquiry does not aim at theoretical knowledge like the others (for we are inquiring not in order to know what virtue is, but in order to become good, since otherwise our inquiry would have been of no use)".[26] Yet he also says that the book will bring "no profit" to the ethically immature—the young, the incontinent, those who are ruled by their passions (1095^a2-13, pp. 3–4)—the ones whose lives seem to be most in need of regulation. Thus Aristotle envisions the philosophical analysis in his *Nicomachean Ethics* as regulating the lives of his contemporaries and posterity not directly, by the reading of the text, but for the most part indirectly through the work of leaders such as city planners, governors, and teachers who will have read the book and thus gained insights into what virtue and the good life are and how things should be arranged to promote virtue. We might call this the social engineering model of the regulative philosopher's role.

At the other end of the directness continuum is Søren Kierkegaard, who crafts a diverse literary *oeuvre* designed to influence the reader directly. Even the parts of Kierkegaard's writings that are most indirect—the pseudonymous ones—aim to influence the reader without human intermediary, and the most direct of his works are discourses that he calls "upbuilding" because they are intended to build up the character of the reader. He addresses these discourses to what he calls "that single individual whom I with joy and gratitude call *my* reader". His discourses explore virtue concepts such as love, patience, gratitude, hope, faith, humility, and

---

[26] Aristotle, *Nicomachean Ethics*, trans. W. D. Ross, rev. J. O. Urmson and J. L. Ackrill (Oxford: Oxford University Press, 1998), 1103^b26-29, p. 30.

courage. The conceptual work in them is clearly philosophical, in that they explore with great finesse the web of conceptual connections in which the virtue concepts have their definition,[27] but the hierarchizing characteristic of modern ethical theory is entirely absent.

Where does the present work fit among these alternatives? We would like to think that it will serve both the individual reader who wishes, by becoming more conscious of the structure of intellectual virtues, to be "built up" in the intellectual life, and the educational leader or teacher or deviser of curriculum who wishes to know more about intellectual character so as to "engineer" the school, the classroom, his own pedagogical activities, or the curriculum for maximum educational benefit. It is also, of course, for the professional epistemologist who might be interested in exploring another way of doing epistemology, perhaps in the wake of indecision about the state of the discipline.[28]

A Map of the Map

The chapters of Part I lay out some considerations that will orient our analysis of the particular virtues, and they introduce some general theses about epistemology for which the book as a whole will serve as an argument. In Chapter 2 we will examine the intellectual goods—the aims of the intellectual life—and suggest that, for purposes of regulative epistemology, and indeed for an adequate understanding of the intellectual life, we need a broader and richer conception of the epistemic goods than has characterized recent epistemology. In Chapter 3 we will try to refine the concept of an intellectual virtue, in a general way, and suggest that, for purposes of drawing a useful map of the intellectual life, we need to be more sensitive to the rich diversity of structure among the intellectual virtues than virtue epistemology has been heretofore. The virtues themselves come in integrated sets in which particular virtues, some pairs of which

---

[27] See Robert C. Roberts, "Kierkegaard, Wittgenstein, and a Method of 'Virtue Ethics' ", in Merold Westphal and Martin Matustik (eds), *Kierkegaard in Post/Modernity* (Bloomington: Indiana University Press, 1995), pp. 142–66.

[28] See Jason Baehr's "Character in Epistemology", *Philosophical Studies* 128, 3 (April 2006): 479–514, in which he argues that, while virtue epistemology is not very promising as a strategy for addressing the routine questions of late twentieth-century epistemology, it is promising for taking epistemology in quite different directions.

may initially seem to be opposites, balance one another and support, enrich, and qualify one another in a variety of ways. Chapter 4 examines the natural faculties on the basis of which intellectual virtues are built up, and we will argue for diversity here as well. In particular, while most of the faculties play a role something like that of *equipment* for the activities of intellectual virtues, the will—a faculty much neglected in discussions of the intellectual virtues—plays quite a different and central role. The virtues that enable the highest kinds of epistemic functioning involve the *integration* of the faculties, especially the "will", and crucial epistemic virtues have this integrative character. Lists of faculties are controversial, and the virtues are relative to schemata of beliefs about human nature and the nature of the universe, so that epistemology is inescapably shaped by metaphysical commitments. Chapter 5 addresses the topic of intellectual practices, since these are the activities that the virtues fit us to pursue. William Alston has brought the notion of epistemic practices into epistemology, but his concept is not the full-blooded commonsense concept of practice that we see at work in sciences, for example. While recent epistemology has devoted almost exclusive attention to the role of the virtues in *acquiring* the epistemic goods, we think that a more adequate guide will need to pay attention to their role in the transmission and application of those goods as well. Part I can be regarded as a sort of general or high-altitude map of the intellectual life, one that provides a perspicuous representation of the relations among the major parts of the territory in question. Part II zooms in on a series of areas within that territory, with attention to their placements in the whole.

2

Goods

Introduction

Intellectual activities, like other human activities, have aims. We collect information and ascertain facts: What is the migratory pattern of the Northern Mockingbird? How many people voted a straight ticket in the last American presidential election? Who murdered President Lincoln? We seek to explain things: How do plants grow? Why do some children develop into delinquents? We seek to predict the future: When will the stock market improve? Will it rain tomorrow? We like to know the truth-value of counterfactual conditionals: If an election were held next week, would the President be re-elected? All of the foregoing is a matter of acquiring and improving beliefs, and the quality of beliefs as beliefs (assuming that they are true) is perhaps well described as their *warrant*.[1] Do we have good reasons for what we believe? Is our information well grounded in some canonical procedure? Do we have good reasons for thinking that the procedure by which our information was generated is likely to yield truths? Do our explanations really explain, or only seem to do so? Have we stopped the regress of explanations prematurely? Are we being too demanding in pushing the regress back? Are our predictions and counterfactual beliefs well-founded, or just guesses? Do the newcomers among our beliefs cohere well with other beliefs that we are pretty confident

[1] We adopt Plantinga's word here, and intend it to be very encompassing. Thus it covers both what philosophers have called "justification" and what Plantinga calls "warrant". Plantinga himself sometimes uses the word this way (see Alvin Plantinga, *Warrant and Proper Function* (New York: Oxford University Press, 1993), p. 3). "Warrant" is better than "groundedness", because it includes more naturally the excellence in beliefs that coherentists favor; and it is better than "justification", because of the voluntarist and deontological associations that some people feel that word carries. However, we will occasionally use "justification" in the same broad sense, if it seems more natural in the context. It is often used this way (see William P. Alston, *Perceiving God* (Ithaca, NY: Cornell University Press, 1991), esp. ch. 2).

about? As efforts to improve or test ourselves intellectually, these are all questions with respect to actual or possible *beliefs*.

But we also have intellectual aims that are not belief-oriented. We sometimes seek to improve our minds by way of the immediacy of experience. Even if, by going to Italy, I were to gain no additional warranted beliefs about Italian Renaissance architecture than I had before, nor improve the warrant for the ones I have, I might still want to go to Italy and feast my eyes on the buildings themselves, get a sense for what it is like to walk from one end to another of a great hall, to see the buildings from the various angles that are afforded by bodily presence in a place, to sniff the odors of the centuries. And I may well think my *knowledge* supplemented by the experience. Such immediate experiences do often give me new beliefs or improve the warrant for my beliefs about the buildings, but this need not be the whole point of my wanting the experience. In experiencing the buildings for myself, I come to know the buildings better, whether or not I gain new propositions or improve the warrant for my beliefs.

Again, we may take a course in nineteenth-century Russian literature to deepen our understanding of its novels, and may think that this deepening improves at the same time our understanding of human nature. We also find that as we grow older, we understand the novels of Tolstoy and Dostoevsky in improved ways. We have a perspective on the dialogue and actions that is deeper, broader, and richer than when we were twenty, perhaps because of intervening personal experiences. We think too that our emotional development makes it possible for us to understand these novels in more fitting ways. The same is true in the natural sciences. As a scientist progresses in her research, she does not just accumulate more and better warranted beliefs, or better and better warrant for her beliefs; nor is this the only aim or chief lure of science. The scientist gains, in addition, a deepened understanding of the part of nature to which she directs her attention, and this may be the most satisfying aspect of scientific endeavor. Science is not just about collecting information and proving things. The understanding at which science aims is an explanatory power, no doubt, and in that way is a matter of belief warranting; but it is also a kind of systematic *appreciation* of things.

So we have identified three large rough categories of epistemic goods: warranted true belief, acquaintance, and understanding. These goods don't generally come isolated from one another. Understanding and warranting are often joined in explanation, and we will argue that an important kind of understanding is exemplified in a certain sophisticated kind of acquaintance. We think that greater attention to the connections between warranted true belief, on the one hand, and acquaintance and understanding, on the other, can help epistemology plumb its potential depths and help it be the serious and important discipline that it can and ought to be.

Routinely, epistemology is denominated the "theory of knowledge". Are all the epistemic goods that we call aims subsumable under the concept *knowledge*? That may depend on what one means by "knowledge". That well-established information about the migratory patterns of the Northern Mockingbird, gathered in ordinary contexts, counts as knowledge is uncontroversial except among philosophical skeptics. Many ordinary speakers of English are comfortable calling the deepened understanding of Russian novels (or even of human life) "knowledge" even if they do not have in mind just the plain information they gained about the historical background of the novels, or biographical information about their authors, or "factual" knowledge about the characters and the novels' plots. "I know more now than I did when I was twenty" can mean "My understanding is deeper". Nevertheless, "understanding" does seem a better word than "knowledge" for this deepened cognitive grasp. As for the immediate experience of the Italian Renaissance buildings, it seems natural to say, "Before the trip I had a lot of book learning about those buildings, but now I have first-hand knowledge". Here we are reminded of the distinction in French between *savoir* and *connaître*. To *connaître* something is to have personal, direct experience of it in some way; the word is particularly used of knowing people, and the person who *connaît* another does not just know *about* him or her (have lots of warranted beliefs about him), but knows *him*, usually by having met and interacted with him.

The kind of knowledge in which twentieth-century English-speaking epistemology specializes is almost entirely some form of belief, where belief is regarded as a propositional attitude. In particular, the definition of knowledge that is tested and debated in, and lies behind, the vast majority of discussions is that knowledge is belief that is good in two ways: it is both true and warranted (justified, well-grounded). And most of the discussion in recent decades has been about the second of these two good-making properties. Is a belief warranted by something like reasons (having reasons, giving reasons, contemplating reasons, being in a position to give reasons, contemplating the fact that one has reasons, knowing that one is in a position to give reasons, etc.), or is it more like being the seat of a process or mechanism that strongly tends to spawn true beliefs? William Alston has pointed out that the seeming interminability of the debate between internalists and externalists about justification can be explained by the fact that the two main camps do not have the same concept of justification.[2] They trade on different paradigm cases and have divergent intuitions about the same cases because they are really focusing on different epistemic goods, or what Alston calls epistemic "desiderata". In a moment we will look at Alston's "iconoclastic and revolutionary" take on the debate, and will suggest some ways in which it can be extended and exploited in the interests of our own project.

But our current point is that the focus on belief in these debates seems to sideline some of the epistemic goods that must be kept in mind if one is to see "knowledge" fully in the context of the fullest human life. Neither acquaintance nor understanding is adequately understood as a qualification of belief. Did Adam, upon "knowing" Eve, acquire some new beliefs, or ground better some that he already had? Perhaps, but that hardly seems to be the most outstanding aspect of his epistemic progress. Does the person who at age 40 understands *War and Peace* better than he did at 19 do so in virtue of having more beliefs about it, or better warranted ones? Maybe so, but this is far from being the most important part of the story. So the epistemology that focuses exclusively on knowledge and makes knowledge some kind of belief or other has tended to neglect some of the most interesting and important aspects and kinds of knowledge. In the present book we want to do some kind of justice to the whole range of epistemic goods, in particular by thinking about how the personal virtues of the epistemic agent contribute to their acquisition and transmission.

Warrant of Beliefs

Much of the late twentieth-century debate about the nature of knowledge was about just what kind of warrant (or justification) a true belief had to have to count as knowledge. Alvin Plantinga opens his *Warrant and*

---

[2] William Alston, "Epistemic Desiderata", *Philosophy and Phenomenological Research* 53 (1993): 527–51.

Proper Function with a list of twenty-one "epistemic values" and observes that rival conceptions of warrant "appeal to different epistemic values". Then, in a prodigal gesture of pluralistic liberality, he ends his list by saying "there are a thousand other[s]". Among the "values" that Plantinga lists, some have more obviously to do with warrant (in the broad sense that we are using) than others. Some of the most obviously relevant are "doing one's subjective epistemic duty, doing one's objective epistemic duty, and doing both;... having a set of beliefs that is coherent to one or another degree;... [or] the disposition to have coherent beliefs;... having adequate evidence or good reasons for your beliefs;... having a reliable set of faculties or belief-producing mechanisms,... knowing that you have a reliable set of epistemic faculties" (p. 3). The schools or theories in late twentieth-century epistemology form by picking *one* such kind of warrant and trying to defend the thesis that their own favored brand satisfies both the necessary and the sufficient conditions for *any* true belief's being a case of knowledge.

With similar openness to variety in the kinds of warrant, William Alston has responded to the apparently undecidable debates between internalists and externalists, and between different kinds of internalists, and between different kinds of externalists, by saying, in effect, that most of the camps have identified *some* kind of genuine good-making property of beliefs in the general area of warranting, but, suffering from a philosophical monomania about warrant, have overgeneralized their own favorite "necessary and sufficient" conditions. For any of the more reasonable kinds of warranting that are proposed as generally necessary for beliefs to be in good epistemic shape, some beliefs will actually need it, or at any rate can profit from it; but there may be no single set of conditions that all beliefs must meet to be warranted, and that are sufficient to warrant any belief. We think Alston's broad-minded pluralism is a recipe for liberation, health, and a new lease on profundity in epistemology. A natural way to bring together the diverse epistemic desiderata is in a *person* who has the power, inclination, and intelligent flexibility to meet the demands for these desiderata *as occasion arises*. So let's illustrate our point by looking at some of the main kinds of warrant, with a view to showing their necessity in *some* cases, and the general need for agents to be able to achieve these kinds of warrant if they are to be epistemically high-functioning.

Consider first *the basing condition*. Justified beliefs are based on such grounds as perceptual experiences (seeing the bird in the tree), rational insights (seeing the necessity in the truth *no prime minister is a prime number*), and other beliefs. On most views of justification, it is not enough that the ground be present, in some sense; the justified belief has to be *based on* the ground. To use an example from Alston, I believe the true proposition that my wife is not home at the moment, and the ground of that belief is that she told me she'd be out with her friend Suzie. The basing condition says that justification requires that my belief that my wife is not home at the moment be *based on* the belief that she told me she'd be out with Suzie; it would not be enough for me just to *have* the belief that she told me she'd be out with Suzie *and also* the belief that she is not home at present. We could also say that the first belief has to be *my actual reason* for believing the second.

Now consider the following scenario. I have a good reason (she told me she'd be out with Suzie), but I have temporarily forgotten it and now believe the proposition on the basis of the inadequate reason that it is a beautiful spring day. The latter reason is inadequate because it does not, let us say, make the belief that my wife is not at home probable enough (it is too low in what Alston calls "*truth-conducivity*"). The belief that would justify it—that she told me she would be out—is still present but has slipped, for the moment, out of consciousness. So my true belief, that my wife is not at home, is based on an inadequate ground, and thus is not justified, even though an adequate ground is somewhere in the neighborhood.

More than one story might be told about this case. One possibility is that my *real* reason for believing my wife is not home is the good ground that I have forgotten: it is, unbeknownst to me, what is causing me to believe that she is not home, and I am making a mistake of introspection in thinking that the other belief—that it's a beautiful spring day—is my reason for thinking she's not at home. An externalist might think that as long as the truth-conducive reason for believing the proposition is the actual cause of my believing it, my true belief is justified (thus knowledge), while one sort of internalist might think that if I'm not currently applying the one belief to the other, then my belief is not based on its (potential) ground, or that my mistake in identifying my reason for believing my wife is not at home is enough to vitiate the basing relation. In other words, the internalist may see a necessary connection between the agent's *access* to the basing relation and the basing relation *itself*. For such an internalist, the access is necessary to establishing the basing relation (a weaker internalism requires only that one be *able* to access the basing relation). But for the externalist, the basing condition can be satisfied independently of such access.

The internalist and the externalist will agree that the basing condition needs to be met, but they are of different minds about what it is. What shall we say about the case in which I am being caused, by a truth-conducive ground, to believe that my wife is away from home at the moment, but think, mistakenly, that my belief has another ground which, as it turns out, is not sufficiently truth-conducive? Am I justified in believing that my wife is away from home at the moment, or not? Intuitions will differ. Some will be inclined to think that I am justified, others that I am not. We think that these different intuitions reflect attention to different kinds of case. I will not be able to explain my belief, so if we are in a context where such explanation is a test of knowledge, then I will not be justified in believing the proposition; but in contexts where that ability is not required for knowledge, I will count as knowing. Imagine a context where the stakes are very high. My wife is accused of burning our house down, and when the police ask me how I know that my wife was not at home on the day of the crime, I say it was because it was a beautiful spring day. Here we have reason to think that I am not justified in my belief, because the standards of justification are higher when the stakes are higher. Here I will not only have to have the right reason, but will have to know what it is. But in the usual case, with rather low stakes, most people will happily admit that I was justified in believing that my wife was not at home, and indeed knew it, as long as her having told me she would be out was the real cause of my believing that she was not at home.

So we say that neither the internalist nor the externalist is right insofar as he is making a theoretical generalization about all cases; but that each of them is focusing on a kind of case which does occur, and each has an intuition that is right for that kind of case. Both epistemologists probably use both concepts in their daily lives, but when it comes to philosophizing, they become theorists and give monistic, legislative preference to one of these kinds of justification. Excellent epistemic agents are disposed to practice and accept both kinds of justification, depending on context.

The disposition to form warranted beliefs on the basis of true beliefs that I may not at present be able to access consciously[3], and the disposition to form warranted beliefs by consciously accessing adequate belief bases, are two aspects of epistemic virtue. Through long intellectual discipline, excellent epistemic agents come to have a store of true beliefs that tend to cause them to generate other true beliefs; it would be very cumbersome and intellectually disabling to have to access consciously all the beliefs on the basis of which any new belief is formed. Of course, it is also epistemically virtuous to be able to give an account of current beliefs in terms of earlier established ones, and for some purposes we may want to rule out, as insufficiently warranted, cases like my failure to access consciously the real reason for my belief about my wife's absence from home. For optimal functioning, we need to be able to call some of these earlier beliefs to mind and thus become conscious of their efficacy in bringing about new beliefs. The virtuous agent will have both of these powers of warrant, and will tend to exemplify them at the appropriate junctures of noetic life. Thus Alston's and Plantinga's openness to distinguishing epistemic goods and allowing for a plurality of them, in combination with the virtue epistemologist's focus on the powers of an intellectual agent, makes for a better picture of knowledge than either internalist or externalist theories provide; and it does so by eschewing the typical theoretical project. The virtue epistemologist just looks for an epistemic virtue—or more likely a dimension of intellectual virtues—out of which each of the legitimate kinds of justification might issue, and refrains from generalizing any of them as necessary and sufficient conditions for justification.

Coherence in one's belief set is another epistemic value that helps to warrant beliefs. I walk into the house and see that my wife's tennis racquet is hanging in the closet. I have other beliefs: She told me she'd be playing tennis this morning; she has only one racquet. I seem to have an inconsistent set of beliefs. I am epistemically uncomfortable and set about trying to form other beliefs that will resolve the puzzle. Did she in fact buy that new racquet she's been wanting? Or was it tomorrow she was to be playing tennis? Did she borrow somebody's racquet? Once I resolve the apparent

---

[3] For some vivid illustrations of this kind of case, see Malcolm Gladwell, *Blink: The Power of Thinking Without Thinking* (New York: Little, Brown, and Company, 2005).

incoherency in my belief set, either by eliminating one or more of my beliefs or by finding another belief that shows the coherency of the original set, each of the beliefs in the set gains warrant.

As long as we do not try to defend coherent*ism*—the view that coherence is a necessary and sufficient condition for any belief's being warranted—we can easily add the coherence disposition to our picture of excellent epistemic character. Human beings have a natural coherence disposition: we are susceptible to puzzlement if our beliefs do not cohere. This natural disposition can be developed into a mature trait that regularly issues in explicit investigations of the coherence of one's beliefs. People can be more or less subject to puzzlement when their beliefs seem incoherent, and more or less resolute and skilled at ferreting out incoherencies and resolving them. Notice that the coherence disposition is not just an ability, but what we might call a "passion". It is like a desire or concern: the concern that my beliefs form a coherent set, that they hang together in relations of implication and non-contradiction. This is an example of a phenomenon that we will be stressing in this book: the functioning of the "intellect" is shot through with "will". The life of the intellect is just as much a matter of loves, concerns, desires, emotions, and the like as the other parts of our lives. A person might have a very great ability to detect and correct incoherencies in his belief sets, but if he didn't *care* about coherence—if he were not subject to discomfort with incoherencies in his belief set—he would not function well intellectually. A mature concern for intellectual coherence will not be an indiscriminate tendency to be fussy about incoherencies, but will be governed by good judgment about which apparent incoherencies are *important*, and about whether they are important *for oneself*, and about whether now is the *time* to be concerned about them. In addition to having the seriousness to care rather intensely about the coherence of one's beliefs, and the practical wisdom to discern which incoherencies are worth getting worked up about, it can take a cultivated imagination and logical skills to notice incoherencies in high-level intellectual contexts.

If firmness is a virtue (see Chapter 7), one also needs to be able to live with incoherence in one's belief system. It is seldom virtuous to give up large numbers of one's important beliefs because of anomalies in one's experience. High intellectual functioning sometimes requires living for periods of time with what appears to be an incoherent set of important beliefs. So intellectual virtue includes the ability to live with the discomfort of puzzlement: if it is a defect for a person to be able to dismiss from his mind the discomfort associated with having an apparently inconsistent belief set, but also less than excellent to give up too easily on important beliefs and beliefs that seem obviously to be true, then one needs to be able to live with a certain amount of intellectual anxiety. This disposition is akin to courage, which is an ability to function well despite fear and cognate emotions (see Chapter 8). The dialectic between the puzzlement sensitivity, firmness, and courage requires a kind of intellectual practical wisdom to determine when to jettison a belief for coherence's sake and when to live with apparent incoherence. It is noteworthy how much intellectual virtues in this area involve a proper adjustment of emotion dispositions.

A desideratum stressed by some internalists is the fulfillment of *epistemic obligations*. The theory would be roughly that a belief is justified if and only if its holder has performed all his subjective or objective obligations, or both, with respect to its warrant. Since on one view or another of intellectual obligations, we could be obliged to have good reasons or evidence for our beliefs, or consciously to access such reasons, or to have good reasons for thinking that our reasons are good ones, or to have coherence in our belief set, or to be aware of the coherence of our belief set, etc., etc., it is clear that intellectual obligations can include a number of other desiderata. Yet the notion of an obligation does seem to add something to the notion of these other desiderata. It adds the notion of *requirement*, of the agent's being under some kind of *authority*. This might be conceived as the requiring authority of Reason, of Truth, maybe even of God.

What shall we say about intellectual obligations? We happily admit that we have some, but we would make at least three points about them. First, it does not make sense to speak of intellectual duties in every case of knowledge. In knowing that the lights have gone out, by virtue of having open, properly functioning eyes in a room where the lights have just gone out, it seems a stretch to say that I have fulfilled any obligation, and even more of a stretch to say that my fulfilling some obligation is what makes my belief a case of knowledge. Second, intellectual obligations are contextual: *what* I am obliged intellectually to do will depend very much on my circumstances—for example, the circumstance that my belief has been effectively challenged, or that I have been given reason to think that I may have formed it too hastily—and so doing what I am obliged to do will depend on my having a power of good judgment as to what I am obliged to do. Sometimes I will be obliged to examine critically my reasons for believing what I believe, and sometimes not. Sometimes I will be obliged to give up a belief because it fails to cohere with others of my beliefs, but not always. So the application of the notion of intellectual duty requires the virtue of intellectual practical wisdom, as an ability to judge correctly what is required from situation to situation. And third, we point out a passional virtue that is associated with obligations: namely, intellectual conscientiousness or the sense of intellectual duty. People vary in how strongly they feel the compulsion to do their intellectual duty. The person who is reliable in doing whatever intellectual duties present themselves is a person who not only recognizes and distinguishes duties in context, but who cares about doing what he ought to do intellectually, and so sometimes acts, not just in *accordance* with his epistemic duties, but *from* the sense of duty.

We have argued for abandoning the project of e-defining propositional knowledge by reference to some particular conception of warrant. Every conception of warrant or justification that has been proposed by epistemologists identifies some way in which beliefs are in fact warranted, but none works as a basis for e-defining knowledge. However, all of these legitimate epistemic desiderata can be brought together in one conception—that of the excellent epistemic agent, the person of intellectual virtues. The virtues are traits that include both the abilities and the drives that tend to deliver these epistemic goods, these aspects of propositional knowledge.

Understanding

However, the intellectual virtues are more than the personal basis for attaining propositional knowledge. In fact, we will argue in the rest of this chapter that propositional knowledge, as it is understood by many contemporary epistemologists, is something of an abstraction from knowledge. It is seldom by itself the kind of knowledge that fully functioning human beings (including, we believe, most epistemologists) seek.

Several recent writers have noted that thinking of intellectual virtues as traits of character encourages us to expand our conception of epistemic goods beyond warranted true belief.[4] Understanding is often named as one of the bonus goods, and in this section we offer some thoughts on that topic. Then in the next section we will discuss an epistemic good that is equally tied to virtues. And we will argue throughout that these diverse goods are frequently so intimately intertwined as to be inseparable. That is why treating propositional knowledge as a separate topic without regard to the knowledge that surrounds and supports it turns it into something artificial.

Consider, first, two related features of propositional knowledge as it is usually treated in contemporary epistemology. The first is that it is knowledge *of a relatively isolated proposition.* The proposition is true, and the subject holds it in an attitude of believing (that is, of attributing truth) and is warranted in holding it with that attitude. The second feature is that, for any proposition, you either know it or you don't; this kind of knowledge *does not come in degrees.* Both of these properties are differences between propositional knowledge and understanding, which is often of complex bodies of propositions (stories, theories, books) or things other than propositions (a drawing, a symphony), and which does come in degrees (a person can increase in his understanding of a proposition or a text or a symphony).

In connection with this last point, it is also instructive to compare understanding's relation to truth with that of propositional knowledge. Something like truth is typically a condition of understanding: If we think that somebody's understanding of a text is incorrect, then we say he doesn't understand it. We admit that he has an interpretation, maybe even an intelligent and highly coherent one (and thus *an* understanding of it), but we say nevertheless that he doesn't understand it. Just as a proposition is thought to be true in virtue of matching the state of affairs that it is about, so understanding anything typically has to be more or less adequate to

[4] See Linda Zagzebski, *Virtues of the Mind: An Inquiry into the Nature of Virtue and the Ethical Foundations of Knowledge* (Cambridge: Cambridge University Press, 1996), pp. 43–50, and *idem,* "Recovering Understanding", in Matthias Steup (ed.), *Knowledge, Truth, and Duty* (New York: Oxford University Press, 2001), pp. 235–51; John Greco, "Virtues in Epistemology", in Paul Moser (ed.), *Oxford Handbook of Epistemology* (New York: Oxford University Press, 2002), pp. 287–315; Jonathan Kvanvig, *The Value of Knowledge and the Pursuit of Understanding* (Cambridge: Cambridge University Press, 2003), ch. 8; and Wayne Riggs, "Understanding 'Virtue' and the Virtue of Understanding", in Michael DePaul and Linda Zagzebski (ed.), *Intellectual Virtue: Perspectives from Ethics and Epistemology* (Oxford: Oxford University Press, 2003), pp. 203–26. See also our report of Plantinga's words at the end of our paper "Humility and Epistemic Goods", ibid. pp. 257–79.

what it is about. When the object is complex and deep, like one's wife or a great text, the understanding of it can be indefinitely *more* right, *more* adequate, *closer* to the "truth". People differentiate understandings of texts with such qualifiers as "deep", "insightful", and "penetrating", and with some objects there seems to be almost no limit to the quantity of depth, insight, and penetration that an understanding can have.

Hugh Benson argues convincingly that Socrates' concept of knowledge in the early dialogues is a concept of understanding.[5] But that concept is not satisfied by an ability to make *some* true connections concerning the object of understanding (say, piety); it requires that its subject be able to produce "an interrelated coherent system of true cognitive states involving that object" (p. 190), thus one that is entirely free of false beliefs and so of any incoherence. So the kind of understanding that Socrates takes knowledge to be does not have the gradual character that we have just ascribed to understanding. Benson tries to make the case that in modern English we have at least *a* concept of understanding that corresponds to this one of Socrates: "We say things like Albert Einstein understands gravity, Richard Feynman understands quantum mechanics" (p. 212), and we contrast their cases with those of people who know a bit about these subjects, but don't *understand* them. Benson is right that we say this sort of thing, in some contexts; but in other contexts we say that Benson's high school physics teacher understands gravity, and if pressed, we would always allow that understanding could be greater: we think that Einstein could have understood gravity even better, had he been able to see how general relativity fits with quantum mechanics.

Not all understanding is deep or insightful, not even potentially so. Consider the understanding of linguistic representations. "I understood what he said, but I don't know what he meant [that is, I don't understand his meaning]." A person says this when he (a) recognizes the uttered sounds as particular words of a language known to him and (b) grasps the syntax of the speech, but either does not know (c) what proposition is being expressed by the sentence or (d) how that sentence fits with other sentences (say, what it follows from or what it implies) and how it fits with particular other sentences that it is supposed to fit with (say, how it

⁵ Hugh Benson, *Socratic Wisdom: The Model of Knowledge in Plato's Early Dialogues* (New York: Oxford University Press, 2000).

is consistent with them). Another feature of understanding a sentence is brought out by (e) a person's ability to paraphrase it. The paraphrase may merely trade on a grasp of vocabulary and syntax, but it may also depend on, or be an extension of, grasping how the sentence fits with other sentences; here we are talking about the agent's ability to "go on".[6] (a) through (e) are all matters of understanding. To understand in all five senses is thus a complicated and rich epistemic accomplishment, one which ordinary shallow people succeed at countless times daily. All five of these senses or levels of understanding language involve *grasping connections* or *fitting things together*. To recognize a sound as a particular word in a known language is to "place" it within that language; to grasp the syntax of a sentence is to connect the words of the sentence in a grammatical, logical, sense-making way. To hear a proposition in a sentence is to pick out a place in logical space (though not in Wittgenstein's atomistic understanding of that space's structure). To know what the sentence implies or what implies it is to place the proposition it expresses within a system of propositions. To be able to formulate heretofore unformulated propositions that are nevertheless implications of or proper extensions of the system of propositions is to grasp the connections among both the previously formulated propositions and the new ones. (c) blends into (d) and (e), and (d) and (e) are extensions of (c). A person might understand a sentence well enough to formulate its denial, or to identify some simple implication of the proposition it expresses, without being able to go very far or very creatively. Again, understanding admits of degrees of depth. Consider the following.

A person might be said to understand Schleiermacher's theology well. Maybe this means that if you give him a paragraph of Schleiermacher, or even just a sentence, he not only understands the words, and how the words go together syntactically; in addition to this he can draw the connections of this passage to a number of other things the theologian says or would say. He can perhaps answer, after the manner of Schleiermacher, questions that Schleiermacher didn't actually answer, because he knows how to think like Schleiermacher. Here again, understanding is an ability to grasp or draw connections. And again it admits of degrees. We can imagine people who can do this just a bit, and people who can do it quite a bit more, and then

---

[6] See Ludwig Wittgenstein, *Philosophical Investigations*, trans. G. E. M. Anscombe (New York: Macmillan, 1953), Part I, §§151-5.

also people who understand Schleiermacher's thought as well as or better than Schleiermacher understood it himself—people who might surprise Schleiermacher by extending his thought in ways that are authentically Schleiermacherian but which never occurred to the theologian himself.

Zagzebski, accepting the epistemologists' convention of identifying knowledge with propositional knowledge, tries to keep knowledge and understanding quite separate and distinct from one another. She admits that Plato has no analogous distinction, that his discussions of *epistēmē* blend the two concepts that she wants to distinguish. "But since knowledge these days almost always means propositional knowledge, and since I have proposed that understanding has no propositional object, understanding differs from knowledge as normally understood."[7] But the kind of cases we have just considered refute the generalization that understanding is non-propositional. They present a mixture of propositional and non-propositional understanding. The case of understanding the sentence from Schleiermacher is surely a case of understanding a proposition in the sense of (c) and (d); it is a matter of grasping the significance of a sentence and seeing its connections with other propositions in a body of propositions expressed in the sentences of Schleiermacher's theology. On the other hand, (a) and (b) do seem to be non-propositional (or perhaps pre-propositional?). The identification or placing of a word in the vocabulary of a language is not itself the grasping of a proposition, although a case might be made that to grasp a word as a word presupposes the *ability* to construct at least rudimentary sentences. Similarly, but perhaps less clearly, to understand the syntactical structure of a sentence is not itself to understand a proposition. Consider, for example, the sentence "Every first-order theory with an infinite model has models of every infinite cardinality". The present authors think we have no problem grasping the syntax of this sentence, though we do not understand the proposition that it expresses. And we would resist the claim that what we understand in understanding that syntax is a bunch of implicit propositions about English grammar.

So on our view, understanding can perfectly well be directed at propositions, and this is one of the most common kinds of case. But there are also plenty of cases of non-propositional understanding. You can sometimes tell, when amateurs play instrumental music, that they don't understand

---

[7] Zagzebski, "Recovering Understanding", pp. 243–44.

it, or don't understand it very deeply. And clearly, what they are failing to understand are not propositions. When we say that someone knows Beethoven's Pastoral Symphony well, we don't mean that he knows some proposition about it; we mean that he understands it, and also, no doubt, that he is acquainted with it (see the next section of this chapter). Not everything that an excellent basketball or football player understands can be captured in sentences. Maybe understanding how a lawn mower engine works is not propositional. If one is working on the engine, and knows what to do next, propositions may be pretty remote from one's mind. One knows how to get the thing apart and back together, and knows why it won't run if you leave out the camshaft, and so forth. One can imagine someone with excellent mechanical understanding who is unable to put his understanding into words. Again, such understanding is clearly a matter of seeing connections among things. It is also, in most or all of the cases we have mentioned, knowing how to do things (with words, with a lawn mower engine). At least, it is an ability to recognize things (e.g., a word as belonging in a language); understanding is ability.

So understanding differs from propositional knowledge, not in being necessarily non-propositional, but in not being necessarily propositional. Another way it differs is in not necessarily being true (except in the sense we identified a few pages back). One can understand Schleiermacher's theology without its being true, but one cannot know that p without p's being true. Very commonly we understand propositions, stories, and theories that we take to be false. We would be in quite a fix intellectually if we couldn't.

Related to the difference between understanding and propositional knowledge is the possibility of alternative understandings of the same text or artwork. Ancient texts like the works of Plato and Aristotle, and the Bible—indeed, all "great texts"—are subject to somewhat divergent interpretations, some of which, though divergent, may be equally validated by the text itself. (Even here there is something like truth, since not every such interpretation is equally true to the text.) In every period of history, the interpretations of these texts are somewhat different, and the reason seems to be that people read the texts in terms of their own questions and concerns, in relation to other things they know and believe, in accordance with their own patterns of thought. It is a mark of the great texts that they have this intergenerational (or inter-epochal) versatility. And because understanding is a graded good, a text that has great depth may be read and reread by a single individual over a lifetime with changing and possibly increasing understanding.

Given what we've said so far about understanding, it is clear that propositional knowledge cannot stand on its own. Our beliefs often gain their justification via inference, and inference is a phenomenon of understanding—of seeing connections between conclusion and premises. And of course you can't very well know a proposition without understanding it. Even if what you know is not expressed in a sentence—"The bird outside my window is red"—to see a red bird out of one's window involves something like understanding: recognizing the situation as having the elements and structure that it has: namely, that it is a bird, sitting on a branch, outside your window. It involves grasping connections between things, making sense of an array. This involvement of understanding in perception is made more obvious by considering gestalt drawings. Some of them are such that when you first look at them you don't understand them at all: you just see a jumble of lines or patches, of which you make no sense. Then, perhaps as you stare at the figure, you come to see how it works, how the lines or patches make some kind of coherent whole, how the parts of the figure go together.[8] So we see a third way in which understanding is involved in propositional knowledge: not only do you have to understand to believe a proposition, and to ground one belief in another; you have to understand even to have perceptions that give rise to propositional knowledge by way of basic belief formation. Part of the analysis of the proper functioning of basic belief-producing faculties is understanding: a faculty like vision or hearing functions as it was designed to do only if the possessor of the faculty recognizes to a sufficient degree its deliverances.

Some may be inclined to associate understanding with reflective awareness of understanding—to think that one cannot understand something without being aware of understanding that thing. Perhaps this inclination

---

[8] Here the relation of understanding to truth seems to differ from that of propositional knowledge to truth. Clearly, the person who sees the gestalt figure in one way, and then in another, understands it in the one way, and then the other; but since there seems to be no truth of the matter in this case, there is no such thing as getting it right and getting it wrong. One might think that a figure like the old-woman young-woman figure has two correct ways of being seen, and only if you see it in one of these ways do you understand it (or maybe you fully understand it only if you can see it in both ways). But we think that if an especially virtuosic visualizer were able to see it as a hot air balloon collapsing into a valley, it would not be right to say that she had failed to understand it.

comes from thinking of high-end instances of understanding (understanding a complex novel, a difficult scientific theory), or perhaps from focusing on "aha!" experiences, in which one is vividly aware of the difference between what one now understands and what, prior to the insight, one understood. But we understand many things without being aware of understanding them. We understand the words of an interlocutor even if our attention is entirely on the inferences in the argument he is making. In reading a text we follow most of its logic without ever noticing the many unproblematic inferences we are following in it. When we make the "aha!" transition from seeing the gestalt figure as just a jumble of lines and patches to making sense of it, we are vividly aware of understanding it, but this is the relatively rare case. Most of the time we are unaware of the connection making that goes on moment by moment in our everyday experiences of pictures and the world.

Greco, Zagzebski, and Kvanvig[9] all emphasize the connection of understanding with explanation. The ability to give an explanation of what one believes indicates understanding, and the better the explanation, the deeper the understanding. Of course, the explanation itself expresses an understanding of what is explained only if the explanation is understood. Here too we see a connection with propositional knowledge: in many cases, a proposition is known only because it is based in a justifying proposition; and often the latter constitutes an explanation of the former.

Understanding as we have briefly sketched it is a good that pervades knowledge from bottom to top, from the most modest instances of perceptual recognition to the grasp of the deepest scientific, conceptual, and narrative truths. It is understanding in the upper reaches of this range whose acquisition is likely to profit from intellectual virtues. The understanding of deep and difficult texts and of natural phenomena by the practices of humanistic inquiry and natural science is achieved, typically, only after long and arduous effort, so that the virtue of perseverance seems eminently necessary. When texts are from a period other than our own, so that a cultural divide yawns between us and the writers, a courageous, empathic, and charitable imaginativeness may be required really to get into what the texts are saying, a humble willingness to learn from people we might be inclined to think of as naïve or primitive. Some scientists,

---

[9] See Kvanvig, *The Value of Knowledge and the Pursuit of Understanding*, ch. 8.

like Barbara McClintock, think that even in the study of such a "lowly" organism as corn, a kind of love and sympathy for what one is studying is an aid or even *sine qua non* of a certain depth of understanding. Where one's intellectual community has a deeply entrenched method, paradigm, or style of interpretation, new understanding may require considerable intellectual autonomy, perhaps even courage. Though one does not always need to be aiming at the truth of the matter in pursuing understanding, one will probably be seeking an interpretation that is true to the text, and in science one *will* be pursuing the truth of the matter. For these reasons, a love of knowledge will be an enormous aid in driving excellence of understanding. Understanding often emerges only with concerted intellectual activities like exploring, testing, dialectical interchange, probing, comparing, writing, and reflecting. These practices require virtues for their best prosecution.

Acquaintance

John Locke comments that

Knowing is seeing, and, if it be so, it is madness to persuade ourselves that we do so by another man's eyes, let him use ever so many words to tell us that what he asserts is very visible. Till we ourselves see it with our own eyes, and perceive it by our own understandings, we are as much in the dark and as void of knowledge as before, let us believe any learned author as much as we will. (*Of the Conduct of the Understanding*, §24, pp. 200–1)

Locke's generalization is a bit wild. We often know by other people's eyes. As Thomas Reid taught, reliable testimony is a perfectly legitimate way to know some things. Furthermore, we know some things we don't understand. The Babylonian astronomers, by meticulous record keeping, knew in advance when eclipses would occur, without understanding what they are or why they happen (though, as the previous section suggests, one cannot justifiably believe that a lunar eclipse will occur in three days' time without understanding *something* about lunar eclipses—as embodied, say, in knowing one when you see it). But if we take Locke to be making just the more modest point that seeing for yourself, and "seeing" for yourself, is one very important kind of epistemic good, his point is well taken. It would be extravagance in the other direction to claim that in no case is seeing for yourself a necessary condition of knowing. When the apostle Paul speaks of "knowing the fear of the Lord" (2 Cor. 5: 11), the knowing has different conditions than knowing the price of corn or even knowing a phobia when you see one; here, a condition of knowing is having the experience oneself. In this section we want to explore briefly the good we call "acquaintance", experiencing for oneself.

When we say that someone is acquainted with something, we do not mean that she is currently in immediate cognitive contact with it. We mean that she *has had* such contact and carries within her, via memory, aptitudes of recognition, belief formation, and understanding that are consequent on that earlier contact. This is the kind of cognitive advantage that we ascribe to someone by saying that she has had "a lot of experience"—with, say, deep-sea fishing or the financial markets.

Sensory experience is a necessary condition of some kinds of knowing. It is hard to see how one could know what coffee tastes like without tasting some, and at a more sophisticated level, how one might know a Brahms symphony (in a certain sense of "know") without having heard it. As we commented in the opening section of this chapter, such "acquaintance" has a role or roles in our noetic life that only partially overlap with propositional knowledge. The acquaintance, along with memory, may, all right, form the warrant for believing that what I am now smelling and hearing are coffee and the Brahms symphony. But the epistemic value of being acquainted with the smell and sound is not exhausted in their forming grounds for beliefs. The epistemic point of the acquaintance may be just the "cognitive contact with reality" (to narrow the meaning of a phrase from Linda Zagzebski). In this book we will treat acquaintance not just as a justifier in propositional knowledge, but as an epistemic good in its own right for which virtues are often an interesting kind of condition.

We want to think of acquaintance as separable from belief in many cases. It is true that if I see the bird in the tree, I will most likely believe there is a bird in the tree. This is the force of the Reidian idea that perception is a belief-forming mechanism or faculty. But I don't always or necessarily form a belief as a result of acquaintance. For example, when I become aurally acquainted with a Brahms theme, it is not clear that I come to believe anything. And if I know that I am subject to bird-in-tree hallucinations, I may have the immediate first-hand experience of seeing a bird in a tree without believing that there is a bird in the tree. When I look at a stick in a bucket of water, I am acquainted with its bent look; but after a bit of this kind of experience, I no longer form a belief that the stick is bent. I "don't believe my eyes". So acquaintance is a kind of knowledge that typically involves understanding, and does not necessarily involve belief, even when it is propositional. (This last occurs when, upon becoming acquainted with the bent look of the stick, I consider the proposition *the stick is bent*, which is the propositional form of my perception, and then deny it or withhold assent.) Here acquaintance is propositional but non-doxastic.

The smell of coffee may be an exception to our observation in the preceding section that most of what may appear to be simple deliverances of the senses are actually constructions that exhibit something like understanding—the placing of things in relation to one another, a grasp of the significance of an entire (if quite circumscribed) situation. Considering what it is to see the gestalt drawing for what it is alerts us to the synthetic complexity of many of our perceptions. Seeing, hearing, smelling, tasting, feeling (tactile), feeling (emotional) are all subject to subjective conditions of objectivity, and sometimes these conditions are very sophisticated. Only the trained mechanic can reach into a dark corner of your car's engine compartment and discriminate tactilely just the nut that needs to be loosened. Only the expert wine taster can discriminate subtle differences among closely related wines. Only the highly trained geneticist can see, through the microscope, the telltale knob on a chromosome. So Locke's phrase "perceive ... by our own understandings" is apt. What we understand, in a dispositional sense, conditions what we perceive, and, as we intend to argue in this book and preview in the present section, our character often conditions what we understand.

Imagine two equally intelligent people witnessing the following scene: Because of his race, a member of a racial minority is being subtly directed away from a majority-race neighborhood in which he would like to buy a home, by his real estate agent.[10] The action is subtle enough to require intelligent discernment on the part of the two observers. They both understand the real estate agent's action, but they have different emotional reactions to it. One of them is highly displeased. He feels angry at the agent and sad for the home buyer, whom he sees as representing a long

---

[10] This example is borrowed from Robert C. Roberts and W. Jay Wood, "Proper Function, Emotion, and Virtues of the Intellect", *Faith and Philosophy* 21 (2004): 3–24, p. 9.

history of senseless suffering at the hands of prejudice. The other observer feels no displeasure, but is mildly amused by the agent's adroit maneuvers and even feels a little admiration for his skill in handling such "problems". In one sense both observers understand what is going on, but only one of them "tastes" the injustice in the situation. Even the morally indifferent observer may be able to subsume the current case under the category *injustice*, thus showing her mastery of the concept of injustice, her moral understanding of the situation. But we want to say that by contrast with the angry observer, she is still missing something epistemically: she does not *appreciate* the injustice, feel it or perceive it as the nasty thing it is. She has a notional understanding of the action as an injustice, but in a moral or spiritual sense there is something she's not "getting". Thus the emotion is a peculiar and indispensable vehicle of knowing something, and the kind of knowledge in question is acquaintance. Emotional acquaintance of this sort is perception which is not sense perception, though the subject also has sense perceptions (sees the neighborhood, hears the real estate agent's voice, etc.).

In the moment of feeling the injustice in that situation, the morally sensitive observer expresses a virtue, his sense of justice. His having this perception depends on a complex background of beliefs, of understanding, and of concern. He has mastery of the concept of justice, easily discriminates justice from injustice in many cases, and cares about just states of affairs. This complex of abilities and inclinations goes into what we might call his understanding of justice, and is his virtue; and his virtue of justice makes injustices salient to him. The perception of the nastiness of an injustice is thus no simple receptivity or the proper functioning of mere faculties. It is the product, above all, of a virtue.

Consider another example. The following passage from Paul's Letter to the Ephesians also illustrates how complex acquaintance can depend on traits of character. Paul prays that his readers will be given first-hand knowledge of the greatness and goodness of God's gifts.

I do not cease to give thanks for you, remembering you in my prayers, that the God of our Lord Jesus Christ, the Father of glory, may give you a spirit of wisdom and of revelation in the knowledge of him, having the eyes of your hearts enlightened, that you may know what is the hope to which he has called you, what are the riches of his glorious inheritance in the saints, and what is the immeasurable greatness of his power in us who believe. (Eph. 1: 16–19a)

This passage is full of terms for epistemic goods: "wisdom", "revelation", "knowledge", "enlighten[ment]". It also has words for the mediators of these goods, perhaps something like what we will call faculties: "spirit", "eyes of the heart". But these faculty words are *encompassing*: They refer not to an isolated faculty—hearing, sight, touch, inference—but to the whole person. (In Paul's vocabulary, the spirit and the heart of a person are the central personal core.) The things that are known are very important: our hope, the riches of the glory of our inheritance in Christ, the greatness of God's power in us. And the way they are known seems to be through emotional response: to have the eyes of our hearts enlightened about these important things is to respond with gratitude, awe, reverence, admiration, love. The kind of knowledge in question here is a sense of appreciation. Expressions like "revelation" and "eyes of your hearts" suggest an immediate appearing or direct acquaintance analogous to sense perception but different from it. The virtues that condition the reception of these epistemic goods are faith, hope, and love. Only a person whose heart is oriented in these ways will "see" the things of which Paul speaks. Such direct acquaintance with the greatness of God's gifts is not necessary for warranted belief in them, but it helps the appreciation. This seeing with the eyes of the heart is a concentrated, perceptual, episodic sort of understanding. Like the moral example above, understanding and acquaintance converge in a way they do not (or do much less) in the smell of coffee.

One of the chief Greek verbs for "know" (*oida, eidō, eidenai*) has strong associations with "see", and the word from which we get "epistemology" (*epistēmē*) means "acquaintance with, skill, experience".[11] Another important word for "know", *gignōskein*, also has perceptual overtones. If you put together the ascent to the Forms in Plato's *Republic* with the ascent described in his *Symposium*, you see that love is an indispensable part of the highest epistemic access. A case can be made that in Plato the intellect and the will are integrated for epistemic purposes. This knowledge is also a kind of seeing, a kind of direct acquaintance by immediate beholding of what is real, including, all-importantly, its value: the object of knowledge (something ever so odd for the modern philosophical temperament) is the

---

[11] *An Intermediate Greek–English Lexicon*, founded upon the 7th edn. of Liddell and Scott's *Greek–English Lexicon* (Oxford: Clarendon Press, 1996; 1st edn. 1889).

Good. Something formally similar to this is found in the Ephesians passage we just discussed and in the idea of Adam's "knowing" Eve.

Knowledge

Contemporary epistemology has been overwhelmingly preoccupied with knowledge on the model of "knowledge that p": that is, knowledge of propositions taken pretty much in isolation; and knowledge is conceived as warranted or justified true belief. In this chapter we have tried to show that such knowledge is only an aspect of knowledge. We say "only an aspect" rather than "only a kind", because propositional knowledge is thoroughly entangled with understanding and acquaintance. Even the most rudimentary cases, in which a true belief is generated by a properly functioning faculty in a congenial environment, require that the subject of the belief recognize something in consequence of the functioning of the faculty, and thus require a rudimentary understanding. In such cases, the understanding is delivered as an acquaintance. The dependence of propositional knowledge on understanding is only the more obvious in cases where the true belief counts as knowledge in virtue of its being inferred from some other belief; for in that case the subject must understand the relationship between the based belief and the basing belief—that and how the one is fit to serve as a basis for the other.

But, as we have seen, acquaintance and understanding do far more than serve as parts of the justification or warrant of beliefs. While they play crucial roles in warrant, they are proper epistemic aims independently of those roles. We often rightly wish to understand even where we are confident that the representations we are trying to understand are not true, and acquaintance often has epistemic value beyond what it adds by way of warrant. Furthermore, as we pointed out at the beginning of this chapter, understanding and acquaintance are classified as knowledge in ordinary, non-philosophical speech. What we seek, as intellectual beings, is not the abstraction that we have been calling propositional knowledge, but the fully orbed package that ordinary people, including educators, and indeed, we must charitably suppose, most professional epistemologists when off the job, call knowledge. If we take epistemology to be about knowledge in this rich, deep, and ordinary sense, the project of providing an e-definition of it looks even more hopeless than we made it out to be in Chapter 1. We see, then, that the concept of knowledge is like the concept of a game as Wittgenstein describes it—held together not by a *single set* of properties that are individually necessary and jointly sufficient for anything's being a case of knowledge, but instead by a *fund* of properties some of which will be necessary, and enough of which will be sufficient, in any given case. Among these properties will be truth, belief, acquaintance, grasp of coherence relationships, and various kinds of justifiers or warrants.

Like Zagzebski, Jonathan Kvanvig argues that understanding is not a kind of knowledge. To this end, he argues that one can have knowledge without understanding. He says,

The central feature of understanding, it seems to me, is in the neighborhood of what internalist coherence theories say about justification. Understanding requires the grasping of explanatory and other coherence-making relationships in a large and comprehensive body of information. One can know many unrelated pieces of information, but understanding is achieved only when informational items are pieced together by the subject in question. (*The Value of Knowledge and the Pursuit of Understanding*, p. 192)

Later (p. 202), Kvanvig describes "the distinctive element" in understanding simply as "grasped coherence relations", and this broader formulation is better, since, as we have seen, the relations in question need not be either explanatory or involve a large and comprehensive body of information. The central feature of understanding is the grasping of coherence in something complex; and a body of information about a subject-matter is *one* kind of complex. Kvanvig is right that people can be said to "know" bits of trivia about, say, Abraham Lincoln, without having any very deep understanding of Lincoln's personality and life, or the historical context. Perhaps they know these by testimony: they looked them up in a reliable book in the course of playing Trivial Pursuit, and have a good memory for such fact-bits. But understanding is required even for this trivial kind of knowledge. If the fact-bit is that Lincoln was elected President in 1861, or that he was the sixteenth President of the United States, the knower will surely have to be able to place *president* among political leader concepts and *United States* among names of nation-states, and *elect* among political mechanism-concepts, etc. A parrot that had been taught to say "Sixteenth US president" when given an authoritative cue would not know even this bit of trivia, and one reason is that it wouldn't understand what it was saying.

In his effort to show that understanding is not a kind of knowledge, Kvanvig also argues that one can have understanding without knowledge. He imagines someone whose historical understanding of the Comanche dominance of the southern plains of North America from the late seventeenth until the late nineteenth centuries consists in her ability to answer correctly any question you might ask her; that is, she grasps all the coherence relations among the truths about this subject (p. 197). However, her beliefs are only accidentally true: among the history books from which she might have got her information, three out of the four give incorrect accounts; she happens to have read the one that gives a correct account, but without any basis for preferring it. So, because of this Gettier-like situation, she does not have knowledge of these historical truths, though she does understand the field. We have defended a "family resemblance" concept of knowledge that allows for differing sets of necessary and sufficient conditions for knowledge, depending on differences of cases (e.g., low-end/high-end) and differences of context (e.g., casual versus rigorous). We have also seen reason for thinking that an ordinary careful speaker of English would have no hesitation in calling this woman's mastery of Comanche history "knowledge". And we might speculate that such an intelligent non-epistemologist, if asked why he calls her accomplishment knowledge despite its somewhat accidental character, would point to the following: she did, after all, get her facts right, she got them from a reliable source, and she grasps the coherence relations among them. Surely this is enough to claim that she knows that history!

Conclusion

In closing this chapter, let us think again briefly about the nature of epistemology. It is the study of knowledge and the conditions of its acquisition, transmission, and application. We have proposed, in outline, a concept of knowledge that is broader, richer, and deeper than the one on which most English-speaking epistemologists focused during the latter half of the twentieth century. In this book we are especially interested in the role of character traits in facilitating the acquisition, transmission, and application

of knowledge. How is our epistemology related to "internalism", "extern-
alism", "reliabilism", "virtue reliabilism", "virtue responsibilism", "proper
functionalism", "agent reliabilism", "pure virtue theory", "coherentism",
"foundationalism", and other such theories? Our offering in this book is
none of the above theories, and is not the same kind of discourse as such
theories. Yet it is clear that each of those proposed definitions captured
something important about at least some cases of knowledge. We will not
hesitate to talk about reliability, proper functioning, coherence, responsibility, motivation, and indeed just about anything that any epistemologist
has proposed as a condition of knowledge. We hope to show how such
things are related to the epistemic virtues and the knowledge that they can
condition, and our aim in sketching these connections and exploring this
conceptual territory is to make ourselves, through philosophical thought,
more excellent intellectual agents and to help others do the same.

3

Virtues

Introduction

The central concept in our study—though not its theoretical basis—is that of an intellectual virtue. Part II contains discussions of several intellectual virtues, selected with a view to representativeness, to breadth of coverage, and to displaying both the diversity and the interconnection of the virtues. We hope that Part II will give the reader a balanced view of excellent intellectual character; it is the heart of the book and the place to go for a detailed understanding of the concept of an intellectual virtue. In the present chapter we intend merely to outline that concept, to discuss it somewhat abstractly and by way of introduction.

We propose that in general a human virtue is an acquired base of excellent functioning in some generically human sphere of activity that is challenging and important. Virtues have both intellectual and non-intellectual bearing, though in one way or another all virtues have a cognitive aspect. We will explore the relations of the virtues to cognition. Many virtues are "perfections", or mature completions of natural (that is, given) human faculties; but some are dispositions that correct for pronenesses to dysfunction and error in certain common situations. Many virtues are dispositions of the will—that is, of desire, goal seeking, concern, attachment, willpower, emotions, and choice; and again, all virtues bear some relation or other to the will (sometimes, as in the case of courage, virtuous motivation derives from other virtues). The will is so important that we will devote a section of this chapter to sketching it. Virtues can also be skills, or involve skills, though not all skills are virtues, since many skills fit us for functioning excellently, not in generic human contexts, but in specialized ones. Again, all virtues bear some relation or other to skills by which we negotiate generically human activities or situations for activities.

Intellectual virtues, as we understand them here, are simply acquired bases of excellent intellectual functioning—this being one of those important and challenging generically human kinds of functioning. We find it unhelpful to try to draw a strict line between the intellectual and the moral virtues. So we will speak of intellectual humility, intellectual courage, intellectual generosity, where more traditional usage might speak of a moral virtue applied to an intellectual context. If the classical division of theoretical from practical reason is artificial, given the enormous importance of practices in intellectual life (see Chapter 5), so is the division between intellectual and moral virtues. So all the virtues are intellectual (as well as "moral" and "civic"). The difference between our study and a study in virtue ethics is simply that we are interested in the relations between the virtues and the intellectual goods.[1]

We realize that our way of using "virtue" is not the only legitimate way. Earlier we mentioned some epistemologists who think of properly functioning cognitive faculties as epistemic virtues. While we do not deny that properly functioning faculties can be called "virtues",[2] they are not what *we* call virtues. Chapter 4 will explore the concept of a faculty and the relations of faculties to virtues in our preferred sense.

Will

Before we sketch our concept of a virtue, let us reflect on a notion that will be important throughout our discussion of virtues in this book. We propose that the will is a central epistemic faculty, and that its proper formation is crucial to intellectual character. What do we mean by "will"?

---

[1] Zagzebski considers four arguments for a distinction in kind between moral and intellectual virtues: (1) they belong to different parts of the soul; (2) the moral, but not the intellectual, virtues are dispositions to experience pleasure and pain; (3) moral, but not intellectual, virtues are dispositions to feelings; (4) a person can be intellectually virtuous but morally vicious, or vice versa. She convincingly refutes all four arguments. See Linda Zagzebski, *Virtues of the Mind: An Inquiry into the Nature of Virtue and the Ethical Foundations of Knowledge* (Cambridge: Cambridge University Press, 1996), pp. 137–58. In a moment we will consider yet another argument.

[2] Ernest Sosa points out that the Greeks used *aretē* for excellences even of such things as knives (*Knowledge in Perspective: Selected Essays in Epistemology* (Cambridge: Cambridge University Press, 1991), p. 271). An analogous usage of "virtue" is natural to speakers of modern English. But when Aristotle speaks of *human* virtues, he says that they are not faculties. "We have the faculties by nature, but are not made good or bad by nature" (*Nicomachean Ethics* II. 5). But maybe the "virtues" of inference, coherence, etc. are not to be regarded as human virtues.

People have abilities or aptitudes: for example, the ability to lift a certain amount of weight, to do calculations of a certain degree of complexity, to see very small objects with the naked eye, to play the guitar, etc. But these aptitudes are not put into play unless their possessor has the will to do so. Someone might be the best guitarist in the world, and yet never play, because he doesn't want to, isn't motivated, doesn't find the prospect attractive, doesn't have a reason that moves *him*. Thus we might say, as a first point, that the will is that in the human mental repertoire that motivates, that impels towards action. In English we have an extensive array of words that capture aspects of will: "desire", "attraction", "concern", "care", "appetite", "preference", "enthusiasm", "interest", "love", "urge", "inclination", "motivation", "attachment", and "goal", to mention some of the main ones. And the negative counterparts of many of these terms also refer to states of the will: "repugnance", "repulsion", "disinclination", which we might call positive negative counterparts, and then the simple negative counterparts (indifference), which we express with the word "lack": lack of inclination, lack of concern, etc., which are also states of the will, states in which the will is in abeyance with respect to some object or other.

So we might say that the will *moves* us. The notion of motion is built into the etymology of some of the will vocabulary: "motive", "motivation", "emotion", and, of course, "move". But the idea that the will moves us may not be quite right in this connection. We might better say that the *object* moves us *because of* the state or condition of our will. I am moved to play the guitar because the prospect of playing attracts me; I am moved to help a sufferer because I care about him. The passive language seems appropriate here: I *am attracted* to playing the guitar because I like to. Will in this sense is crucial to the intellectual virtues, because the intellectually excellent person must be one who finds knowledge attractive, enjoys it, is moved to seek it both for himself and for others, and enjoys the epistemic practices.

The foregoing paragraph doesn't describe the will of an adult human being. Such a person is not simply a set of aptitudes plus a set of susceptibilities to be attracted by this or that prospect or object. People are not just moved to action or behavior by being attracted to this or that in virtue of some state of their likes and dislikes. People *assess* the objects of their urges and desires and attractions for their *eligibility*, and then *choose* what to do. People often have conflicting desires, and they may judge some of their desires to be inappropriate or inopportune, or just plain bad. This capacity to choose is also a function of the will. Someone may object that this is confusing because, clearly, choosing is not just a matter of being attracted to something and "going for it", so to speak, but involves thinking, deliberation, considering reasons pro and con; and that's not part of the will, but part of reason. But this objection makes the mistake of thinking that the will and reason have to be separate. Even the first aspect of the will that we mentioned—being attracted to something or some prospect—typically involves the "intellect" in human beings. For example, a person can't want to play the guitar unless he knows what a guitar is and what it is to play it. Will as the power of choice depends on will as attraction. Even if I choose to do what I don't want to do, because it is my duty, I have to want to do my duty. And generally, any consideration on which a person makes a genuine choice must have a certain attractiveness for him (which is not to say that it has to be the alternative that feels most attractive to him).

Here the passivity that we noted in connection with the first function of the will is mitigated. In deliberately choosing, a person takes some command of his desires and attractions and exercises his agency in adjudicating among them. But choice is more than adjudication of reasons. It is, upon such adjudication, the undertaking of action. It is acting on deliberation. Merely having settled on what to do is choice only if the person acts (or would have acted, in case he was prevented by circumstances, or compelling new reasons have brought about a change of mind). We include in the choosing function of will that of making an effort. Actions are sometimes not completed, but they count as fully chosen if the agent has made a sufficient effort. Let us call the first function of the will *attraction*, and the second (that of choice and effort) *execution*. Since this second function of the will is involved in many actions, and since intellectual practices (see Chapter 5) are made up, in part, of deliberate actions, the second aspect of the will is clearly relevant to intellectual virtues. With respect to both of the functions of the will that we have glanced at so far, the will can be well or ill formed. For example, in the attraction function, the will is well formed intellectually if it finds genuine intellectual goods sufficiently attractive (see Chapter 6), and in the executive function, the will is well formed if it is disposed to make good intellectual choices. We do not mean to suggest doxastic voluntarism; the choices we have in mind are not of beliefs, but of actions that are involved in intellectual practices, such as searching for more evidence and getting one's interlocutor to clarify his statement before launching into a criticism.

A third aspect or function of the will we call "willpower". Mature people engage in impulse management. They become wise about their emotions, their appetites, and their desires, and through self-management practices and efforts and the strengths that accrue from these, they come to be able to suppress unwanted behaviors and actions and to extinguish or modify unwanted deliverances of their wills. For example, a mature person will usually be able to conquer fear in situations where he or she needs to act in spite of the fear. This presence of mind may take the form of acting through the fear; but more typically, it will involve calming it. The same will be true of anger, shame, impatience, and physical appetites or social urges. The mature person is more or less constantly monitoring his own desires and other affects in situations where these are most aroused, and is not just monitoring, but also managing these, enhancing some and mitigating others. This aspect of the will is as important in the intellectual life as elsewhere. For example, in dialectical exchange, in classroom teaching, in reading (say, criticisms of one's work, or the irritating work of people from other disciplines or of people with a very different approach to one's own discipline), emotions and urges will arise that need to be managed in the interest of excellent intellectual practice.

In a fourth aspect or function, the will as we understand it is the source of emotions. As in the other three functions, here too the "intellect" is involved. We take emotions—at least the paradigm cases of adult human emotions, the ones that chiefly interest us in our epistemological explorations—to be construals or "takes" on situations. The subject of anger, for example, perceives his situation as containing an offense (what he is angry about), an offender (the one he is angry with), and an offended one (this might be the subject himself, or someone he cares about, or a community or even some non-personal object such as a mountainside, in case the subject is angry about something the offender has done to the mountainside,—e.g., strip-mining). Furthermore, the subject construes the offender as culpable (if, through new information, the subject comes to construe the offender as not culpable of the offense, he ceases to be angry). What has this to do with the will? Emotions are not just any kind of construal, but are concern-based construals. A person will not be angry unless he cares about what is offended, and cares about the offense against him (her, it). So the emotion is based in the will (based on concerns), but it also generates a consequent concern—in the case of anger, the desire that the offender "get what he deserves". Other emotions have other consequent concerns—embarrassment, the urge to hide; fear, the urge to avoid a danger, etc.[3] Emotions are relevant to intellectual functioning in a variety of ways, some of which we will review later in this chapter.

These, then, are the four functions of the will as we conceive it in this book: (1) attraction, desire, concern, attachment, etc.; (2) choice, effort, and undertaking; (3) willpower; and (4) emotion.

What is a Virtue?

Certain activities or situation types for activities are generically human. Virtually every human group exchanges goods, pursues intimate interpersonal relations (friend–friend, spouse–spouse, parent–child), worships the divine, acts in the face of impeding or diverting impulses (fear, impatience, fatigue, irritation, anger, etc.), inquires, and passes knowledge from one person to another. Such activities, or activities in such situations, can be performed well only by people in whom certain capacities and dispositions have been formed by education (in a broad sense). Properly functioning faculties are not enough. The education in question is not just "technical"—a training in specialized skills—but is also a formation in *human* excellence. The trait products of such an education for life are called virtues.

As a way of introducing our concept of the intellectual virtues, we will consider, in this chapter, several questions that might be raised about their nature. What makes a trait of personality a virtue? How are the intellectual virtues related to human nature? What explains competent, but divergent, accounts of the virtues? What makes an intellectual virtue more than just an intellectual application of a virtue? Are virtues all "perfections" of human nature? How are the tasks of the intellectual virtues divided among them? How are virtues individuated? How does motivation figure

---

[3] For a defense of this view of emotions, see Robert C. Roberts, *Emotions: An Essay in Aid of Moral Psychology* (Cambridge: Cambridge University Press, 2003), ch. 2; for the analysis of anger, see pp. 202–21.

in the constitution of an intellectual virtue? Do all the virtues have a "motivational component"? If so, do they all have it in the same way? To what extent must an intellectually virtuous person be "autonomous" in his possession of the virtue—that is, independent of communities that support his virtue in a variety of ways? We will pay close attention to the particular intellectual virtues, trying to avoid the abstraction and overgeneralization characteristic of recent discussions of them.

Virtues and human nature   In the history of philosophy virtues have often been thought of as fulfillments, realizations, mature states, or "perfections" of human nature or some aspect thereof. Thomas Aquinas, for example, defines a human virtue as a "maximum of a [human] power [*potentia*, faculty]" (*Summa Theologiæ*, 1a2æ 55,1)[4] and, again following Aristotle, makes most central the distinctively human power of reason (see *Nicomachean Ethics* I. 13). We draw on this tradition in developing our concept of a virtue. We think of human beings as persons and of the virtues as excellences of persons, traits that make one excellent as a person. The classical idea is that, like other biological species, the human species has a set of potentials and developmental parameters that must be respected if the individual is to become an excellent specimen of its kind. If the DNA of any species is or contains a set of instructions for what the mature individual is *supposed* to be like (no guarantee that it *will* be like this, since many influences from the environment have their effects on development; the environment can fail to cooperate with the instructions, so to speak), then human nature is a sort of psychological DNA, a DNA of the personal life (no doubt conditioned by the physical DNA). The instructions are an internal disposition or tendency of the organism, tuned to the kind of environment in which the organism will live out its life. As psychological, the instructions have to be honored in a process of education; the devices of education or upbringing are, in this case, the relevant environment, social and otherwise. If the education is right, the human nature will be realized, within the limits particular to the individual; if it is poor, the development and outcome are very likely to be poor too, no matter how excellent the instructions in the nature of the person.

---

[4] *Summa Theologiae*, translated by the Fathers of the English Dominican Province (Westminster, MD: Christian Classics, 1981), 1a–2ae, question 57, article 1, p. 828.

Human nature is tailored for an environment of certain specifications, both physical and psychological. Physically we do very poorly if we lack water or the right nutrients or an atmospheric temperature within certain bounds. Socially we are made for a set of relationships with parents initially, then with peers and friends, and very likely with a spouse and then children of our own. And these relationships need to be of a certain positive and benevolent nature if we are to develop properly and thrive. Here already environmental and developmental parameters, and consequently the shape of maturity, are somewhat contestable. The concept of virtue in the Stoics (what they call *apatheia*) is that of a fulfillment of human nature, all right, but the concept of human nature is not quite what it is among Christians and adherents of several other outlooks. The Stoics tend to think of human nature as that of a highly individualized rational psyche to which concerns—especially highly intense ones focused on changeable objects such as health and wealth and friends—are intrinsically foreign, and therefore vicious. This concept of human nature, with its corresponding virtue of *apatheia*, has consequences for the nature of the social relationships of the mature individual. Whereas Christians think it perfectly appropriate and mature to care about others to the extent of making oneself subject to intense grief at their loss, the Stoic thinks of such attachments as immature and vicious. Such a metaphysics of the person has obvious consequences, as well, for moral knowledge and any virtues that may be supposed to foster it. It also involves an understanding of the relation of the individual to his environment: The real environment for the Stoic is not so much an immediate society of friends and relatives and associates, and tasks relating to these, as the universe at large, thought of as a rational (ordered, law-governed) whole.

In Christianity, the redemption of the world through Jesus Christ makes most central and basic the virtues of faith (in that redemption and in God as the source of it), hope (for the completion of that redemption in the new world of resurrection), and love (as the reciprocation, towards God, and the imitation, toward one's neighbor, of the love that God has shown in that redemption). But, tied as these virtues are to the Christian story, they do not even occur in other outlooks. Furthermore, they influence the structure of the other virtues. If we think of ourselves as redeemed from sin by God and destined for an "eternal weight of glory", courage and humility and other virtues will be quite different than if we thought of ourselves as simply mortals in an indifferent universe. Because of the belief that we are creatures of a loving God, we are encouraged to stress our dependence and thus our interdependence in a way that Aristotle, for example, does not. Thus, gratitude is a virtue on the Christian conception of human nature, but not on Aristotle's; and consequently Christian generosity is an attitude significantly different from Aristotelian liberality (see our discussion in Chapter 11).

Thus, different conceptions of the human person and his place in the universe yield strikingly different pictures of proper human functioning, and thus of the virtues. We have offered a general characterization of human virtues in the second paragraph of this chapter, but in light of the dependence of any human virtue on some conception of human nature, we see that this general characterization is only formal. If we actually analyze particular virtues, we see that at some point in the development of the specificity of the concept, we will have to advert to some contestable view of human nature. This fact is often hidden from view, in the writings of philosophers about the virtues, either because they do not admit the contestability of the conception on which their own analysis rests, or because their analyses remain too abstract to bring out the special features. One of our complaints about the literature on the virtues—intellectual and otherwise—is the paucity of analysis of particular virtues.[5] This deficiency is not just a gap, but a hole that causes structural weakness throughout the discussions. We hope that Part II of this book will begin to remedy this deficiency in the literature.

In our initial characterization of a human virtue we stressed the way in which virtues fit us for excellent functioning in generically human situations. We can see now that what one takes to be a generically human situation can vary from outlook to outlook. For example, non-Christians do not think that the situation in which all human beings find themselves is a universe ruled by a loving God who has offered redemption to us through Jesus Christ. So non-Christians do not think Christian faith is a virtue, but Christians do. By contrast, we can probably count on far more cross-outlook agreement that being inquirers and passers of knowledge and understanding to and from one another are generic features of our human

---

[5] For a collection of exceptions to the tendency, see Clifford Williams (ed.), *Personal Virtues* (Houndmills and New York: Palgrave Macmillan, 2005).

nature and situation. Consequently, we may be able to secure quite a bit of cross-outlook agreement about features of traits that fit us to function well in those activities and situations.

Regardless of what, precisely, one thinks a human being is and what her generic situation is, we take virtues to be traits that make a person excellent *as a human being* rather than, for an example, *as a scientist, as a lawyer,* or *as a basketball player.* And this provides an answer to a possible objection to the notion of intellectual virtues as we conceive them. Having denied the classical distinction between moral and intellectual virtues, we might seem to have laid ourselves open to the following *reductio* argument:

> If courage is an intellectual virtue just because it fits one to pursue well the intellectual goods, then why are there not such virtues as ice hockey courage and tree-climbing courage and hostess courage? It is just as absurd to think that intellectual courage is a special virtue as it is to think that courages in these other contexts are special virtues.

We don't think so. Ice hockey, tree climbing, and hosting can be challenging, and they may be important for particular individuals, but they are neither generic nor as important to human life as intellectual activities are. We are not at all denying that courage can be applied in these special contexts; courage is nothing if it is not applicable in the special circumstances of an individual's life. We are saying only that courage in hosting contexts does not have a general claim to be set aside for special treatment in the way that courage and other intellectual virtues are being privileged for special treatment in this book.

What about the idea that virtues are "perfections" or "completions" of human nature? We have no objection to the idea if it is taken in a somewhat weak or casual sense, but both words have an absolute ring. We do not think that a trait can be called a virtue only if it is as good as possible. Aristotle is ambivalent about calling the traits of moral strength virtues. A person who is reliably able to control his untoward anger has a trait that we could call self-control (*enkrateia*), and Aristotle agrees that this trait is good conditionally: that is, it is good for someone who is disposed to episodes of untoward anger. But since the condition for self-control's being a good trait is a defect, Aristotle is reluctant to call *enkrateia* a virtue. He is pretty optimistic about the possibility of some people becoming "perfect" in the ordinary sense—entirely without defects. We are not optimistic about this. It seems to us that everybody is defective in one way or another, and thus in need of virtues that are not exactly "perfections", but "correctives". The virtues of strength of will are such corrective traits. Another implication of "perfectionism" that some thinkers feel is that no virtue can be expressed in evil action. This principle rules out such actions as courageous theft and compassionate injustice. We will argue in Part II that such actions may express virtues. Furthermore, we think that virtues come in degrees or amounts. Thus one person can be more humble or courageous than another, and an individual can grow in honesty and self-confidence. So we do not exactly endorse a definition of virtue that attributes to virtues perfection or completion of the faculties.

Virtue and virtues   Thomas Aquinas points out that a disposition is called a virtue for one or both of two reasons: (a) it *enables* us to do something, gives us an aptitude; (b) it induces or *motivates* us to practice the aptitude (*Summa Theologiae* 1a2æ 57.1, response). Under the influence of the Aristotelian tradition, Aquinas goes on to say that the intellectual virtues other than practical wisdom are called virtues for the first reason only. They have the character of an aptitude, but do not, in themselves, motivate. Linda Zagzebski's conception of a virtue has the same two elements, which she calls a "success component" and a "motivational component"; but, disagreeing with Aquinas, she insists that virtues, including the intellectual ones, each have both components. Thus she defines a virtue as "a deep and enduring acquired excellence of a person, involving a characteristic motivation to produce a certain desired end and reliable success in bringing about that end" (*Virtues of the Mind*, p. 137). These claims raise questions about how the individual virtues are related to the whole personality, and in particular the whole configuration of virtues in the virtuous personality. How are virtues related to virtue? How are the virtues interconnected in the personality? What justification have we for distinguishing particular virtues, as our ordinary language does when we speak of justice, humility, courage, charity, tenacity, and many others as distinct virtues? How do the success and motivation aspects of the virtuous life relate to the particular virtues? Do all virtues have both components, as Zagzebski thinks? Do the chief intellectual virtues lack the motivational (appetitive) component, as Aquinas thinks?

Let us start with Aquinas, who says:

Now since the speculative intellectual habits do not perfect the appetitive part nor concern it in any way, but have regard only to the intellectual part, they may be called virtues insofar as they confer an aptitude for good operation, namely, for considering truth, for truth is the good work of the intellect; however, they are not called virtues in the second way as though they made a power or a habit be used well (57,1, response).

But since the *use* of the intellectual virtue presupposes a movement of the will, Aquinas seems to be saying that a person would never actually achieve the goods proper to the speculative intellectual virtues if he did not have a properly disposed will. And if we look at people of extraordinary intellectual excellence, we see that they have both aptitude—well-trained intellectual powers—and a drive or concern or will to understand, to discover truth, to ground their beliefs ever more firmly. Richard Feynman had extraordinary powers of imagination and inference in his field of particle physics.[6] But these aptitudes were not separable from his love of figuring things out, his awe before the magnificence of the universe, and his drive to understand more and more about it. It is true that we can imagine Feynman in the situation of Antonio Damasio's "Elliott", a man with normal or above average intelligence as measured by the standard intelligence tests, who, because of damage to the frontal lobes of his brain, lacked motivation to put his intelligence to use.[7] Had Feynman suffered "Elliott's" kind of brain damage, he would, presumably, have retained his extraordinary *ability* to do the work, while ceasing to *care* about doing it. But in the normal, virtuous non-brain-damaged Feynman, aptitude and will were bound together.

Aquinas admits that one cannot actually bring the goods of the speculative intellect to fruition if the will is not contributing its bit, but he still wants to insist that virtues that fit people to do the kind of work that Feynman did are seated entirely in the intellect, and not in the will. We can offer at least two arguments to the contrary. First, notice the etiological reciprocity between these aspects of a person's intellectual constitution. Without the will to understand, one will not have developed one's powers of observation

---

[6] See Richard P. Feynman, *You Must Be Joking, Mr. Feynman,* as told to Ralph Leighton, ed. Edward Hutchings (New York : W.W. Norton, 1985).

[7] See Antonio Damasio, *Descartes' Error* (New York: Avon Books, 1994), and the discussion of the Elliott case in Roberts, *Emotions,* pp. 148–51.

and inference, and without developing such powers of success in getting insights and truths, one will become discouraged and will lose the will to proceed. Second, notice that the objects of a person's intellectual *abilities* are the very same things as the objects of one's intellectual *will*: in the case of Feynman, the facts about the fundamental physics of the universe. What he knew was the very thing he wanted to know, and what he wanted to know was precisely what his intellectual powers allowed him to know. A third argument for the inseparability of these faculties in the virtues of the intellect applies less obviously to the case of physical science than it does to moral and religious knowledge. Aquinas says that faith is a virtue of the speculative intellect, and that it cannot do its job unless moved by the consent of the will; but when the apostle Paul speaks of knowing the glorious things of the gospel by seeing them with the eyes of the heart (Eph. 1: 18), he seems to suggest that the truths come across to the knowing subject via such emotions as joy and hope; it is not just that the will *moves* the intellect *into operation*, but in this kind of case the will (as the seat of these *affectiones*) is *part* of the intellect. The operation of the intellect is itself affective; the will itself functions intellectually. The emotions of faith are a power of "seeing".[8] Something analogous could be said about our case of the person who, only through his indignation, appreciates properly the injustice of a racist real estate agent. (For both of these examples, see Chapter 2.) We grant the usefulness of distinguishing intellectual and other faculties, and will discuss this issue in Chapter 4. But it seems to us gratuitous to posit that each virtue must be "seated" in one and only one faculty. Damasio's Elliott, in losing his will for inquiry, has lost his intellectual virtue, even though his "intellect" remains intact. In what follows, we will suppose that virtues reside, not in faculties, but in people, and that they integrate functions from more than one faculty.

What about Zagzebski's claim that every intellectual virtue has both a success component and a motivation component? Our denial of Aquinas's

---

[8] Alvin Plantinga reaches a similar conclusion when considering the question, Which is prior, intellect or will in seeing the glory and beauty of the Lord? His answer is Neither, or There's no saying. "The structure of will and intellect here is perhaps a spiral, dialectical process: heightened affections enable us to see more of God's beauty and glory; being able to see more of God's beauty and glory and majesty in turn leads to heightened affections. There are certain things you won't know unless you love, have the right affections; there are certain affections you won't have without perceiving some of God's moral qualities; neither perceiving nor affection can be said to be prior to the other" (*Warranted Christian Belief* (New York: Oxford University Press, 2000), p. 303).

principle might seem to imply our acceptance of Zagzebski's, but we think that a close look at the structure of intellectual virtues shows considerable variety among the virtues as to both the success and the motivation components.

It is beyond dispute that intellectual motivation dispositions and dispositions to epistemic success are components or aspects of the excellent intellectual life *as a whole*. The epistemically virtuous person values, cherishes, seeks, and appreciates intellectual goods. She wants to know important truths and to understand how things work; among the things she wants to understand is how the "whole" of reality works, so she is internally driven towards "wisdom", and thus considerations in the neighborhood of theology. She craves insight, or what we have called "acquaintance", in these matters; she wants to "see for herself" in some kind of striking, relatively unmediated way; she is not satisfied with operating on mere hearsay or induction or inference, but for some things wants contact with reality. Ultimately, perhaps, she wants to combine knowledge, understanding, and acquaintance in "the beatific vision". If we are Augustinians, we will think that the drive towards this worshipful contact with ultimate reality, a contact that is at the same time "epistemic" and "moral", is planted in the nature of every human being, whether that person is aware of the drive or not. In that case ultimate intellectual excellence will involve an *awareness* of the drive and an *intentional* pursuit of its object. And if such epistemic goods are the agent's desire, clearly she must be equipped to approximate success. She needs approaches to questions that will yield answers; she needs epistemic habits and skilled faculties that will accomplish the work of justified believing, seeing, and understanding. She needs the ability to oppose or circumvent obstacles, internal and external, to her coming to know. She needs education and training and formation to these ends. And she needs practices that are well designed for harvesting the epistemic goods.

But to say that *each* intellectual virtue has its *own* distinct motivation and success components, and that this motivation and success are distinctively intellectual, seems to us as awkward as the supposition that each virtue must be seated in one and only one of the intellect, the will, or the sensory appetite. Let us sketch briefly some of the intellectual virtues, to display the variety of ways in which motivation and success dispositions characterize intellectual virtues. (Some, but not all, of the virtues sketched here receive more extended treatment in Part II.)

Consider first *love of knowledge,* a virtue that is basic to the whole intellectual life. Love of knowledge is a disposition to take an interest in information, understanding, and direct epistemic contact with reality, to enjoy intellectual activities as such, to be excited by the prospect of learning, and so to engage in actions that aim at the acquisition, maintenance, transmission, and application of knowledge. It is eminently a formation of the will. Anyone who loves knowledge in a mature (virtuous) way will inevitably have some skills for acquiring knowledge and passing it on to others, because the love of knowledge matures in the context of intellectual practices. For the same reason he will also, very likely, have some degree of virtues such as intellectual autonomy, firmness, and courage. But if we are to think of the virtues as at all plural and distinct from one another, the love of knowledge will have to be thought of as *associated* with other virtues and skills rather than as *including* them. These coordinated skills and virtues supply various aptitudes for intellectual practice. If we ask what is the motivational component of love of knowledge, the answer is that this virtue is itself a motivational structure. It is not exactly a component of a virtue, since it is the whole virtue. It *is*, of course, a component of intellectual character as a whole.

Intellectual *charity* has a distinct motivation component, but unless we confuse it with love of knowledge (both being loves in some sense), charity's motivation does not seem to be directed at an intellectual good. A person is not said to be charitable on account of loving and seeking intellectual goods. Charity is love of *God* and/or fellow *human beings* and such objects are not intellectual goods. No doubt, the person of full intellectual virtue will have not only charity, but also virtues that involve loving the intellectual goods and the means to achieve them. Charity becomes intellectual charity when it applies in contexts of the intellectual life, so charity is an attitude toward, most notably, interlocutors and authors of texts. If one reads a text charitably, one is reading the text *as* coming from an author who would like to be treated with respect and goodwill. Such charity is an *intellectual* virtue because of its applicability to intellectual activities like text reading, and because it (presumably) enhances the agent's prospects of achieving the aims of the intellectual life.

Consider an act of intellectual charity. I am discussing someone's philosophical book, and I disagree pretty fundamentally with what I take the author to be saying. If I am reading a certain passage charitably, I interpret it so as to attribute as much validity and intelligence to the passage as I can, compatibly with a careful and therefore critical reading. The act of charity in this case is the interpretation. The motive distinctive of intellectual charity (as contrasted with other intellectual virtues) is here my concern to treat the author as I would like to be treated were I the author. It is goodwill towards him, a valuing of him as a person and as an author. If I am broadly intellectually virtuous, I will also be motivated by the prospect of deriving intellectual goods from my reading of the book: I want to understand, to learn, to be better informed, and I take pleasure in such intellectual progress as accrues to me. But this motive is distinctive not of charity, but of the love of knowledge. The fact that I interpret the passage so as to attribute as much validity and intelligence to it as I can does not by itself make the act an act of intellectual charity, because as charity, the act has this motivational condition: I must act out of goodwill towards the author. If I make a "charitable" interpretation of the passage, because doing so will enable me better to crush the author in the noetic dust under my feet, then I have not acted charitably, even if I have acted "charitably". But even if I "use" charity in the interest of knowledge and understanding, rather than of crushing my opponent, I do not act from the virtue of charity, since the characteristic aim of charity is the well-being of a person.

What about the success component? What is it to be successful in one's goodwill towards an author? If goodwill towards the author *as author* is the desire that the author be right, then the success of the motivation will be *that the author is right*. But surely I do not need to desire that the author be right for me to have acted with intellectual charity towards him. We might think that the success in question would be the achievement of some intellectual good, since that is the characteristic goal of the virtuous intellectual personality taken as a whole, in reading a text. But such success is not the object of intellectual charity *as charity*. It may become clearer what success would be if we switch from the case of charitably reading a text to conducting charitably a debate face to face with an interlocutor. In such a debate, the goal of my charity (as distinguished from the goal of my love of knowledge) will be such things as not embarrassing my interlocutor, making him aware of my respect for him, staying on friendly terms with him, and bringing it about that he gets some genuine intellectual goods out of our conversation. If I achieve such things as these in the course of my conversation with him, then my charity will have succeeded. In reading a text charitably, if the author is dead and/or will never be affected by my charity, I cannot realistically aim at any such outcome. In such cases, the charity has a virtual, or as-if, goal: it does not really aim at anything, though it is *as if* it aims as charity would aim if in conversation with a live interlocutor.[9]

What is the relation, in the intellectually charitable person, between the motivation to get the intellectual goods and the motivation of charity (goodwill towards the author or interlocutor)? Presumably the virtuous person does not behave charitably *just so as* to get some intellectual goods *for himself*, since this would deprive his behavior of the motive required for it to express genuine charity. On the other hand, he might behave charitably just so as to secure some intellectual goods *for his interlocutor*, because one perfectly fitting way to wish another well is to wish him to have some intellectual goods. In this case, love of the intellectual goods and charity for the interlocutor come together in a special way: wanting the intellectual goods (for the other) *is* the motive of charity.

How is the motive of charity related to the motive of getting the intellectual goods for oneself? We assume, as we have been doing, that having charity for the interlocutor does in fact promote one's getting the intellectual goods for oneself. Furthermore, the intellectually virtuous person may be aware of this connection. But he will try to keep the consideration that charity for his interlocutor is good for his own intellectual life in the background, where it does not come to the fore as a motivation for charitable behavior. We might describe the relation between the motivation characteristic of charity and charity's proneness to foster the epistemic goods as follows. If it is true that goodwill towards fellow intellectual agents promotes the acquisition, maintenance, and application of the intellectual goods, then someone who was designing epistemic agents of roughly the human kind for proficiency would design them with charity. He would also design them as seekers of the epistemic goods. But he would not design them to exemplify goodwill towards their fellow

---

[9] Zagzebski seems to admit the possibility that some acts of virtue do not aim at any end, inasmuch as her definition of *act of virtue* includes the phrase "bringing about the end (*if any*) of virtue A" (*Virtues of the Mind*, p. 248, italics added).

epistemic agents *for the sake of* acquiring, maintaining, and applying the epistemic goods. The instrumentality of the designer–agent would not be perfectly reflected in the reasoning governing the practices of the designed agent.

Intellectual *courage* is an ability to perform intellectual tasks well despite what one takes to be significant threats. The threats may be such things as loss of employment or other opportunities, loss of reputation or status, loss of home and friends, even bodily harm or loss of life. Intellectual courage is often needed in contexts where a political régime fears and represses critical thought and research, or in religiously reactionary contexts that ostracize, or in anti-religious contexts such as many present-day universities, or scientific contexts dominated by some defensive orthodoxy, and in many other contexts. Acts of courage may be speaking one's mind, continuing one's research, publishing one's ideas, thinking carefully, refusing to suppress data and arguments.

Although courageous acts must be motivated, no one type of motivation is characteristic of courage. Zagzebski speaks of "the emotions characteristic of the virtue of courage" (p. 131) that motivate acts of courage, but she says they have no name, and she does not describe them except to say that they are not just the absence of fear. We think that our inability to name or describe such supposed motivation indicates that there isn't such a thing. People can be motivated to perform acts of courage by any number of things—love, hate, fear, anger, patriotism, concern for justice, the desire for gain, the desire for knowledge and understanding, the desire that others should have knowledge and understanding. These last two motivations make it possible for courage to be an intellectual virtue, but we think that it is better to think of these motivations as coming from another virtue, which we call the love of knowledge. A person can act with intellectual courage because he loves the intellectual goods, but that love does not distinguish intellectual courage from intellectual tenacity, humility, fairness, generosity, or any other intellectual virtue. Zagzebski sometimes seems to identify the motivation component of a virtue with the motivation *to have* the virtue in question (see, for example, pp. 246–7). But one might desire to be courageous without being courageous, and one might be courageous without desiring to be courageous (except, perhaps, in a purely dispositional and counterfactual sense). And certainly, many acts of courage have primary motives other than the desire to be courageous. It seems to us that the motive characteristic of a virtue is in no case, or almost no case, the desire to have the virtue.

What about the aptitude component? What is courage an aptitude to do? We began by saying that courage is an ability to perform intellectual tasks well despite what one takes to be significant threats. Thus it is an aptitude to do a wide variety of things, such as we mentioned before, but none of these is distinctive of courage. What seems distinctive is that these things are done in spite of what one takes to be a significant threat. So maybe courage is an aptitude for doing *whatever* one does, *well* by some standards for that kind of doing, *despite* a sense of being significantly threatened, *if* one does that thing. That is, the courageous person is one who, knowing that doing X has a significantly high probability of bringing some kind of adversity on himself or something he cares about, can manage to do X well anyway. "Doing X well" here does not mean doing X successfully. If a newspaper publisher courageously undertakes to publish an article so as to expose some fraud in the city government, his act can count as courageous even if he fails to expose the fraud (say, the fraudulent city fathers have concocted a seamless defense), and even if he fails to publish the article (say, the newspaper offices are dynamited just as the type is being set, and all who know the truth die in the explosion). All that is necessary for the action to count as courageous is that the agent have undertaken the action, or at any rate genuinely decided to do so.

Consider next the virtue of intellectual *humility*. In the analysis that we will present in Chapter 9, humility is marked by an absence of a range of vices that you might call the vices of pride: vanity, arrogance, domination, superciliousness, conceit, and others. Several of those vices are structures of motivation: a desire to be highly regarded for purposes of social status, a desire to dominate others, etc. Arrogance is a motivated disposition to infer illicitly some entitlement from one's superiority to others, though the motivation can vary (it can be vanity or sensuousness or perhaps other things). Where humility marks the absence of a vicious motive, it is characterized neither by a particular kind of motive (as charity is) nor by a circumvention of a kind of motivation (as courage is). Humility presupposes an overriding interest in something, and in the case of intellectual humility, that will be an interest in the epistemic goods. But that interest seems to be auxiliary to humility rather than part of the virtue. Christ's humility is shown by his willingness to forfeit or set aside his divine standing (Phil. 2: 6–8).

It presupposes his charity towards sinners, which is what motivates him to undertake the task in which he exhibits his humility. But it seems to make sense to say that he is motivated, not by his humility, but by his charity. Similarly, in the intellectual life, the humble person is motivated by his enthusiasm for intellectual goods, not by his humility. The function of the enthusiasm, in humility, is to overwhelm motives like vanity. And similarly, it seems odd to talk about the aptitude aspect of humility, since humility does not set a task in which one can be successful or not, the way courage, charity, and perseverance do. The goal of the actions in which Jesus Christ expresses his humility is not the goal *of his humility*. One might, of course, say that *humility* has a goal—the goal of ruling out the vices of pride—but this goal is not one that the humble person characteristically has in view. And then the aptitude aspect of humility would be its power actually to elbow out these vices. But thinking of it in this way, the "success" of intellectual humility *as humility* will not be the achievement of some intellectual good, but the ruling out of those vices that in fact frees up the agent in her pursuit of intellectual goods. But in the most perfectly humble person, this will not be a success at which he aims, but a success that comes so naturally to him that he neither intends the success nor notices it. If anyone "uses" humility to aim at the goal of humility, it is the designer of humility, not its subject.

Finally, let's take a brief look at intellectual *conscientiousness,* because it exemplifies yet another structure of motivation and aptitude. We have intellectual duties—to examine some of our beliefs, to question our motives in arguing for one position or another, to collect evidence for our beliefs, to deepen our understanding of important things when we have opportunity, and so forth. We are not in all circumstances obligated to act on all of these duties; but obligations do arise in contexts, and it is part of practical wisdom as it applies to the intellectual life to discern our duties as they become applicable. Many if not all of our epistemic duties are discharged in the course of exemplifying the intellectual virtues, but to exemplify conscientiousness is not just to exemplify the other virtues. Immanuel Kant famously distinguishes acting *in accordance* with duty from acting *from* duty. Presumably a person with the epistemic virtues will often, in acting from such virtues as intellectual honesty and charity and love of knowledge, act in accordance with his epistemic duties. But he does not thereby act *from* duty—that is, moved by the consideration that such-and-such is his duty.

One exemplifies the virtue of intellectual conscientiousness only in acting from intellectual duty.

At our best, we are motivated "directly" by the intellectual goods, and by other goods connected with them, to do what it takes to acquire, maintain, communicate, and apply the intellectual goods. Understanding, propositional knowledge, and acquaintance with various things *attract* us; we love knowledge and cherish its possession by others and want these goods; we are spontaneously disposed to respect others as sources of purported intellectual goods, etc.; and thus we act. Sometimes, however, this more direct, and more directly virtuous, kind of motivation fails us. In a circumstance where the transparent love of knowledge would, ideally, impel us to check the data one more time, we just don't feel like checking the data one more time. Or we just don't feel like adding that extra scruple about our argument that we know is needed, or reading one more book before we finalize a paper to send off to a journal. Perhaps we're impatient, or tired, or beginning to get bored with a project. At this point, where the mature, spontaneous attraction to the intellectual goods fails or partially fails us, we may still be virtuously motivated to do what we ought to do, if we have a sense of intellectual duty—a sense of "ought" about intellectual actions. Intellectual conscientiousness is the susceptibility to be motivated by the consideration that behaving well epistemically is *required* of us, is what we *ought* to do, is our *duty*. It is a character trait like the other intellectual virtues, with the difference that it supplies this indirect, substitute motivation.

This indirect desire, under the description of "what I ought to do", is the motivational component of conscientiousness. What, then, is the aptitude involved? It is not full epistemic success, in the sense of actually getting propositional knowledge, understanding, or acquaintance, or being justified, warranted, or rational, etc. As supplier of a supplemental motivation, the virtue of intellectual conscientiousness is aimed, from the designer's point of view, at getting required intellectual actions done. Thus, we would describe this aptitude in much the way we described that of courage: conscientiousness is an aptitude for getting certain actions performed, now not under conditions of fear, as in the case of courage, but under conditions of insufficient intrinsic motivation.

We have argued that different virtues are structured quite differently from one another. No one-size-fits-all analysis—no theory in the sense of a simple reductive or monolithic account—will describe the actual variety within the virtuous character.

Individuating virtues   The preceding discussion is an attempt to illustrate the diversity of psychological structure among the virtues. We assigned a variety of functions to the virtues we discussed, this function to one virtue and that to another, and withheld other functions from the same virtues, assigning them instead to other items in the intellectual character, either to other virtues or in one case to skills. Thus courage, but not humility, provided for acting well in the face of perceived threat, and humility, but not charity, was constituted by the absence of motives of vanity and arrogance. We pointed out that a courageous act might be motivated by charity, and illustrated a certain kind of humility by an action of Jesus Christ that was motivated by charity. Thus, in illustrating the diversity of the virtues, we also began to illustrate their interdependence—what has sometimes been called the unity of the virtues. The emerging picture is that of a character fitted, capacitated, attuned, and oriented in a variety of ways for a variety of life situations and activities in situations, such that the possessor of that character lives well.

We began our discussion of the nature of a virtue by pointing out that some activities and situations in which activities are pursued are generically human. The familiar virtue categories seem to track these areas, with variations. Situations of threat that tend to impede action are generic to human life, so courage is a virtue. Impulses of vanity and arrogance are generic to human life and destructive or degrading of it, so humility is a virtue. Gift giving (in the broad sense of gratuitous purveyance of goods from one person to another) is generic to human life, and promotes it if well done, so generosity and gratitude are virtues. Imperfection of intrinsic motivation in situations where good actions need to be performed is generic to human life, so conscientiousness is a virtue. Inquiry is generic to human life, and some situations of inquiry are characterized by threats that tend to impede inquiry, so intellectual courage is a virtue; inquiry can also be impeded by arrogance and vanity, so intellectual humility is a virtue; intellectual goods can be passed from one person to another, so intellectual generosity and gratitude are virtues; inquiry can be undermined by deficits of intrinsic motivation for the intellectual goods, so intellectual conscientiousness is a virtue. And so on.

The question of the individuation of the virtues is the question about what principles govern the assignment of a function to a virtue. What are the criteria by which we decide that such-and-such a function belongs to the virtue of intellectual firmness but not to intellectual charity, while another belongs to autonomy but not to caution? The answer, it seems to us, is largely "ordinary language". We have a vocabulary of the virtues, of which the chapter titles in Part II are representative, which is made the more determinate the more we locate ourselves within a tradition that includes a particular understanding of human nature and the nature of the universe. This is not to say that virtue epistemology can be prosecuted by consulting a dictionary or even books of theology or some equivalent expression of the canons of a world view. Ordinary language has considerable potential depth and subtlety, and thinking hard about this part of ordinary language requires a kind of psychological reflection and insight that is not available in dictionaries or usual in books of theology. Exploring such conceptual connections and disconnections has always been a large part of the business of philosophy, whether or not it was acknowledged as such. The analyses of the particular virtues in Part II of this book are proposals of this sort.

Virtues and situations   At the beginning of this chapter, we proposed that a virtue is an acquired base of excellent functioning in some generically human sphere of activity that is challenging and important. But the "functioning" in question always occurs in some situation or other, and there are limits of normality for such situations. Virtues do not fit us for functioning well in situations that are very abnormal for human beings. Distributive justice would not help us to live in a situation of sheer abundance of all transferable goods. Generosity does not fit us to function well in situations characterized by very efficient con-people; in a situation containing a very efficient con-person, generous people are liable to function less well than ungenerous ones. Similarly, a person with intellectual charity may be at an epistemic disadvantage in a situation dominated by hardened egoistic hyper-autonomous cut-throat intellectuals, and the same could be said about intellectual humility and generosity. We are more Aristotelian than Stoic on this issue, and so believe that the environment has to cooperate by being more or less "normal"—that is, the kind of environment for which the virtue in question was designed.

This is a corollary of our point that virtues are always indexed to some conception of human nature: that love of knowledge would not be a virtue if truth were in principle inaccessible to human cognitive operations, that intellectual conscientiousness would not be a virtue if human beings had perfectly reliable intrinsic motivations, and faith would not be a virtue if God did not exist. Both points are about "context" or "situation" or "environment" or "sphere" in a broad sense of these words, and what they say is that in exemplifying virtues we are always at the mercy of our situation. The example of conscientiousness brings out the fact that part of the "situation" may be a fact about human nature in a narrow sense—in this case, that high-quality intrinsic motivations are not always available, even to the best formed of human beings.

When we say that the sphere of activity of a virtue has to be challenging, we have in mind such things as that it is natural, in a way, not to stand one's ground in situations of threat, that it comes quite naturally to interpret one's intellectual opponent uncharitably, that it takes long discipline against the grain to become intellectually cautious, and so forth. Virtues involve concerted discipline, both self-imposed and imposed by others. Virtuous actions are extraordinary for human beings, especially worthy of admiration, and it is features of the situation in which the action is performed that make the action challenging. This point may seem somewhat in tension with the normalcy condition mentioned in the preceding paragraph; but in fact it is normal for life to be challenging, and so for excellence not to come easily. The point of the last paragraph is that the difficulty of performing excellently must be a limited difficulty. By virtues, people become more human, not superhuman. Virtues fit us for excellent functioning in *this* world, given *human* nature, not for any possible world, given any possible nature.

However, the situations of our lives present not only challenges for virtues to rise to, but supports for virtue. A human life is lived in the presence of other human beings, and is not just made difficult by them, but is also educated by them, supported by them, kept on the straight path by them. If we are doing science or scholarship, our colleagues keep us honest by challenging us, keeping an eye on us, threatening us unspokenly with embarrassment or even ostracism if we are too lax in our epistemic practices. Very few if any of us ever achieve sheer emotional and practical autonomy, a complete lack of need for encouragement from others.[10] Yet, if we are too much in need of this environmental regulation and support, we do not possess the virtues. The virtuous person is more than a child who "behaves" because he is being watched. He also has autonomy, an ability to stay honest for intrinsic reasons (see Chapter 10).

Thinking about the Virtues in Epistemology

We began this chapter by saying that the concept of a virtue is central to our book, but not its theoretical basis. As we noted in Chapter 1, most of the virtue epistemologies proposed in the past twenty years do attempt to make the concept of virtue in some sense the basis for a theory of knowledge. Thus the concept of a virtue is crucial to the definitions of knowledge offered by Sosa, Greco, and Zagzebski, and the similar concept of a properly functioning faculty serves this purpose in Plantinga's epistemology. We have called our virtue epistemology *regulative*, and have said that we are not interested in a definition of knowledge in the typical style, one that specifies the broadly logically necessary and sufficient conditions for anything's being a case of knowledge—though in Chapter 2 we did propose a concept of knowledge, and one that we think especially suits a regulative virtues epistemology. We think that that concept of knowledge is more interesting and truer to people's real epistemic aspirations than the concept of propositional knowledge that has dominated recent discussions.

In this chapter we have tried to clarify the concept of a virtue, and this effort will continue throughout the remaining chapters of the book. Earlier in this chapter we sketched the crucial faculty of the will, and in the next chapter we will look further at the human epistemic faculties, since these are the naturally "given" basis of the acquired aptitudes and attitudes that make up the intellectual virtues. Then, in the last chapter of Part I, we will look at the concept of an epistemic practice and some examples of practices, since these practices are the activities in which the virtues are exemplified, and thus shape the virtues and are shaped by them in turn.

---

[10] We thank Robert Merrihew Adams for stimulating this comment.

This analytic policy of relating a concept to connected concepts is evident in the present chapter, in which we have expounded the concept of an intellectual virtue by relating it to such other concepts as human nature, the human will, and the human environment. Instead of making the concept of a virtue into a theoretical *basis* from which to derive other concepts, we have tried to *locate* the concept of an intellectual virtue with respect to the other concepts.

Another thing we did in this chapter was to look at some examples of virtues, with a special interest in showing the structural diversity among them. Virtues are not interestingly susceptible to a one-size-fits-all analysis in the style that is so popular among theoretical philosophers. But the very brief analyses that we have offered in this chapter are only the beginning of what we want to do. Our regulative purpose in writing this book is to bring analytic attention to the intellectual virtues so as to deepen our own and our readers' understanding of the life of the mind, from the inside, as it were. To accomplish this purpose, we must focus concerted attention on a range of particular virtues, in that process also showing the rich connections they bear to one another. That is the task of Part II.

4

Faculties

Introduction

An intellectual virtue is an acquired base of excellent epistemic functioning. But whenever we function intellectually (or in any other way), we do so on a further basis of given powers, powers that are natural to us as human beings, and not acquired through practice. We do not sprout legs as a result of extensive walking. Nor do we, by practicing, acquire eyes or ears or the basic power to draw inferences or to form concepts or to see one thing in terms of another. By practicing, we learn to do these things *well*, but we would never get started without a given basis of powers. These powers are innate, given with our nature as human beings. "Innate" here does not mean that we are born with the capacity, any more than men are born with beards. Some of the faculties accrue only as the human organism matures; but they are given with nature in the way the beard is, not as a result of cultural influences and practice. Nor does "innate" imply possession by every individual human being; it implies possession by every *normal* individual. In a traditional word we call these natural, given powers "faculties". So faculties lie behind, or beneath, virtues. They are presupposed. We would never become able to act courageously, generously, charitably, justly, cautiously, conscientiously, wisely, and autonomously if we did not have the basic equipment to perform in these ways.

A faculty is not just any natural or innate disposition, but one that is potentially a base of *proper* functioning. If, for example, we have a natural but fallacious tendency to believe that basketball players shoot in streaks[1]—more likely to hit the basket on any given shot if they've hit it on the preceding one—the tendency is not a faculty. The simplest examples of faculties are the senses. Vision is a way of getting information about

---

[1] See Thomas Gilovich, *How We Know What Isn't So* (New York: Free Press, 1991), pp. 11–16.

things. Unlike Plato in the *Republic*, Books 6–7, most of us do not think of vision as a fundamentally misleading disposition from which we need to turn away if we are ever to have real knowledge—though we admit that we are sometimes misled by our eyes. Thus we think of vision as a faculty, an innate basis of potentially proper functioning.

Vision and the other senses are especially salient to us as faculties because they are associated with easily identifiable organs on the surface of the body. But we also have faculties that do not have an obvious, external location. Epistemologists have identified several epistemic faculties in addition to our senses: memory, introspection (the ability to know directly that one exists and who one is and some of one's own states of mind), inference (the ability to derive one thought from another, logically), induction (the ability to generalize from cases), a priori intuition (the ability to recognize necessary truths for what they are), testimonial credulity (the disposition to believe what others tell us), language (the ability to learn and understand languages), construal (the ability to see, hear, etc., or think, of one thing in terms of another), coherence (the disposition to demand consistency and a mutual supporting among one's beliefs), the desire for understanding, and the *sensus divinitatis* (the disposition to seek and to be aware of God). The last three items in this list are intellectual appetites, dispositions not so much of aptitude as of motivation, or perhaps a combination of the two.

The above list makes it clear that identification of faculties can be contestable. Perhaps no one would deny that human beings have an innate tendency to believe in God, but non-theists will deny this tendency to be an epistemic faculty. Sigmund Freud, for example, notes the tendency, but thinks it a disposition to illusion,[2] much like our tendency to think that basketball players shoot in streaks. Thus it is not to be developed into a virtue (say, the virtue of faith), but needs to be trained out of us, in much the way that we try to eradicate or circumvent other natural tendencies to cognitive distortion. Similarly, Thomas Reid posits a faculty of testimonial credulity, but John Locke is inclined to think it a faulty tendency, which must be strongly controlled if we are to do our epistemic best, by an insistence on seeing the evidence for ourselves. Reid also believes controversially that judgments of aesthetic taste are true or false,

---

[2] See Sigmund Freud, *The Future of an Illusion*, trans. W. D. Robson-Scott, rev. and ed. James Strachey (Garden City, NY: Doubleday, 1964).

and that the mature ability to judge correctly of aesthetic matters is based on a faculty of taste. For Plato in the *Republic*, all the modalities of sense perception seem to be mere rungs on a disposable epistemic ladder. In that case the sensory organs would play a role in the development of the intellectual virtues, but the virtues would not be modes of functioning that make current and continuing use of the senses. Most virtue epistemologists will disagree with Plato here. It seems clear that Freud's rejection of the *sensus divinitatis* as a faculty, and Plato's unwillingness to give the sensory organs an ongoing place in virtuous epistemic practice, are traceable to other commitments of theirs concerning the nature of reality.

In this chapter we will argue, contrary to some recent epistemologies, that the proper functioning of the epistemic faculties in congenial environments is not sufficient for the most interesting and important kinds of knowledge. Or, to put our point another way, the conception of proper functioning in these epistemologies needs to be broadened.

Coming to know, as well as maintaining, transmitting, and applying our knowledge, depends on the skillful deployment of these faculties, on culture-bound cultivation of the faculty or of parts of the mind that function in deployments of the faculty, and depends in the typical case on the personal aims, desires and attachments, emotions and actions, of the epistemic agent—dispositions of the will. As knowers or would-be knowers, we are not just a coordination of faculties, analogous to an automobile which *is* nothing but a coordination of functional parts. People are epistemic agents—beings equipped with faculties for knowing things, who pursue knowledge by various means which centrally involve those faculties. To the extent that epistemic faculties are equipment, they may sometimes function magnificently and yet not generate knowledge of the kind they were designed to yield, just as a car may function perfectly with respect to engine, brakes, and other parts, yet not function very well as transportation if driven by a driver who doesn't care where he is going, or now and then depresses the brake pedal just to enjoy the sensation of being precipitated forward in the seat.

The analogy of car and driver has limited application, since epistemic faculties are not all equipment. They depart from this category in at least two ways. First, the will is a special case among the faculties. If we wish to think of it as a faculty, the will is not, for the agent, a piece of equipment on a par with eyesight or hearing or the ability to draw valid inferences. It is, instead, something like the very heart of a person. A deaf or blind person can be an excellent person, but to have a perverted or non-functioning will—chronically inappropriate desires, emotions, and attachments, and a disposition to make bad choices, or nearly a lack of any of these powers—seems to be almost a definition of the deepest human dysfunction. It is odd to speak of *using* the will well or badly. It is true that a person can dissociate from some deliverances of his will, such as some desires and emotions (thus criticizing and/or controlling them), but there is always some perspective of the will that is not dissociated from and thus cannot be regarded as "used" even in this attenuated sense. By contrast, it makes perfectly good sense to speak of using inferential powers, or hearing or memory. So in the automobile analogy, the will, or at least its center, is not the car, but the driver. But most epistemologists who speak of epistemic faculties do not include the will among them.

So not all faculties are equipment. But, second, even faculties that are straightforwardly equipment-like, such as vision and the power of a priori reasoning, are subject to development and deep integration into other aspects of life, and in this way are unlike ordinary equipment. As we get better at driving, the steering wheel and the engine do not improve, but only the driver. By contrast, we do not just get better at *using* our hearing and vision, but the faculties themselves seem to become more discriminating, say with musical ear training and training in the visual recognition of plant species.

What is it for vision to function properly? There seem to be broadly two kinds of answer to this question. In one sense our visual apparatus functions well when the lenses focus sharply on the retinas and the retinas and other parts of the neurological equipment function in the way that an ophthalmologist would consider normal. Proper functioning is 20–20 vision. This is the sense in which vision is most like a steering wheel. It does not get better with training, at least not much better. But vision can be trained in many ways, and the standards of proper functioning here will be laid down by the field in which the eyes are used: ambulation and throwing in basketball, information gathering in various fields of microscopy, distinguishing copies from originals of old paintings, and so forth. In this deeper kind of seeing, vision in the equipment sense is integrated with motor skills, conceptual schemata, and complex bodies of information. An important social kind of visual acuity is the recognition of others' emotions through facial expressions. By seeing others' emotions on their faces, we are enabled to respond sensitively and appropriately to their emotions, and thus to pursue proper interpersonal relationships with others—relations of mutuality, friendship, and harmony, as well as of suspicion and critical judgment. Since the subject's own moral-emotional maturity lies behind her ability to see in this way, here vision becomes much more than a faculty in the sense of equipment, and becomes an epistemic function of the whole person.

Faculty Epistemologies

In the last few decades several major epistemologists, not happy with efforts to define knowledge by specifying rules of duty for belief formation, turned to the faculties as a possible locus of conditions of justification. The idea, roughly, is that all and only beliefs that result from the working of a reliable or properly functioning epistemic faculty have warrant or justification. In the present section we will discuss a leading advocate of this approach. In the next section we will show how certain shortcomings of a faculty epistemology are overcome by a virtues approach.

Ernest Sosa's work in epistemology relies heavily on an account of faculties and faculty competence to analyze central epistemic notions like knowledge and justification. He does not make the classic distinction between faculties and virtues, but uses the words interchangeably. By defining faculties as abilities or powers to attain certain kinds of accomplishments relative to certain kinds of circumstances, Sosa acknowledges that our faculties are indebted to supporting environments. "One has a[n epistemic] faculty only if there is a field F and there is a set of circumstances C such that one would distinguish the true from the false in F in C."[3] Thus, for example, vision is a faculty for Sosa, since it allows us to distinguish truths from falsehoods in a field—viz., the size, color, and spatial location of middle-sized objects—in a kind of circumstance, viz., adequate light. In addition to perception, Sosa names introspection, memory, intuition, and reason among our intellectual faculties.

---

[3] Ernest Sosa, *Knowledge in Perspective* (Cambridge: Cambridge University Press, 1991), p. 274. The paper from which the quotation comes is "Intellectual Virtue in Perspective". All references to Sosa in the present chapter are to this collection.

Sosa does not define *faculty* as we did earlier in this chapter. He defines it not as the innate basis of an ability to perform some task, but as the ability to perform the task well. "How now shall we think of faculties: as dispositions or as grounding intrinsic characters of dispositions? Faculties seem [to be] abilities to do certain sorts of things in certain sorts of circumstances rather than what *underlies* the possession of such abilities" (p. 235). Historically, philosophers have viewed intellectual faculties as the innate or underlying powers by which we come, through practice, to be able to accomplish various intellectual acts. In contrast, for Sosa a faculty is a power already perfected to a certain level of competence: "To each faculty there corresponds a set of accomplishments of a distinctive sort. Indeed the faculty is defined as the ability to attain such accomplishments" (p. 235). This way of speaking has some odd consequences. For example, it seems to imply that infants, who cannot yet infer, speak, or introspect, lack the faculties that enable those activities. And it seems to preclude the notion of bad vision or hearing; faculties are by definition excellent. Sosa's unusual concept of a faculty helps to explain his unusual identification of faculties with virtues. On his reading, a faculty is a sort of skill, a learned ability to *use* what others would call a faculty.

The question of which faculties we have is important for the epistemologists who are called "reliabilists"—those who think, roughly, that a belief is justified just in case it is produced by a faculty that reliably produces true beliefs. Only if a faculty is epistemically reliable will it justify any belief that it produces. So these epistemologists are faced with "the generality problem". Were they to identify a faculty merely as "vision", it would not be a basis for epistemic justification, since there are so many situations in which vision is not reliable: for extremely small or distant objects, in situations of very dim or bright lighting, etc. On the other hand, were they to define a faculty very specifically—say, as the ability to recognize beer bottles at a distance of three feet in daylight—it would be highly reliable but would hardly serve its purpose in a general definition of epistemic reliability. So Sosa's strategy is to limit the scope of a faculty in several ways that will achieve just the right degree of generality for it to be usable in a reliabilist definition of justification.

He distinguishes two aspects of an environment, and calls them "environment" (E) and "conditions" (C). Chris Evert, for example, has the ability to perform stellarly, in the tennis sort of way, under certain "conditions", but only under them. These conditions will include such things as having a racquet of a certain quality, being on a tennis court, not being in a hurricane, having a relatively skilled opponent, a fairly fresh ball, and not carrying a 75-lb backpack. When in these and other required conditions, Evert has a high reliability of performing stellarly in the tennis sort of way, and that is her tennis-faculty or -virtue.

What Sosa calls "conditions" are relatively episodic: they come and go in Evert's life; she is not always on a tennis court facing a skilled player. What he calls "environment", by contrast, is "relatively stable background conditions" (p. 284). Such "environmental" conditions include being on the surface of the Earth with just its gravitational conditions, having an adequate supply of environmental oxygen, not being dehydrated, and so forth. Such conditions are much less episodic, in Evert's life, than what Sosa calls "conditions"; but as he remarks, "the distinction between C ["conditions"] and E ["environment"] is not sharp or important" (p. 284). A third element in a faculty or virtue according to Sosa is an "inner nature" (I). This includes "certain stable states of [Evert's] brain and body" (p. 285): namely, such things as the tone of her muscles and the acquired synaptic conditions that underlie her ability to play tennis well. Just as E and C are not sharply differentiated, but overlapping categories, so I overlaps with E. Like other aspects of E, the training that Evert's brain and muscles have acquired through long-term tennis practice are stable background conditions rather than more episodic ones. So one might think of the trained state of Evert's brain as part of E, and of that brain minus its trained condition as I. "If (in the corresponding account of virtues generally) conditions C are allowed wide compass while the environment E is narrowly circumscribed, then, as a newborn, Chris Evert already had the virtues of a tennis player" (pp. 284–5). This is because a faculty or virtue is an inner nature (I) that disposes one to perform excellently in a circumscribed kind of way (in Evert's case, the tennis sort of way) in certain episodic conditions (C: on a tennis court) given certain background conditions (E: oxygen, etc., but now also the very specific training of her muscles and brain). Since baby Evert had, in her neurological and muscular endowment, the potential to take on that specific "environment" that yielded the mature Evert's abilities, we could say that baby Evert "had the virtues of a tennis player". The particular C of Evert's early life (proper nourishment, athletic opportunities) were such that her infantile I could take on the relevant part of E. "But", as Sosa remarks, "it is much more plausible to restrict the scope of conditions C in such a way that only after a period of maturation and learning does she come to be in an environment E with an inner state I (a total relevant epistemic[4] state, including certain stable states of her brain and body) by virtue of which she would then perform stellarly when in the conditions C of a tennis match (on the surface of the earth, etc.)" (p. 284).

Now, applying this schema to the notion of an "intellectual virtue or faculty", Sosa writes,

Because subject S has a certain inner nature (I) and is placed in a certain environment (E), S would most likely be right on any proposition X in field F relative to which S stood in conditions C. S might be a human; I might involve possession of good eyes and a good nervous system including a brain in good order; E might include the surface of the earth with its relevant properties, within the parameters of variation experienced by humans over the centuries, or anyhow by subject S within his or her lifetime or within a certain more recent stretch of it; F might be a field of propositions specifying the colors or shapes of an object before S up to a certain level of determination and complexity (say greenness and squareness, but not chartreuseness or chiliagonicity); and C might be the conditions of S's seeing such an object in good light at arm's length and without obstructions. (p. 139)[5]

It is plausible that Evert would not be a reliable tennis player were she not a reliable judge of oncoming tennis balls. Thus her tennis-playing faculty or virtue implies her intellectual faculty or virtue of vision. So when Evert, on the basis of the performance of her eyes and allied resources, forms the belief, *a tennis ball is coming towards me and will soon arrive*, she is very likely to be right. Because of this reliability, when she forms such a belief, she is *justified* in doing so. If knowledge is justified true belief, then when Evert forms this belief and it is also true, then she *knows* that a tennis ball is coming towards her. In accordance with the restrictions in the above-quoted schema, the belief in question has to fall in a field of propositions (F), say, about oncoming medium-sized physical objects rather than their chemical composition, and is restricted to an environment (E), say, the surface of the Earth rather than some environment with gravitational conditions strong enough to pull the ball down well before

---

[4] Surely Sosa here intends "tennis-playing" rather than "epistemic".
[5] This quotation comes from "Reliabilism and Intellectual Virtue".

it gets to her. The belief also has to be formed under certain normal conditions (C), say, *not* the condition of having a virtual reality helmet strapped over her head, and not the condition of the ball being two miles away or its coming towards her in the dead of night. This belief-forming power depends on Evert's having an "inner nature" (I) that meets certain specifications—"good eyes and a good nervous system"—but the scope of the I of Evert's power of vision is subject to the same variability as the scope of the I of Evert's power of tennis playing. We can include in the I of Evert's power of vision the trained condition of her eyes and brain that has enabled her to judge prospective arrival of tennis balls with the rapidity and accuracy needed for expert tennis playing, or alternatively, we may assign that trained condition to E and restrict I to the genetically given basis of her mature ability. In the former case, we have conceived I as, in ordinary parlance, a skill, a trait that, being a "habit", bears some resemblance to a virtue. In the latter case, we have conceived I as what would ordinarily be called a faculty.

Our ordinary way of thinking about virtues is strained less by thinking of Evert's disposition as including her training; it seems very odd to say that, as an infant in the crib, she had the virtues of a tennis player. We are more likely to say that she had the potential to acquire these qualities ("potential" comes from the Latin word that philosophers used for faculty: *potentia*). On the other hand, our ordinary way of thinking about faculties is strained less by thinking of her disposition as not including her training; in the ordinary sense of "faculty", it takes much more than excellent faculties to play tennis well.

Sosa's account has the resources for distinguishing a faculty from its excellent functioning or its development into a virtue, but it does not systematize its vocabulary to make the distinction clear. Sosa knows the difference between an undeveloped base that has the potential for excellent performance (the "bare" I—what most people would call a faculty, and which he calls a "fundamental" virtue or faculty) and the developed state of that base (an "environmentally" extended I—what would usually be called a virtue, or at least a skill, and which he calls a "derived" virtue or faculty (see p. 277)). From the point of view of the present work, the shortcoming of Sosa's account is not so much its confusing virtues with faculties as its expository obscurity and the thinness of its concept of a virtue. In particular, Sosa gives no hint of the involvement of the will in mature epistemic character; indeed, his "virtues" are hardly traits of character. And corresponding to this thinness is the low level of the kinds of knowledge to which the account is relevant. His examples are such things as knowing that "it rains" (p. 273), and knowing that "this before me is white and round" (p. 139). He also mentions a bird-watcher's refined visual acuity, but we think that a fuller account of the character that is capable of acquiring and deploying such epistemic skill would have to refer to such personal characteristics as enthusiasm about learning and perseverance.

Besides the reliabilist's theoretical need to identify the faculties specifically enough to guarantee that they are reliable truth-producers, philosophers have an occupational compulsion to divide what they are studying into neat categories. So Sosa distinguishes between "generation faculties" and "transmission faculties", the former leading to beliefs from various experiences we undergo, the latter leading to beliefs from already held beliefs (p. 225). These categories can crisscross with others; for instance, reason can function both as a generation faculty, as when it makes self-evident truths known, and as a transmission faculty, as when we deduce a belief from already held beliefs. Sosa further distinguishes faculties from "sub-faculties", the latter being a delimited part of a faculty's total range of operation. Following this division, reason is a faculty, and inductive inference a sub-faculty. (One might wonder whether every kind of reasoning we engage in—abducting, analyzing, hypothesizing, synthesizing, thought experimentation, etc.—should be represented as a sub-faculty.) Sosa also distinguishes "faculties" from "more-refined sub-faculties", where the subject field of the latter ranges over more content than the mere faculty alone. "Thus the visual faculties of an expert bird-watcher would presumably include many more refined sub-faculties of the faculties of color and shape perception that he shares with ordinary people. Moreover, the visual faculties of a bird-watcher with 20–20 vision would presumably include many more refined sub-faculties of the faculties that he shares with those who fall short of his visual acuity" (p. 236).

We do not think there is any single systematic way, independent of contestable metaphysical commitments, to decide which of the natural belief-forming tendencies of the human mind are faculties and which are not. Cognitive psychology can pinpoint fallacious dispositions, like the tendency to believe that basketball players shoot in streaks, because it can identify the disposition, statistically, and then apply statistical techniques to assess the accuracy of the disposition's doxastic outputs. The truth-value of the judgment that basketball players do not tend to shoot in streaks is determinable to the satisfaction of just about anybody who knows the data and considers the matter. But for an account of the faculties that takes into consideration the more contestable kinds of judgments—judgments about such matters as God, morality, and aesthetics—the right approach is to start with what, upon careful consideration, we believe we know, and then develop as best we can our account of the virtues and of the faculties that underlie them, supposing these to be dispositions that enable us to practice well the practices that lead us, as we believe, to the truth.

This seems to be the approach taken by Alvin Plantinga in *Warrant and Proper Function*. In the next section we will consider Plantinga's consideration of some faculties, and try to show how his faculty epistemology leads naturally to completion and fulfillment in a virtues epistemology.

The Relations of Faculties and Virtues

a. Non-epistemic faculties

We have seen that epistemologists who attempt to define knowledge by reference to the functioning of faculties need to restrict these to contexts in which they are highly reliable true belief-producers.[6] Another restriction is that the belief-producing faculty must be one that is aimed at truth. Plantinga points out that some faculties that influence or produce beliefs are aimed, not at truth, but at such other functions as preventing mothers from swearing off second pregnancies and making us more likely to survive diseases. Since these faculties fairly frequently produce falsehoods, the proper functioning of such faculties must be excluded from the definition of knowledge. Consider Plantinga's discussion of a passage from John Locke, who imagines a seasoned professor confronted all of a sudden with a bright student who makes a point that undermines a fundamental principle of the professor's life's work.

---

[6] Some material in this subsection has been adapted from Robert C. Roberts and W. Jay Wood, "Proper Function, Emotion, and Virtues of the Intellect", *Faith and Philosophy* 21 (2004): 3–24.

Would it not be an insufferable thing for a learned professor, and that which his scarlet would blush at, to have his authority of forty years standing wrought out of hard rock Greek and Latin, with no small expense of time and candle, and confirmed by general tradition, and a reverend beard, in an instant overturned by an upstart nouelist?[7] Can any one expect that he should be made to confess, that what he taught his scholars thirty years ago, was all error and mistake; and that he sold them hard words and ignorance at a very dear rate?

Since the professor's belief "that the young upstart is dead wrong" is produced by the proper functioning of a defense mechanism, rather than of a faculty aimed at truth, his belief "has little by way of warrant".[8] His properly epistemic faculties may be unimpaired, but because the defense against shame disinclines him to think carefully about the objection, and thus to appreciate its force, he is unwarranted in his belief.

The virtues epistemologist will point out that the professor—the person, the epistemic agent—is not functioning well epistemically.[9] Each of his faculties, taken individually, may be, in a sense, in good order: the defense mechanism is defending him against shame, and there is nothing wrong with his eyesight, his powers of inference and logical intuition, etc., though in the present case the defense mechanism is suppressing the use of some of the crucial epistemic faculties. The virtue epistemologist's invitation to focus attention on the whole agent is made more attractive by considering the case of another professor. After arguing that the search in recent epistemology for the single correct concept of epistemic justification has been a mistake, William Alston comments:

It will, I hope, have become clear by now that the thesis of this paper is an iconoclastic and revolutionary one, a bold departure from the well-trodden pathways of the discipline. It implies that a large proportion of contemporary

---

[7] Novelist: "†2. One who is inexperienced; a novice. 1630 Lennard tr. *Charron's Wisd.* II.VII §18.305 There is not anything so easie that doth not hurt and hinder vs, if wee bee but nouelists therein" (*OED*).

[8] Alvin Plantinga, *Warrant and Proper Function* (New York: Oxford University Press, 1993), p. 12.

[9] The mere fact that the professor has formed a false belief does not imply that he is unwarranted, or that he is not functioning well intellectually. Since firmness (tenacity) is an intellectual virtue, a person who holds onto a belief against contrary evidence may be functioning well intellectually, even if the belief is false. If Locke's professor, in holding onto his belief against the rather compelling argument of the novelist, is expressing proper scholarly tenacity, it seems that he is warranted in this false belief. However, in Locke's rather jocose description of the professor we are invited to see something other than the working of proper tenacity (a virtue which, after all, Locke counts a vice), and Plantinga follows Locke in making the professor out to be epistemically off base. We do too, but see our discussion in Ch. 7.

epistemologists, including myself, have been misguided in their researches, fighting under a false banner, engaged in a quixotic tilting at windmills.[10]

It is true that Alston goes on to confess the pleasures of iconoclasm and to show how a good portion of the epistemological windmill tilting over recent decades can be redeemed, after all, by reconceiving somewhat the goals of epistemology. But still, it is an impressive intellectual attribute to be able to see and admit that what one has been laboring at for the past several decades and enshrining in ink, and what one has been lionized for, is pretty fundamentally misconceived. The difference between Locke's professor and Alston is, as Plantinga's language suggests, not a difference of the excellence of epistemic faculties. It is a difference in epistemic functioning, and one that is important for a philosopher. Locke's professor is blinded to truth by the deterrent of shame, by the stake of his honor and status and image and identity as professor that, as he sees it, will be compromised by so fundamental an admission of error. Alston, by contrast, is willing to suffer the embarrassment because of his overriding interest in getting epistemology right. Or perhaps he sees more clearly that there is not much shame in disowning a significant part of his work in the interest of truth.

So we need to assess not just faculties, but their integration into the character of the intellectual agent. Perhaps people need a psychological defense against devastating shame, but adjustments are possible here, and normatively called for. One might think that the professor is overly ashamed, or ashamed of what is not really or deeply shameful; or that it would be better for his defenses to be more permeable. Locke's professor's defense mechanism is functioning properly if construed in isolation from the larger purposes of his life, but its functioning is making *him* something of an intellectual wimp. His defense mechanism is functioning properly in the way that the eyesight of a person with 20–20 vision is functioning properly, despite the fact that her visual assessments of people's emotional states are skewed. It is functioning properly in an abstract sense, but it is frustrating one of the larger purposes of his life as a human being: namely, knowledge.

---

[10] William Alston, "Epistemic Desiderata", *Philosophy and Phenomenological Research* 53 (1993): 527–51; pp. 541–2.

On a plausible description of the professor's mind, taking cues from Locke's references to his authority and his "reverend beard", the professor's failure to hear the student's point is due to the emotional structure of his personality (his self-image as important and learned and his emotional attachment to that self-image; the subordination of the concern for truth to the concern to be respected). By contrast, on a plausible description of Alston's mind, it is not just that he did his epistemic duty in forming the belief that the jig was up for monolithic theories of justification. Instead, the order of his concerns was somewhat different from that of the professor; his character was differently formed. Getting it right philosophically was a powerful enough concern to override the concern to maintain the full luster of his previous accomplishments. Guiding his intellectual choices and emotional responses was a practical wisdom concerning the relative importance of reputation and truth. Or, if he felt a shame like that of Locke's professor, perhaps he had a greater ability to dissociate from it, to objectify it and set it aside for purposes of intellectual practice. If the difference between these professors is in the excellence of their faculties, it is largely a difference in the functioning of their wills. And this difference, which bears quite directly on the warrant of their beliefs, is a difference in the quality of their functioning as epistemic agents.

b. Self-knowledge

At least since the days of David Hume, philosophers have sometimes doubted whether people are ongoing centers of consciousness, or at any rate whether we have the wherewithal to know that we are such. In Plantinga's discussion of self-knowledge,[11] he deploys his faculty epistemology to defend the proposition that we can know ourselves to be ongoing centers of consciousness.

The skeptical argument goes something like this: When I introspect, I find myself having various experiences—perceptual experiences, emotions, thoughts, kinaesthetic sensations, and so forth. But if I canvass the things I thus have experiences *of*, I don't find myself among them. That is, I find no datum, among the other data, that I would call "myself", no experience that is the experience of *me*, in addition to the experiences of thoughts, sensations, and the like. Yet I find myself, quite naturally, believing not

---

[11] Plantinga, *Warrant and Proper Function*, pp. 48–55.

just that *there are* all these experiences, but that *I am the subject* of them, that they are *mine*. Derek Parfit[12] and his ilk say that since I don't find myself among the data, I am not warranted in thinking I am an ongoing subject of experiences, so I ought to suspend my belief about this.

Plantinga answers that the conclusion doesn't follow. It is true that I am not among the data, and that all my experiences could be exactly as they are without my being an ongoing subject of experiences; but from these considerations it doesn't follow that my belief that I am an ongoing subject of experiences lacks warrant. The fact that this belief is, for us human beings, a natural product of our experiences is warrant for believing it. The belief that I am an ongoing subject of experiences, as occasioned by introspection, is as naturally compelling as the belief that there is a bird in the tree before me, in response to being appeared to in the bird-in-a-tree sort of way. If it is, as it seems to be, the result of a belief-forming process that is aimed at truth, functioning properly in a congenial environment, then I am warranted in holding it. The mere fact that I can imagine being in error about this is not warrant for thinking I may actually be in error.

True to his formulations for warrant and knowledge, Plantinga's discussion of self-knowledge remains at the level of faculty function and does not require any unusual or hard-to-achieve epistemic capacity such as an intellectual skill or virtue. If *anybody* has self-knowledge in this sense, then pretty much *everybody* has. (Maybe some lunatics don't, and presumably very young infants don't. And philosophers may be able to talk themselves out of their warrant for believing it; e.g., when Parfit acquired his belief that he has a defeater for the belief that he is an ongoing subject of experiences, he may have forfeited his warrant for believing that he is.)

At the beginning of Plantinga's brief discussion he comments that "an even reasonably complete account of self-knowledge...would require a book all by itself" (p. 48). No doubt, in a book-length discussion Plantinga would discuss moral self-knowledge, accurate assessment of one's own abilities and limitations, understanding of one's own actions and motives, awareness of how one is seen by others, and facing up to such facts as that one's life is a disaster. These topics are the loci of "self-knowledge" that is a somewhat rare and often a difficult and impressive achievement. They are the kinds of knowledge that anyone but a professional philosopher would

---

[12] Derek Parfit, *Reasons and Persons* (New York: Oxford University Press, 1985), ch. 11.

expect to hear about when a discussion of "self-knowledge" is advertised. No one unacquainted with the arcane and ultimately pointless worries of the likes of Hume and Parfit would take an interest in such a discussion. By contrast, the kind of self-knowledge that marks human maturity should be of profound interest to everybody, because of its intrinsic importance.

The acquisition of this kind of self-knowledge requires far more than properly functioning faculties in a congenial environment. It *presupposes* the kind of self-knowledge that is pretty much guaranteed by the proper functioning of the faculty of introspection. A person who didn't know that he was an ongoing subject of experiences would not be able to have deeper moral and spiritual self-knowledge, or to assess accurately his capacities and limits. But this is the bare beginning of self-knowledge. A normal 5-year-old knows he is the same person who went to sleep in his bed last night and will have to go to the dentist tomorrow, but he has, as yet, little self-knowledge. As Peter Goldie comments,

One of the many horrible things about being young, and especially about being a teenager, is that we don't really know who we are. Of course we know who we are in one sense (barring amnesia, being a foundling, and the like), but we don't know what *sort of a person* we are.[13]

Deeper self-knowledge requires virtues, and an epistemology capable of throwing light on this kind of self-knowledge will need to study the virtues that it presupposes. Our thesis can be formulated in either of two ways: (a) that proper function of the faculty of self-knowledge is not sufficient for deeper self-knowledge—proper *faculty* function must be supplemented with proper *person* function (expressions of virtues); or (b) that proper function of the faculty of self-knowledge, when applied to the deeper kinds of self-knowledge, requires the "perfection" of that faculty in some intellectual virtues.

Socrates went about trying to promote self-knowledge in his fellow Athenians, and many of them found his efforts annoying and embarrassing, since he invited them to see clearly the limits of their own understanding. Nicias is about to get involved in one of Socrates' searching conversations, when he comments, rather bravely,

---

[13] Peter Goldie, *On Personality* (London: Routledge, 2004), p. 19.

"…anyone who is close to Socrates and enters into conversation with him is liable to be drawn into an argument, and whatever subject he will start, he will be continually carried round and round by him, until at last he finds that he has to give an account both of his present and past life, and when he is once entangled, Socrates will not let him go until he has completely and thoroughly sifted him. Now I am used to his ways, and I know…that I myself shall be the sufferer, for I am fond of his conversation, Lysimachus. And I think that there is no harm in being reminded of any wrong thing which we are, or have been, doing; he who does not fly from reproof will be sure to take more heed of his afterlife." (*Laches* 187e−188b)[14]

Nicias realizes that as he lets the conversation with Socrates begin, he is opening himself to increased self-awareness, and that what he will see about himself is likely not to be an unmixed pleasure. Yet he overcomes his apprehensiveness in the interest of personal growth. He is open to the very real possibility that what he doesn't know about himself is harming him, and he is willing to suffer pain for the sake of the improvement. This desire for self-knowledge and the courage to expose himself to examination are dispositions of the will that in the individual case may be necessary for deepening self-awareness. And they are virtues—indeed, virtues of the intellect, insofar as the source of pain and the object of fear is knowledge, and they facilitate increased knowledge. For a contrast, a case of someone who is not open to increased self-knowledge, see Euthyphro in the dialogue named for him. Euthyphro differs from Nicias in not seeing the value of increased self-knowledge, and in responding to its prospect with avoidance. The kind of self-knowledge that many of Socrates' contemporaries resisted was not exactly propositional knowledge of their ignorance and other fallibility (though some of them no doubt gained that), much less propositional knowledge that they are ongoing centers of consciousness, but the sort of personal and emotional *appreciation* of it that we called "acquaintance" in Chapter 2. Socrates seems to have caused people to *face* themselves, and probably would not have been satisfied to leave them with mere warranted true belief about themselves.

A similar kind of self-knowledge comes up in the Hebrew−Christian tradition. For example, when the psalmist says (Psalm 51.3−4a),

---

[14] Trans. Benjamin Jowett, in Edith Hamilton and Huntington Cairns (eds), *The Collected Dialogues of Plato* (New York: Bollingen Foundation, 1961), pp. 131−2.

> For I know my transgressions,
>   and my sin is ever before me.
> Against thee, thee only, have I sinned,
>   and done that which is evil in thy sight,

he is not talking about mere warranted true belief that he is a sinner, but about a sort of direct emotional acquaintance with its gravity, an appreciation of its import. His knowledge is a deep *impression* of the heinousness of what he has done and of its close clinging to him ("in sin did my mother conceive me", v. 5). Again, this is the kind of knowledge that in Chapter 2 we called "acquaintance". A person might have a warranted belief that he has seriously transgressed, that he is responsible in the appropriate degree for the transgression, and so forth. He might have perfectly good evidence for this, but still not know his transgression in the sense intended by the psalmist ("my sin is ever before me"). And it seems clear that the personal qualifications needed for this kind of knowledge go far beyond the proper functioning of the faculty by which we know ourselves to be ongoing centers of consciousness. A "contrite heart" (v. 17) is a necessary subjective qualification, and the disposition to have a contrite heart on appropriate occasions consists of such virtues as love of moral purity, humility, and openness to correction. We said just now that one can be warranted in the belief that one is a sinner without this intimate knowledge. But the latter could supply warrant or be part of the story about warrant. This is something like seeing for oneself the moral significance of what one has done and is; it is a moral analog of sensory experience. And one might think that for this reason it's a better kind of warrant.

Sometimes self-knowledge is just a warranted true belief. It is an achievement for a creative person to assess accurately his own abilities and accomplishments. Søren Kierkegaard knew he was extraordinary and occasionally commented about how he would be read by future generations; but he also said that the importance of his pseudonymous authors was "once again to read through solo, if possible in a more inward way, the original text of individual human existence–relationships, the old familiar text handed down from the fathers".[15] This self-assessment seems to be right on target. Far less significant authors have sometimes thought themselves and

---

[15] Søren Kierkegaard, *Concluding Unscientific Postscript*, I, trans. Howard Hong and Edna Hong (Princeton: Princeton University Press, 1992), pp. 629–30.

their contributions quite original and important. It seems that they would be less likely to have these unwarranted beliefs, and instead to have some warranted ones about their degree of importance and accomplishments, if they had the virtues of humility, generosity, honesty, and justice, as these apply to assessments of intellectual credit. These virtues involve caring about epistemic goods—insights, contributions, felicitous formulations—in just the right way (for example, with a certain degree of detachment and "objectivity", a certain "disinterested" care) and caring about the good these goods can do, but caring about them in such a way that one's *self*-importance is not too great an ingredient.

Here is a more mundane kind of case. Bill is buying paint at the home supply store. He sits at the counter for a minute and lays his color samples on the counter. The clerk is helping someone else and turns to him and says, "I'll be with you in a moment." So he leaves his samples on the counter and wanders across the aisle to look at the ladders, watching out of the corner of his eye the progress on the other side of the aisle. A man comes up and starts waiting to be served by the paint clerk. Bill thinks to himself, "With me over here by the ladders, that fellow might think he's next in line, after the present customer." So Bill goes back and sits at the counter, and in a moment the clerk starts helping him. When he is well into the process, the newcomer interrupts indignantly and says that he is next in line, and he should be served ahead of Bill. The clerk tells him that Bill was ahead of him, and he contradicts the clerk. When the clerk tries again to explain that Bill was ahead of him, the man storms off in anger.

This case too involves a kind of self-knowledge, or lack thereof. The man did not know his place in line, and when given an opportunity, and then a repetition of that opportunity, to find out the truth about his place in line, he passed it up and remained in the dark about himself. Why? He seems to have been strongly disposed to insist on his own way, to be quick to claim his rights. He didn't really listen to the clerk's assertion, listen in the sense of take seriously for a moment's pause to inquire. So maybe if he'd had slightly more cautious attitude about appearances, he would have figured out what was going on. He seems to make an arrogant presumption of personal knowledge, manifesting overconfidence in his own powers of observation. A weaker disposition to insist on his own rights might have freed him to exercise a bit of healthy self-skepticism. And this not insisting on his own way might have been fostered by generosity:

"Why not let somebody in ahead of me, even if it's not quite fair? We all have our business to do, and this fellow who has somehow got ahead of me in line no doubt has his." So a cluster of intellectual and moral virtues—generosity and humility and caution about appearances—would be a ground of self-knowledge in this very ordinary and common case. A more virtuous man might have left the store with more truths and fewer falsehoods.

c. Testimonial credulity

Thomas Reid pointed out that we humans tend to believe what we're told. He considered this tendency "a good gift of Nature",[16] and the goodness he had in mind was in the first instance epistemic. Because the intellectual life is profoundly cooperative, this gift is important to us. It is a faculty, not something to suppress, eradicate, or bypass, but something to refine and develop, because we depend, and must depend, heavily on the unsupported testimony of others. Without this natural tendency, children could not get started in their cognitive lives, nor could adults come close to collecting all the truths they need to function well intellectually.

Plantinga follows Reid in considering testimony a perfectly legitimate, and practically necessary, source of warranted beliefs. A person is not functioning sub-properly just because he believes what others tell him, without further evidence. Since people do sometimes give false or misleading testimony, either intentionally or otherwise, we develop, as we mature, ways of sorting out testimonies and trusting some of them more than others.

I believe you when you tell me about your summer vacation, but not when you tout on television the marvelous virtues of the deodorant you have been hired to sell. We learn not to form beliefs about a domestic quarrel until we have heard from both parties; we learn to mistrust pronouncements of campaigning politicians, lawyers arguing a case, and people with a strong financial interest in our believing what they tell us. (Plantinga, *Warrant and Proper Function*, p. 79)

Plantinga no doubt speaks for himself and for others who are intellectually mature. Those of us who have been hanging around universities most of our life may be under the impression that the kind of discrimination Plantinga

---

[16] Thomas Reid, *An Inquiry into the Human Mind on the Principles of Common Sense*, in *Thomas Reid's Inquiry and Essays*, ed. R. Beanblossom and K. Lehrer (Indianapolis: Hackett, 1983), ch. 6, sec XX, p. 87.

describes is virtually universal among adults. It isn't. Lots of grown-ups are pretty gullible, and the university types may be gullible outside their natural habitat. So for adults, an untutored faculty of testimonial credulity is a source of little, if any warrant. To function properly, it must be fitted with a sophisticated filtering device consisting of various epistemic skills and virtues.

Catherine Z. Elgin elaborates on Plantinga's point.[17] She argues that the way to vindicate testimony as a source of warrant is neither "piecemeal" nor "wholesale". The piecemeal approach says that I am warranted in accepting a testimonial p only if I have good inductive evidence that p's testifier is trustworthy vis-à-vis sentences like p. This approach is unrealistically restrictive. The wholesale approach says that since people usually tell the truth, then unless we have particular reasons for suspecting the testifier, we are warranted in believing his testimony. This approach is unrealistically liberal. "To understand the message a speaker's testimony conveys and the level of epistemic warrant it transmits requires sensitivity to contextual factors that affect both the content and strength of the claim" (p. 291). She summarizes:

Rather than concluding that testimony is in general warranted or that only the testimony of informants who are known to be reliable is warranted, we assess testimony in light of a variety of factors that bear on its warrant. We consider not just who is talking and what she is saying, but also what is at issue, what is being assumed—about the facts, the circumstances, the testifier, the audience, and the cognitive context. We also consider whether the shared assumptions are themselves justified. A testifier can transmit no more warrant than she has. But her audience may have epistemic resources that she lacks. If, for example, they have additional relevant information or better methods of assessment, they, as it were, filter her testimony through a finer mesh. ... To make effective use of testimony requires that we be neither too gullible nor too skeptical. We should neither accept nor reject every offering. Rather, we need to consider whether the information attested to meshes with our other cognitive commitments to yield a system that, as a whole, is reasonable in light of what we already had reason to believe. This requires that we attune ourselves not just to the bald statement of fact, but also to the speaker, the context, and the institutions that underwrite it. (p. 307)

---

[17] Catherine Z. Elgin, "Take it from Me: The Epistemological Status of Testimony", *Philosophy and Phenomenological Research* 65 (2002): 291–308.

The "attunement" or "sensitivity" of which Elgin writes is of course an acquired trait—or better, a set of traits—of the individual agent. Sensitivity to context has sometimes been called "circumspection". The good judgment by which one avoids both gullibility and skepticism is a kind of practical wisdom that presupposes epistemic humility and boldness, generosity and charity, openness to new ideas, caution, and concern to get the truth. Unless a person has acquired these refined aptitudes and concerns, the bare faculty of testimonial credulity is not a very reliable source of warranted beliefs. To express the point in Aristotelian terms, testimonial credulity is a disposition that admits of, and demands, perfecting.

The threat posed by an undisciplined credulity disposition is gullibility, but in some intellectual ambiences a wholesale fastidiousness about belief formation may be the problem. Plantinga's discussion of testimony is less polemical than his discussion of self-knowledge, but it might have been directed against a tendency suggested by some of the writings of Descartes, Locke, and Kant. These epistemologists are suspicious of testimony because it seems to compromise the principle that each person should be responsible for his own cognitions and because testimony may seem to be a generally low-grade kind of evidence. But, given natural human limitations, and the way things go according to the human cognitive design plan, the early modern tendency to prescribe a general suspicion of tradition and testimony could be read as an endorsement of epistemic arrogance and fastidiousness—an insistence on the right and duty always to "see for oneself". A character that made us generally suspicious of testimony or overly insistent on having in our own possession all the evidence supporting each of our beliefs, would be a paralyzing intellectual paranoia, a hyper-individualism that would be both unrealistic and, to the extent that it actually got instantiated as a personality trait, detrimental to our cognitive functioning. The virtues of intellectual humility and gratitude could be regarded as a liberation of the credulity disposition from unwarranted intellectual suspicion and distrust, and thus as dispositions promoting warrant in testimony circumstances.

Among the dispositions that enable a person to discriminate warranted from unwarranted testimony are emotional sensitivities. Consider the following scenario. At a cocktail party another guest, whom you have just met for the first time, tells you a story about a common acquaintance. The story casts your acquaintance in a mildly uncomplimentary light. You wonder whether to believe the story, but you think you detect in the narrator's facial expressions and voice just a little too much enjoyment, of the wrong kind, at that moment in the story when the derogation to your acquaintance becomes manifest. In the suspicion engendered by this impression, which may be thought of as a suspicion of a lie or of self-deception or of biased reporting, you withhold assent from the story and its implication. If this sensitivity tends to filter out false testimonies, then it is epistemically advantageous. This emotional sensitivity makes you a more reliable recipient (and thus transmitter) of testimony, and is thus epistemically virtuous.

The qualities of transmitters of testimony are just as important as the qualities of recipients. Consider the following apparently autobiographical comment of Thomas Reid:

I believed by instinct whatever they [my "parents and tutors"] told me, long before I had the idea of a lie, or a thought of the possibility of their deceiving me. Afterwards, upon reflection, I found they had acted like fair and honest people, who wished me well. I found that, if I had not believed what they told me, before I could give a reason for my belief, I had to this day been little better than a changeling. (*Inquiry*, ch. 6, sect. XX, p. 87)

Reid's credulity disposition gave him warranted beliefs in his early years and allowed for a smooth transition to refined filtering capacities as he grew, because he had virtuous parents and tutors, who treated him fairly in epistemic matters, told him the truth as best they could discern it, and loved him. We might add, speculatively, that these people were relatively free of the vices of gullibility and epistemic fastidiousness. Thus they fed mostly warranted beliefs into the little guy's credulity disposition, giving him a trustworthy fund on which to build a distinguished intellectual career, but just as importantly encouraging in him traits of the same virtuous kind as their own: honesty, fairness, love of truth, humility, gratitude, caution, and all the rest. The point can be generalized. The proper functioning of an adult's credulity disposition depends not just on his having some of the intellectual virtues, but also on his coming from and belonging to a community of persons who have those virtues.

Catherine Elgin points out how standards of precision in testimony, and thus what it means to believe a testimonial proposition, vary from context to context. For example, scientists have concluded that humans and Neanderthals did not interbreed, on the basis of comparing "human DNA with a sample of one Neanderthal's mitochondrial DNA" ("Take it from Me", p. 301). This is pretty slim evidence, but it's the best available. Insiders of the scientific community appreciate both the slimness of the evidence and the importance of the fact that it's the best we have. Thus they know how to "take" the testimony. But somebody outside the community, not understanding these factors, will probably ascribe to the testimony a rather different weight and will be, to that extent, less qualified recipients of the testimony. In general, by coming to know things in a field of inquiry, we become better able to determine which testimonial deliverances have the ring of truth and which don't, how much and what kind of credulity to accord them. We develop a sense for who is an expert and who is not, and for differences in the ways that experts and non-experts express themselves. In Chapter 3 we distinguished intellectual skills from intellectual virtues, in part, by saying that skills are more context-specific intellectual excellences, while virtues are more generic. On that reading, the scientist's superiority as a recipient of testimony is an intellectual skill, while a more general disposition to be cautious in receiving testimony, but also to trust others and not to arrogate to oneself undue entitlement to doubt expert and other testimony, would be virtuous. Both skills and virtues are crucial to the proper functioning of the testimonial credulity faculty, for the adult acquisition of important kinds of knowledge.

The Definition Project, Once Again

For several reasons we have eschewed the main project that drives the faculty epistemologies: namely, the effort to specify the necessary and sufficient conditions for a belief's being justified or warranted and, by extension, an instance of knowledge.[18] First, we think that the concept of knowledge is not susceptible of that kind of analysis, since it is not univocal (see Chapter 2). But second, we think that the project is hopeless even if we limit our discussion to propositional knowledge, since we suspect that any interestingly informative definition can be undone by contriving

---

[18] We are grateful to Jason Baehr for prompting us to write this section.

a Gettier case or other counterexample (see Chapter 1). And third, we think that such a definition, even if possible, would have only minimal philosophical interest, because it would not, of itself, contribute much to our understanding of knowledge (see Chapters 1 and 2). Philosophical analysis can reveal much about the concept, but all its revealing can be done without formulating a successful e-definition. In fact, efforts to define knowledge have shed some light on the concept—though far from everything that might be revealed if we concentrated more on upper-end kinds of knowledge and reintroduced understanding and acquaintance into our discussions.

Nevertheless, let us think for a moment about how the faculty epistemologists might respond to the proposals in this chapter about the place of the faculties in producing knowledge. We have admitted that faculties, functioning properly in suitable environments, may be sufficient for warranting the beliefs they produce in case these beliefs are on the lower end of the knowledge spectrum—for example, that the lights have just gone out, that a white round object is before me, that my wife is at home, and so forth. At least this is so if we allow a minimal conceptual background and development of skill with the faculties in question. But for interesting kinds of knowledge—self-knowledge in a deep moral sense, scientific knowledge, religious knowledge, complex historical knowledge, for example—considerably greater powers are needed: in particular, epistemic skills and virtues. In other words, if we consider the whole range of kinds of things that people know, it becomes clear that the faculty epistemologies have not specified generally sufficient conditions even for propositional knowledge.

Or is it clear, after all? Any specification of sufficient conditions for knowledge will be literally incomplete. Oxygen, for example, is presumably a necessary condition for knowledge, yet no one thinks that a definition of knowledge would be incomplete if it did not mention that people can know nothing without oxygen. If we started requiring the mention of *all* the background conditions for knowledge, we would never finish the mentioning. So maybe perseverance and courage and humility are necessary to the acquisition of some warranted beliefs, but it does not follow that such virtues need to be mentioned in a definition of knowledge. The faculty epistemologist might say that just as the cognitive faculties will not function properly in an oxygen-free environment, so they will sometimes not function properly in a virtue-free "environment" (see Sosa's flexible notion of environment, discussed above). Perseverance, humility, and charity are sometimes required for the proper functioning of the faculties, but virtues need not, for all that, be mentioned in a definition of knowledge. The essential causes of epistemic warrant are still the properly functioning faculties.

This response is perhaps implicit in Sosa's concept of a virtue, but no one has made it explicitly, as far as we know. It raises the question of just what distinguishes conditions that must be mentioned in a definition of knowledge from those that can go unmentioned. For some reason, externalist definitions of knowledge pick out conditions like eyesight and a priori intuition, but let equally necessary conditions like oxygen and nutritional protein go unmentioned. Why? We think that this is because the epistemic faculties, unlike oxygen and protein, are specifically *aimed at* the epistemic goods. This rationale is reflected in Plantinga's clause "aimed at truth".[19] Only properties of the human constitution that are aimed at truth properly enter into the definition of knowledge. But if being directly aimed at the epistemic goods is what distinguishes the conditions that merit mention from all the ones that are only incidentally necessary, then surely intellectual virtue, which encompasses love of the epistemic goods, perseverance in pursuit of them, humility in contexts of intellectual endeavor, and any other such epistemically relevant character traits, belongs among the conditions that merit mention. Being aimed at the epistemic goods, these traits are much more like the cognitive faculties than they are like oxygen and protein. It looks to us as though the program of the faculty epistemologists needs to be broadened to encompass a more complete range of positive cognitive dispositions.

Another approach that a faculty epistemologist might take is to include virtues and epistemic skills under the heading of the proper functioning of the faculties. In the lower-end cases, they might say, the faculties may function fine, and thus yield warrant, without the support of intellectual virtues; but in the upper-end cases they simply do not function properly without the virtues and skills. Such a faculty epistemologist might, then, welcome what we have said as a helpful supplement to his conception

---

[19] See Plantinga, *Warrant and Proper Function*, pp. 11–17.

of a properly functioning faculty, without changing his formula defining justification in terms, say, of reliable belief-producing processes. The virtues are just a part of the story about reliable belief production. We do not object to this response, but we would point out that someone who takes this approach has given up the spirit of a faculty epistemology no less than one who responds by turning virtues into background conditions. Faculty epistemologists who are willing to accord to character traits a major and essential role in the acquisition of some epistemic goods have wandered far from the original idea of a faculty epistemology, because what is doing the work in the new permutation of their view is no longer just the faculties but, in the upper-end cases at least, the epistemic agent who *uses* the faculty virtuously for his or her purposes. The epistemologist may wish to keep the virtues in the humble role of supplementing the functioning of faculties, but in reality he has reduced the faculties to appliances in the hands of a person.

Conclusion

We have argued that epistemologies that try to account for the human ability to achieve the epistemic goods by reference to faculties cannot ultimately succeed unless they appeal to the maturation and mature use of those faculties. In their undeveloped state, the faculties yield only the most minimal and uninteresting of epistemic goods, if any at all. The mature functioning of the epistemic agent depends on and makes use of the faculties, but the dispositions that are needed for high-level functioning are not the faculties alone, but the epistemic skills and virtues that are built on them. Current faculty epistemologies move implicitly and tentatively in the direction of a virtue epistemology, but do not arrive at the goal. One of the main impediments to this conceptual fulfillment is the failure of these theorists to acknowledge the human will—the innate basis of our ability to have concerns, desires, and emotions, and to make choices and efforts—as an important epistemic faculty. Indeed, we think that a virtue epistemology that does full justice to the functioning of the epistemic faculties in producing the most interesting and important kinds of knowledge will have to make the will the central intellectual faculty. The reason is that the epistemic goods are acquired, ultimately, not by faculties but by agents, and the will is the locus of our identity as agents.

How is our regulative epistemology related to the analytic epistemologies of the late twentieth century? It is both significantly continuous and deeply discontinuous with them. We have argued that the search for an e-definition of knowledge, which was so dominant in the last decades of the century, is a hopeless and not very interesting project, yet we certainly think that clarification of the concept of knowledge (see Chapter 2) is an important task for the epistemologist, and we regard the task of regulative epistemology as, in a broad sense, an analytic task. The one-size-fits-all concept of justification that analytic epistemologists tended to seek is, again, a chimera, but virtually all the ideas of justification that were proposed have merit as aspects of a concept of justification. The propositional knowledge on which analytic epistemologists lavished their time is, from our point of view, an abstraction, yet, seen as such, it is an enormously important aspect of knowledge. Finally, we have argued in this chapter that the faculty epistemologies that were popular in the late twentieth century were incapable of explaining the most important kinds of knowledge; yet it is in a way a small step from the idea of properly functioning faculties to that of a properly functioning epistemic agent. Our aim in this book is not to replace all the activities that have characterized epistemology in recent decades, but to let the concept of an excellent intellectual agent reshape those activities and concerns in the direction of analysis that will serve intellectual communities far beyond the borders of professional epistemology.

5

Practices

Introduction

As the concept of a function suggests, the epistemic faculties are means by which things happen or get accomplished. By the eyes, things are seen; by reason, conclusions are drawn; by construal, one thing is grasped in terms of another; and so forth. Some of what faculties accomplish happens automatically, and some of it results from actions or activities of the cognitive agent, though we argued a while ago that little of epistemic importance is achieved—automatically *or* deliberately—without the training and formation of both the faculties and the whole persons who possess them. This formation arises largely in the pursuit of determinate activities that we call practices. In turn, the virtues and skills, so formed, are required for the proper and successful practice of the practices. Some examples of intellectual practices are observation, hypothesis formation, hypothesis testing, critical discussion, teaching, interviewing, reading, and prayer.

We could call the items in this list practice categories, because each of them has many subspecies. The practice of observation, for example, takes many forms, some highly disciplined and others rather casual, some performed with the naked eye (ear, tongue, skin, intellect) and others with elaborate instrumentation (microscope, telescope, oscilloscope, computer) that requires special skills to manipulate. Hypothesis testing can take many forms, for example: casual observation, empirical experimentation, thought experimentation, critical discussion, and trial by counterexample. No doubt many, if not all, of the practices listed at the end of the preceding paragraph have parts that are also practices. For example, critical discussion involves listening to one's interlocutor(s), giving criticism, receiving criticism, and responding to criticism, among other things. Many practices are thus in fact practice clusters. Teaching (say, in the humanities) would be a practice cluster encompassing such practices as lecturing, leading discussion, expounding and interpreting texts, demonstrating and using visual aids, and grading and commenting on student work. But leading discussion could also be regarded as a practice cluster, encompassing questioning, listening, responding to questions, responding to criticism, analyzing, interpreting, paraphrasing, and expanding what an interlocutor has said. And no doubt some of these practices could also be regarded as clusters of practices. Intellectual practices form a network or mosaic of partially discrete but also overlapping parts, variants, and subspecies, so that a tight schema for individuating them would be hopeless, confusing, and useless.

Some practices are explicitly social (classroom teaching, dialectical interchange), others are implicitly social (reading, writing), and still others are solo (single-person laboratory science, journaling, meditative reflection like that of Descartes before his stove). But even solo epistemic practices have a social dimension: the laboratory scientist will belong to a tradition of experimentation; Descartes's thoughts are responses to a historical intellectual and political situation.

The intellectual life is fraught with practices; they are its medium. The distinction, dating from Aristotle and enduring even to the present day, between the intellectual and the practical (theoretical versus practical reason, contemplative versus practical wisdom) is ill-drawn, because the intellectual life is fully as much a matter of practices as any other part of life. In earlier chapters we have spoken repeatedly of "the intellectual life"; the intellectual practices fill the moments in which the goods of that life are pursued. Whether epistemic practices are executed well or badly depends on the qualities of their practitioners—a mixture and interaction of aptitudes and skills, on the one hand, and concerns and tastes and desires, on the other. So we are back to proper functioning and its bases. In this book we are especially interested in the virtues as bases of excellent noetic functioning, so we will try to show how each of several practices is enhanced (for the delivery of epistemic goods) by the agent's possessing the virtue base. And the virtues are to a large extent products of the practices.

William Alston proposes a "doxastic practice" approach to adjudicating principles that "lay down conditions under which one is justified in holding beliefs of a certain kind".[1] We prefer to speak of "epistemic" rather than "doxastic" practices, since we think that the goods these practices promote are not limited to beliefs (see Chapter 2). Alston's paper is in the reliabilist tradition, which, as we have seen, focuses firmly on faculties, mechanisms, and processes. He thinks he can make headway on developing a reliabilist conception of justification by shifting the focus slightly from epistemic principles to epistemic practices. His chief example is the "sense perceptual doxastic practice" (SPP).

The term "practice" will be misleading if it is taken to be restricted to voluntary activity; for I do not take belief-formation to be voluntary. I am using "practice" in such a way that it stretches over, e.g., psychological processes such as perception, thought, fantasy, and belief-formation, as well as voluntary action. A doxastic practice can be thought of as a system or constellation of dispositions or habits, or, to use a currently fashionable term, mechanisms, each of which yields a belief as output that is related in a certain way to an "input". (p. 5)

If we take sense perception to be a single faculty, then perhaps Alston is following in Aristotle's footsteps; but if we take it, more plausibly, to be five faculties, then already SPP integrates the functions of several faculties, and Alston points out that "we have to rely on the output of memory and reasoning for the overriders of perceptual beliefs" (p. 6). So it seems pretty clear that SPP involves a lot more than the functioning of one faculty. But the mention of memory and reasoning as practices suggests that sometimes Alston means by "practice" just about what Plantinga calls the functioning of a faculty. This accords nicely with his warning against taking "practice" to imply "voluntary" and his openness to the word "mechanism". However, he also mentions practices that are voluntary, and can not be tied very definitely to any one faculty—for example, the "Christian doxastic practice" and the "scientific doxastic practice" (p. 18). These expressions seem to encompass more than anything we would call "*a* practice". Both Christianity and science have many intellectual practices, which it would not occur to us to group together as a single practice.

By contrast with Aristotle and Alston, we are not interested in practices that are faculty-specific. Nor are the practices that interest us dispositions,

[1] William Alston, "A 'Doxastic Practice' Approach to Epistemology", in M. Clay and K. Lehrer (eds), *Knowledge and Skepticism* (Boulder, CO: Westview Press, 1989), p. 1.

mechanisms, or habits, though the skilled or virtuous practitioner will have dispositions to practice the practice, and will no doubt possess relevant mechanisms and habits that are brought into play in the practice. Further, we do think of practices as primarily voluntary activities, undertaken with a more or less explicit intention of acquiring or transmitting warranted beliefs, understanding, and firsthand insight. They are activities, in a robust sense, and not just "processes". The denial that people choose their beliefs needs to be refined, since, for example, a major purpose of undertaking to read the literature on virtue epistemology is to *decide* what to think about various issues in virtue epistemology. Of course, as in any activity at which we become proficient, much is carried on automatically, spontaneously, intuitively. Activities like reading, philosophical conversation, scientific experimentation, and prayer are practiced voluntarily, while resultant occurrences, like belief formation, increase of understanding, and the dawning of insight, may be quite involuntary.

Another emphatic theme of this book is the cultivation of the would-be knower's will in the formation of the intellectual virtues. We can divide intellectual goods into two kinds, using a distinction that Alasdair MacIntyre has made current, though its predecessors go back at least to Plato's *Republic*.[2] MacIntyre distinguishes goods internal, from goods external, to a practice. Some goods internal to the practice of violin playing would be a beautiful tone, an excellent performance of a piece, musical understanding of a piece in the violin repertoire, and enjoying executing a run excellently. Some goods external to this practice would be the money, honors, and other perquisites that sometimes devolve on its best practitioners. Roughly, goods are internal to a practice if and only if they belong to a class such that, to practice the practice well, one *must* aim at them. Goods are external to a practice if they accrue to its excellent practitioners with some regularity, but one can practice the practice without aiming at them. For example, it is perfectly possible for someone to attain the very highest powers of violin playing without ever aiming to become rich or famous; but it is not possible to attain such powers without aiming to understand the musical logic of pieces in the violin repertoire, to execute runs and trills well, to produce a beautiful sound, etc.

---

[2] See Alasdair MacIntyre, *After Virtue*, 2 edn. (Notre Dame, IN: University of Notre Dame Press, 1984), pp. 187–96. All citations in this chapter are of this edition.

Intellectual practices aim intrinsically at such goods as understanding (of texts, of natural processes, of historical events, of historical human actions, of human nature and its conditions of flourishing and conditions of dysfunction, etc.), acquaintance, and confirmation of beliefs (evidence, insight about coherence with well-established beliefs). Intellectual practices aim at the justification and warrant of beliefs. Other intellectual practices (those of education, broadly speaking) aim at the communication of the above goods and at nurturing the powers and skills by which people gain more of the intrinsic epistemic goods for themselves. So communication skills and the personal powers by which agents acquire understanding, knowledge, and justification and warrant of beliefs become, themselves, goods that are intrinsically sought through intellectual practices. Also, self-directed practices by which one acquires the knowledge and skills needed to pursue intellectual activities (study, self-discipline, and techniques of skill and knowledge acquisition) are valued. These, then, are some of the goods that are internal to intellectual practices. Such practices also have external goods. People make money from their research; scientific discoveries and book sales can be financial bonanzas. Honors come to people who perform well intellectually (or seem to do so): named university chairs, Pulitzer and Nobel prizes, and on a smaller scale, tenure, promotion, Teacher of the Year awards, recognition as expert by smaller or larger populations, grades, and the $10 gift certificate to MacDonald's that goes to the spelling bee winner. Some of the extrinsic rewards may further the intrinsic goods: money may free one for further, less fettered inquiry, and tenure and other positions may do the same. But, as before, the very highest of intrinsic intellectual goods may be achieved with little or no associated extrinsic goods, and occasionally large amounts of the extrinsic intellectual goods may come to persons of modest intrinsic achievements.

In general, intellectual virtues are dispositions to use our epistemic faculties well—in the excellent pursuit of the goods internal to cognitive practices. The person who pursues these goods, but pursues them only as means to goods external to the practices, is unlikely to achieve the internal goods as well as the person who pursues them at least partly for their own sake; a greater preponderance of intrinsic motivation is not only a mark of greater intellectual virtue, but is also, we judge, more "efficient" at realizing the goods. So if these goods really are the ticket to achieving the goods external to the intellectual practices (and it is abundantly clear that they *need not* be treated as such), then intellectual virtue will be the more reliable way to achieve the goods external to the practices. Through James Watson's and Francis Crick's discovery of the structure of DNA (certainly an intellectual good internal to their practices of inquiry), they won the Nobel prize (a good external to those practices). But it is arguable that an important part of the value of the Nobel prize is the high scientific reputation that it entails. Watson's account of the discovery of the structure, and the fallout of his account, effectively lowered the scientific esteem in which other scientists and the larger public hold Watson and Crick. Their shenanigans and their motivations, when known, reduced the luster that the Nobel prize would have conferred had they made the discovery with full intellectual integrity. So it looks as though the very highest degree of the external good of reputation is achieved only when the internal intellectual good is achieved via intellectual virtue (or at least appears to have been so achieved). This would not be true of other extrinsic goods such as money. The pursuit of the internal goods can conflict with the pursuit of the external goods, and when conflicts arise, excellent intellectual practice may require a kind of self-denial, in the interest of the intrinsic goods, that is also the exercise of intellectual virtues.

However, our concept of a practice also differs somewhat from Mac-Intyre's. He writes:

By "practice" I am going to mean any coherent and complex form of socially established cooperative human activity through which goods internal to that form of activity are realized in the course of trying to achieve those standards of excellence which are appropriate to, and partially definitive of, that form of activity, with the result that human powers to achieve excellence, and human conceptions of the ends and goods involved, are systematically extended. (*After Virtue*, p. 187)

MacIntyre tells us that bricklaying is not a practice, but architecture is; planting turnips is not a practice, but farming is. We can imagine him saying that slide preparation and pathology microscopy are not practices, but medical research is; reading is not a practice, but historical research is. But it is not clear that bricklaying and turnip planting are excluded by his formulated definition of "practice". Both are coherent, modestly complex, and socially established in a broad sense; they have standards of excellence and aim at such internal goods as well-made walls and first-rate turnips.

It seems to us a bit arbitrary to make it definitive of practices that they systematically extend "human powers to achieve excellence, and human conceptions of the ends and goods involved". Even if turnip planting and bricklaying did not evolve (and it's far from clear that they don't), they would still count as practices in our book. The stipulation that no activity is a practice if it does not extend human powers to achieve excellence seems to be motivated by the role MacIntyre assigns the concept of a practice in his neo-paleo-foundationalist ethics: the role of grounding the concept of a virtue after the demise of the Aristotelian biological foundation. Our concept of a practice is not designed to provide any such conceptual foundation. Finally, while the practices that interest us have internal goods, this feature is not necessary to our concept of a practice. Stock trading could be a practice on our concept, even if its goods are all external to it.

Nicholas Wolterstorff, taking a cue from the Alston paper that we cited earlier, proposes that we understand John Locke's basic epistemological project as that of reforming the epistemic practices of his contemporaries. According to Wolterstorff's interpretation, in the Middle Ages Europeans consulted a more or less canonical set of traditional texts when they wanted to form judgments about religion and morality, but during and after the Protestant Reformation it became more apparent than ever before that this body of texts, which included "Saint Paul and Virgil, Aristotle and Augustine",[3] did not speak with one voice, and could not be made to do so. The religious wars of Locke's time provided urgent motivation to fashion new practices that would settle the disputes that could not be settled by interpreting authoritative texts. The latter part of Book IV of Locke's *Essay Concerning Human Understanding* and his pamphlet *Of the Conduct of the Understanding* are devoted to a discussion of his proposed epistemic practices. It seems to us that the practices that Locke discusses, such as seeking evidence for one's beliefs, informing oneself broadly, listening to people with opposing viewpoints, critically assessing one's own prejudices, and reading, are the kinds of activities that we wish to call intellectual practices. In the interest of connecting these practices with virtues, we would like to propose a little extension of Wolterstorff's interpretation of Locke. Virtue concepts seem to be integral to Locke's discussions of epistemic practices.

[3] Nicholas Wolterstorff, *John Locke and the Ethics of Belief* (Cambridge: Cambridge University Press, 1996), p. 2.

For example, the disposition that Locke calls "indifferency" (*Conduct*, §§11, 14, 34, 35, pp. 185, 188–9, 211–14), which is a freedom from passionate attachment to particular beliefs combined with an intense concern that one's beliefs be true, is clearly a quality of the will or heart of the agent, and not merely a skill. If it is also an excellence, as Locke thinks it is, then it is a virtue. And it is a virtue clearly relevant to the practice of seeking evidence for one's beliefs. In Chapter 6 we will see that Locke also advocates a virtue that we could call love of knowledge. In Chapter 1 we noted the contrast that Wolterstorff draws between the regulative epistemology of Descartes, which is oriented toward rule following, and that of Locke, which is oriented to education. Education—including but not limited to training in skills—links practices to character formation, and thus is more than habituation of rule following. Let us look at some intellectual practices and try to discern some of their connections to the virtues.

Reading

People read with a variety of aims, some of which are not epistemic goods, either finally or instrumentally. We sometimes read for sheer entertainment or escape, though even here may lurk a hint of an epistemic or quasi-epistemic good. The murder mystery into which one escapes presents a puzzle to be solved—clearly an intellectual challenge of a sort—and the reader becomes engrossed in "finding out" who done it. A comedy book presents incongruous juxtapositions and characterizations that strike us as funny, with something like what we earlier called acquaintance, and in fact even the lowest work of fiction, if it has the power to interest or titillate, brings "pictures" before our minds. But here we are interested primarily in reading aimed at understanding, warranted belief, and acquaintance with truths, and in seeing how these aims gain, from the virtues, in prospect of success.

Our ability to get knowledge from our reading depends on aptitudes, skills, and accomplishments other than virtues. Clearly, a decently quick intelligence is important. The ability to pay close attention to what one is reading is one such skill, and background knowledge in the subject-matter is important to the acquisition of any kind of new knowledge. But our question right now is whether, and if so, to what extent, virtues such as honesty, truthfulness, charity, generosity, respect, diligence, justice, openness, and caution figure in the acquisition of intellectual goods from reading. To what extent is the practice of reading promoted by the reader's virtues? Consider, as a first example, reading this passage from Tolstoy's *Anna Karenina*:

> Vronsky's life was particularly happy in that he had a code of principles, which defined with unfailing certitude what should and what should not be done. This code of principles covered only a very small circle of contingencies, but in return the principles were never obscure, and Vronsky, as he never went outside that circle, had never had a moment's hesitation about doing what he ought to do. This code categorically ordained that gambling debts must be paid, the tailor need not be; that one must not lie to a man but might to a woman; that one must never cheat anyone but one may a husband; that one must never pardon an insult but may insult others oneself, and so on. These principles might be irrational and not good, but they were absolute and in complying with them Vronsky felt at ease and could hold his head high. Only quite lately, in regard to his relations with Anna, Vronsky had begun to feel that his code did not quite meet all circumstances and that the future presented doubts and difficulties for which he could find no guiding thread.[4]

The mature reader who grasps the irony of this passages experiences a sort of perceptual acquaintance with the character of Alexei Vronsky from Tolstoy's moral point of view. It is an experiential appreciation of the solidity of morality as it is brought into relief by the silliness and folly of Vronsky's outlook. One might hesitate to call this experience new knowledge; yet appreciative acquaintance is a kind of knowledge that is always new, a fresh re-seeing of a truth of whose propositional form one may have dispositional knowledge already. We think it plausible to suppose that possessing some of the moral virtues that belong to Tolstoy's outlook—or virtues similar to them—contributes to the reader's ability to hear the irony in these passages. And, supposing that Tolstoy's moral judgments concerning marital relations, payment of debts, and so forth are correct, this perception of the fictional Vronsky as rather ridiculous will count as acquaintance with moral truths.

True, a person with a very different outlook from Tolstoy's—say, a confirmed Vronskyite—might also hear the irony in the passage. If so, it

---

[4] Leo Tolstoy, *Anna Karenina*, trans. Rosemary Edmonds (New York: Penguin Books, 1954) Part 3, ch. 20.

would be by virtue of a power of empathy with Tolstoy's viewpoint, an ability to put oneself into that viewpoint in a hypothetical way. It would be acquaintance with *how Vronsky looks from Tolstoy's viewpoint*, not with *how Vronsky is*. This power of empathic self-transcendence is itself a virtue or quasi-virtue; an inability to see from alien perspectives is a cognitive deficit that is also a personal failing. But we think the empathic acquaintance of a confirmed Vronskyite with Tolstoyan moral truths is unlikely to be as rich experientially as that of someone with a moral viewpoint, because the individual with the moral virtues *cares* about marital relations and debt payment in a way that even the most empathic Vronskyite does not. The concern is an important aspect of the moral virtues, and this caring gives the knower's acquaintance with the irony of Vronsky's judgments an emotional depth and appropriateness that lends understanding to the acquaintance. In other words, the emotional dispositions of moral character are themselves epistemic powers, powers of appreciative acquaintance with moral truths.

Consider now an academic person reading a text by an author of a very different theoretical persuasion or academic style—for example, an analytic epistemologist reading Hans-George Gadamer's *Truth and Method*. We don't mean just sniff around in it for something to make fun of or turn easily to one's own purposes; we mean, really read it, from start to finish (more or less), seriously intending to understand it. It is, admittedly, difficult to imagine, but to do so is to imagine the reader as exhibiting something on the order of heroic virtue. Virtues that come to mind are charity, open-mindedness, patience, humility, perseverance, and self-control. By charity the analytic reader treats Gadamer with respect, reading him as she would want to be read, were the roles reversed. By open-mindedness she reserves judgment about phrases and indeed whole pages that at first blush seem utterly opaque or irrelevant or implausible, and by patience and perseverance she continues to read on when the rewards seem meager or elusive. By humility she reads carefully where a person of only normal arrogance would feel entitled to skip and dismiss. By self-control she sets aside her anger and impatience with the jargon and slow pace of the book and pays real attention in an effort to understand. All such activities seem likely to promote the extraction of epistemic goods from Gadamer's book. Of course, it would be imprudent of the analytic epistemologist to lavish her intellectual virtues on just any work with the outward and inward appearances of *Truth and Method*. Presumably, in her prudence she has some reason (and no doubt increasing reason as she reads it virtuously) to trust that there is epistemological gold in that Teutonic mountain.

Reading is one of the intellectual practices on which Locke, in his role of regulative epistemologist, comments again and again in *Of the Conduct of the Understanding*. He emphasizes that reading is much more than just taking in what is on the page and remembering it. Excellent reading is digestion, critical assessment, and systematic assimilation of what is read to a coherent view of things. That is, reading is a process of understanding.

There are those who are very assiduous in reading, and yet do not much advance their knowledge by it. They are delighted with the stories that are told, and perhaps can tell them again, for they make all they read nothing but history to themselves; but not reflecting on it, not making to themselves observations from what they read, they are very little improved by all that crowd of particulars that either pass through or lodge themselves in their understandings. They dream on in a constant course of reading and cramming themselves, but, not digesting anything, it produces nothing but a heap of crudities. If their memories retain well, one may say they have the materials of knowledge, but, like those for building, they are of no advantage, if there be no other use made of them but to let them lie heaped up together. (*Conduct*, § 13, pp. 187–8)

The really good reader's reading is integrated into a larger intellectually excellent life. Locke might say, "Take the speed-reading course if you like, but do not expect it to teach you how to *read*." The good reader loves knowledge and understands that knowledge is not just a collection of facts; he critically insists on good reasons for affirming what he affirms and denying what he denies. He does not just seek support for his prejudices but is open to learning, willing to take a critical look at his own preexisting views. But these dispositions are all virtues: love of knowledge, love of truth, an open willingness to hear another side. Insofar as tutoring can teach these things in the course of a curriculum of reading, it is not just skill purveyance, but an education, a nurturing in the intellectual virtues.

Locke's inveighing against passive reading invites a conversation with a recent theory of textual interpretation. In an essay entitled "The End of the Book and the Beginning of Writing",[5] Jacques Derrida heralds the end of

---

[5] Jacques Derrida, *Of Grammatology*, trans. Gayatri Chakravorty Spivak (Baltimore: Johns Hopkins University Press, 1976), pp. 1–26. Our discussion bears on the early Derrida. On the distinction between the early and the later Derrida, see Bruce Ellis Benson, *Graven Ideologies* (Downers Grove, IL: InterVarsity Press, 2002), pp. 110–12.

what he calls "logocentrism". Logocentrism is the slavery of presupposing
that language is *about* things—the bondage of the word to its object. The
sad history of logocentrism goes back at least to Plato, and its idea is that the
point of language is the "presence" of one thing to another. For example,
when a person has the sensation characteristic of hitting his thumb with a
hammer, he rather spontaneously says "ouch" or some local variant thereof,
thus creating a presence of "ouch" and the sensation. But some sensations
seem to be about external things, such as trees, so when a person, upon
having an arboreal visual sensation, utters the word "tree", he creates (or
seems to create) a mediated presence of the tree itself to the word "tree"
(ordinary people might say instead that the word *refers to* the tree). This
presence is mediated, because the visual sensation comes between. But now
imagine that this same person writes down his experience: "I saw a tree
in the backyard." In writing, he makes a mark (inscription) on something.
It might be an ink mark on paper, or a carved mark on a piece of wood,
or a little rut in the sand; or in place of these primitive technologies he
might make a "mark" on the screen of a computer. The important point
about any such inscription is that its "presence" to the thing it is supposed
to make present is even more attenuated (mediated) than the "presence"
of the spoken word, in either the "ouch" case or the "tree" case, to the
things whose presence those words are supposed to mediate. The written
signifier signifies the thing in the world only by signifying the oral signifier
which signifies the thing in the world only by signifying the mental state of
being arboreally appeared to, which signifies the thing in the world. The
written signifier is thus a signifier of a signifier of a signifier of the signified.

For Derrida's purpose of undermining logocentrism, the attenuation of
presence effected by writing is a boon. But now he claims that, in our day,
we are coming to think of all language (and, we would add, much that we
do not think of as language) as writing:

... one says "language" for action, movement, thought, reflection, consciousness,
unconsciousness, experience, affectivity, etc. Now we tend to say "writing" for all
that and more. ... thus we say "writing" for all that gives rise to an inscription in
general, whether it is literal or not and even if what it distributes in space is alien to
the order of the voice: cinematography, choreography, of course, but also pictorial,
musical, sculptural "writing." One might also speak of athletic writing, and with
even greater certainty of military or political writing in view of the techniques that
govern those domains today. All this to describe not only the system of notation

secondarily connected with these activities but the essence and the content of these activities themselves. (p. 9)

In the broadest sense of "inscribe", all human activity inscribes. For example, when the basketball player makes a goal, his movements on the court and with the ball are a sort of inscription (admittedly, not a preserved one). Dancers write on the dance floor, painters write on canvas, architects write on the earth and sky with stone and steel and wood, political campaigners write on the minds of the voters, and sailors use their vessels to write on water. In generalizing writing to encompass all human activity, Derrida stretches still further the natural distance between the "written" and the "signified". In fact, he disconnects writing from a signified, thus depriving it of its status as signifier, as having reference. Writing becomes sheer non-referential expression.

Logocentrism, on which Derrida's construction is an attack, is a limitation of human freedom. For those who think of writing in the old logocentric way, writing is under the discipline of its referents. The writer cannot write just anything, but is in moral bondage to the truth, thought of as the real state of the referent; writing is in disciplined servitude to the thing written about. By contrast, in the situation of Derridean post-logocentrism, human beings are freed from this bondage.

What has this to do with reading? Reading is a human activity like any other. If basketball and politics and sculpture and sailing are anti-logocentric writing, surely reading, too, is such writing. Reading too is a free activity, not bound by any referent, not subject to the slavish necessity of making something "present". This picture of reading is quite radically opposed to Locke's, where it is assumed that there are truths of the matter about which one is reading and truths about what the text says about that matter, thus possible correct understandings and more numerous possible incorrect ones. To understand correctly the words written on the page is to know what they are about (to experience via them what they "present") and thus to put oneself in a better position to adjudicate their truth. The virtues that would aid a Lockean, logocentric reader to read well include love of truth, a respectful openness to the writer's intended meaning, a humble willingness to consider possibilities (of understanding and of truth) that may conflict with one's initial opinions, to revise one's own opinions in the light of such criticism, and so forth (we might call these the virtues of humble respect for the text and for the world the text is about). By contrast, the virtues that make a Derridean reader excellent are creativity, imaginativeness, and autonomy from the text and the world that the text is about (we might call these the virtues of instrumental domination). For the Derridean, the text is to be not the reader's master, but an occasion or instrument for the reader's creation of her own world.

This is not to say that the reader makes no disciplined reference to the text. To say just anything that came to mind in the presence of a text—say, upon reading *Hamlet* to launch into a discourse on the domestic habits of the Black Widow spider or the recent history of the stock market—might not count as an *interpretation* of the text, and Derrida is, after all, bent on interpretation. The creativity, imaginativeness, and autonomy would be cheap and unimpressive without the discipline of classical hermeneutics. Thus he can say:

To recognize and respect all [of a text's] classical exigencies is not easy and requires all the instruments of traditional criticism. Without this recognition and this respect, critical production would risk developing in any direction at all and authorize itself to say almost anything. But this indispensable guardrail has always only protected, it has never opened a reading. (p. 158)

Thus, a kind of "as-if" logocentric reading is presupposed by the non-logocentric reading, as a guardrail to protect the creativity, imaginativeness, and autonomy of the latter from failing to be an interpretation by floating uncontrollably off into empty space.

The aims of logocentric and non-logocentric reading are so divergent that one might wonder whether they are really in competition with one another. Why shouldn't someone who was generally committed to careful, Lockean reading of texts adopt, on some occasion, the non-logocentric attitude of playful inventiveness? During such activity, the usually Lockean reader would not, presumably, be aiming to find out the truth about the text's meaning or the truth about what the text was about. Instead, she would be interested in playing with the text, letting it suggest to her whatever it might suggest, but always with the concerted purpose of creating a world of her own thoughts, not the text's. But one could imagine the two kinds of reading combining, so that the Derridean reading became a "moment" in a Lockean reading: after, perhaps, some disciplined Lockean reading, the reader starts free-associating on the basis of what he has understood, playing with the thoughts that emerge; and then, with the cultivated imaginings, he returns to a search for sober truth about the text and about what the text is about. We suspect that very good readers sometimes read in something like this way. On this reading of reading, an important virtue for the excellent reader would be the practical wisdom of when to read playfully and when to read in disciplined submission to the text and its subject-matter. Such judgment would take into consideration the reader's immediate and longer-range purposes in reading as well as the particular character of the text at hand.

It is clear, however, that Derrida does not regard the non-logocentric stance as just one possible attitude in the excellent reader's repertoire of attitudes. Instead, it excludes the logocentric stance. So we might be inclined to think that Derrida's agenda is a different set of virtues governing excellent reading: namely, the virtues of creative instrumental domination. (We assume that any ordered, established human practice requires enabling excellences in the human agents who practice it.) This interpretation of Derrida's program comes naturally to a virtues epistemologist, but it faces an internal problem. Derrida's anti-logocentrism is not confined to a rejection of external reference of the sort that has been our focus so far (e.g., the reference of "tree" to a tree). He is also critical of Jean-Jacques Rousseau's logocentric Romantic expressivism, which centers on the idea that language has a kind of internal or reflexive reference. For the Romantic, even if a poem, say, makes no significant reference to the outside world (it is purely "expressive" of the poet's mind), still this expression is a kind of reference—to the poet's mind. If in the logocentric perspective the purpose of language about a tree is to make the tree "present", the purpose of language expressive of the self is to make the self "present"—first to itself, then perhaps to others. But for Derrida, genuine writing can be no more in thrall to a preexistent self than to a preexistent world. Instead, it is freely creative of both.

If reading is writing in Derrida's extended sense, then the excellent reader not only freely improvises a world on the basis of the text; he also freely improvises himself as reader. Definition in what the text is about, definition in what the text says about what it is about, and definition in the reader are all dimensions of logocentric slavery. Locke's idea that the reader comes to the text with a certain psycho-ethical-epistemic character that is more or less definite and fixed, a knowledge of which impinges on his ability to acquire other epistemic goods and out of which he performs excellently or otherwise the practice of reading, is just one more feature of logocentric bondage. But virtues—even the virtues of creative instrumental domination—have to be *some* kind of orientation, some kind of stability, some kind of partially defining semi-fixity in the reader. So it looks as though Derrida's rejection of logocentrism implies a rejection of the very notion of stable personal identity, and thus of virtues, and thus of a consistent and principled practice of anti-logocentric reading. A characteristically anti-logocentric reader must have *some* self-defining attitudes. (Derrida himself seems to have a fairly definite self-understanding as a reader.) A Derridean reader with no character at all could not be counted on to be Derridean; she might fall back into logocentrism at any moment. We do not understand how de-centering Derridean characterlessness can be combined with a thoroughgoing anti-logocentrism. We suspect that the position is internally incoherent. We also recognize that the Derridean may wear the attribution of incoherence as a badge of honor. What neater escape from logocentrism could there be than the thorough unpredictability of sheer irrationality?

So for the sake of our project of exploring the virtues of the excellent reader, and also to be charitable (in our own way) to Derrida, let us assume, un-Derrideanly, that the Derridean reader will have some virtues, and consider what these virtues of creative instrumental domination will be like. On this we speak lamely, because the stance is quite foreign to us, and discourse about virtues is not native to it. It is perhaps helpful to delineate these virtues in contrast to ones that we have been advocating. Our first example of reading was that of hearing the irony in Tolstoy's descriptions of Alexei Vronsky in *Anna Karenina*, and we said that this irony is probably best heard by someone who shares the moral concerns that Tolstoy expresses through his irony. In this picture, the reader is solidly oriented by his own moral position and takes himself to be listening to an author similarly solidly oriented by his. For the Derridean reader, by contrast, the situation on both sides is much less determinate. She is not unacquainted with the moral position of Tolstoy, and may well find in herself some resonances with it; but as a reader whose project is free creative instrumental domination of the text, she is ever disposed to transcend these "meanings", to hold them in awareness but at the same time to place them "under erasure" (*Of Grammatology*, p. 60), in the interest of making of them something new, something utterly her own. To honor Tolstoy's morality by simply and vividly construing Vronsky in its terms would be to fall back heavily into logocentric stolidity; the kind of respect for the text and humility before it that are characteristic of excellent logocentric readers are vices by Derrida's lights, dispositions to a bad, unfree, uncreative, non-dominating practice of reading. The virtues of the Derridean reader are playfulness, inventiveness, defiance of custom and convention. The ideal outcome of such reading is not understanding the text or getting information from it, but weaving, out of the text, a shimmering fabric of thoughts, construals, and images that are all one's own.

On our conception, intellectual virtues often involve both aptitudes to accomplish intellectual ends and motivating dispositions of the will to accomplish them. The will aims at epistemic goods, and aptitudes facilitate their achievement. The kinds of goods that we identified in Chapter 2—propositional knowledge, understanding, and acquaintance—are quite foreign, even anathema, to Derrida. He does not believe in well-grounded true belief; understanding (a text, say) is at most an erasable way station on the road to invention; and acquaintance is the very concept of that "presence" that he wishes to expunge from the human scene. So the Derridean agent does not aim at the epistemic goods as we have identified them.

She aims instead at clever, unpredictable "readings" that the text subserves as a pre-text for her inventiveness. We might name the excellent Derridean reader's cardinal virtue *lectorial playfulness*. Even the Derridean must have some regard for the text, because reading is a game in which one shows one's stuff, and no one who thumbed her nose at the rules of a game would show her stuff in playing it; the idea is to perform spectacularly *while following the rules*. This, then, is what we might call the aptitude side of sportliness: the clever ability to come up with something recognizable as an interpretation while placing the "normal", logocentric sense of the text under the exploitative erasure of one's inventiveness. The best reader, then, is the cleverest, the one with the most "stuff" to "show".

So it seems that, despite the thoroughly Derridean reader's loss of the substantive identifiable dispositional self, her ego is really center-stage: she is an intellectual show-off, and her will is to show brilliantly—especially in comparison with others. Egoism is thus a virtuous motivational structure, an admirable orientation of the will, in the Derridean scheme of things. But this cannot be the whole story; another side of the virtuous Derridean reader's will is closer to what we, from our point of view, might call intellectual purity of heart—a love of the epistemic goods for their own sake. In addition to her love of self-display, the Derridean reader simply loves to play at thought. She takes joy in interpretive invention in much the way a runner in his prime takes joy in the speed and endurance of his body, or a basketball player in a beautifully executed defense or three-point basket. The best and purest joy of the Derridean reader is not so much in the *product* of her inventiveness (which in the next moment after its production is anyway reduced to a "pre-text" for further invention), but rather in the *activity* of invention, the sheer exuberant creativity of her mind. This joy in intellectual invention is the Derridean analog of the virtue that we call love of knowledge (see Chapter 6).

In *Truth and Method*,[6] Hans-Georg Gadamer offers an account of reading that is similar to Locke's, though he has less than Locke to say directly about the virtues of the excellent reader. Gadamer models the process of reading on that of a conversation in which the partners focus their discussion primarily on the subject-matter (*die Sache*) of the text, rather than on the historical, linguistic, psychological, and stylistic peculiarities of their discussion partner. Like Locke, Gadamer thinks that the reader comes to the text with both an interest in the subject-matter and an already formed (albeit perhaps primitive) set of opinions about it, and that having *some* such set of opinions (Gadamer calls these "prejudices" (*Vorurteile*, prejudgments)) is necessary if the reader is to understand the text. Understanding the text is a matter of processing what the text says in terms of what one already thinks about the subject-matter. Much of Gadamer's book is critical of what he calls "historicism", a method of reading texts in which the reader tries to prescind from his own historical situation and individual particularity (setting his own mind aside, so to speak) and seeks to understand the mind of the author by informing himself about the language and historical background of the text. In a genuine, respectful conversation, the interlocutors do not analyze one another's minds, historical background, and language (a psychotherapy interview or an oral examination is not a genuine conversation), but rather, they try to understand what the other is saying about the topic of conversation

---

[6] Hans-Georg Gadamer, *Truth and Method*, 2nd rev. edn., trans. Joel Weinsheimer and Donald G. Marshall (New York: Continuum, 1993); see esp. Part II, sect. II.

by listening to what the other has to say, by asking questions about the subject-matter, by asking for clarification, by adjusting their own views in light of what the interlocutor has made plausible—by seeking the truth about the subject-matter.

As one reads, one gathers information about what is said and construes it in a certain way, always in terms of one's current noetic structure; and as one continues to read, some of one's construals of what is said are confirmed, some disconfirmed. In the latter case, one revises the construal and goes on until a new revision is needed, thus deepening one's understanding of the text. Furthermore, some of what one previously thought about the subject-matter is confirmed, but some of it is called into question, inviting critical reflection. Upon such reflection, the reader may revise his own views about the subject-matter, or he may resist what the author says, or he may suspend judgment for the moment and keep reading. Especially when the reader runs up against an alien viewpoint on the subject-matter, his own "prejudices" are highlighted, and he has an opportunity for a deepened acquaintance with his own mind, which heretofore may have been mainly implicit. By becoming clearer (more reflective) about what he himself thinks about the subject-matter, and the role of those "prejudices" in forming his impressions of the text, he becomes better able to grasp what the text itself is saying.

Although Gadamer has little or nothing to say about virtues in connection with the practice of reading, it seems clear that by the standards of his account not all people are equally good readers, and that a significant differentiating factor will be personal traits. He holds that excellent reading has an important potential to call the reader's "prejudices" into question and to commend certain revisions of them. Such revisions may be difficult, even fear-inspiring, and so courage will be an epistemic asset in a reader. People tend to be conservative with respect to some of the beliefs and understandings that may be called into question through genuine reading; so openness to confront alien standpoints and really to grasp and consider them is a virtue in a reader. Part of such conservatism may be the reader's pride in his intellectual accomplishments, which to the intellectually immature makes revision seem demeaning; in which case humility will facilitate his reading. The historicism that Gadamer objects to at such great length is a strategy for bracketing the personal beliefs and commitments of the reader in the interest of "objectivity", with the effect that the reader shields himself against being called personally into question by the text. Historicism tries, thus, to replace virtues like courage, openness, and humility with a "method" that can be applied by anyone who takes the time to develop the requisite scholarly skills. But if Gadamer is right, the cost of such evasion is forfeiture of significant intellectual goods. So if one is to read very well, there is no substitute for intellectual virtues.

Gadamer's model of reading as a sort of respectful conversation between equals suggests that respect for authors who are at a distance of culture or time may be an unusual trait, and one that is certainly a virtue for human beings who have a natural tendency toward cultural and historical chauvinism. A piece of writing may deceptively seem simple or naïve, hiding profundities as it were; and so the generous-spirited reader, the reader disposed to lavish "credit" on texts and authors for having something to say, may have an advantage in the harvest of epistemic goods. And behind all of these reading-enhancing traits is a disposition of the will that we call love of knowledge: an interest in understanding, an eagerness for acquaintance, a desire for significant information and the solid support of actual or possible beliefs.

We began this section by noting the variety of people's purposes in reading. Gadamer focuses on *one* important sphere of reading: the reading of worthy texts with significant humanistic content (excellent histories, novels, correspondence, philosophy, psychology, etc.), mostly at some historical or cultural remove from the reader's time and culture. These qualifications seem necessary to make sense of Gadamer's stress on how the text, when properly read, engages the reader's "prejudices" and can call the reader personally into question. Were the text fully contemporary with the reader, its engaging his "prejudices" would perhaps be too obvious to warrant comment; and if the content of the text were not broadly humanistic and significant, the sense in which it would or should call his "prejudices" into question would be tenuous indeed.

Gadamer's account seems less relevant to second-rate texts, texts written by maniacs, and technical texts. A good reader can often detect inferiority in a text upon reading a paragraph or two, and may virtuously read only enough to dismiss the text. Here the reader properly sits in sovereign domination of the text, and does not submit himself to examination by it. A university professor might be required, in the line of duty, to read the whole of a long bad piece of work, and for the most part take very much a "judgmental" rather than submissive attitude as he reads. A good reader might read *Mein Kampf*, not so as to enter into a conversation with Hitler about *die Sache*, but so as to assess Hitler psychiatrically. A scholar might read a Babylonian bill of sale, not to "fuse horizons" with an ancient merchant, but just to answer some fine question about Babylonian business practices. Reading need not always aim at gaining a correct understanding of whatever the text is about. People can virtuously read even the greatest texts with other purposes—say, to understand the customs of the period, or the linguistic usages of the author. These are all practices of reading that can be pursued more or less virtuously without fitting Gadamer's model.

Some texts are treated as authoritative by a community, and so, within that community, are accorded a special respect that may bear epistemic fruit. In Eleonore Stump's Gifford Lectures, she interprets various biblical texts, asking what they might say about the problem of evil.[7] When we read the story of the Israelite judge Samson (Judges 13–16), most of us (including as great a reader as John Milton) suppose that the sin for which God abandons Samson is that of telling Delilah the secret of his strength. But to suppose that Samson tells the patently treacherous Delilah what he takes to be the truth by which he can be overcome by the Philistines is either to make Samson unbelievably dim-witted or suicidal, or to impute incoherence to the story. But for Stump, this story is Scripture and so *must* make sense (whether or not she is able to find that sense). The special respect that Stump, as a Christian, has for Scripture moves her to read the text very closely, very patiently, and very openly, with the result that she not only makes sense of the story in its own terms (that is, without imputing mistakes in redaction, transmission, etc.), but finds a sense that is spiritually uplifting to the reader and glorifying to God and the text. The sin for which God abandons Samson, on Stump's reading, is not that of telling Delilah the secret of this strength, which he does not think lies in his being unshorn; Samson's sin is that of presuming on God's faithfulness and treating that faithfulness as a convenient protection for his dalliance with Delilah rather than for carrying out his appointed mission of rescuing Israel from the Philistines. And Samson's abandonment by God is ultimately for

---

[7] The lectures will be published as *Wandering in Darkness: Narrative and the Problem of Evil* by Oxford University Press.

Samson's good, as it precipitates repentance and a return to God and God's return to Samson.

The respect that Stump directs to this text and the others that she treats in the Gifford Lectures might, in principle, have been lavished on them without their being Scripture for her; but that would be very unlikely. Behind this respect is faith that God has embodied in these stories crucial insights and truths about his dealings with humanity. For Stump, the practice of reading these texts is part of the larger set of practices of the Christian life. Connected with the special respect that is due the Samson story, in light of the fact that it is Scripture, is the fact that reading it might be combined with prayer concerning its meaning; after all, its being Scripture gives it a special role in God's communication with the reader and the reader's with God, and a central practice of this communication is prayer. The practices of prayer and Scripture reading depend for their excellent prosecution on such Christian virtues as faith, humility, and love of God. Within the Christian community, then, the distinctively Christian virtues come to be virtues of a reader.

The canons of reading vary enormously with the nature of the text, the reader's purposes in reading, and the status of the text in the practices of the reader's community. This variety suggests that a virtue of practical wisdom governs the practice of excellent reading and determines which of the other virtues come into play at any given moment in the pursuit of that practice. The excellent reader constantly adjusts, as she moves from one text to another, or even from one part to another part of the same text. Much of the exemplification of such practical wisdom happens automatically, "without thinking" (obviously, however, not without thinking about what one is reading).

Public Debate

The economist Glenn Loury has written about social and psychological obstacles to clear and truthful transmission of ideas among persons in the context of public debate.[8] These obstacles have the nature of social

[8] Glenn Loury, "Self-Censorship in Public Discourse: A Theory of Political Correctness and Related Phenomena", in *One by One from the Inside Out: Essays and Reviews on Race and Responsibility in America* (New York: The Free Press, 1995), pp. 145–82.

pressures and the accompanying emotions. People who communicate too clearly or in the wrong "language", or present unwelcome facts, are subject to social sanctions like anger, ostracism, condemnation, and being labeled an "outsider". The clarity-impeding response to these potential sanctions is fear or a utilitarian caution. Loury's essay is longer on clarification of the problem than on solutions, but he himself hints at the kind of solution a virtues epistemology would propose: needed are people with some virtues of communication. The hints are at the beginning and end of Loury's paper.

The epigraph is a quotation from George Orwell that attributes the failure to speak and write clearly in political contexts to insincerity, an untruthfulness that is motivated by fear or a desire to have the fruits of misunderstanding. "The great enemy of clear language is insincerity. When there is a gap between one's real and one's declared aims, one turns as it were instinctively to long words and exhausted idioms, like a cuttlefish squirting out ink" (p. 145). Then at the end of the paper Loury speaks the language of virtue:

How, then, are the demagogues and the haters to be denounced? How can reason gain a voice in the forum? How can the truth about our nature, our party, our race, our church come to light when the social forces of conformity and the rhetorical conventions of banality hold sway? How can we have genuine moral discourse about ambiguous and difficult matters (like racial inequality in our cities or on our campuses) when the security and comfort of the platitudes lie so readily at hand? Though it may violate the communal norms of my economics fraternity to say so, I believe these things can be achieved only when individuals—first a few, and then many—transcend "the world of existences" by acting not as utilitarian calculators, but rather as fully human and fully moral agents determined at whatever cost to "live within the truth". (pp. 181–2)

What, exactly, is the epistemic problem? And how might moral character be a solution?

We might think initially that communication and discussion are just matters of people making utterances, and others understanding the utterances and perhaps objecting to them or accepting them or suggesting refinements of them, as though *who* is making the utterances, and *how* he is making his points, and the *particular* points he is making do not matter. But Loury points out that much of our speech is loaded with a "meaning-in-effect". The way we say things, and what we say, the kind of vocabulary we use and the kinds of facts we emphasize, often tell something about us the speakers. And how the listener takes the *speaker* will partially determine what the listener takes *from* the speaker. Where we speakers "stand" is always in principle available to be known, and often is known, by our hearers. In virtue of this meaning-in-effect, our listeners size up both us and what we have to say. They may conclude that we are "of them", or that we are execrable outsiders, not worthy to be listened to because we are bad people. Or we are somewhere in between, meriting a cautious and guarded ear. At the same time, if we are slightly sophisticated, we realize that we are being sized up by our listeners, and we have preferred ways to be sized up. So we adjust our speech to have, as much as we can, the meaning-in-effect that we want to convey. (We say politicians and their advisors are spin doctors and impression managers, but we all do it more or less all the time.) And of course the audience is aware of this tendency to adjustment as well, and will be looking for signs of insincerity in the way we present ourselves in our speech.

Loury posits that a discussion community reaches an equilibrium in which people who want to be accepted by the community will censor their own speech, making the meaning-in-effect as acceptable as possible to the party, despite doubts they may have about the party line. They will tend not to raise certain questions which might mark them as unfaithful or fringe members of the community. Then those who are not faithful members of the community (the real Nazis, the real male chauvinist pigs, the real racists) come to be just about the only ones who do speak in "incorrect" ways, and so the political correctness or incorrectness of everybody's speech becomes an even more reliable indicator of group membership. This equilibrium tends to stifle discussion and learning, and to veil truth. If Loury were an orthodox social scientist, he would regard this equilibrium as the last word on the subject; but he is also a moralist, and at the end of the paper he calls on individuals to disturb such vicious equilibria so as to be agents of truth.

Here a very fine line needs to be hewn to in the interest of the epistemic goods. On the one hand, if in cunning self-protection we succumb to the equilibrium, truth and light are sacrificed, and along with them, most likely, justice. If, on the other hand, in unworldly purity of heart we are what Loury calls "naïve speakers", the police state of mind created by the guardians of political correctness will deprive us of our forum. What traits of character would fit us to be agents of understanding, warranted belief, and acquaintance in the world that Loury sketches? Intellectual virtue here will not be naïveté, in either the speaker or the hearer; but neither will it be cynically manipulative or crassly utilitarian. It will be hermeneutical sensitivity to "meaning-in-effect", and skill at negotiating its strategies, combined with a concern for truth and justice, a concern both to know and transmit truth, and a concern both to receive and to give justice, and whatever epistemic skills will promote the satisfaction of these concerns. Both over-suspicion of others' communications and over-trust of them are intellectually unvirtuous. The phrase of Jesus comes to mind: "wise as serpents and innocent as doves" (Matt. 10: 16). What are some traits that, in combination, satisfy these conditions?

Consider truthfulness, which is a concern to *convey* the truth as one understands it—not just to "tell" it any which way, but to make it clearly known. This purity of heart with respect to truth is opposed to insincerity, which is compatible with uttering nothing but true sentences. But truthfulness is more than just the concern to communicate the truth clearly; it is also a skill. It takes practice and finesse and empathy with others' point of view to get the truth across in such a way as to evoke genuine understanding on the part of one's receivers, and often the "naïve speaker" is inept at putting the truth in such a way that *it* will get across, rather than some irrelevancy that triggers prejudice. Truthfulness is also a concern to *know* the truth. In some of Loury's examples, inquiry is short-circuited because of evasive expression in response to the pressures of PC; if you are on the recipient side of the discussion, the drive to know the truth will tend to correct such shorts, to pursue the truth, to promote getting the noetic electricity where it needs to be. Here again, in addition to a strong concern to know, you need hermeneutic sensitivity to the communication dynamics of the social context.

Justice, as a personal virtue, involves a concern that justice be done and injustice avoided or corrected, that individuals be treated justly and institutions justly constituted. Because in political contexts the clear statement of truth is often a key to achieving justice, the desire for justice can be the motivation for clear and truthful expression. In fact, clear truth telling is itself a kind of justice, if it is unfair to one's hearers to mislead them or leave them in the dark when one could tell them some relevant truth. In this way, justice can be an epistemic social virtue.

Loury imagines a university president in the days of apartheid who has genuine concern about justice for South African blacks, but would like to see open debate about the advisability of divestiture as a strategy for promoting that justice (see pp. 162–4). In other words, this president has not only the virtue of justice, but also the allied virtue of intellectual caution: he is inclined to be careful about his and other people's important beliefs. But he knows that in the present political climate, even to raise the question of whether his university should withdraw from its South African investments is to brand himself, in the eyes of the students, as less than fully committed to racial justice. And he doesn't want to risk damaging his reputation as a good liberal.

What kind of epistemic character would it take for optimal performance in this situation? The goal is to keep the debate open, so that the decision about the use of sanctions can be as rational as possible. The last sentence of Loury's essay—which prescribes that individuals act "as fully human and fully moral agents determined at whatever cost to 'live within the truth'"—suggests that this president needs courage. If he raises the questions, he will perhaps tarnish his liberal reputation and lose some credibility with the ideologues who from their careening bandwagon throw caution to the wind. But if his associates are so immature, maybe he shouldn't care too much about tarnishing his reputation with them. If they are students, one might think that his role is to teach them something; and if he doesn't show some courage, he may miss an opportunity to model intellectual caution. But his courage is likely to be more fruitful, intellectually, if it is allied with some traits that we might call virtues of diplomacy and their brands of practical wisdom.

It takes insight to know when we are being pressured or manipulated by the subtler sanctions of PC; we often accommodate to the pressures almost without noticing what we are doing. Insight into how strategic self-expression works, and a nuanced understanding of how to speak truthfully, without losing one's forum, in an environment that is highly charged with unspoken threats against the "incorrect", is an important aspect of epistemic practical wisdom. (Loury's chapter can function as a primer in this bit of practical wisdom.) The speaker who loves truth and justice but knows the dynamics of strategic self-expression will be less a passive victim of the dynamics, but he will not become simply a "naïve communicator". He will count the cost of candor and forthrightness and clarity, and use these sparingly and strategically. He will *prudently* transcend "the world of existences" in the interest of truth and justice. This is not because he would at any cost preserve his good standing with the less intelligent members of his community, but because he will not want to cut off communication too soon by ham-fisted clarity. He will know how to be "diplomatic", as a way of keeping the lines of communication open, but in the end he will not let diplomacy keep him from getting the truth across.

But such diplomacy is not all deliberated PC counter-strategy. Some of it is in the emotional dispositions of the epistemic agent. Both Aristotle (*Nicomachean Ethics* $1125^a25-1126^b10$) and Jesus (Matt. 5: 5) commend a virtue that goes by the name of *prautēs*, which is variously translated as "gentleness", "meekness", "good temper", and "mildness". It is a disposition to be relatively calm or mild or gentle in response to offenses, including inflammatory or insensitive language, insult, and political incorrectness. It is akin to forgivingness, which is a disposition to look past offenses (forgiveness is not a naïve failure to notice or evaluate the offenses).[9] As an epistemic virtue in the context of discussion, gentleness is a disposition to listen to offensive language without ceasing to "hear" the arguments it expresses, perhaps even an ability to "hear" arguments that are only incipient and not at all well expressed in the heat of invective, an inclination not to be too defensive when you realize you are being verbally assaulted or when somebody is saying something that is ideologically repugnant to you. This would be the ability to discern the truth in statements that are not couched in polite terms, and to respond to them in a measured and reasonable way. Intellectual meekness is a form of openness. It is not the same as noetic spinelessness; the intellectually meek person has integrity, and will, we hope, have the virtue of firmness as well. Gentleness is not just a disposition to "hear"; it is also a disposition, in heated contexts, to express oneself mildly, conciliatorily—or as much so as possible—while nevertheless speaking what one takes to be the truth. One is reminded of the apostle Paul's injunction to "speak the truth in love" (Eph. 4: 15). Such gentleness, on either the receiving or the expressing side, can do much to defuse the resentment that often makes a barrier to mutual understanding in public debate.

---

[9] See Robert C. Roberts, "Forgivingness", *American Philosophical Quarterly* 32 (1995): 289–306.

Another virtue, in the neighborhood of gentleness, that counteracts the liabilities of meaning-in-effect, is intellectual friendliness. This trait is a disposition to like other people, to find them attractive and enjoy interaction with them despite an awareness of fundamental disagreement. Intellectual friendliness is an immunity or resistance to the mentality of "us versus them" that arises when people see themselves as not agreeing on important questions. It supplements intellectual courage, inasmuch as, after one has courageously jeopardized one's forum, friendliness, in either the speaker or the hearer, is as good a bet as any that one will keep the forum. Friendliness, and all the virtues we have sketched in this section, do their work by unbalancing the equilibrium of dialectical isolation that Loury describes.

Teaching and Learning

The teacher   Consider the epistemic practice cluster of teaching, say of teaching a college class. It may well involve the practices of lecturing, leading discussion, and commenting on students' work, both in writing and in one-on-one consultation in the teacher's office. It is conceivable that all of these practices be practiced well in a merely skillful way—by competent application of "techniques" characteristic of this occupational specialty. We can imagine a person who pursues all these activities with a high degree of skill, and is thus a successful teacher, but who possesses none of the virtues: for example, he is not generous, but self-seeking; he does not care about the well-being of his students, but only about the goods external to teaching; he is not interested in his academic subject, but only in what competence in that subject can net him. Perhaps he wants to be a dean one day, and so develops all the requisite skills and does everything as well as he can, with a view to achieving this status; or perhaps in his society college teachers are paid more than anybody else, and the best teachers are the best-paid members of the teaching profession. And so on for all the virtues. This individual's behavioral dispositions are only as firm as his interest in the goods extrinsic to the practices and the astuteness with which he can govern his behavior with a view to gaining those goods.

Or *is* this conceivable? We say that this picture, even if logically possible, is psychologically implausible to a high degree. We think it very unlikely that the teaching practices of lecturing, leading discussion, and commenting on students' work will be executed with maximal excellence in the complete absence of intrinsic motivation. It is very likely that where intrinsic motivation is low, performance quality will also be low. That is, the teacher's genuine interest in the subject-matter of the teaching, combined with a genuine interest in the intellectual well-being of his students, is likely to make for the most effective execution of the practices of teaching, and thus also for whatever extrinsic goods may accrue to the teacher—assuming, of course, other factors such as talent and resources.

Consider the practice of class discussion. The teacher raises a question, and a student attempts an answer. An important part of this practice is that of listening to the student's answer as a stage in the conversation. This can be done in a variety of ways. For example, the teacher listens closely enough to detect whether the answer is correct or partially correct, and responds with a mini-lecture in which he affirms what is right, corrects what is wrong, and in doing both amplifies and enriches the student's answer for the benefit of the whole class. This is not bad. But it may be made better, pedagogically, by the teacher's willingness to probe the student's mind further. Rather than launch immediately into the mini-lecture, the teacher might express the virtues of empathy, attentiveness, courage, love of knowledge, humility, and patience by staying with the student a little longer, trying to draw out of her more thought about the question and its answer. By contrast, to take the student's response as just a cue to launch into the mini-lecture could express the teacher's vanity (desire to show his stuff), lack of interest in the student (not listening *very* carefully to what she says, not desiring very much that *she* perform well), insecurity (fear of the discussion's getting out of the area in which the teacher feels intellectually comfortable), and impatience (disinclination to control the urges of frustration and boredom at having to draw the student along at such a slow pace).

Gentleness also supports the activity of teaching. Some students are pretty easily intimidated or discouraged, and even the toughest of them respond favorably to encouragement, personal attention, and judicious praise. In discussion and in comments on written work, an important part of the teacher's job is critique, correction, and challenge to greater things, but the teacher who is disposed to couch her faultfinding in gentle terms and to intersperse her critique with praise for things well done is likely, at the end of the day, to have transmitted more epistemic goods than her harsher counterpart. Here, as elsewhere, practical wisdom is essential. The excellent teacher will be judiciously harsh from time to time, and will not be above scaring a student out of his complacency and lassitude. She will learn to discriminate the students who need a little harshness from the ones who may wilt under it, and will avoid a sappy gentleness that may induce a quick fix of transitory self-esteem in some, but an inclination, in more discerning students, to retch into the collar of their forward neighbor. Again, it is possible (just barely) to imagine a teacher who practices such "gentleness" simply as a professional skill. But a genuine concern for the students' cognitive well-being such as characterizes the virtue of intellectual gentleness is usually more reliable and always more praiseworthy.

The recipient of teaching   Students are often young people, and when they are, it is perhaps too much to ask full-fledged virtues of them. Still, some virtues are especially relevant to the student in the student–teacher relationship, and clearly promote his acquisition of the epistemic goods of understanding, acquaintance, and warranted belief. Even if full-fledged virtues are rare among 14- to 22-year-olds, approximations of them are not terribly rare. Aristotle says that all people by nature desire to know, but people differ considerably in how intensely and steadily and discriminatingly they desire to know. A robust appetite for serious learning is part of what the medievals called the virtue of docility, or teachableness. Such an appetite tends to make the student discriminating about teachers and enthusiastic about the ones who know lots and are able to impart what they know. A certain boldness and trust in his own ability to learn, combined with an awareness of his ignorance, tend to make the student active in intellectual pursuits. A humility and/or courage that allow him to show his ignorance to others frees him to put himself in positions to learn that the fearful, vain, or obsequious student may avoid. These virtues will also allow him to express a critical independence of mind that makes him vulnerable to being shot down but also trains him in intellectual autonomy and toughness and an open imagination. A disposition to respect the teacher, both as a human being and for what she knows, and to be grateful to her for what she imparts, is an encouragement to the teacher, and thus promotes both the teacher's teaching and the learner's learning.

Sciences

The sciences—from anthropology to zoology, from biochemistry to pale-ontology, from astronomy to sociology, from ethology to particle physics, from ecology to neuroscience, from entomology to social psychology—are constituted of a dizzying array of evolving research practices. In the present section we want just to hint, rather speculatively, at a few ways in which virtues enhance such practices, and then take a more particular look at the work of the ethologist Jane Goodall.[10]

Science always involves difficult, potentially discouraging, time-consuming work whose outcome is seldom if ever assured. These facts of life suggest that a good scientist is likely to exemplify patience, perseverance, industriousness, a capacity for self-denial, and even courage. Furthermore, as human beings, scientists are not just technicians, but have one or another attitude of heart toward their subject-matter and toward the human beings with whom they pursue their science. For some, the science may be primarily a way of dominating and controlling nature and their fellows. They may see nature as a sort of challenger to be vanquished by finding out its secrets, and their relation to their colleagues as one of cut-throat competition for preeminence. Or, alternatively, the scientist's attitude toward nature may be awe, reverent humility, loving respect, deferential questioning; and the attitude toward colleagues may be generous cooperation in the pursuit of the shared goods of understanding and information.

We do not deny that the will to power over nature and colleagues may strongly energize certain personality types among scientists, but we don't think this kind of motive is either necessary, sufficient, or optimal as a drive for scientific excellence. Even the most hubristic scientist will not stay in the game without a certain amount of intrinsic fascination with the subject-matter; and intrinsic love of nature and interest in knowing it are in fact sufficient drive in some scientists (for examples, see Chapter 11). Intellectual adventurousness is a virtue that stems from intrinsic fascination with nature. Better scientists, we think, are ones who are attuned to nature in its complexity and surprisingness, and thus can be excited when they encounter anomalies, rather than just irritated by them. This openness to

---

[10] We are grateful to Susan Bratton, Gerry Cleaver, and Jim Marcum for discussions that informed the present section.

being surprised, this welcoming attitude toward the unexpected, can make the difference between a real scientist and a plodding technician. Again, a welcoming excitement over anomalies can be motivated by competitive opportunism, but it may also be motivated by a love of knowledge and pleasure in the arduous process of acquiring it.

Another fact about the sciences is that they are social enterprises, pursued by collaboration, by cooperative division of labor, by sharing of information and insights, and by debate. This fact suggests that better scientists will have social virtues such as generosity and gratitude to facilitate sharing of intellectual goods, humility and openness as they seek and receive information and insights from one another, and gentleness and charity combined with independence of mind as they interpret one another's work in the course of disagreement and debate.

What shall we say about the fact that highly productive scientists sometimes—even often—exhibit such vices as arrogance, vanity, domination, and selfish ambition? First, we think that successful scientists with these traits could be even more successful if their character were such as to elicit trust and cooperation from their fellow scientists. Second, while they may garner considerable epistemic goods and the attendant prestige for *themselves*, they probably do less than they could do for their fields and for the general advancement of knowledge by nurturing and helping others. (Our thesis is that virtues foster the delivery of the epistemic goods in general, not just that they foster their possessor's acquisition of them.) Third, even the egotistical successful scientist is by no means bereft of virtues, for he would never have succeeded at the scientific practices were he not persevering, interested in the truth about nature, and at least somewhat honest. Fourth, given the teamwork characteristic of modern science, the character deficiencies of a scientist may be compensated by traits of another scientist working on the same team. An abrasive scientist may have a colleague who functions as peacemaker on the team; an egotist may be less epistemically dysfunctional than he would otherwise be if some of his colleagues are forbearing, humble, and have a sense of humor. So, as we look for the epistemically effective virtues among scientists, we should not locate them only in individuals; a whole team may have a personality and a configuration of character traits. Fifth, even when two scientists are not exactly working as a team, a virtue of one may supply an epistemic power whose lack in the other would have barred the latter's access to epistemic goods. Rosalind Franklin's patience and perseverance and love of truth are clearly effective virtues on which the success of James Watson and Francis Crick was parasitic (see Chapter 11).

Alasdair MacIntyre comments: "It is no part of my thesis that great violinists cannot be vicious or great chess-players mean-spirited. It is just that the vicious and mean-spirited necessarily rely on the virtues of others for the practices in which they engage to flourish and also deny themselves the experience of achieving those internal goods which may reward even not very good chess-players and violinists" (*After Virtue*, p. 193). It seems to us that the last claim in this quotation is not quite right. The vicious ambition of Watson and Crick to get the Nobel prize for discovering the structure of DNA, their injustice and greed in using Rosalind Franklin's data without her knowledge and without giving her credit, do not seem to have prevented their enjoying the intrinsic intellectual pleasure of discovering and knowing the structure of DNA. Perhaps the quality of their enjoyment of that good internal to the practice of molecular biology was inferior to what more virtuous investigators might have experienced, but we do not know how to adjudicate that question.

As of 1990, when Jane Goodall published *Through a Window*,[11] she had spent thirty years observing chimpanzees in the wild in Gombe, Tanzania, on Lake Tanganyika. She learned many things that could not be learned by observing captive chimpanzees or ones that had been domesticated by human beings. She learned that, without human intervention, chimpanzees make simple tools; for example, they will trim a wide blade of grass to use as an implement to fish termites or ants out of their mounds. They pass such skills on to the next generation, thus creating something analogous to culture within their social group, a culture that may differ from that of other chimpanzee groups. She discovered that they sometimes hunt, kill, and eat meat—colobus monkeys, baby baboons, young bushpigs and bushbucks. Sometimes they hunt cooperatively and share the kill. She found that individual chimpanzees vary, in much the way humans do, along various dimensions such as sociability, mothering skills, sexual desirability, intelligence, and ambition for social status. She learned that some, but not all, chimpanzees can learn to control their emotional expressions—say,

---

[11] Jane Goodall, *Through a Window: My Thirty Years with the Chimpanzees of Gombe* (Boston: Houghton Mifflin Company, 1990).

learn to suppress vocalizations of delight at finding bananas, so as to avoid having the bananas stolen from them by larger chimps. She learned that some practice cannibalism—for example, one mother stole the babies of other mothers and then ate them, sharing the meat with other members of her family. Chimpanzees live in territorial communities, and will wage war against other communities. She learned that chimpanzees sometimes adopt orphaned young of the community. She discovered that, as males vie for the status of community alpha, they sometimes form alliances with other males. They also sometimes develop individual techniques of performing their dominance display (one used large tin cans that had been left lying around by the humans), and sometimes a younger male observes, and then imitates, an older, successful male's ritual and can be seen practicing the technique, in clear imitation of the older animal. Chimpanzees of lower social status practice deception to get what they want. Many chimpanzee behaviors suggest that they plan ahead.

By what practices did Goodall gain these epistemic goods? A sort of mega-practice, one encompassing all more particular practices, was that of living among the chimpanzees. Since chimpanzees are naturally shy of humans, Goodall had to gain their trust, and she did this by a constant unthreatening presence in their habitat. A more particular practice was that of following individuals and groups as they went about searching for food, courting, fighting, waging war, etc. Goodall used very much a narrative approach, focused on a particular community and on particular individuals within that community, of which she wrote histories encompassing three decades. Crucial to this practice was to name each chimpanzee and to get to know each as an individual, so as to write biographies. As she comments, "since we cannot know with the mind of a chimpanzee we must proceed laboriously, meticulously, as I have for thirty years. We must continue to collect anecdotes and, slowly, compile life histories. We must continue, over the years, to observe, record, and interpret" (p. 11). Another of Goodall's practices, one that is typical of many sciences, is that of collaboration and the use of assistants. Within four years of starting her research at Gombe, Goodall began to assemble a research center, and by 1972, twelve years after the work's inception, she had as many as twenty American and European students working with her, as well as increasingly knowledgeable Tanzanians. "... there was no way in the world that one person, no matter how dedicated, could have made a really comprehensive study of the Gombe chimpanzees. Hence the research centre" (p. 26).

It is not difficult to see that certain traits of character were necessary for the successful pursuit of Goodall's intellectual practices. From her childhood, Goodall loved animals, and it seems safe to say that the chimpanzees are among those dearest to her. In the opening pages of *Through a Window*, Goodall records her excitement and delight in being back in the presence of her chimps after three months of lectures, meetings, and lobbying in the USA and Europe. This love motivated her to spend the vast amounts of time, in gentle association with them, needed to garner the animals' trust, which in turn made it possible for her to observe things never before recorded by humans. But her love of the animals is more complex than that of an ordinary animal-lover; for she also loves them as a scientist. That is, her love of the animals is at the same time a love of knowing about them in considerable, rigorous detail. This love is an *epistemic* virtue.

The practice of following the chimpanzees in the mountains and through the bush was not for pantywaists, as the following description makes clear:

Clearly Fifi had been waiting for Fanni—now she climbed down and set off, and the children [young chimps] followed after, playing as they went. The family moved rapidly down the steep slope to the south. As I scrambled after them, every branch seemed to catch in my hair or my shirt. Frantically I crawled and wriggled through a terrible tangle of undergrowth. Ahead of me the chimpanzees, fluid black shadows, moved effortlessly. The distance between us increased. The vines curled around the buckles of my shoes and the strap of my camera, the thorns caught in the flesh of my arms, my eyes smarted till the tears flowed as I yanked my hair from the snags that reached out from all around. After ten minutes I was drenched in sweat, my shirt was torn, my knees bruised from crawling on the stony ground—and the chimps had vanished. I kept quite still, trying to listen above the pounding of my heart, peering in all directions though the thicket around me. (p. 8)

But sometimes observing the chimps from up close required more than an ability and willingness to suffer discomfort; sometimes there was real danger, since these animals, though smaller than human beings, are several times as strong, and are emotionally "immature", by human standards. For example,

Goblin leapt down and charged past me, slapping and stamping on the wet ground, rearing up and shaking the vegetation, picking up and hurling a rock, an old piece of wood, another rock. Then he sat, hair bristling, some fifteen feet away. He was breathing heavily. My own heart was beating fast. As he swung down, I had stood up and held onto a tree, praying that he would not pound on me as he sometimes does. (p. 2)

[Frodo] wants me to play, and, because I will not, he becomes aggressive. At twelve years of age he is much stronger than I am, and this behaviour is dangerous. Once he stamped so hard on my head that my neck was nearly broken. And on another occasion he pushed me down a steep slope. I can only hope that, as he matures and leaves childhood behind him, he will grow out of these irritating habits. (p. 4)

So another virtue requisite for Goodall's scientific practices is courage.

She comments on the difference between her construal of the chimpanzees and the ways of construing them typical of ethologists when she began her studies. At that time, the chimps were seen as very different from human beings, as not having minds, intellectual abilities, or emotions—hard as this now is to conceive. Her approach, by contrast, was to construe them very much on an analogy with human beings, as is reflected in her giving them individual names and attributing to them differential personalities and motivations closely analogous to human ones. Thus, attitudinally, Goodall used empathy with the chimps in her science about them, and this enabled her to see in them mental sophistication that in the 1960s was not being perceived by most ethologists. We see in this intellectually fruitful openness to the minds of the chimps a kind of inter-species generosity, in contrast to the stingy attitude that says, as it were, "We insist on reserving dignity for us human beings alone."

Goodall comments on the cognitive importance of generosity towards fellow humans, as well. Writing about her research center at Gombe, she says,

There was a spirit of cooperation among the students, a willingness to share data, that was, I think, quite unusual. It had not been easy to foster this generous attitude—initially many of the graduate students were, understandably, reluctant to contribute any of their precious data to a central information pool. But clearly this had to be done if we were to come to grips with the extraordinarily complex social organization of the chimpanzees and document as fully as possible their life histories. (p. 25)

It sounds as though Goodall was teaching these students not only ethology, but also a lesson or two in virtue epistemology!

Conclusion

The substance of the living of the intellectual life is its practices; they are what the life of the mind is made of. That life is fully as much a matter of activity as the moral life, and aims just as concertedly at goods. The practices that constitute our cognitive life are extremely diverse and interwoven and, it seems, highly subject to historical evolution, at least in the particularities of the activities and of the auxiliary equipment that we use in pursuing them. But the need for virtues, where the highest goods are concerned, is constant across time. Virtues of character such as humility, patience, tenacity, fairness, love of knowledge, and generosity, or at least some approximation or facsimile thereof, need to be exemplified by the practitioners of the practices by which such goods are acquired, maintained, transmitted, and applied. We have considered only a few examples, and examined them in only a cursory way. In the chapters of Part II we will enter into a deeper examination of some of the main virtues that enable these practices to yield epistemic goods.

PART II
Intellectual Virtues

6

Love of Knowledge

Introduction

The dispositions of desire, emotional response, and choice that constitute the excellent formation of the will have been, from ancient times to the present, much noticed in discussions of ethics, but remarkably less so in epistemology. A central contention of Part I has been that the formation of the will is crucial to an agent's intellectual functioning. So we begin the more substantive part of our book with a discussion of a virtue that consists in an excellent orientation of the will to knowledge. We mean "knowledge" to express the concept that we sketched in Chapter 2: namely, the richly intertwined bundle of understanding, acquaintance, and propositional knowledge. In using the phrase "love of knowledge", we do not mean strictly to follow ordinary usage, but to express a virtue concept that we will develop in this chapter.

Despite omitting the will from his account of the intellectual virtues, Aristotle begins his *Metaphysics* by attributing to human nature an appetite for knowledge.

All men by nature desire to know. An indication of this is the delight we take in our senses; for even apart from their usefulness they are loved for themselves; and above all others the sense of sight. For not only with a view to action, but even when we are not going to do anything, we prefer seeing (one might say) to everything else. The reason is that this, most of all the senses, makes us know and brings to light many differences among things.[1]

[1] Aristotle, *Metaphysics* I. 1, 980ª20–8, trans. W. D. Ross, in *Basic Works of Aristotle* (New York: Random House, 1941), p. 689.

Human beings have several natural dispositions of attraction. We are attracted to food and drink, to members of the opposite or our own sex, to beautiful sights and sounds, to activity (moving, doing, making), and, as both Aristotle and Nietzsche note, to the exercise of power over things, other people, and ourselves. Aristotle points out in this famous passage that our species is also attracted to knowledge. We enjoy knowing things; we spend money on books; we take pleasure in noticing differences and similarities, say, in being able to distinguish the plants and birds in our surroundings, in being able to associate some birds with one bird group, others with another. Taxonomy satisfies. Aristotle here emphasizes a simple variety of the kind of knowledge that we have been calling "acquaintance": the baby explores with his eyes, his ears, his hands, his mouth; but even in our remotest maturity we take pleasure in the kind of contact with reality that we call seeing for ourselves. Sometimes this seeing is literal sensory experience ("Let *me* look in the telescope"), sometimes it is mathematical or conceptual insight or religious experience. And even when it is sensory, it may be at the same time conceptual (scientific, moral, religious). But acquaintance is not the only kind of knowledge we thirst for and enjoy. We take pleasure in deepened explanatory competence, in the ability to interpret texts, in the confirmation or disconfirmation of beliefs and hypotheses. Aristotle here points to a natural disposition—what we called a faculty in Chapter 4. This natural appetite for knowledge needs to be matured, formed, realized, completed. Everyone has the faculty, presumably, but only a few people ever come to possess its full and mature realization. In the present chapter we will explore the structure of this mature disposition of the will towards knowledge.

In the very young infant the appetitive orientation of which Aristotle writes is perhaps an indiscriminate penchant for sensory stimulation and the activities that promote it. But discriminations soon emerge, and the appetite becomes exploratory—the child wants to know things, to understand how things work. It is as though she is asking questions, thus focusing her desire for knowledge in very personally particular ways (*this* is what *I* want to know). And with further maturity, crucial distinctions come to guide the child's epistemic activities. She wants true perceptions and beliefs, not false ones; she wants well-grounded beliefs, not vagrant, floating ones; she wants significant rather than trivial, relevant rather than irrelevant, knowledge; she wants deep rather than shallow understanding; and she wants knowledge that ennobles human life and promotes human well-being rather than knowledge that degrades and destroys; she wants to know important truths. The development indicated in the previous sentence is often compromised or arrested short of its highest reaches, but the individual who loves and desires knowledge according to the discriminations of significance, relevance, and worthiness has the virtue that we are calling love of knowledge.

Christian tradition, starting with the Bible, has commended a discriminating appetite for knowledge. The apostle Paul writes, "Whatever is true, whatever is honorable, whatever is just, whatever is pure, whatever is lovely, whatever is gracious, if anything is excellent, if anything is worthy of praise, think about these things" (Phil. 4: 8). Saint Augustine says that not only our bodily appetites need to be properly channeled if we are to avoid self-ruin, but we must do the same for the appetite of the mind, which is "subject to a certain propensity to use the sense of the body ... for the satisfaction of its own inquisitiveness. This futile curiosity masquerades under the name of science and learning, and since it derives from our thirst for knowledge, and sight is the principal sense by which knowledge is acquired, in the Scriptures it is called *gratification of the eye*."[2] Thomas Aquinas continues this tradition in distinguishing a virtuous love of knowledge (*studiositas*) from an unvirtuous one (*curiositas*). (See *Summa Theologiæ* 2a2æ, Questions 166 ("Of Studiousness") and 167 ("Of Curiosity").) The present chapter is not an exposition of this Christian tradition, but it is inspired by it; the analysis of this virtue, like that of the others in this book, is in part controversial because of the way in which virtues are indexed to metaphysical commitments and world views.

Knowledge among the Human Goods

Locke describes a virtue marked by "an equal indifference for all truth, I mean the receiving it in the love of it as truth, but not loving it for any other reason before we know it to be true" (*Of the Conduct of the Understanding*,

---

[2] Augustine, *Confessions*, trans. R. S. Pine-Coffin (Harmondsworth: Penguin, 1976), Book X, ch. 35, p. 241; the biblical quotation is from 1 John 2: 16.

§12, p. 186).[3] We will try to understand what this loving indifference amounts to, but we can begin by specifying one thing that it cannot reasonably be. Many propositions of which a person could have knowledge are, absent very special circumstances, of no interest whatsoever, so that a person who equally loved all of them would not thereby display virtue, but instead a weird intellectual pathology. Imagine a lover of truth who with equal indifference wanted to adjudicate the truth-values of (1) a charge of capital crime against his mother and (2) the proposition that the third letter in the 41,365th listing in the 1977 Wichita telephone directory is a "d". The world is rife with truths of the latter sort, and a person who aspired to know them with indifference of enthusiasm would not be a model epistemic agent. Instead, the healthy, well-functioning agent loves some propositions (is interested in them, that is) far more than others—before he knows which ones are true. Epistemic goods are not all created equal; in fact some of them are so far down the value scale as hardly to be goods at all. So discrimination among epistemic goods is essential to the virtue that consists in loving them.

One kind of principle of discrimination is the set of criteria for propositional knowledge. The lover of knowledge wants his beliefs to be true, and to be adequately supported, in whatever way of supporting is appropriate to his particular belief in its particular circumstances. So the virtuous epistemic agent will insist on these conditions and will choose practices that tend to satisfy them, and will feel emotional discomfort when his desire for them is frustrated. Given a certain aptitude, he will tend to get truth and adequate support because he wants and pursues them. But an agent whose passion for knowledge involved only these principles of discrimination would exemplify the kind of indifference that we condemned in the preceding paragraph. So other criteria of discrimination must be essential to the virtue of love of knowledge.

If beliefs often need support, then beliefs can gain in value by being supports for other beliefs. So not only is *having* support a sometime desideratum in beliefs; a belief's *providing* support for other beliefs can also make it more interesting than some others, and a belief can be trivial because of its utter lack of a supporting role. One reason why the belief about the

---

[3] In John Locke, *Some Thoughts Concerning Education* and *Of the Conduct of the Understanding*, ed. Ruth W. Grant and Nathan Tarcov (Indianapolis: Hackett, 1996), p. 186.

Wichita phone book lacks allure is that, barring very special circumstances, nothing rides on it. By contrast, explanations of anomalies in biology are usually highly significant, in that they press for revisions of other biological beliefs, on which, in turn, still other beliefs depend. Acquaintance and understanding can also be valued for the load they bear. Perceptions and insights can support important beliefs or important understandings of things. Compare, for example, the microbiologist who is excited by seeing something telltale on a chromosome with an accident gawker on the highway. Both exemplify the human appetite for perception that Aristotle indicates, but the gawker's desire and delight are going nowhere. They are idling; the perceptions they seek support nothing in particular. Seeing something or not seeing something through the microscope can make all the difference for the formation of a belief or for the coming together of understanding, and a scientist often spends much time and energy putting herself in a position for an acquaintance as a basis for some such epistemic good. In science, theology, history, and individual self-knowledge, the understanding of one thing often contributes to the understanding of another, or helps to warrant some belief. A philosopher or mathematician may expend great energy and time developing his understanding so as to put himself in a position to have basic insights within a given range.

The fact and extent of some knowledge's bearing an epistemic load is thus one of the criteria by which the lover of knowledge discriminates in her appetite for knowledge. She will tend to be more resolutely attached to more load-bearing beliefs, acquaintances, and understandings, and more interested in assessing the truth-value of proposed ones that seem to her to bear more of a load. However, load bearing *by itself* is not much of a value, since the load that a belief bears may itself be trivial or irrelevant. The fact that an expert witness has told me *the third letter in the 41,365th listing in the 1977 Wichita telephone directory is a "d"* supports the proposition, but the supporting role of the testimony does not lend much value to it if the proposition it supports is utterly without interest. The lover of knowledge discriminates pieces of knowledge by reference to their load bearing, but only by virtue of other bases of discrimination.

A more fundamental basis is one that we call worthiness. Propositional knowledge, understanding, and insight are important, not taken in abstraction, but in connection with their bearing on human flourishing and the intrinsic importance of their objects. Knowing the truth in a criminal trial, understanding the mind of the accused, hearing the emotion in his voice, are important because justice is important. Getting a diagnosis right and understanding how a disease agent works are important because people's health is at stake. Warranted true beliefs and understanding of history may be important because our understanding of present-day institutions and current policies may depend on it; this knowledge is important also because the events it recounts were important to the people concerned in them. So, in the epistemically virtuous person the disposition of caring about the intellectual goods will derive in part from a disposition of caring about other goods such as justice, human well-being, and friendship. Love of the intellectual goods properly resides within the concern for what Aristotle calls eudaimonia—the broadest and deepest human well-being. So love of the epistemic goods is not a virtue in abstraction from other virtues, like justice, compassion, and a sense of civic duty.

But we are not saying that knowledge is valuable only if it is "practical". Some things are worth knowing even if the knowledge has no "application". Why is it worth knowing how old the universe is, while it is not worth knowing how many grains of sand are in a particular cubic centimeter of the Sahara Desert (assuming that both truths are "useless")? Why is it worth having a map of the entire human genome, even apart from the medical applications? Why is it worth understanding the details of the evolution of some organism? Is it just that these questions are very difficult to answer, and thus a challenge to human ingenuity, in the way some logical puzzles are? Is it just a challenge, like a crossword puzzle, so that once the puzzle is solved, the fun is over? The value of inquiry often turns on the value of the thing to be known. Organisms are excellent and beautiful things in their own right; human beings are glorious and important (to us, but just as some insect is also glorious, the value of human beings is not simply a parochial human affair). The universe, with all its processes, is worthy of respect. And this worthiness of the objects of knowledge is tied to their particular character—their particular complexity and simplicity, the particulars of their structure and composition and functions. The human genome is interesting because of what it is, whereas the cubic centimeter of the Sahara, simply as so many grains of sand together, is uninteresting because of what *it* is. And the epistemic correlative of complexity–simplicity functioning is not "knowing facts" but "understanding". The point of knowing the age of the universe is not that of having a number to put on it, but of the web of connections on which that number depends, the other parts of the story of the development of the universe, the explanation and the grasping of it. Again, the value of the epistemic goods is interconnected with other goods—now not just with human eudaimonia, but with the value of the universe, of the things that are known. But the value of the thing known does not guarantee the virtuousness of the love of knowing it.

The criterion of the intrinsic value of a potential object of knowledge is vague, and we have certainly not developed it significantly here. But we can say one more thing. Fictional objects—say, the *Star Wars* series or J. R. R. Tolkien's *Lord of the Rings* trilogy—sometimes have a complexity and simplicity, a structure, that is analogous to the human genome or the evolution of the universe. Their intrinsic character may render them worthy to be studied, but this worthiness seems much less than that of something that is real; and we think that much of the legitimate interest that such fictional objects have depends on their reflecting reality in one way or another. We should not be taken as suggesting that the intrinsic worthiness of a real object trumps the worthiness of any fictional object. We want to allow, for example, that a knowledge of *Middlemarch* may be more worthy than a knowledge of a real car.

The proper lover of knowledge will value some knowledge more than others because some knowledge is more worthy. People differ as to the kinds of truths they take an interest in, and the differences can be differences of intellectual virtue, according to the quality of the goods the people care about. Individuals who are concerned about the truths they read in *Science* magazine, or the *Atlantic Monthly*, the *National Geographic*, the *New York Review of Books*, or *Books and Culture*, are in this respect more virtuous than people who are most interested in the truths they read in *People* magazine or the gossip columns, because the truths that are found there are mostly trivial or even salacious and invidious (that is, the truths aren't vicious, but it is less than virtuous to care about them, or to care much about them). This may sound elitist, but if it is, this is an elitism we cannot avoid. Surely anyone acquainted with intellectual culture knows the distinction between important and trivial knowledge. The aim of liberal arts programs in colleges and universities is not just to transmit a bit of the higher kind of knowledge to their students, but to nurture in them a discriminating love of knowledge and thus to create in them a distaste—or at any rate, a limited patience—for trivial knowledge. It would be elitist not to spread this kind of education as broadly as possible through the population, but the aim of such an education is *properly* elitist. It is to produce people with a taste for what is excellent, and this will necessarily distinguish them from people who lack this taste. The right attitude of the educator is what Michael Platt has called "elitism for everybody".

A third principle of discrimination is relevance. Beliefs, understandings, insights, and perceptions can be very significant in the sense that other epistemic goods rest on them, and worthy in the sense that their objects are intrinsically important or bear on human eudaimonia, without being of much interest to a given person or group at a given time because these are not relevant to their current concerns. It is not for everyone to know the details of Samuel Johnson's life or important facts in quantum mechanics, despite the ramifications and intrinsic value of such knowledge, because some bits of important knowledge are necessarily restricted to a small community of specialists. No human being can know all important knowledge. People's special placement in society and their already existing fund of knowledge can make certain pieces of knowledge relevant to them which are not relevant to many other lovers of knowledge. Conversely, knowledge can be highly relevant without bearing much epistemic weight or being generally very worthy. Sometimes the most relevant question is "Where are my keys?" or "How can I get some food for my family?" (Of course, the relevance of where my keys are does and must bear, in at least a small way, on my human flourishing.) The intellectually virtuous person is acutely circumspect—that is, has a strong and sharp sense of the relevance of the parts of his knowledge to his current circumstances and his finitude—and his appetite for knowledge will be governed, in part, by his sense of relevance.

It would be a mistake to attribute to the lover of knowledge a too methodical approach to its acquisition, one whereby she governed her intellectual behavior by an explicit and rigid appeal to principles of load bearing, worthiness, and relevance, carefully and decisively shunning all experiences, insights, and beliefs that did not satisfy the criteria for properly lovable knowledge. Even the most brilliant and best-educated human being is not in a position to recognize with sufficient reliability the beliefs, insights, and understandings that have the property of proper lovability.

Experimentation, trial and error, and muddling about are unavoidable features of the life of the mind. It will be part of the flexible practical wisdom of the intellectually virtuous individual to know when to play with ideas, hypotheses, interpretations, images, experiences, and formulas, often with only a vague sense of the positive value of the objects of play. Thus the lover of knowledge, whether she is a scientist, an interpreter of texts, a historian, or a layperson interested in any of these fields, will on occasion exemplify something like the Derridean–Nietzschean virtue of epistemic playfulness (see Chapter 5), letting her mind go on outrageous creative wanderings. And it will be part of the formation of her intellectual taste that she takes pleasure in such activity. The difference between the lover of knowledge as we describe her in this chapter and the authentic Derridean-Nietzschean is that in the lover of knowledge epistemic playfulness is just one of the many virtues which, in her practical wisdom, the agent exemplifies as occasion calls for.

A similar topic is the enjoyment of problem solving. People who are talented at puzzle solving often take great pleasure in exercising their brains, sometimes without discriminating regard to subject-matter. Thomas Kuhn points out that a leading motive for doing "normal science" is the joy that certain smart people get from solving the numerous puzzles that are created by a scientific paradigm.[4] Human beings' attraction to intellectual puzzles—regardless of the significance of the subject-matter—is a natural expression of the love of knowing that Aristotle mentions. But if getting solutions to the puzzles had no significance beyond amusing smart people, the enthusiasm for doing so would not be much of a virtue. We credit chess masters with intellectual brilliance of a sort (thus a virtue in the thin sense promoted by some virtue epistemologists), but their interest in chess is at best a minor intellectual virtue. Some scientists' love of puzzle solving may be little more than an enthusiasm for highly technical and challenging amusement. But the enterprise is communally ennobled by the fact that their work contributes to an understanding of nature, and we think that most cases of scientists' motivation for their work contains at least an admixture of joy in understanding the universe. The taste for puzzle solving is itself virtuous, in a mild way,

---

[4] Thomas Kuhn, *The Structure of Scientific Revolutions*, 2nd edn. (Chicago: University of Chicago Press, 1970), pp. 35–42.

but it gains enormously in value if integrated into an overall intellectual will or project that is governed by load-bearing significance, worthiness, and relevance.

If the love of knowledge is governed by these kinds of discriminations, what can Locke mean by "equal indifferency for all truth"? He identifies the counterpart intellectual vice as "prejudice". A person who suffers from prejudice adheres to certain beliefs for inadequate reasons, such as that he likes believing them, that it would cause him anxiety to give them up, that this is what people in his tribe have always believed, and that the investigations leading to the revision of these beliefs would cost him more trouble than he wants to spend. The lover of knowledge is free from prejudice. Described in our terms, prejudice is a malformation of the epistemic will. The four examples of inappropriate reasons that we have just attributed to the prejudiced are all appetitive states—aversions, preferences, attachments—which may not always be bad, except as they override the good of knowing the truth. The lover of truth, by contrast,

must suppose ... that his persuasion is built upon good grounds, and that his assent is no greater than what the evidence of the truth he holds forces him to, and that they are arguments and not inclination or fancy that make him so confident and positive in his tenets.

And the test of whether he really and honestly loves belief-as-adequately-grounded above all such competitors as we mentioned above is his openness to hear criticism and revise his opinions:

Now if, after all his profession, he cannot bear any opposition to his opinion, if he cannot so much as give a patient hearing, much less examine and weigh the arguments on the other side, does he not plainly confess it is prejudice governs him? (*Conduct*, §10, p. 184)

What shall we say about Locke's sketch of the lover of knowledge in the light of the three principles of discrimination that we have laid out? We note first that Locke seems to be concerned primarily with the discriminations associated with the structure of propositional knowledge. We have argued that commitment to such knowledge is not enough for someone to count as a lover of knowledge. Furthermore, Locke's conception of adequate grounding is evidentialist, and we would propose a more pluralistic, Alstonian understanding of warrant (see Chapter 2). We concur that where evidence is called for, the lover of knowledge will discriminate among beliefs on the basis of the evidence for them; but in addition to allowing for a variety of kinds of warrant, whose adequacy varies with the beliefs in question and their circumstances, the lover of knowledge will have a more complex set of principles, which he will apply with practical wisdom according to kinds of beliefs and their circumstances. We also agree that mere preference for a belief, fear of emotional distress, and aversion to exertion are usually not adequate reasons for retaining an important belief that one has been given some reason to abandon. While we do not want to rule that retaining a belief for any of these reasons is incompatible with love of knowledge, we agree that they are uncharacteristic for a person with the virtue. We also want to allow that the lover of knowledge may have some of the impulses of the prejudiced—an anxiety about putting his pet beliefs in jeopardy, a certain aversion to long drawn-out investigations, and so forth—but he also has a counterbalancing love of the intellectual goods, discriminated according to their significance, relevance, and worthiness, and he has a toughness of self-discipline that allows him to override these less worthy motivations when they threaten his intellectual life, with more or fewer efforts of self-management.

Locke is right to accord great importance to discriminating truth from falsehood; the lover of knowledge does love truth as such, even if he doesn't love truths indiscriminately. Bernard Williams points out that just as a person can love music as music without loving all kinds of music, so the fact that a person wants his knowledge to have other qualities besides truth does not imply that he desires truth only incidentally or instrumentally.[5]

But Locke is far from advocating an indiscriminate obligation to ground our beliefs in argument and evidence. He says that since life is short and knowledge hard to come by,

it becomes our prudence, in our search after knowledge, to employ our thoughts about fundamental and material questions, carefully avoiding those that are trifling. ... How much of many young men's time is thrown away in purely logical inquiries ... is much worse than for a young painter to spend his apprenticeship ... in examining the threads of the several cloths he is to paint upon, and counting the hairs of each pencil and brush he intends to use in the laying on of his colors.... superficial and slight discoveries and observations that contain nothing of moment

---

[5] See Bernard Williams, *Truth and Truthfulness* (Princeton: Princeton University Press, 2002), p. 90.

in themselves, nor serve as clues to lead us into farther knowledge, should be lightly passed by, and never thought worth our searching after. (*Conduct*, §43, p. 222)

And he gives as an example of a fundamental piece of knowledge "that admirable discovery of Mr. Newton, that all bodies gravitate to one another."

Purveyance

Among human beings, knowledge is very much a social affair, and the two main kinds of social roles people occupy with respect to it are those of *acquiring* it from others and *purveying* it to others. For example, these two functions constitute the social side of the teamwork characteristic of modern science. Throughout this study, we are interested in what we might call the *general* delivery of the epistemic goods, the role of the virtues not just in fostering the single virtuous individual's own knowledge, but the general human acquisition of these goods—or rather, their acquisition, maintenance, and application within a community. The love of knowledge would not be in the fullest sense an intellectual virtue in a person who loved it only for himself. So now we need to comment briefly on the love of knowledge as it characterizes people in the various roles of purveyor—for example, those of witness, teacher, and supporter of epistemic enterprise. To think of an intellectual virtue as a disposition that fosters the goods in this general way is to bring social attitudes into the analysis, to include in the disposition concerns for the cognitive well-being of other people. Let us consider the love of knowledge as a motivation for purveying it through testimony, teaching, and support of epistemic enterprises.

According to Thomas Reid, among the inborn epistemic dispositions with which human beings are equipped by nature is a

propensity to speak truth, and to use the signs of language so as to convey our real sentiments. This principle has a powerful operation, even in the greatest liars; for where they lie once, they speak truth a hundred times. Truth is always uppermost, and is the natural issue of the mind. It requires no art or training, no inducement or temptation, but only that we yield to a natural impulse. Lying, on the contrary, is doing violence to our nature; and is never practised, even by the worst men, without some temptation. Speaking truth is like using our natural food, which we would do from appetite, although it answered no end; but lying is like taking physic, which is nauseous to the taste, and which no man takes but for some end which he cannot otherwise attain.[6]

Reid's sentiment is a credit to the persons in his range of observation; perhaps they were unusually truthful. It is true that a person needs *some* motivation to lie, as one needs some motivation to do anything at all, but we have known people who at the slightest hint of being in a "political" situation spontaneously adopt the strategy of deceit or evasion. However, even if the disposition that we have observed is always a positive perversion of our native condition, the disposition to tell others the truth, if it amounts to no more than Reid describes here, is not the virtue of truthfulness—in part because the natural impulse to tell the truth is not tough enough to make truth telling highly probable when the going gets rough (the temptations are a fact of life), and in part because it does not require a love of something good. The disposition that Reid describes is not an appreciation of the epistemic goods and the importance of others' possessing them. Here again, we see the gulf between a faculty—a natural propensity to some kind of behavior—and a virtue, a state of mature character that is somehow the development and realization of that faculty.

Truthfulness is a love of the intellectual goods as they may be lodged in other people by way of one's own communication. It is a concern that what one tells the other be true, not just in some legalistic sense of being a true proposition, but that what one is communicating actually become a true belief or correct understanding lodged in the other person—that she know and understand the truth. Here love of knowledge is not just a love of epistemic goods as such, but of other people's having them. So what we would ordinarily call a moral motivation is involved in the structure of the virtue—benevolence, *agapē*, justice, generosity, or the like—but the virtue is intellectual inasmuch as the good or the justice that is wished for the other is an epistemic one.

This is not to say that the truthful person never knowingly deceives or allows an interlocutor to continue uncorrected in a false belief, but it is to say that she does not do so without good reasons, and she is subject to emotional discomforts in many cases of withholding truth, or allowing or

---

[6] Thomas Reid, *An Inquiry into the Human Mind On the Principles of Common Sense*, ed. with an introduction by Timothy Duggan (Chicago: University of Chicago Press, 1970), ch. 6, sect. 24, pp. 238–9.

conveying falsehood. This animus against purveying or allowing falsehoods is not indiscriminate; the practical wisdom of truthfulness is a sense of which falsehoods are important to avoid, or especially important to avoid, and why, and which, truths urgently need to be told. The criteria governing this wisdom are the ones that govern the love of knowledge, except that now the judgments are made by virtue of empathy with the interlocutor's situation: One judges for the other as to communication as one would judge for oneself as to inquiry—according to the discriminations of truth, load bearing, worthiness, and relevance. And the last two criteria, especially, reach out beyond the "purely epistemic" to the broader concerns for human well-being. Consider the case of Socratic irony.

History has given us, perhaps, no greater lover of knowledge than Socrates, and yet in the course of his ironical proceedings in the *Euthyphro* and other dialogues Socrates plays rather fast and loose with the truth of particular propositions. He is on his way to the law court to be prosecuted by Meletus for impiety and leading the youth astray when he meets Euthyphro, who is going to the same place to prosecute his father for a "murder". Euthyphro discloses that his motive for prosecuting his father is piety to the gods, who, according to him, require utterly impartial justice. He displays such confidence in his knowledge of what piety requires that Socrates proposes to become his pupil so that when he appears in court he can tell Meletus that he has learned the truth about piety and so is in a position to reform and lead a righteous life hereafter. All of this is literally false. In truth, Socrates functions throughout the dialogue as a potential teacher of Euthyphro. The topic is the nature of piety, and the upshot is that Euthyphro is much less clear about what piety is than he thinks. What Euthyphro might have learned is the highly ramified, worthy, and relevant truth that Euthyphro does not know what piety requires. Socrates makes a good-faith effort at teaching Euthyphro this truth, and his strategy is irony: falsely presenting himself as Euthyphro's pupil so as to engage him in a conversation from which Euthyphro may learn this truth. On the surface the effort seems to fail miserably, with Euthyphro as ignorant at the end of the dialogue as he was at the start—maybe even worse off epistemically, inasmuch as he seems to have developed a more defensive posture against Socratic questioning.

Socratic irony has epistemic victims in the sense that it sometimes leads people to believe falsehoods; furthermore, Socrates employs it intentionally, in full awareness that it may have this effect. Is the practice compatible with truthfulness and the love of knowledge? We think so, and we think that the justification can be explained in terms of some of the discriminations that we take to govern the love of knowledge. The false proposition that Socrates risks introducing into Euthyphro's doxastic structure—namely, *Socrates wants to learn from me*—is trivial compared with the ramified and worthy understanding that might be engendered by their conversation. Furthermore, if deceit is brought on by the irony, it is very likely to be temporary; on one reading of the dialogue, by the end Euthyphro realizes that he has been tricked into the rather deep conversation he has just had. If, in addition, seeds of intellectual and moral humility have been sown in his constitution, then perhaps nothing has been lost, and something gained. Euthyphro is not likely to forget soon his conversation with Socrates, and the probability is pretty high that it will have more durable effects than the ones recounted in Plato's literary product. Besides these considerations, Euthyphro may not be the only person to be considered. In many of Socrates' dialogues, while the irony may be lost on some interlocutors, it may be transparent to others, yet not unimportant in the economy of communication even for those who see right through it. The irony presumably has pedagogical power for many of the millions who have read and will read the dialogue across the ages. Another plausible justification is that a more direct communication of the important truth that Socrates tried to communicate to Euthyphro would have had even less chance of success than the ironic approach.

We have argued that the lover of knowledge is motivated, in her role of purveyor, by the value of knowledge in itself and its value for the ones to whom it is supplied. In connection with purveyance, then, the love of knowledge is a kind of benevolence, generosity, or justice. People communicate epistemic goods to others, as well as a great deal of epistemic trash, for reasons other than these ideal ones. Some of these lesser motivations are exploited in social structures to encourage the communication of epistemic goods, while others would be better omitted altogether from life. Teachers teach reasonably responsibly, at least in part for salaries and prestige, and institutions are contrived to reward excellence in these extrinsic ways. People speak the truth from fear of a bad reputation, and that is often better than lying or keeping the truths to themselves. People pass on information about others from malice or envy. Some people teach out of a love of showing off. Most people's motivation for teaching has at least some admixture of the vice that we will call "domination" in Chapter 9—the hubristic desire to be the author of somebody else's mind. All these kinds of motivation differ from the virtue that we have been calling the love of knowledge.

Even apart from the currently growing specialization of knowledge and narrowing of disciplinary expertise, no one can care in the same way about all important truths. It is not indicative of intellectual vice not to care much about knowing for oneself, say, the chemical properties of some rocket propellant or the rice yield in the Mekong Delta, even though it may be very important for somebody else to know these things. The fully mature lover of knowledge will, in a necessarily abstract sense, love all knowledge, even the knowledge which she knows only by hearsay and with respect to which she will thus not have the powers of discrimination that we outlined in the second section of this chapter. If such a lover of knowledge is to contribute to its purveyance, she will have to ally herself with and trust others for judgments about load bearing, worthiness, and relevance, as well as for the more immediate purveyance of the knowledge. Such a lover might send her children to a university to which she herself would not have been admitted; she might give money so that a student could study a subject that she would not want to know (or at any rate, know deeply) herself; she might support research on a question that she barely understands. Of course, such actions may be motivated by vanity, domination, or other vicious or non-virtuous motives. The point is that a person need not be particularly intellectually accomplished, or have tasted very directly any particular kind of knowledge, to have something like the virtue that we are describing in this section.

Faulty Epistemic Will

We can deepen our understanding of the love of knowledge by reflecting on shortfalls and deviations from it. Faulty epistemic will encompasses immaturity and vice. Immaturity is a fault, not among the very young, whose immaturity is perfectly normal, or among the congenitally defective, whose "immaturity" is inevitable, but among those who are old enough and well enough endowed to be properly developed, but aren't. The difference between immaturity, when it is a fault, and vice is not very sharp, but one criterion is the positiveness of the fault—is it in the direction of the perverse, or is it just a shortfall from the good?—and another is blameworthiness, though this is not a strict criterion, because some cases of immaturity are blameworthy and some cases of vice may not be. With these provisos, we want to retain the distinction between immaturity and vice.

We have the following reservation about Aristotle's distinction between weakness of will and vice. Bad motivation that will count, in a given person, as contributing to no more than what Aristotle calls weakness of will, since the person is also virtuously motivated to struggle against the bad motivation, can be both blameworthy and positively perverse, and thus clearly vicious. That is, we want to attach the word "vicious" not just to overall behavioral dispositions, but to motives. However, we gladly acknowledge the heart of Aristotle's distinction: namely, that between a disposition to struggle against a vicious motive, and to regret failing in the struggle, and a disposition simply and cheerfully to act on the vicious motive. Roughly, immaturity relative to the love of knowledge will be a shortfall of proper love for the epistemic goods or of proper aversion to epistemic harm, while vice will be a perverse love for or aversion to the epistemic goods and/or perverse attraction to other things that affect epistemic performance. Accordingly, our discussion can be divided along the following lines: (1) failures of concern to know, (2) unvirtuous concerns to know, (3) failures of concern not to know, and (4) unvirtuous concerns not to know.

Failures of concern to know We have seen that while mature love of knowledge is the development of a natural, faculty-like disposition of the human will which at the beginning is little more than a love of cognitive stimulation, the virtue itself is a desire or concern that discriminates its objects along several dimensions. Since the original disposition is an inbuilt aspect of human nature, we are not likely to find many members of the human race who lack interest in all kinds whatsoever of cognitive stimulation or activity. In this respect the sheep diverge from the goats along the lines of discrimination that we outlined in the second section of this chapter. Consider some of the more typical kinds of faulty cognitive indifference to be met with among human beings.

Locke comments that some people, while not by any means "indifferent for their own opinions" (indeed, these people are passionately attached to their own opinions), are not "concerned, as they should be, to know whether [their opinions] are true or false" (*Conduct*, §12, p. 187). One sign of insufficient concern for truth is that when such people are given an opportunity to test their more cherished beliefs, they decline it, or apply it too casually, or offer defenses of the beliefs that are weaker than any that these people would accept in other contexts. From time to time we hear of scientists who intentionally falsify data in favor of their own hypotheses. It is not that these people have no concern at all for truth, but that they do not care about it enough to be fully excellent epistemic agents. When other motives conflict with the concern for truth, these defective individuals tend to forsake truth to satisfy the other motives. Locke seems to underestimate, consistently, the rightful place of intellectual firmness and personal advocacy of beliefs in the intellectual life. We will discuss this point in the next chapter. Not everyone who seems to his colleagues rigid in his beliefs is in fact intellectually immature or vicious; intellectual practical wisdom may dictate that one person hold on where another, because of *his* placement in the intellectual history or community, should forfeit. Both individuals might be exemplars of both firmness and love of truth. The fact that firmness is a virtue does not diminish the importance of the love of truth.

Connected with the intellectual defects of caring too little about truth and grounding is a casualness about understanding, a complacency about letting certain things, which one could understand with effort, go ununderstood. The very best intellectual agents are alert to deficiencies in their understanding and continually seek to untie the knots in it and deepen it. Most intellectual endeavors afford plenty of scope for improvement of understanding, and a person who insists inordinately on understanding everything can, admittedly, become discouraged or tire himself to the point of sickening. So again, judgment and balance are requisite. A person can be uninterested in deepening his understanding in some area without exemplifying a vicious intellectual complacency. A student might wisely elect to settle for a "B" understanding in microbiology if this is not central to his own intellectual development and if getting a deeper understanding here would entail sacrifice of development in other more important areas. Yet a very common defect of the intellectual will is complacency of understanding. The agent reaches a level that enables him or her to "function" (say, to keep his job, to get a "B" in the course, to do the tasks that daily life requires), and settles for his intellectual *status quo* until forced by the threat of no promotion, a lower grade, or the inability to perform some task, to go a little deeper.

A similar complacency about important kinds of acquaintance is an immaturity in the same vein. Let us mention just a couple of notable kinds. Facing our own emotions is often difficult for people, and important. We do not like to admit that we are feeling guilty about something we have done; we give ourselves "justifications" for our action that shield us a bit from the experience of the emotion, yet it is there waiting with its impact were we to look straight at it. Or we avoid feeling the envy that is working in us, again telling ourselves stories about our situation that are calculated (in an unexplicit sort of way) to shield us from full perception of the emotion. Feeling these emotions (as compared with a mere "intellectual" acknowledgment that we have them) is an important part of self-knowledge; in the feelings we may have access to a clear and distinct idea of what we are like.[7] But some of us systematically shield ourselves from this self-knowledge, and while in a sense we "know" these emotions are present, we keep our back turned and so remain in the twilight about ourselves.

Another kind of acquaintance that is subject to complacency is the perception of anomalies in science and other intellectual endeavors. Thomas Kuhn points out that scientists working within a paradigm are sometimes quasi-blind to phenomena that resist explanation within the paradigm. But as in the emotion case we just mentioned, this dimness of insight is not a sheer blindness, but partly a phenomenon of the will, a deficit of desire, pleasure, and choice. Scientists differ from one another in the extent to which they find anomalies attractive, exciting, interesting, enjoyable. For some scientists anomalies are chiefly an annoyance, an impediment to getting on with the day's work, while for others they illustrate the comment of Johannes Climacus that "a thinker without a paradox is like a lover without passion".[8] A passion for paradoxes is a disposition to be

---

[7] For more on feelings of emotion as a source of self-knowledge, see Robert C. Roberts, *Emotions: An Essay in Aid of Moral Psychology* (Cambridge: Cambridge University Press, 2003), ch. 4.

[8] See Søren Kierkegaard, *Philosophical Fragments*, trans. Howard Hong and Edna Hong (Princeton: Princeton University Press, 1985), ch. 3. Climacus might have formulated his point more accurately

acquainted with them, a principle of their saliency. A fear of paradoxes, or a lack of interest in them, is a defect of the epistemic will. Again, proper formation of the will is governed by practical wisdom: some paradoxes, while intractable, seem to be tricks of formulation, while others invite solutions that yield genuine progress of understanding.

What is the cure for these complacencies, these deficits of intellectual passion? How can one who lacks a sense of the value of something be brought to love it? The answer lies in a certain kind of education, one that treats goods like truth, grounding, understanding, and significant insight as intrinsic goods and not merely as means to other goods like employment, grades, and the accomplishment of tasks. Such an education leads the agent into the presence of the good, thus inviting him to appreciate it. In the middle of Plato's *Theaetetus* is a digression (172c–177c) in which Socrates compares the character and education of a philosopher with the character and education of a lawyer. The lawyer learns to argue in court, where topics are determined by the exigencies of the legal system, where truth-claims and the arguments for them are subordinate to prosecutions and defenses, and where strict time limits are set for the arguments. Such an education, says Socrates, is not likely to lead to the love of knowledge. The philosopher, by contrast, learns argument in the context of a free and leisurely search for the truth itself, so that if one line of argument does not deliver the goods, it is abandoned, and another is taken up. The student here learns through an endeavor that is directly and ultimately aimed at the epistemic goods themselves, in the company of others who value these goods for their worthiness. If the inquirer achieves some understanding (and in the *Theaetetus* the participants do, even though they discover no adequate definition of knowledge), he delights in it for what it is. So in the process of such an education, the value of the epistemic goods becomes evident to the student. We hope that such acquaintance can also be fostered by thinking hard about the epistemic goods, as we are trying to do in this book.

Unvirtuous concerns to know   We have argued that loving knowledge as good in itself is compatible with discriminating grades of knowledge, where the

---

but less poetically thus: "A thinker indifferent to paradox is like a lover indifferent to his beloved," thus showing himself a little more clearly to be a virtues epistemologist.

grading is determined by human well-being and the importance of the objects of knowledge. These ways in which the value of other things affects the value of knowledge make possible unvirtuous or even vicious concerns to know. Let us distinguish instrumental from non-instrumental unvirtuous concerns to know.

People desire to know things for a wide variety of instrumental reasons. Knowledge can be the way to finishing that damned dissertation, getting tenure, getting a job at Yale, making lots of money, getting a Nobel prize, scaring other people, plumbing the basement, and cooking up a first-rate soufflé, to mention just a few. In some of these cases, desiring knowledge solely for the kind of reason in question is perfectly compatible with the highest intellectual virtue. The knowledge of how to make a soufflé seems to *have* no value beyond its instrumentality in mediating soufflés. So you're none the less virtuous for desiring that knowledge with nothing more than the crass intention of puffing up a terrific soufflé for yourself and your honey. But in other cases there is something intellectually immature, to say the least, about somebody who seeks the kind of knowledge in question solely for instrumental reasons. If the knowledge in the dissertation is worth writing a dissertation about, then something is wrong if your only interest in it lies in finishing the dissertation. If a piece of knowledge merits a Nobel prize, one who desires that knowledge only for the Prize has a defective epistemic will. The point is not that wanting the Nobel Prize is in itself perverse (though it's not particularly admirable either), but that wanting something as worthy as important scientific knowledge less than one wants the incidental good that it procures shows a corrupted or immature spirit.

Some goals for which high-level knowledge is instrumental are, however, much more worthy than the goals of fame and fortune embodied in the Nobel prize. The medical applications of biological knowledge would be an example. A person who seeks biological knowledge solely for the sake of its medical applications is more mature, intellectually, than one who seeks the same knowledge solely for a Nobel prize, for at least two reasons. First, the medical applications are the kind of eudaimonia-integral rationale that more broadly contributes to the value of knowledge in the first place; second, medical knowledge is internal to such applications, in the same way that a knowledge of justice is internal to justice in court cases. By contrast, biological knowledge is not internal to prestige and money. Note that, in this book, we formulate the broad powers afforded by the intellectual virtues as the acquisition, maintenance, transmission, and *application* of knowledge. Our rationale for including the application of knowledge among the aptitudes essential to virtuous intellectual character is our sense that knowledge's instrumentality to application of knowledge is quite different from knowledge's instrumentality to making money or gaining a prestigious position. Still, biological entities are astoundingly beautiful and ingenious, and a biologist who found knowledge about them utterly uninteresting apart from its medical applications would have a defective intellectual character.

Non-instrumental desires for knowledge can also be vicious or immature, through lack of circumspection. Circumspection is a concern for the values that the knowledge, or the pursuit of it, would affect, along with good judgment about the possible effects of the research or the resulting knowledge. Nazi medical researchers using concentration-camp prisoners as subjects in experiments with obvious and horrendous harmful consequences for the subjects provide clear examples of extreme vice. Nuclear physicists or biologists working on weapons of mass destruction provide more ambiguous examples. Since intellectual circumspection has both a motivational and a "success" component, an individual scientist could fall short of virtue either by caring too little about the possible consequences of her researches or by lacking good judgment about those consequences. The present point is just that such vice or immaturity is compatible with desiring the knowledge in a purely non-instrumental way.

Another perversion of the love of knowledge is that of being a willing purveyor or consumer of gossip. While the concept of gossip stresses, perhaps, the giving of information, the practice includes collecting it. The gossiper enjoys passing on gossip, but equally enjoys collecting material, and may become very skilled at research, learning to drop comments and ask questions that tend to elicit gossip from others, and entering into transitory quasi-contractual relationships in which gossip is traded. He takes pleasure in learning and passing on information about other people that is inappropriate for him to learn, possess, or pass on to another. Much gossip is only pseudo-knowledge, but nothing in the idea of gossip prevents its being perfectly warranted true belief. Since gossip is not necessarily defective as propositional knowledge, the standard by which the love of it is faulty must be some principle of discrimination other than those governing propositional knowledge. The proper response to gossip is, "It's none of his (her, my, your, our) business." That is, the gossiper lacks an epistemic (life) context for his acquiring or passing on the information in question. The knowledge is idling in his cognitive establishment. But to say that it's none of his business is not just to say that his interest is idle; the gossiper is more vicious than a mere lover of trivia. Among the more sophisticated and "sensitive", gossip is often couched in benevolent and compassionate terms, in a tone of solicitude and caring for the objects of their discourse and researches, but what makes it gossip is that it is nosey. It is invasive, voyeuristic, and often has an invidious edge of put-down about it; and even if it expresses no bad will, it is often to the unjust hurt of another's reputation or to the violation of his privacy. The gossiper exhibits a deficit of circumspection, of seriousness about the question: Is this something I, in my circumstances, am permitted to learn, or to pass on to this other in his circumstances? That gossip is circumstantial, and that the vice betokens a deficit of circumspection is obvious from the fact that the very same propositional knowledge may be perfectly legitimate if kept to oneself, or if inquired after by a priest, police officer, doctor, or teacher.

In Toni Morrison's novel *Beloved*, the slave-narrator comments on a slave-owner who was a cut above the average, that he looked away when the slave women were nursing their infants. This intentional forgoing of acquaintance expresses respect for the women's privacy and a sense of the limits that human proprieties set to appropriate knowledge. It is not that acquaintance with the appearance of the women's breasts is a bad thing in itself, knowledge that no human being ought ever to have; rather, the epistemic virtue here consists in an appetitively qualified sense of context, determined in part by social conventions concerning modesty and in part by universal facts of human nature such as the need to be dignified by respectful treatment. To be an indiscriminate ogler is a trait of bad intellectual character, a failure of discipline of the will to know.

The unvirtuousness of desire for acquaintance need not turn on the interpersonal dimension of knowledge. One of us (Roberts, in case you want to know) was recently subjected to the previews in a movie theater. Half a dozen movies were excerpted which, if the sampling was represent-ative, consist in a series of flashing lights, raging fires, exploding buildings, speeding cars, crashing cars, cars falling over cliffs, cars chasing other cars, burning cars, exploding cars, fistfights, gunfights, fights with unidentified high-tech weapons, and deafening booms from unknown sources. Here were various series of cognitive inputs (if this is not too exalted a term) of such a sort as to get the attention, easily, of the least epistemically developed among the animals. We should not say that no principles of discrimination were employed in selecting the inputs; but the principles were not truth, warrant, significance, relevance, or worthiness, but instead decibels, brightness, speed, suddenness, destruction, and violence. What kind of education grounds the enjoyment of prolonged exposure to this sort of thing? What sort of formation does a person have to have to find this worth paying $11 and a couple of hours of one's life for? Roberts thinks that ordinarily, a person with a proper intellectual education, a lover of knowledge, will find this pretty hard to tolerate for more than a couple of minutes because his cognitive interests make demands, shaped by the discriminative criteria that we have been expounding, that this sort of fare fails woefully to satisfy.[9]

Still, distraction by arresting but noetically low-grade sights, sounds, and thoughts can have its place in the life of the mind. Norman Malcolm, in his memoir of Ludwig Wittgenstein, tells how, after grueling sessions of philosophy in which Wittgenstein would exert his investigative powers to the utmost, he would invite Malcolm to go to a "flick". The movie would be some mindless American western with, no doubt, lots of galloping and shooting and Indians falling off horses and cowboys being pushed over cliffs and forts being burned down and the like, and Wittgenstein would sit as close as possible to the screen so as to fill his visual and auditory fields with the images and hullabaloo. Such distraction appears to have been therapeutic for Wittgenstein, allowing him to pry his mind off philosophy, to which it had become almost obsessively stuck during the seminar session. Wittgenstein's use of the mindless cognitive stimulation of movie theaters is remarkably similar, in some ways, to the use Roberts imagines that people of low intellectual virtue make of it. For Wittgenstein, as for the intellectually immature, it was paramount that the stimulation be mindless. Like the others, he did not go to the theater for an intellectual challenge.

---

[9] Thomas D. Kennedy traces the apparent increase in people's tolerance and appetite for mindless sensory stimulation and other kinds of contextless knowledge to the vast increase, in recent decades, in the power and availability of contemporary information technologies. See his "Curiosity and the Integrated Self: A Postmodern Vice", *Logos* 4 (2001): 33–54.

He wanted his attention to be riveted in as passive and effortless a way as possible. The difference between him and the intellectually immature was the place that this intake of acquaintance had in the rhythms of his larger intellectual life. For some people, viewing the movies that Roberts previewed may constitute the cognitive high point of their day, the moment at which their mind is most engaged; for Wittgenstein such movies functioned like ballast on a hot air balloon, pulling hard downward with the effect of arresting dangerously uncontrolled flight. By letting his attention be absorbed by the sights and sounds, he could quiet a mind too passionately riveted on the higher epistemic goods. Few people have had greater powers of concentration, or a more integrated intellect, than Wittgenstein. So again, virtue and vice are not just a matter of "behavior" (of, say, sitting enthralled before a flashing, screaming screen), but are determined by patterns of motivation and of the relations of patterns of behavior to one another. Here Wittgenstein's use of distraction is intelligently in the service of concentration, integration, mental health, and the pursuit of high intellectual goods.

Failures of concern not to know We have seen that because of the criteria of worthiness and relevance by which the mature lover of knowledge selects propositional knowledge, understanding, and acquaintance, he actually has a will *not* to know certain things that he could know but ought not to know. Examples illustrating this point have been given in the preceding subsection, where we stressed perverse or immature concerns to know what is irrelevant or unworthy; so here we need comment only briefly on them from this new angle. The faulty epistemic will is characterized not only by inappropriate concerns for knowledge, but by a deficit of those concerns that might override the inappropriate ones. We have considered the possibility of a scientist's improper desire for understanding, the gossiper's improper love of nosey propositional knowledge, and the ogler's improper love of a certain kind of acquaintance. In the virtuous lover of knowledge, these kinds of knowledge are discriminated against by a certain orientation of taste, a concern for other things that rules out (or at least rules against) the improper love.

Very likely, a human being who is intensely interested in high-level scientific questions and sees the likelihood that she (or her contemporaries) will be unable to handle the proposed knowledge, will still, at some level or in some degree, want the knowledge. So here, temptation will be normal for the lover of knowledge. A biologist involved in cloning research or a physicist working on nuclear fission, even if, as mature reflective lovers of knowledge, they are fully aware of the difficulties that humanity will have handling the potential new knowledge, will desire it. But if they have a strong sense of the place of knowledge in human eudaimonia, their sense of the knowledge's potential for evil will also give them a cautioning concern that countervails against the desire in the particular case. So the concern for human well-being and the ability to make this concern activate one's powers of discrimination of worthiness or relevance in the pursuit of knowledge make the difference between a Frankenstein or a Nazi medical researcher, on the one hand, and a virtuous lover of knowledge, on the other. Here the moral and the intellectual come together in the virtue of practical wisdom. Knowledge is only one of the important goods constituting human flourishing, but it is deeply entangled with those other goods.

Since cases in which the lover of knowledge chooses to eschew high-level but eudaimonistically unfitting knowledge are likely always to involve conflicting motives, the lover of knowledge will have to have, not just these two conflicting concerns—the love of knowledge thought of more abstractly and the love of human well-being—and the practical wisdom to know how to balance these in particular cases; he or she will also have to have the potential for self-denial, the power of self-mastery, that makes it possible for him to do what he takes to be best despite strongly wishing to do something else. The person who falls short of the virtue of love of knowledge will, therefore, fall short in one or all of these three ways: he will lack a clear and intense concern for the well-being of humanity, or he will have abstracted that concern so thoroughly from his intellectual life that he is undisposed to recruit this concern in decisions of the present sort, or, while he both has the concern and recruits it, he suffers so from weakness of will that he cannot implement his practical wisdom in this regard.

Consider now the rather different cases of the gossiper and the ogler. Here also the virtuous lover of knowledge forgoes knowledge because it is not right in the circumstances; but a major difference is that the forgone knowledge is quite low-grade. Insofar as it appeals to the lover of knowledge, it does not appeal to his highest concerns. The propositional knowledge in which the gossiper trades and the acquaintance that attracts the ogler are rather uninteresting "intellectually", yet both kinds of knowledge have a widespread, primitive appeal. So here, too, the lover of knowledge is likely to have to struggle, in a way that lovers of knowledge do not have to struggle against the temptation to watch loud, flashy, and mindless movies all the way through. And again, the deficit of the person who doesn't exhibit the virtuous love of knowledge seems to be that he does not grasp, appetitively, the place of the illicit knowledge in life. He is deficient in aversion to this kind of knowledge in this kind of context.

Unvirtuous concerns not to know When we were discussing unvirtuous failures of concern to know, some of the cases involved a concern *not* to know, a positive aversion to the epistemic goods. Thus sometimes people do not want to know the truth about their bank balance or whether their kids are on drugs. Or they want not to perceive their own emotions or the anomalies to their scientific hypothesis. Or they want not to understand the causes of their obesity or the arguments against their religion. Such anti-epistemic motivational dispositions are principles of intellectual vice or immaturity. Our earlier point was that such bases of vice can be mitigated by an increase in sensitivity to the goodness of the epistemic goods, a deepened appreciation and desire for truth, warrant, understanding, and acquaintance. But it seems clear that one could also approach motivational improvement or repair by reducing these aversions. Such positive aversions are rooted in personal interests: I don't want to know the truth about my bank balance because I want to continue to spend freely; I don't want to know that my kid is on drugs because then I'll have to do something about it and I have no idea where to start. I don't want to perceive my own guilt or envy because it will indicate my personal nastiness. I don't want to see the anomalies to my hypothesis because I have invested years in this research and I'm afraid to change paths.

It is not hard to see that a number of these anti-epistemic personal interests are morally substandard, or would threaten my intellectual life less if I had more of a virtue like courage. If I were more responsible in spending my money, I wouldn't be averse to knowing my bank balance. If I were more committed to helping my kid and more courageous in facing her problems, I would want to know what she is doing with drugs. If I had greater trust in God, I would have no interest in hiding behind an ignorance of the objections that can be made to my religion. So we see that, at least in many cases, positive aversion to intellectual goods is mitigated, or corrected for, by an increase in the virtues that are usually regarded as moral. One of the main theses of this book is that no strict dividing line can be drawn between moral and intellectual virtue.

Love of Knowledge, Metaphysics, and Wisdom

If the virtue of the love of knowledge includes a sense of what is important among truths—if it is a kind of wisdom—then different moral and metaphysical communities will promote different versions of this virtue. Truths that are of overriding importance for the Stoic may not even be truths in the Marxist's opinion; nor will the theist's most important, and thus organizing, truths be of much interest to a Bertrand Russell. This seems to be a substantive difference in virtue, with ramifications over the whole personality; these people's personalities are differentially related to the truth. We have seen that there is no such thing as a simple love of the truth; this virtue is always oriented upon truths (of different kinds). We have to reckon with the possibility that what some serious people take to be knowledge is not knowledge, and thus that what some people take to be intellectual virtues are not virtues. If they are vices, they need not be such in any blameworthy sense; but if they systematically lead one away from the epistemic goods, they are intellectual vices nonetheless. Religious faith would be an example of an intellectual virtue that might be an intellectual vice; it is related to the supposed intellectual good of knowing God, which, if it is not an intellectual good, cannot properly be aimed at by an intellectual virtue. Similarly, a certain version of the virtue of caution—one that entails metaphysical naturalism, for example—could in fact be a vice or at least a virtue that has an unvirtuous dimension to it, a spoiled virtue. All of this could be decided only by a sort of metaphysical adjudication which is in all probability unavailable to human beings. So we are stuck with the situation of somewhat variant systems of traits that in charity we call virtues, which may not be such—indeed, which cannot all be such.

Locke's exposition of the virtue of the love of knowledge emphasizes the discriminations associated with propositional knowledge, though we have noted that he acknowledges the discrimination of significance and presupposes that of worthiness. Being a Christian, Locke has a healthy respect for truth and for the created world that is the object of so much of the knowledge we aspire to. Accordingly, our account of this virtue differs from his primarily in emphasis. In the interest of seeing how different metaphysical commitments yield diverse versions of intellectual virtues, perhaps it is worthwhile here to glance briefly at a rather different case. Friedrich Nietzsche also endorses a virtue that we might call love of knowledge, and like us, he stresses that the epistemic goods that are hereby loved are inseparable from the other goods of human life. He rejects what he calls "dogmatism", examples of which are the doctrines of "the Vedanta in Asia and Platonism in Europe".[10] Nietzschean love of knowledge is decidedly not an aspiration for cognitive contact with the eternal Forms. Dogmatism posits a system of unchanging verities whose existence depends in no way on human thought or activity or concerns, to which the knower relates by humbly conforming his mind in a kind of contemplative receptivity (this attitude of receptivity is perhaps something like Locke's prejudice-renouncing indifference). For Nietzsche, by contrast, knowledge is always perspectival and interested. On his psychology, human beings are interested chiefly in power—our basic drive, from which all other drives derive, is to create, to control, to dominate—and the chief epistemic expression of this desire is the creation of interpretations. What he calls "the will to truth", which is an expression of the will to power that is misguided by such "dogmatic" outlooks as Platonism and Christianity, eventually gives rise to the truth(!) that there is no truth in the dogmatic sense; "truth" is interpretations that people make up in the interest of their will to power—unselfconsciously at first, and then self-consciously (with the advent of philosophers like Nietzsche). "The falseness of a judgment is to us not necessarily an objection to a judgment.... The question is to what extent it is life-advancing, life-preserving, perhaps even species-breeding" (Part I, §4, p. 17). Strictly speaking, Nietzsche does not believe in what Locke calls "knowledge", but he does believe in a counterpart epistemic good: namely, life-affirming, life-giving, exuberance- and power-expressing interpretations.

---

[10] Friedrich Nietzsche, *Beyond Good and Evil*, trans. R. J. Hollingdale (Harmondsworth: Penguin, 1990), Preface, pp. 13–14.

It might be thought that, compared with the trait of character that we have delineated, Nietzsche's intellectual virtue lacks discipline. We expounded several principles of discrimination that govern the passion for knowledge in our framework. Does Nietzsche's virtue exhibit counterparts of our principles? In a way it does. He certainly distinguishes correct from incorrect interpretations. For example, Plato and Christian thinkers think that they are telling truths, whereas they are really expressing their will to power. The person who knows that his interpretations are expressions of his will to power is expressing his will to power more frankly, more nobly, more freely than the muddle-headed Christians and Platonists. The will to power is a rather frightening essence of ourselves; it is easier and more comfortable just to be humble and go on taking oneself to be seeking truth in the dogmatic sense. The discipline of acknowledging the centrality of the will to power in one's epistemic activities is a counterpart of Locke's discipline of indifference; you stand still sometimes and say, "Don't take the easy route of prejudice (dogmatism); remember that you are a knower!" Another of our principles of discrimination is relevance. We have no reason to think that this principle does not guide the selection or invention of interpretations; one interpretation can be more or less relevant to another, or to a situation that arises in the course of life. Nietzsche is very astute in seeing the relevance of a variety of intellectual movements of his day and of preceding intellectual history to his own interpretation of human nature—and of his interpretation of human nature to those movements. He is circumspect in this regard, and his writings teach a Nietzschean style of circumspection to those who would like to learn it. We noted in Chapter 5 that Derridean interpretation requires a moment of "as-if" classical interpretation; the purpose of this is to prevent the interpretation from becoming so "playful" that it becomes irrelevant to the text. Another of our principles is worthiness. Whereas Christians and others might eschew gossip as unworthy knowledge because we think it incompatible with respect and *agapē* for the neighbor, a Nietzschean might eschew it as expressing a servile, petty, competitive spirit—that is, insufficient self-respect. But both outlooks distinguish worthy from unworthy knowledge, and do so by appeal to values embedded in the outlooks' conceptions of eudaimonia.

7

Firmness

Introduction

We have been writing about the general love of the epistemic goods, but we human beings have a natural, conservative tendency of attachment to some of the particular putative epistemic goods currently in our possession. We tend to cling to our theories and research programs and resist giving up our own understandings and beliefs, and we tend to continue to perceive in the ways we have perceived before. Tenacity with respect to one's own epistemic acquirements is natural and good. We cannot and must not be open to change our deeper views at the first appearance of contrary evidence. It is proper, then, that the first thing we do on confronting a putative reason for deeper epistemic change is to look for ways to refute the objection or accommodate the anomaly to our current understanding of things. At the same time, this conservatism is not completely rigid. The natural urge to seek perceptual input, support for our beliefs, and deeper understanding is a disposition that opens us to epistemic change. Our imagination, in concert with our senses and the vicissitudes of epistemic circumstance, contrive flexibility of perception, and of belief and understanding formation. And so they must do. Practices like investigating, studying, looking, listening, reading, conversing, and soliciting testimony are by their nature openings to change. In these activities we aim to acquire new knowledge, and sometimes such knowledge revolutionizes our noetic structure.

These opposite and complementary tendencies in our epistemic will divide roughly along lines of structural depth. We tend to be more conservative about the more foundational parts of our epistemic establishment (what we have called the goods with more load-bearing significance), and the ones in which we are more personally invested (ones that strike us as more worthy). Initially, we are interested only in supplementing and fine-tuning our fund of knowledge—making adjustments on the periphery, rather than rebuilding our noetic structure.

Our natural conservatism and openness derive from the nature of the epistemic goods. Beliefs are, after all, some kind of commitment to the truth of the believed propositions. Perceptual dispositions (without which no real perceiving occurs) are particular ways of perceiving things, ways that naturally exclude other possible ways of perceiving. Similarly, our understandings of things are dispositions that belong to us and exclude other understandings. Not to be at all conservative about them would be not to believe, not to understand, not to have ways of perceiving. On the other hand, a natural openness is entailed by the fact that these dispositions are good and are felt to be good. Every day we find ourselves wanting to learn things (that is, to *acquire* beliefs, understandings, perceptions). And acquisition entails newness. We can't very well acquire something we already have. So insofar as we participate in the intellectual life at all, we are perforce and naturally both conservative and open. But that does not mean that we have the virtue that this chapter is about. That virtue is a trait of individual character, an acquired tuning and balancing of these natural tendencies.

In this chapter we expound a trait of intellectual character that is right with respect to the issues of "hold" on individual epistemic goods. For want of a better term, we call this virtue "firmness", by which we mean to suggest something like an Aristotelian mean between flabbiness and rigidity. Muscles are most healthy and functional when they are supple without being flaccid, firm without being "tight". In their proper condition of being well-toned, certain muscles in the body (the grasping and hugging and biting ones) enable a full range of "grips", from the tightest to the lightest, as occasion warrants. Jesse Bjoraker has pointed out that, with its trunk, the elephant can both uproot a good-sized tree and pick up a potato chip without breaking it. We say that the idea of firmness is something *like* an Aristotelian mean, but the muscle analogy shows that the "mean" here is not just a midpoint between a strong and a weak grip. It is instead a potential for a range of grips, in between and including very strong and very weak as adapted to the particularities of our epistemic situations. People are subject to a variety of dysfunctions in this area of the intellectual life, such as gripping all their epistemic goods too lightly, gripping too lightly particular goods that should be gripped more tightly, and gripping some beliefs too tightly. The word "firmness" may seem to stress the potential for tight grip, but we want it to refer equally to the potential for light grip; the idea we have in mind is that of a potential for *right* grip across the whole range of proprieties. In a living animal such as an elephant or human being, differential grip is of course governed by judgment and sensitivity; that idea will also be important in our analysis and signals a limit on the muscle metaphor. Let us begin by reflecting about noetic flaccidity.

Flaccidity

An extreme and amusing example of intellectual flaccidity is found in George Eliot's novel *Middlemarch*, in the character of Mr Brooke, the uncle and guardian of Dorothea Brooke, the heroine. Eliot describes Brooke diagnostically as a man of "miscellaneous opinions", "uncertain vote", and a "rambling habit of mind". In this "glutinously indefinite mind" the "Puritan energy was clearly in abeyance".[1] Brooke reports the following of himself:

"I remember when we were all reading Adam Smith. *There* is a book, now. I took in all the new ideas at one time—human perfectibility, now. But some say, history moves in circles; and that may be very well argued; I have argued it myself. The fact is, human reason may carry you a little far—over the hedge, in fact. It carried me a good way at one time; but I saw it would not do. I pulled up; I pulled up in time. But not too hard. I have always been in favour of a little theory: we must have Thought; else we shall be landed back in the dark ages. But talking of books, there is Southey's *Peninsular War*. I am reading that of a morning. You know Southey?"[2]

This snippet of Brooke's conversation is a snapshot of his noetic flabbiness, and Eliot's terms of description are the beginnings of an explanatory analysis of his condition. Clearly, to judge by the topics that "interest" him and the books he reads, Brooke is an intellectual of sorts. He isn't stupid—at least,

---

[1] See John Locke, *Of the Conduct of the Understanding*; ed. Ruth W. Grant and Nathan Tarcov (Indianapolis: Hackett, 1996): "Some men's tempers are quickly weary of any one thing. Constancy and assiduity is what they cannot bear: the same study long continued in is as intolerable to them, as the appearing long in the same clothes or fashion is to a court lady" (§17, p. 191).

[2] George Eliot, *Middlemarch* (New York: Book of the Month Club, 1992), Book I, ch. 2.

not in a way that would show up on an IQ test. He does not squander his reading time on fatuous romances or even, overmuch, on newspapers. Yet his intellectual accomplishments put us in mind of Locke's comment that unless one processes what one reads so as to make it one's own by reference to some organizing principles, the result is less a house than a pile of lumber. Brooke's opinions are "miscellaneous", and his vote "uncertain", because no intellectual particularities (ideas, beliefs, understandings) occupy the appetitive center. By habit his mind "rambles" because it has no favored pathways or destinations. It is glutinous, all right, picking up much that it contacts in its rambles, but always in vague generalities because nothing is followed up or pursued to an end, as the focused enthusiasm characteristic of the Puritan mind, now lapsed, would have insisted. Its perceptions are vague because perception is not just sensory glutinosity but an active, oriented, concerted *making something* of what one sees or hears.

The firm mind is glutinous too, but with a focused insistence that tends to sort its various acquirements into the incidental, the worthwhile, and the all-important, and to create a structure of them. Thus it does not so much ramble as travel, and what it assembles on its travels is less a hodgepodge than a body of thought, and its votes are fairly predictable to someone who knows its principles, and what it sees on its way is sharply focused and differentiated. Thus the firm mind, not the flabby one, delivers the epistemic goods.

Another flaccid mind in literature is that of Leo Tolstoy's Stepan Arkadyevich Oblonsky. Stepan Arkadyevich, the brother of Anna Karenina, is an amiable hail-fellow-well-met whose "convictions" track the views that prevail among the fashionable people of his social class. As their views change, so do Stepan's.

Oblonsky subscribed to and read a liberal paper, not an extreme liberal paper but one that expressed the views held by most people. And although he was not particularly interested in science, art, or politics, on all such subjects he adhered firmly to the views of the majority, as expressed by his paper, and changed them only when the majority changed theirs, or rather he did not change them—they changed imperceptibly of their own accord.

Oblonsky never chose his tendencies and opinions any more than he chose the style of his hat or frock-coat. He always wore those which happened to be in fashion. Moving in a certain circle where a desire for some form of mental activity was part of maturity, he was obliged to hold views in the same way as he was obliged to wear a hat. If he had a reason for preferring Liberalism to the Conservatism of many in his set, it was not that he considered the liberal outlook more rational, but because it corresponded better with his mode of life. The Liberal Party maintained that everything in Russia was bad; and in truth Oblonsky had many debts and decidedly too little money. The Liberal Party said that marriage was an obsolete institution which ought to be reformed; and indeed family life gave Oblonsky very little pleasure, forcing him to tell lies and dissemble, which was quite contrary to his nature. The Liberal Party said, or rather assumed, that religion was only a curb on the illiterate; and indeed Oblonsky could not stand through even the shortest church service without aching feet.[3]

Oblonsky is even less intellectually serious than Brooke; he does not even rise to the level of a dilettante. It is not very clear what Brooke gains by holding on so lightly to his beliefs and understandings. He just seems to have got into a dilettantish habit, perhaps as a result of a bad education; intellectual frivolousness seems to have worked itself into his grain. Or maybe he is vaguely uncomfortable with intellectual "enthusiasm", especially when the commitments threaten to issue in expensive actions, as those of his niece Dorothea tend to do. But it's clear what Oblonsky gains by his epistemic flaccidity. Oblonsky's mind is spineless on principle, so to speak, though rather unreflectively. When Tolstoy says that Oblonsky does not choose his opinions, he means that Oblonsky's changes of mind are not consequent on careful deliberation; for Oblonsky does choose his opinions, perhaps even more robustly than the intellectually firm person, for whom each newly acquired belief or understanding is heavily regulated by his rich and firm noetic structure. Tolstoy makes clear that Oblonsky follows principles, however automatically, in the selection of his beliefs and ways of understanding, and the principles are (1) let each belief facilitate my fitting in socially, and (2) let each belief correspond with my existing mode of life.

One might wonder whether beliefs chosen on this basis are really beliefs, or just policies of assertion, acquiescence, and behavior. Similarly, for purposes of political and scientific conversation in Oblonsky's circles, only a very minimal understanding of the views he "espouses" is required, and he is not likely to get beyond this minimum if all he wants from his understanding is social acceptance. Indeed, a few platitudes and stock phrases may serve Oblonsky's social purposes. Oblonsky's flaccidity, like Brooke's,

---

[3] Leo Tolstoy, *Anna Karenina*, trans. Rosemary Edmonds (New York: Penguin Books, 1954), Part 1, ch. 3.

deprives him of real intellectual goods; both men are intellectually shallow in the extreme. But their deficit extends beyond the intellect, thought of in abstraction from the rest of the personality. Their failure to stand for anything intellectually entails, and is entailed by, their failure to stand for anything at all; an unintegrated intellect is a mirror image of an unintegrated, immature self. Compare Brooke with Dorothea; compare Oblonsky with Constantin Levin.

The exemplars of intellectual flaccidity that we have considered so far are both mature in years, however juvenile they may be intellectually, and both are "educated", so we could have expected them to be better than they are. But flaccidity is also a normal trait of the youthful mind, which we can expect it to outgrow with intellectual and moral exercise. A bright college freshman, taking an introductory course in philosophy, may resemble Mr Brooke. Having a taste for ideas, she treats the survey as a smorgasbord at which she partakes with an appetite. Within a course of sixteen weeks she may have been a Platonist, an empiricist, a skeptic, a Cartesian, a Kantian, a utilitarian, a social contractor, a mind–body dualist, a Berkeleyan idealist, a reductive materialist, a theist, an atheist, and an agnostic. Having scratched the surface of a debate, having followed for a few steps the flow of a dialectical exchange, she commits quickly to each theory, easily relinquishing its contrary, then passing on to the next. She is bright, but under the pressure of successive presentations of ideas, her intellectual character is too soft to hold onto a position. Her memory is glutinous, but a rather different power of retention is needed for her to hold her own in the exchange of ideas (for at the moment she lacks anything of her own to hold on to).

But we may hope that she will not turn out like Brooke. With an education in which she learns to love knowledge, she will also learn where she stands intellectually and will stand firm there. She does not easily change her mind because she understands pretty deeply with an understanding that is integrated into her broader character.

Brooke seems to pride himself vaguely on his general lightness of hold on the intellectual goods; Oblonsky's flaccidity seems to be a half-calculated strategy of social comfort; only the student's cognitive promiscuity seems to be completely unreflective, natural, and without rationale. But some philosophers have actually offered principled reasons for flaccidity. Because they endorse intellectual softness for what they take to be excellent reasons, they regard it as a virtue and would no doubt take umbrage at our term "flaccid", which carries a suggestion of sub-optimal function and is not intended as a compliment. The views of these philosophers provide one more illustration of our claim that virtue and vice concepts must be indexed to conceptions of human nature and the nature of the universe. What they take to be virtues, we take to be variants of the vice of flaccidity.

Consider first the ironist, whose outlook, according to Richard Rorty, fulfills three conditions: (1) She has "radical and continuing doubts about the final vocabulary"[4]—that is, conceptual scheme—by which she conducts her own moral and intellectual life. An example might be the vocabulary of modern democratic liberalism, or that of modern medicine. To have doubts about this is to be in a state of suspended or quasi-suspended belief about whether this vocabulary is the best way to grasp human nature or the world we live in. It is to have doubts about whether this conceptual scheme is *right*. (2) She realizes that "argument phrased in her present vocabulary can neither underwrite nor dissolve these doubts" (ibid.); that is, she cannot, within her ethical or medical vocabulary, either establish or discredit that language as an instrument of life conduct. And (3) "insofar as she philosophizes about her situation, she does not think that her vocabulary is closer to reality than others, that it is in touch with a power not herself" (ibid.). For example, she does not think that her democratic liberal ethical framework reflects *reality* any more than those of Qu'ranic Islam, Maoist communism, or the ancient Aztec religious ethic of human sacrifice; or that her diagnostic and explanatory vocabulary about viruses, bacteria, genes, etc. is any closer to reality than the explanations of Azande witchcraft.

Ironists, says Rorty, "are never able to take themselves seriously because always aware that the terms in which they describe themselves are subject to change, always aware of the contingency and fallibility of their final vocabularies, and thus of their selves. ... The ironist spends her time worrying about the possibility that she has been initiated into the wrong tribe, taught to play the wrong language game" (ibid., p. 75). For a variety of reasons having to do with the nature of language and the powers of human reason, Rorty thinks that none of our beliefs accurately describes the world or captures the essence of persons. We adopt our beliefs because they help

---

[4] Richard Rorty, *Contingency, Irony, and Solidarity* (Cambridge: Cambridge University Press, 1989), p. 73.

us cope with the vicissitudes of life. Irony regarding our own "beliefs" is thus both a radical tentativeness regarding the objective reference of their content and a skepticism about their fitness as coping devices. Whatever the ironist professes, she professes with the perpetual worry that the wrong vocabulary has turned her into the wrong kind of person.

To our current epistemic accomplishments—our beliefs, our understandings of things, our perceptions of the world—Rorty commends a double attitude: on the one side a "solidarity" or commitment to the community to which our vocabulary belongs, and on the other "irony", a kind of non-commitment that seems to us to revoke their very epistemic status. For after all, a belief that is not believed, an understanding that is not taken to be correct, a perception that is not taken to be veridical, is hardly a belief, an understanding, or a perception for the subject who adopts that attitude toward it. This non-commitment to one's epistemic treasury is in some ways very much like Brooke's and Oblonsky's and the freshman student's non-commitments to theirs. But there are differences, especially with the freshman student. Unlike the ironist, who consistently distances herself from her own views by constant reminders that they do not reflect reality and may not even be very good coping devices, the student has serial commitments. (She is committed to Berkeley for two hours, and then to eliminative materialism for an hour and fifteen minutes, etc.) The student appears uncommitted to her own epistemic goods only if we view her dispositionally, over a fairly long stretch of time, say two weeks; at any given moment, she may give headlong assent to the view of the hour. Brooke and Oblonsky, being more conscious and systematic in their dissociation from their beliefs and understandings, are more like Rorty's ironist, because they are aware, at least in principle, of their non-commitment at any given moment. So Brooke, Oblonsky, and Rorty's ironist have a kind of continuity in their intellectual lives and character that the student lacks. They are committed to non-commitment. It may be extremely difficult for older people to have no intellectual character at all (good or bad), as it is possible for young people.

The difference between Oblonsky, who is committed to his own social comfort, and the Rortyan ironist, who is committed to the struggle against cruelty, say, is just in the content of their commitments. Neither of them thinks that what they are committed to is the *right* thing to be committed to in any objective sense; at least, the ironist is not committed to this, for otherwise she would give up her ironist stance and become an ordinary believer. On the other hand, both Oblonsky and the Rortyan ironist, insofar as they are consistent over a fairly long period of time, both in their pragmatism and in the bearing of that pragmatism (on social comfort in the one case, on the struggle against cruelty in the other), do have something like character; but in both cases the character is dissociated, in their own view, from epistemic goods proper in the form of understandings, well-grounded beliefs, and perceptions. On the view of the intellectual life taken in this book—one in which the intellectual goods are integrated with other goods, and intellectual virtues are strongly continuous with the moral virtues—the formation of character represented by Oblonsky and the Rortyan ironist is odd, to say the least. The oddity is in the proposal that the Rortyan ironist be systematically uncommitted to intellectual goods as we conceive them while strongly committed with focused concentration on certain "moral" goods. One suspects that a person who claims to be deeply committed to the struggle against cruelty while stressing the radical contingency of his own beliefs about cruelty is either less committed to the struggle, or less ironic about the proposition, than he says. Oblonsky is less odd because, as we would predict, his intellectual flaccidity is mirrored in his moral flaccidity. Another difference is that in a sense Oblonsky is a more successful pragmatist than the Rortyan ironist if we take beliefs to be coping devices. Because the Rortyan ironist is morally serious, she spends her time worrying that she may have become the wrong kind of person; psychologically, this would seem to be a defect in her coping. Oblonsky has no such worries, but just changes his views as social comfort demands; he copes better because his flaccidity is more thoroughgoing.

Another advocate of principled intellectual softness is the skeptic Sextus Empiricus, who strives for a radical and general suspension of belief for himself and those he teaches. This suspension has a therapeutic aim. In Sextus's view, belief is the root of emotional disturbance. For example, if I am anxious about whether my children are safe, it is because I believe that it would be bad for them to be harmed. If I am angry with someone for smashing my windshield with a hammer, it is because I believe that she smashed my windshield with a hammer and that to do so is bad. In a different way, if I believe the doctrines of Epicurus, then if I hear a strong argument against them, I will be disturbed. Since eudaimonia, as Sextus conceives it, is tranquility, the absence of emotional disturbance, eudaimonia can be achieved by ridding ourselves of beliefs. To this end, the skeptical therapist takes any belief (but no doubt especially any that is currently causing distress) and offers equally strong arguments both for and against it, so as to create in the patient a perfect equipoise between assent and dissent, a perfect suspension of belief. The aim of the therapy is, in Martha Nussbaum's words, "a purgation of all cognitive commitment",[5] a state of being completely undoxastic, unopinionated.

In comparing the character that results from a skeptical therapeutic regimen with the ideal character outcome of other Hellenistic therapies, such as the Aristotelian and the Stoic, Nussbaum exploits an analogy congruent with the metaphors of this chapter. The Aristotelian and Stoic therapies aim to change the patient's noetic constitution by substituting true beliefs for pathological, false ones. Nussbaum says that this goal is like that of providing the patient with a strong but rigid ship in which to weather the storms at sea. The skeptic's response to this goal is that, by arming the patient with a structure of beliefs, the therapist only makes the patient vulnerable in a new way. Just as any ship, because of its rigidity, is subject to breakup in *some* storm or other, so the paragon graduate of Aristotelian or Stoic therapy is always vulnerable to psychological disaster at the hands of someone with a strong enough argument against his position. The right approach, says the skeptic, is to have no position (skepticism, in the skeptic's view, is not a position). The skeptic aims to be invulnerable by virtue of flexing with the storm vicissitudes, by going with the flow and riding the waves, like seaweed or fish. So the perfect graduate of skeptical therapy just goes with the flow of his desires as they arise in response to the impressions that he receives from his environment, completely without beliefs about either himself or his environment. Since he thinks of this state of the intellect as the highest possible human virtue, the skeptic will probably not like our calling it flaccidity (though he will not *believe* that our metaphor is bad). If he accepts Nussbaum's fish analogy, he may point out that a healthy fish, while very flexible in water, is hardly flaccid. Indeed, it is firm: neither flaccid nor rigid. But we would point out that exactly because the fish is able to swim against the flow and is not perfectly flexible, it is vulnerable to the roughest water. In storms at sea, fish do

---

[5] Martha Nussbaum, *The Therapy of Desire: Theory and Practice in Hellenistic Ethics* (Princeton: Princeton University Press: 1994), p. 285. Our information about Sextus's view derives from Nussbaum's excellent discussion.

sometimes get injured on rocks and reefs. Perhaps a more perfect analogy with the perfectly cultivated skeptic would be plankton.

Unlike the skeptic, we believe it to be a non-negotiable fact of human nature that human beings live by believing. Were it possible to form a human being who was not disposed to form beliefs, he or she would not be a paragon of virtue, but a monster of human deformity, a paradigm of intellectual and moral dysfunction. Starting, thus, from a very different conception of human nature than the one entailed by Sextus's skepticism, we think it appropriate to describe his intellectual character ideal as flaccidity. Genuine intellectual virtue is something much stiffer, more resistant, and yes, more vulnerable to anxiety, disappointment, confusion, and error than the character that Sextus proposes.

Thomas Kuhn says that for any given paradigm, recalcitrant data, unexpected results, or other violations of the theory's predictions remain. He says that scientists respond to anomalies by ignoring them, posing *ad hoc* explanatory solutions to them, or making them a part of routine projects for ongoing scientific exploration; but scientists don't abandon their theories at the first sign of trouble. Scientific interests would be greatly impeded were scientists not strongly attached to their theories and research programs in the face of anomalous data. Scientists wrestled for over sixty years with various challenges to Newton's inverse square law, and "this patience with a major anomaly proved justified". Kuhn is clear that firmness is a prerequisite for being a good scientist. "Although history is unlikely to record their names," writes Kuhn, "some men have undoubtedly been driven to desert science because of their inability to tolerate crises. Like artists, creative scientists must occasionally be able to live in a world out of joint".[6] If scientists regularly behaved in the way that sometimes seems recommended by Locke's evidentialism, they would suffer, as Kuhn's unremembered scientists seem to have done, from a crippling deficiency of intellectual firmness.

Rigidity

A person may be defective not only by being too pliable, but also by being too stiff. The intellectual life is a dynamic interaction between

---

[6] Thomas Kuhn, *The Structure of Scientific Revolutions*, 2nd edn. (Chicago: University of Chicago Press, 1970), pp. 81–2.

the epistemic agent and his constantly changing environment, social and otherwise. He needs to be always learning, thinking, taking in new information, intelligently encountering views different from and even opposed to his own, and applying his own framework in new situations that it may fit (or seem to fit) only imperfectly. Because epistemic practices involve continuing adjustment, the agent needs not only a certain tenacity with respect to the putative intellectual goods in his possession, but also an openness to what may occasion revisions and improvements in them. The vice of intellectual rigidity comes in several varieties, but they have in common that they impede the appropriate processing of these occasions for revision and deepening.

Our examples of rigidity will be taken mostly from the lives of "intellectuals". No doubt, less cultivated people are also subject to intellectual rigidity, but a higher education is no guarantee against it. A fully proper and excellent higher education (a "liberal" education) aims at the intellectual virtues, including firmness, but that is an education of the epistemic will that has become a bit foreign in the modern university, where intellectually counterproductive rigidity is frequently exemplified by adherents of such diverse views as atheism, Darwinism, Marxism, capitalism, various feminisms, liberalism, rational choice theory, and (more rarely) Christianity and Islam.

In this section we consider five kinds of rigidity: dogmatism, doxastic complacency, stolid perseverance, perceptual rigidity, and comprehensional rigidity. As we will see, most cases of rigidity span more than one of these noetic pathologies; we distinguish them only for purposes of exposition and analytic clarity.

Dogmatism Dogmatism is a property of people, not of beliefs; that somebody is dogmatic about some belief is a demerit of the person, not of the belief. That some Darwinians are dogmatic about natural selection is perfectly compatible with the truth of natural selection. Dogmatic people are usually quite undogmatic about the vast majority of their beliefs; a person's dogmatism bears not on all her beliefs, but only on ones that rise to the status of doctrines. A doctrine is a belief about the general character of the world, or some generally important aspect of the world, which bears the weight of many other beliefs. Thus a mother who refuses, in the face of what should be compelling evidence, to give up the belief that her son is innocent of a certain crime, is perhaps stubborn, obstinate, or blinded by her attachment, but she is not on that account dogmatic. By contrast, someone who holds irrationally to some fundamental doctrine, such as the basic tenets of Marxism or capitalism or Christianity, or some broad historical thesis such as that the Holocaust did not occur, is dogmatic.

Dogmatism is not just strong conviction or the deep entanglement of a belief with important practices of one's life; for both of these kinds of attachment to a belief are compatible with intelligently considering objections to it and even raising hard testing questions of one's own about it. Nor is dogmatism just strong adherence to a belief for inadequate reasons. It is a disposition to *respond* irrationally to *oppositions* to the belief: anomalies, objections, evidence to the contrary, counterexamples, and the like. Intellectual challenge is dogmatism's native habitat. While the firm person has an intelligent, communicative, open, listening attitude toward criticisms of his position—despite possibly holding very strongly to his belief—dogmatism is a hardened position. And the irrational response must be regular and habitual; desultory irrational persistence makes for something less than dogmatism. This negative social dimension of dogmatism—the irrational resistance to criticism—typically has a positive counterface: a compulsion to recruit others to one's position. Intellectual insecurity or self-doubt is one possible motivation for dogmatism, and this might explain the compulsion to make converts. Dogmatism is sometimes hard to distinguish from firmness because it has psychologically internal conditions. At crucial points in the debate the dogmatic person turns willfully away from insights into the force of his interlocutor's objections and calls to his aid arguments that he knows or half-knows to be dodges. Long and detailed acquaintance with a dogmatist's behavior may be needed to judge rightly of these mental strategies.

What is the difference between firmness in religious faith and dogmatism? In Dostoevsky's *The Brothers Karamazov* Ivan Karamazov, the religious skeptic, presents to his believing brother, Alyosha, a series of stories of suffering, culminating in some about children's suffering, the cumulative conclusion of which is that Alyosha's God does not exist. Alyosha persists in his Christian faith, but his persistence is not dogmatic, because he listens openly and carefully, allowing himself to feel the full weight of the argument. He is like the best sort of Kuhnian scientist confronting a significant anomaly to his theory. He sees the problem of putting together with the Christian doctrine of God the undeniable facts that Ivan presents, and he is honest with himself and Ivan about not having an answer to the objection. He does not, like the dogmatist, hide from himself the force of Ivan's argument or try to convince Ivan and himself of the adequacy of some sophistical response. Like the Kuhnian scientist, he has other reasons, both personal and more objective, for holding tight to his belief: his belief has considerable load-bearing significance in his noetic structure, and both it and the beliefs that bear on it have a great deal of worth for him.

The persistence and force of the opposition is also relevant to attributions of dogmatism. A person who refuses to adjust in the face of occasional or ambiguous opposition, preferring to "wait and see", may just be virtuously firm and not at all irrational; suspicions of dogmatism arise when the believer is regarded as holding out too long, or where the opposition is judged to be so strong and clear as to demand a revision of his view. Again, this is a matter of judgment, and may vary with epistemic standpoint. In situations of what Kuhn calls scientific crisis the line is fine between dogmatism and firmness, the call depending again to some extent on where the parties to the debate stand. Thus what looks like dogmatism to the revolutionary may look like firmness to the old guard. But many cases are unambiguous.

David Irving, the "historian" of the Second World War, presents a case of dogmatism so extreme as to be almost a caricature of the vice. While a caricature is unrealistic in some ways, it offers the philosophical advantage of drawing the distinctive characteristics very saliently. Many of Irving's thirty-some books are about the leaders of Nazi Germany, and Irving's tendency, from early on in his publishing career, has been to minimize the suffering of the Jews and Adolf Hitler's murderous intentions and actions toward them. He argues that Hitler was largely unaware of the killing of Jews, that he intervened to prevent it when he became aware of it, that the large-scale gassing of Jews was a figment of survivors' imagination and faulty memory and British invention, and that the Jews were more to blame for their plight than they want to admit. In 1993 Deborah Lipstadt published *Denying the Holocaust: The Growing Assault on Truth and Memory*,[7] in which she accused Irving of distorting the historical record in the interest

---

[7] Deborah Lipstadt, *Denying the Holocaust: The Growing Assault on Truth and Memory* (Harmondsworth: Penguin, 1993).

of his admiration for Hitler. In 1996 Irving sued her and Penguin Books for libel, and in the spring of 2000 the four-month trial began. As a result of the defense, Irving's work was subjected to more careful scrutiny than ever before, and Lipstadt and Penguin won the case. Richard J. Evans, a historian at Cambridge University, was hired as an expert witness at the trial, and has written an account of the whole affair, *Lying About Hitler: History, Holocaust, and the David Irving Trial*.[8]

The errors in historical argument uncovered by Evans and the other expert witnesses for the defense cannot have been inadvertent, inasmuch as they consistently tend to support Irving's fundamental beliefs about Hitler and the Jews. Irving prides himself on his historical method of basing his judgments on diaries, memos, telegraph communications, memories of contemporaries, court records, and the like, of which he says that he has a better mastery than any other historian of the period. But Evans and others have found, upon carefully examining these sources and comparing them with Irving's use of them, that he has ways of making them seem to say what he wants them to say. For example, he engages in tendentious summary, partial quotation omitting material that runs contrary to his beliefs, hiding information in footnotes, removing material from one context and placing it in another to change its import, misreading handwriting, translating texts tendentiously, exaggerating inconsistencies or errors in evidence so as to draw far-reaching conclusions from them, and raising implausible doubts about the reliability of material that disagrees with his views. One cannot systematically abuse evidence in such ways without knowing the proper use of historical evidence. Given that his methods of historical argument are so ill-suited to secure truth, and that he clearly knows what he is doing in using them, we may find it hard to believe that Irving *believes* the propositions he is defending (as opposed to just trying to get other people to believe them). So we may feel that Irving does not really qualify as a dogmatist, since a dogmatist must believe his dogmas. But Evans, who by now has had a great deal of experience with Irving, both through his writings and in person in court, comments:

The reason why Irving did all this was neither incompetence nor perversity. The evidence was overwhelming that Irving was not merely propelled by a juvenile

---

[8] Richard J. Evans, *Lying About Hitler: History, Holocaust, and the David Irving Trial* (New York: Basic Books, 2001).

desire to shock, although an element of that did seem at times to be present in his personality. He was a racist, anti-Semitic, and neo-fascist ideologue, and an admirer of Hitler, and there was little doubt that he believed what he said and wrote. (*Lying About Hitler*, p. 243)

Let us accept that Irving believes what he says and writes; but the psychology of dogmatic belief is not simple. For Irving not only believes what he says and writes, but also doubts it. The psychology and "logic" of dogmatism is doxastically paradoxical in the same way as self-deception. Just as the self-deceiver "convinces" himself of what he "believes" not to be true, so Irving defends himself against doubt of his Fascist, anti-Semitic doctrine by using arguments he knows to be bogus. Thus the dogmatist, like the self-deceiver, is essentially in a kind of fog concerning himself, in particular concerning his own epistemic states; or to put the matter otherwise, his epistemic states are indeterminate. Irving's confusion came out particularly strongly in the cross-examination to which he was subjected during the trial. Again and again when the contradictions in his web of thought were made explicit, he shifted ground, denying what he had said earlier, retracting and then retracting his retractions; so that in the end it was hard to tell what he did believe, except that his pro-Hitler and anti-Jewish orientation was never undermined. Irving is an extreme case, but we think that his noetic fog is characteristic more generally of dogmatic persons. Paradoxically, dogmatic persons cannot know very clearly what they believe, because of the contrariety between the beliefs they hold dogmatically and their means of defending them. By contrast, the intellectually firm person is more likely to have true beliefs *and* to know where he stands both with respect to his central convictions and with respect to his reasons for holding them. So he tends to get at least two epistemic goods for his virtue: more truth in his beliefs and greater self-transparency.

Doxastic complacency   A related belief rigidity, which differs from dogmatism in being much more passive, is laziness in belief formation. Imagine someone mature in years who responds to recent debates about capital punishment by thinking, "I have neither time nor inclination to follow all the wrangling about the way our justice system metes out capital sentences. I've always thought the death sentence a just and useful deterrent to crime and I'm not about to change my mind at this stage of my life." Even when his beliefs are criticized, the required asceticism and exertion of mind are more than the epistemically complacent person is willing to expend. Long-accustomed lassitude has calcified his mind. By contrast, the intellectually firm individual cares more about knowing the truth, has the habits and skills of critical reflection and investigation to go with his will to know, and is ready to rise above his some-time laziness to do his epistemic duty. *When* does the firm person critically evaluate his beliefs? *Which* of his beliefs is it his epistemic duty to reconsider? These are crucial questions, because unchecked doxastic earnestness could send one to an early grave. In general, the firm epistemic agent will be less inclined to call into question beliefs, the more load-bearing they are in his noetic structure and the more worthy he takes them to be. So when they need to be called into question, the more virtue (openness, courage) it will take for him to do so. There is no general rule, hard and fast, for when an agent must respond with genuine searching and listening to challenges of his most fundamental beliefs; but it is clear that Alyosha judged the powerful and serious challenges of his brother Ivan to be such an occasion. Firmness, like every other intellectual virtue, depends on practical wisdom. The doxastically complacent fail either to know when and how to examine their beliefs or to be willing to do so. (For more on doxastic complacency, see the subsection "Failures of concern to know" in Chapter 6.)

Stolid perseverance   If dogmatism is holding fast irrationally to a putatively already achieved intellectual good, stolid perseverance is holding fast irrationally to an epistemic goal. Henry Casaubon, from the same novel of George Eliot where we met Mr Brooke, makes it his life's work to write a "Key to All Mythologies". "[He] had undertaken to show that... all the mythical systems or erratic mythical fragments in the world were corruptions of a tradition originally revealed. Having once mastered the true position and taken a firm footing there, the vast field of mythical constructions became intelligible, nay, luminous with the reflected light of correspondences" (*Middlemarch*, ch. 3). To determine precisely what the original tradition was and to demonstrate the derivation of all other mythologies from it, Casaubon spends some thirty years collecting mythologies, which he preserves in notebooks amounting to "all those rows of volumes" (ch. 20), in the words of his dismayed young wife. Yet the promised publishable synthesis seems not even close to emerging from this pile of raw material, and Casaubon dies before beginning to write the work.

Clearly, Casaubon has a seriously flawed intellectual character, and one of his vices is in the rigidity neighborhood. But it is less dogmatism than doggedness, a foolish perseverance. Towards the end of his life it seems to become a paralysis, though one that does not prevent his continuing to tread ploddingly in place, expanding daily his notebooks of citations. He gets lost in the detail of his research, even starts collecting things whose relevance he does not see, because he cannot bring himself to pass them up. He finds comfort in doing more of the same, as it creates a sensation of forward motion, even if he realizes dimly that he is making no progress. Casaubon's project supports and is supported by an exalted image of himself whose function is to compensate for his intrinsic smallness of spirit and accomplishment. "All through his life Mr. Casaubon had been trying not to admit even to himself the inward sores of self-doubt and jealousy" (ch. 37). He is preoccupied with the respect, or lack of it, that he has received and will receive from the scholars at Oxford. He is aware that German scholarship may obviate his by its superiority and greater currency, but he does not read German and, as his nephew Will Ladislaw comments, "I saw that he deafened himself in that direction" (ch. 21).

Casaubon has traits which, if combined with others, would be virtues. He is right to look down a nose at those frivolous but brilliant scholars who never had a thought they didn't publish immediately, who trade on their imagination and are satisfied with the barest basis in argument. He is right to look down a nose at those who flit from one project to another without consistent purpose, with no unifying vision of what they are about. But perhaps he should not look down his *own* nose at such people, because in him this perseverance, seriousness about laying the foundation, and consistency of outlook are fatuous. The perseverance is unintelligent, the foundation remains mere materials on which nothing is ever constructed, and there is little more to the consistency of the outlook than the phrase "key to all mythologies". With a bit of help from Will Ladislaw and some interaction with the material and with Casaubon, his young wife Dorothea is able to see all these things pretty clearly, but Casaubon himself never gives up. What is wrong with him?

First, one gets the impression that while Casaubon is very learned in a collecting sort of way (he has the Brookean glutinosity), he is not very bright. He does not have the powers of imagination, intellectual synthesis, and hermeneutic insight to pull off the project he has undertaken, even if there were such a thing as a key to all mythologies. His ambitions are grandiose relative to his native equipment; he would do better to work at tasks that match his talents. So Casaubon's rigidity can be traced in part to a lack of self-knowledge. Ideally, he would come to see, after a period of efforts, what kind of projects best suit his talents, and would give up the grand synthesis as too demanding. But another vice seems to lie behind his failure to undertake the needed self-inventory and draw the required conclusion. Casaubon is vain; his interest in the project derives in very large part from his desire to be important and admired. But he must be careful not to look this motivation straight in the face, so he perpetuates his self-unawareness. A somewhat purer love of knowledge—an urgency to have significant and worthy information and understanding for which a certain humility would have cleared the path—would have made him much more flexible vis-à-vis this particular project. As it is, however, the project seems important to him less because of the epistemic goods in prospect than because of what it means for his importance in the eyes of the world.

Thomas Kuhn writes about intellectual firmness in science, but he stresses less the character of the individual scientist and more the sociology of the scientific enterprise and the impingements on the investigators of the historical developments of the science. Nevertheless, he notes that individuals differ in their ability to get into a new paradigm when the history of their science calls for it (compare Priestley with Lavoisier). Sometimes the stolid perseverance of the older scientists is such that only their death, and their replacement by younger people, will allow the proper advance of science toward the epistemic goods. Here the new generation's openness seems attributable less to their intellectual virtue than to their youthfulness; perhaps they will be as stolidly persevering, in their turn, as their predecessors were in theirs. But older scientists do not always hang on too long to their old ways of thinking, and differences of character do seem to be part of the explanation in such cases. (See the brief discussion of Subramanyan Chandrasekhar in Chapter 9.)

Kuhn alerts the virtue epistemologist that much that is salutary in the intellectual life is guided and channeled by institutions and social pressures that transcend the character of individuals, correcting for vice and supporting virtues. Aberrations like David Irving and Henry Casaubon are often forestalled or made less pernicious by processes of peer review. Early in his career Irving published his books with major publishing houses, but book reviews over the years deprived him of this source of credibility, reducing him in the last few years to publishing his books under his own imprint. His libel suit is an example of how institutions can correct for individual vice.

It would be interesting to know more about the character of scientists who exhibit such vices as dogmatism and stolid perseverance, and those who display the counterpart virtue. A major resource for virtue epistemology in the coming years will be intellectual biographies—of both the most successful and less successful intellectual practitioners. We hope that the present book will stimulate philosophers to read such biographies and will provide some initial guidance in what to look for in them.

Perceptual rigidity   In Chapter 2 we argued for an enrichment of the concept of knowledge from the justified true belief model that has dominated recent epistemology. The concept we proposed, which includes the aspects of understanding and acquaintance, is closer to the concept of knowledge that operates in everyday life and in the lives of the most excellent knowers. It also allows us to see kinds of cognitive rigidity that were less visible in the older epistemology.

If we wanted to coin a Greek name for the perceptual rigidity we have in mind, "eidosclerosis" would be suggestive, because in Greek *eidos* can mean both "that which is seen", and "form" or "concept" or "category"; and it is connected etymologically with one of the chief words for knowing (*oida, eidenai*). Eidosclerosis is a defective *perceptual* disposition, but it is compatible with 20–20 vision and perfect hearing. The deficit of versatility is categorial or conceptual, without being merely a lack of concepts; one's *perceptual* acuity is stuck within certain categories, outside of which one is "blind" or "deaf". A person who is aspect-blind because he lacks the intellectual flexibility to see an anomaly is not thereby dogmatic. But dogmatism and stolid perseverance can cause eidosclerosis, which in turn contributes to these other vices.

Kuhn speaks of the involuntary conservatism that is "built into the nature of the perceptual process itself" (p. 62). That is, people perceive in terms of categories in which they are practiced and prejudiced, and when things are presented that do not fit the customary categories, they tend not to perceive them or to perceive them in the old terms anyway. He illustrates this with an experiment conducted by Bruner and Postman (ibid., pp. 62–4) on the visual recognition of playing cards. Anomalous cards (black hearts and red spades) were mixed in with normal cards, and upon visual exposures of various durations subjects were asked to identify the cards. For the virtue epistemologist, an interesting feature of the results is that people differed in their perceptual flexibility, some being virtually inflexible, that is, unable to see in terms of the unaccustomed categories. "A few subjects... were never able to make the requisite adjustment of their categories. Even at forty times the average exposure required to recognize normal cards for what they were, more than 10 per cent of the anomalous cards were not correctly identified" (p. 63). "In science, as in the playing card experiment, novelty emerges only with difficulty, manifested by resistance, against a background provided by expectation" (p. 64).

Most people have no emotional investment in their playing cards' being normal, but scientists do have an emotional stake in their experiments' turning out right and their theories' being vindicated experimentally. Something analogous is true generally of intellectuals. So, in addition to the perceptual resistance created by expectation, further resistance is created by hope and fear, by attachment to one's own views. The more one attributes worthiness and load-bearing significance (see Chapter 6) to one's current putative epistemic goods, the more resistance, other things being equal, one will display to perceiving in conflict with them. Maybe some people are more categorially flexible than others in what we might call a "technical" sense (this could be a feature of IQ associated with the innate power of imagination); but in addition to this variability, people may be more or less able (willing) to venture, despite deep commitments, beyond the perceptions with which they are emotionally comfortable.

Greater flexibility here is a feature of emotional epistemic maturity. People who are mature in this way will be better able to set aside, for purposes of perception, their personal agendas, hopes, fears, attachments, and preferences, and to see, in a hypothetical way analogous to entertaining a proposition. If Casaubon is to be really in conversation with his field, he needs not only to read the Germans, but to read the mythological texts *as* they do, to see and hear what they see and hear in the texts, to empathize with their take on the texts even when he disagrees with it. If he is so afraid of finding in them something that will refute or obviate his own work that he "deafens himself in that direction", then he is intellectually crippled in any conversation with them. Seeing and hearing outside the box of one's commitments is perhaps more difficult than entertaining propositions, because of the compelling immediacy of acquaintance. Intellectual courage is relevant to such emotional-perceptual flexibility, as is the love of truth in something like Locke's sense ("give me the truth come what may").

But mere flexibility is not firmness. Professors in the humanities are sometimes virtuosi at seeing (reading) from a variety of viewpoints without this suppleness being part of the virtue of intellectual firmness, because their flexibility is not in the service of any serious viewpoint. They simply "play" with texts and with readings thereof. They are like Brooke, but more professional, more proficient; they can talk for hours and make a lot of academic sense, with more depth than Brooke. But their depth, like Brooke's shallowness, is not "theirs". They are like Locke's reader, who by all his labors has collected the intellectual equivalent of a pile of lumber, without constructing a building.

Comprehensional rigidity   With the cases of Casaubon and the humanities professors we make a transition from the more strongly perceptual cases to cases of less perceptual understanding. There is no sharp line here, as is suggested by the fact that the kind of perception we wrote about in the preceding subsection is deeply conceptual and interpretive. Rigidity of understanding is a special kind of stupidity or learning disability, albeit one that many intellectuals suffer from; it is compatible with being well informed, and even deeply insightful, in a narrow, specialized sort of way. In colleges these days we find much concern about interdisciplinary studies and multiculturalism in the curriculum, and one of the deeper values of such studies is the flexibility of understanding that it promises to promote. In general, a liberal education aims to broaden minds as much as to deepen them, and the broadening *is* a deepening, and the deepening a broadening. The vice of narrowness shows up in chauvinisms of academic discipline, of theoretical school, of ethnic and cultural membership, of historical period. It is the inability to grasp theoretical alternatives to one's own; it is the tendency for the views from other vantage points to look stupid or infantile or uninteresting or just opaque. Comprehensionally inflexible is the Freudian who can see no value in cognitive-behavioral psychology, the analytic philosopher who can make no sense of Plato or Hegel or the Continental philosopher unable to appreciate Quine, the neuroscientist who thinks philosophers have nothing to contribute to the study of human emotions, the modern physicist who thinks that Anaximander was just stupid, the modern technologist who thinks that life in the sixteenth-century was not worth living, the nineteenth-century Anglo-American who thought blacks were uneducable, the scientist who finds an alternative paradigm not just implausible but repugnant. The virtue of firmness that we are trying to describe is a kind of intellectual sympathy, an ability to appreciate brilliance and greatness across divides of culture, theory, and time.

Our explanation of comprehensional rigidity has two aspects. On the one hand, it is a lack of acquaintance with and practice in the categories of the alien framework; on the other, it is an emotional discomfort with the alternative ways of understanding. A liberal education gives one some facility in categorial schemes different from one's own, but this can hardly be more than by way of example, given the finitude of the human mind and the usual limit of four or five years in which to accomplish the higher part of the education. The main formative effect of a liberal education has to be the inculcation of sympathy, an open and undefensive will towards alternative frameworks. This book is less about how such an education is accomplished than about what it aims to accomplish: namely, in the present discussion, the character of the intellectually firm person. Virtues are always interlaced, so that the story about one is inevitably about its connections to and dependencies on others. One virtue that underlies firmness is an intellectual adventuresomeness that works against rigidity.

Consider two paleontologists reported on by *National Geographic Magazine* (August 2002, article unpaginated). The skull of a hominid about 1.75 million years old with "huge canine teeth and thin brow [that look] too apelike for an advanced hominid" was recently found under the ruins of a medieval town called Dmanisi in the Republic of Georgia, thus challenging the widely accepted hypothesis that *Homo erectus*, a more advanced hominid than this one, was the first to leave Africa. To abandon that hypothesis would be to revise a great deal of palaeoanthropological understanding. Writing about Philip Rightmire of New York State University at Binghamton, *National Geographic* comments that "Rightmire's world has been turned upside down, and he seems almost gleeful," and then, about another scientist, that "Along with other fossils and tools found at the site, this skull reopens so many questions about our ancestry that one scientist muttered: 'They ought to put it back in the ground.'" This scientist's epistemic will seems to suffer from rigidity, while Rightmire's excitement about potential *new* understanding that this find promises seems to express intellectual adventuresomeness, provided that it is part of firmness.

Another virtue that supports comprehensional openness is a basic respect for others—the assumption that, until proved stupid, the interlocutor from another discipline or another historical period or culture is likely to have something intelligent to contribute. Generosity of spirit has a similar effect. Another supporting virtue is intellectual industriousness, a willingness to work and to keep working; the wishful fantasy of putting the skull back in the ground may express a weary lassitude. And of course the love of knowledge lies behind firmness, as behind every other intellectual virtue.

The firm person is like Socrates, who has a definite viewpoint, but at the same time is eager and open to learn, approaching each new situation with a readiness to examine his own intellectual commitments (as well as others') with the question, "What can I learn here?" rather than "Let me defend my position at all costs" or "How can I squash every objection?" It is the attitude of the perpetual student, and this attitude is a self-understanding: I do not have the final word on things; though I know a few things, my understanding is far less than it might be, and I have much to learn.

What is "hold"?

We opened this chapter by comparing the intellect, and especially the intellectual will, with a muscle which, if in optimal condition, is neither flaccid nor rigid, but firm: capable of a whole range of grips from very tight to very light. The virtue of intellectual firmness is the disposition to grip currently possessed particular intellectual goods, in the various contextual vicissitudes of the epistemically relevant passing show, with just the right degree of tightness/lightness. We must now try to determine a little more precisely what "grip" amounts to. What is it to hold onto a particular intellectual good? Our task here is more complicated than it would have been under twentieth-century epistemology, whose epistemic goods were all beliefs. To grip a belief may not be the same thing as gripping an acquaintance ("perception") or an understanding. But let us start with hold on beliefs.

Holding beliefs   Some philosophers have sought to clarify the metaphorical language of "grip",[9] "embrace", "hold", and related terms with another metaphor: "depth of assent". Assenting is then a mental act whereby we welcome some claim into our noetic structure or a dispositional attitude of hospitality towards it, and assenting comes in degrees, some beliefs being welcomed wholeheartedly while we assent to others in a halfhearted, more tentative, probationary way. John Locke, for instance, writes of

degrees of assent from full assurance and confidence, quite down to conjecture, doubt, and distrust... the mind, if it will proceed rationally, ought to examine all the grounds of probability, and see how they make more or less, for or against any proposition, before it assents to or dissents from it; and, upon a due balancing of the whole, reject or receive it, with a more or less firm assent, proportionably to the preponderancy of the greater grounds of probability on one side or the other.[10]

While Locke has a legitimate concept in mind, it is not what we would call assent. On our understanding of "assent", a "degree of assent" that amounts to doubt is not any kind of assent. Assent, as we will understand it, is a threshold concept: that is, one that becomes applicable when a threshold is reached. The threshold, as we will understand it, is of what we will call *confidence*. We posit a continuum of confidence from strong negative confidence on one end to strong positive confidence on the other. In the middle we have what we may call neutral confidence (which is really no confidence one way or the other). Confidence, not assent, comes in degrees, so that as, on the accumulation of warrant for a proposition, my confidence that that proposition is true moves from negative or neutral to positive, at a certain threshold somewhere in the positive range I am

[9] We will ignore Bayesian claims that ideally rational agents change their degree of belief in accordance with the demands of conditionalization and the axioms of probability. We doubt that agents whom we would all acknowledge to be rational conform their belief holding to such principles. For a brief and clear account of the problems confronting a Bayesian construal of hold, see Philip Kitcher, "Scientific Knowledge", in Paul K. Moser (ed.), *The Oxford Handbook of Epistemology* (Oxford: Oxford University Press, 2002), pp. 385–407, esp. pp. 393–7.

[10] John Locke, *An Essay Concerning Human Understanding*, collated and annotated by Alexander Campbell Fraser (New York: Dover Books, 1959), vol. 2, Book IV, pp. 365, 366.

assenting to the proposition. Similarly, at a certain threshold in the negative range, I am dissenting from it. Thus, one thing we might mean by "hold" is positive confidence; and the more positive our confidence of a proposition, the stronger our "hold" on it. If I do not have enough positive confidence in a proposition to assent to it, I may still hold onto it as a proposition with a certain amount of promise—that is, with a degree of hold less than assent. If my confidence drops well below the neutral point, then I let the proposition go; it no longer plays a role in my considerations. (Hereafter, when we write "confidence" we will mean positive confidence.)

Alvin Plantinga briefly mentions another possible concept of hold, which he calls "depth of ingression".

Some of my beliefs are, we might say, on the periphery of my noetic structure. I accept them, and may even accept them firmly, but could give them up without much change elsewhere in my noetic structure.[11]

Confidence is roughly the subject's dispositional probability estimate concerning the truth of a proposition, whereas depth of ingression is the degree to which giving up the belief would cause reverberations in the subject's noetic structure. A high degree of confidence can be combined with a shallow depth of ingression, and great depth of ingression can be combined with fairly low confidence. For example, I may be perfectly confident that I left my keys on the dresser, yet when I call home and my wife says the keys are actually in some jeans due for the laundry, I easily abandon the former belief because the change has little reverberation in my noetic structure (I don't worry that I'm crazy, or that the KGB sneaked my keys into the dirty laundry). Conversely, a rational choice (RC) theorist who is deeply invested in her theory, yet sees its weaknesses clearly, may have fairly weak confidence regarding its truth, yet remain committed to it, in the sense that she continues to allow it to be crucial in her noetic structure (she continues to see the social world in RC terms, and it remains fundamental to her research). Or a religious person may, at certain periods of her life, have a relatively low confidence that God exists, yet find that so much of what makes life worth living and so much of her understanding of her duties and values depends on belief in God, that she nevertheless holds strongly to the belief. Here we see that worthiness, and not merely

[11] Alvin Plantinga, "Reason and Belief in God", in Alvin Plantinga and Nicolas Wolterstorff (eds), *Faith and Rationality*, (Notre Dame, IN: University of Notre Dame Press, 1983), p. 50.

load-bearingness, contributes to depth of ingression. While confidence and depth of ingression are distinct and can vary independently of one another, they do tend to reinforce one another. Other things being equal, the more confident we are of a belief, the more ready we are to let it bear the load of other beliefs. And since depth of ingression is the degree of a belief's involvement in other beliefs of a person's noetic structure, and this involvement is largely a matter of the belief's cohering with the other beliefs in that structure, and since coherence is one source of justification, and since justification, if known, is a source of confidence, depth of ingression also typically influences confidence.

We propose that hold on beliefs is strength of confidence and depth of ingression combined in a variety of ratios; hold will tend to be indicated by the agent's behavior, epistemic and otherwise, though behavior can be misleading about hold, and in many cases the beliefs a person holds will issue in no symptomatic behavior for long periods of time. The epistemically firm person has a well-developed noetic structure—that is, a system of beliefs the most load-bearingly significant and worthy of which he holds with an appropriately strong confidence. He also has many beliefs on the periphery of this structure, which he gives up neither too easily nor too reluctantly, but in just the right way according to his canons of belief formation and retention (regarding evidence, coherence, which beliefs are properly basic, etc.).[12] These canons reside in his noetic structure. Brooke's problem is that he has an immature noetic structure. His will and mind are so formed that none of his beliefs enjoys much strength of confidence or depth of ingression (especially the latter), with the consequence that he has no framework with respect to which to adjudicate beliefs rationally. His beliefs are pretty much a hodgepodge of items that easily come and go without much rationale. Casaubon's problem is more complex. His noetic structure has a bit of a center. A central proposition is that there is a key to all mythologies, but he seems to hold this proposition with only pseudo-confidence and

---

[12] The canons of belief formation we have in mind are not those suggested by epistemological theories of justification and warrant. In Ch. 4 we argued that the theories tend to pick out one of the many legitimate modes of justification and to make that favored mode the whole story. If, instead, we attend to the actual ways in which excellent epistemic agents form their beliefs, we see that they have a variety of modes suited to the particular circumstances of belief formation, and that they apply or exemplify these modes flexibly and intelligently. The canons of belief formation are supplied not by theories but by the actual practices of the best practitioners of the academic disciplines, traditions of inquiry (such as we find in the religions, e.g.), and such practical disciplines as medicine, counseling, and law.

pseudo-ingression, so that the "structure" itself is sketchy and weak, and thus doesn't provide much wherewithal to adjudicate propositions (he ends by collecting mythological material randomly, including material that seems even to him not to belong anywhere in his project). He is sustained in the project, not by a well-formed noetic structure, but by the intellectually extrinsic factors of his egotism, vanity, envy, and fear. That the supports for whatever beliefs he does form are intellectually extrinsic largely accounts for his intellectual rigidity.

What about revisions of the noetic structure itself? Because of her maturity, the firm person will be very slow to give up parts of her noetic structure, and in any case revisions can be only in *parts* of it; responsible belief change always has some basis in belief. The noetic structure will evolve as the individual develops over time. Note that the line between the center of the noetic structure and the periphery is not sharp. Beliefs are clos*er* to or farth*er* from the periphery. The firm person is, in general, more tenacious with respect to the beliefs that are closer to the center and less so as the outer periphery is reached. But as beliefs closer to the center are revised, the canons for their revision become less definite, since the beliefs closer to the center *are* the determinants of proper revision.

Holding understanding　A mature noetic structure is a set of beliefs, understandings, and memories that is fairly consistent, at the center of which are some especially load-bearing and worthy beliefs and understandings; with maturity, a noetic structure assumes a firmer, more definite shape. Thus it can function as an interpretive schema, a framework for grasping claims and proposals, a set of explanatory connections, a basis for reading, rating, and revising reality. In its reflectively mature state, this interpretive schema is a world view, an orientation for understanding one's world and one's life and for acting. But of course understandings vary in their scope; some are understandings of the world, others are understandings of particular things. Let us distinguish, then, between an understanding of the *world*, which is a noetic structure that provides a framework for a person's character, and understandings that a person will have of this or that *aspect* of the world—of the recent war, of the Israel–Palestine conflict, of the nature of cancer, of a period of history, of a given text, etc.

The expression "hold an understanding" does not ring natural in the way "hold a belief" does; and at least one reason for this is that beliefs seem more negotiable, more the sort of thing one can accept, reject, or revise. But this is not entirely true. Lectures, books, op-ed pieces, editorials, scientific papers, are often offerings of understandings, and they bid to change their recipients' understandings of the topic in question.

Holding an understanding (as we are using this odd locution) can be distinguished from having an understanding. This distinction helps us to understand firmness. When a noetic structure is a *world* view, it is more fundamental than an understanding of something in particular, though we can often discern how the latter is grounded in the former. A person with a Marxist understanding of the world is likely to have a different understanding of the Israel–Palestine conflict than someone with an Islamic understanding of the world. *Holding* a Marxist understanding of the Israel–Palestine conflict differs from merely *having* an understanding of it. To hold an understanding in this sense is to inhabit it, to live one's life in its terms. It is a disposition to repudiate incompatible understandings. Thus it is associated with believing the propositions that are grasped in the understanding. By contrast, merely to *have* an understanding is just to see how it goes, to see what the implications are, within the understanding in question. It is to be able to say what a Marxist is likely to say about such-and-such a situation in Palestine, by virtue of knowing what a Marxist is likely to say about situations like that. One can *have* many incompatible understandings: nothing is to keep one from having both an Islamic and a Marxist understanding, as well as a Nazi understanding and a Christian understanding of something, while a mature person would *hold* only one of these (or some one syncretism of more than one of them). Firmness is abetted, and not violated, by such flexibility of *having* understandings. To be unable to understand points of view that are not one's own is an intellectual deficit, if not a vice. Such inability is the rigidity and narrowness that we called comprehensional rigidity above; it is more often attributable to emotional immaturity than to a lack of basic cognitive talent. Firmness also requires holding an understanding. This statement applies primarily to the most fundamental and basic kind of understanding, the world view; we all necessarily fail to have understandings of more particular items such as the Israel–Palestine conflict, although if we have no particular understandings at all, we must have some defect of cognitive character. But to fail to hold an understanding of the world is to fall short of excellent character, intellectual and otherwise.

So what is "hold" as regards understandings? In relation to beliefs, we said that hold is strength of confidence and depth of ingression in varying ratios. Likewise, hold on a world view involves confidence, depth of ingression, and thus the disposition to live out that understanding consistently over a fairly extended period of time and through the historical vicissitudes that naturally attend the passage of time. It will also involve a certain amount of reflective awareness of the world view and a willingness to endorse it—perhaps not wholesale, since the mature individual will be aware that his world view is likely to have some kinks in it—but in a rough and general way. Hold on an understanding of a particular aspect of the world will be a disposition to endorse it, at least in a rough and general way, spontaneously to see that aspect of the world in its terms, and so to act. Clearly, holding an understanding is not a purely "cognitive" matter, but equally a matter of the will, of how one cares about what is understood and cares to understand it. It should be clear that we view a person's noetic structure as subject to development, culminating in one that is rich and reflectively endorsed.

To be intellectually firm is thus to be very conservative in the holding of one's noetic structure, to be resistant to change in it because it has been well formed. It is not to be utterly impervious to change, though as we noted in relation to beliefs, the change cannot be of the whole noetic structure, but only of parts of it; any change of understanding depends on understanding something, on epistemically "standing" somewhere. The firm person is very open, however, to changing particular understandings of things, compatibly with his world view. He may argue hard for his own particular understandings but he is quick to admit that an interlocutor has a better understanding as soon as he is convinced of this; and the openness and catholicity of the understandings that he *has* (as contrasted with *holds*) make him quick to access better understandings when they are presented.

As regards *having* understanding, no such conservatism characterizes firmness. The intellectually firm individual is practiced and open at grasping, and eager to grasp, alien viewpoints. She is quick to exercise her empathic imagination to "get inside" other viewpoints, to understand them. Because she is well established in her own basic viewpoint, she is not afraid to understand opposing viewpoints deeply, and is even disposed to think that she can deepen her own noetic structure by gaining sympathetic insights into alien outlooks. The openness of firmness is particularly evident in this dimension of the orientation towards understanding.

Holding acquaintance We have argued (Chapter 2) for a three-dimensional concept of knowledge. Besides our beliefs and understandings, our know-ledge is constituted by our acquaintance—that is, perception or experience of things. But what would it be to hold acquaintance, to be able (or unable) to grasp it tightly enough, or to be disposed to hang onto it too long or too tightly? Beliefs and understandings are both dispositions, and dispositions can be maintained, lost or abandoned, or retained in modification. But acquaintance, being episodic by nature, does not seem subject to these operations. Yet we do have perceptual dispositions, and to some extent we can preserve and recall perceptions through memory. Perhaps perceptual dispositions can be held onto or relinquished, and memories can be accessed or revised or given new significance or allowed to fade, in much the way that we can retain our beliefs and understandings of things, or modify or relinquish them.

As we argued in Chapter 2, the three dimensions of knowledge are intimately intertwined. We could not have beliefs if we had no under-standings or acquaintances; nor could we understand anything if we had no beliefs or acquaintances, and our acquaintances are conditioned by our beliefs and understandings. So the hold that we have on our perceptual dispositions is a matter of the hold that we have on the other dimensions of knowledge. Our dispositions to see (say, in biological or historical terms, microscopic animals or antiquities) and to hear (say, in reading texts or in listening to courtroom testimony) are conditioned by our beliefs and understandings concerning the matter in question, and so our hold on these perceptual dispositions is largely a matter of the dynamism of our conviction and the depth of ingression of our beliefs, and of the having and holding of understandings. The degree of development of our noetic structure, in itself and in relation to our will, determines our hold on ways of perceiving. What we see and hear changes with our development as cognitive agents, and the firm flexibility of our perceiving is a matter of the firm flexibility of our believing and understanding.

Still, perception has its own dynamism. Perceptual hold can determine understanding and belief formation. One must *practice* perceiving in such fields as music, literature, history, biology, astronomy; one can develop one's "eyes" and "ears" (not to mention one's "touch" and one's "palate") in such a way that they are firmly and deeply patterned in what they perceive, and yet are also flexible and open to the unusual and unexpected and what does not quite conform to previous belief and understanding. One can control perception through looking, listening, trying to see and hear, trying this or that way of seeing or hearing, using one's imagination, calling this or that fact to mind and applying it to what is before one. One can be stubborn in seeing or hearing in one way or another; one can be willful and grind an axe in perception as well as in argument and interpretation. One can be intelligent and rational in perceptual activities and efforts, firmly grounded in a noetic structure and yet flexible within that structure. The excellent epistemic agent has this flexible perceptual firmness, so that in her, perceptual excellence can drive excellence of belief and understanding as much as flexibly firm belief and understanding drive perception.

8

Courage and Caution

Introduction

A virtue is an acquired base of excellent functioning in some generically human sphere of activity that is challenging and important. Examples of such spheres are the interpersonal, the political/civic, and the intellectual. The spheres intersect and interact; many intellectual activities are interpersonal, as we saw in Chapter 5, and intellectual excellences deeply affect our interpersonal and political practices. Virtues fit us in a diversity of ways to function well in such spheres of human life. Some virtues supply the needed motivation, others fit us to negotiate, with finesse, generic parameters of the sphere in question, while still others fit us to address obstacles and impediments to proper action, both internal and external to ourselves. A virtue must be tailored to both human nature and the nature of the activity it promotes.

Chapter 6 was our first extended analysis of an intellectual virtue, and we found that the love of knowledge is a maturity of the human will with respect to a generically human good—knowledge—whose value is deeply involved with human well-being and the values of the things that may be known. It mainly supplies the peculiar motivation needed for excellent intellectual functioning. The virtuous knower loves knowledge within a variety of discriminations, and thus has an intelligently tuned epistemic will. In Chapter 7 we argued that firmness is a virtue because of two very general features of the intellectual life of human beings: that our knowledge necessarily builds on previously formed beliefs, understandings, and experiences, yet the practices by which we acquire knowledge always carry within them the potential for something new, something requiring adjustment to those very beliefs, understandings, and experiences without which we could not intelligently sort through the new. Firmness fits us to negotiate well the pervasive fact that the acquisition of higher-level knowledge depends both on holding steadily to our understandings, beliefs, and perceptual dispositions and on relinquishing or adjusting them in the face of cognitive vicissitudes. It is a finely tuned disposition to negotiate intelligently, in the concrete circumstances of the life of the mind, these two generic features of the human epistemic situation.

The present chapter is about courage and caution in the intellectual life. In general, courage and caution enable us to find our way among the threats, real and apparent, that we encounter in the course of our practices, sometimes circumventing these threats, sometimes facing them, and sometimes paying their price. When the practice in question is intellectual (research, teaching, investigative reporting, etc.), courage and caution are intellectual virtues. Like other human activities, intellectual ones are fraught with threats—pitfalls, dangers, and difficulties—both apparent and real. The real threats must be respected, yet not allowed to deter the agent from the pursuit of the intellectual goods. The merely apparent ones must be assessed as such, and the resulting fears well managed. In intellectual activities, the threatening harms are often intellectual harms. Let us say that a threat is a potential harm with a fairly high probability of being actual or possibly with a low probability of being actual in case the potential harm is very great. Some threats are obtrusive, obvious, and overt, and some of the most obtrusive are only apparent; others, though real, are stealthy and hidden. Fear and anxiety are emotions whereby we perceive situations as threatening. Sometimes fear needs to be honored or even cultivated; sometimes it needs to be mitigated or expunged, circumvented or transcended. The dynamics and axiology of fear are a fact of life in intellectual practices, and the intellectually courageous and cautious person is one in whom that dynamics and axiology are *right*.

Courage and caution each have two vice counterparts. The vices corresponding to courage are cowardice and recklessness; those corresponding to caution are recklessness and scrupulosity. We will expound courage and caution by examining each of the vice counterparts. But first, let us consider the question of motivation as it pertains to courage and caution.

Motivation

In connection with courage, motivation comes up in two ways: There is the motivation that stands behind the virtue of courage as the characteristic (for the agent) motivation for courageous actions; but there is also the motivation that challenges the virtue, so to speak, and may be overcome or circumvented or transcended in or by the courageous action. This competing or resisting motivation is fear and its cognates: anxiety, terror, fright, dread. In paradigm cases of courageous action, the agent feels some of this kind of emotion, and the emotion offers a resistance to performing the action. The action gets the title of courageous because in performing it the agent overcomes this resistance created by fear.

In contrast, the motivation that stands behind the courageous action is not so definitely specifiable. Aristotle says that the courageous person must aim at "the noble" (*Nicomachean Ethics* 1115^{b}12), but this does not seem right. A person *may* act courageously in the interest of the noble—say, out of concern that justice be done, or out of love for someone, or patriotism. But his motive may be self-interested: perhaps he acts courageously in an effort to forward his career or to make money; or his motive may even be evil, as is that of the suicide bomber who gives his life in the cause of hatred. In holding that courageous acts must be motivated by the noble, Aristotle seems to confuse acting from *a* virtue (courage) with acting overall virtuously. A person who is able to face down his fears so as to perform acts that, of their kind, are well done (whether these be acts of patriotism or of theft) displays a generically human excellence—mastery of his fears. If we distinguish acting with aplomb in the face of fears from acting overall virtuously, we may properly admire the ability to act with aplomb in the face of fears even when it is misused. So courageous actions need not be overall virtuous; they are virtuous *insofar as* they are courageous, since courage is a virtue; but to be overall virtuous, they need to be motivated by some virtuous motive. And this will mean that some virtue other than courage has to motivate the courageous action: justice, compassion, generosity, love of knowledge.

In paradigm cases the agent who exhibits courage feels some fear, anxiety, etc. and then acts with aplomb despite the fear. But we insist on the qualifier, "in paradigm cases". A person who has repeatedly faced down fear and thus become courageous may have become fearless in some of the circumstances in which he acts courageously. Despite the absence of actual fear, we still call him courageous, for at least two reasons. First, he has *achieved* fearlessness in this kind of circumstance *by* facing perceived threats on earlier occasions. He carries the achievement with him into the new circumstance, and so we attribute the new action to the virtue. An essential condition of the virtue—courage's relation to fear—can be met without that condition being met in every action in which the virtue is exemplified, because the trait carries the relation to fear in its history. Second, the circumstance is the kind in which many or most people *would* feel fear. It is a circumstance in which the agent risks some significant harm or loss.

We also said that the fear "may be overcome or circumvented or transcended in or by the courageous action". Sometimes one feels fear or anxiety before undertaking the action, but once the action is under way the fear is effectively sidelined by the concentration of mind and the implementing sub-actions required for the performance. The hump to get over in this kind of case is to move into action despite the fear, and repeated successes at this strategy "encourage" a person, making him more likely to act boldly in the future. They create in him a *disposition* to act in the face of fear. A person may even acquire something of a taste for this, a kind of pleasure of competition in defeating fear, the potential defeater. By "success" we do not mean that the goal of the courageous action is achieved, but that the act is in some sense brought to completion or has proceeded far enough to show that the fear did not overcome it; in some degree of performance the fear has been successfully faced down. If, in addition, the action succeeds in its goal, this is perhaps an added encouragement. Sometimes the fear is not so much charged into as softened up a bit by some mental strategy so that it will be easier to deal with. A person may succeed in using rational techniques to mitigate his fear: "Come now, what's the worst that can happen to me if I face this audience and simply speak the truth?" "I have survived this kind of thing before." "Tomorrow I'm going to be very glad I did this, and if I don't do it, I'll be miserable." Such preparation can make it easier to charge into the threatening situation. Or, rather than addressing the fear directly, the agent may heighten his sense of "calling" by reminding himself of the importance of his undertaking. "Look how much will be gained if I succeed, and how little lost if I fail." And this concentration on the value of the goal may itself mitigate the fear somewhat.

We have denied that any single motivational pattern is characteristic of courage, but we do not deny that an individual *person's* courageous actions will have a characteristic motivational pattern. The idea of characteristic motivation is fundamental to the idea of a virtuous person. Thus some courageous people will be characteristically moved by considerations of justice, of compassion, and so forth. And among such possible motivations is the one that is special to the intellectually virtuous person, the love of knowledge. The intellectually courageous person will be good at acting with aplomb in the interest of significant propositional knowledge, acquaintance, and understanding for himself and others, in face of the perceived hazards of life. What are typical fears that the intellectually courageous person overcomes? We sometimes fear knowledge—for example, self-knowledge, knowledge of criticisms of our pet views, and especially of our own works, and knowledge of facts that are painful to us. We fear others disagreeing with us; we fear challenges to our views; we fear looking bad in front of our colleagues and students. We fear being harmed in the course of intellectual practices—say, being beaten up by a playful chimpanzee or infected with a disease in the course of experimentation with microbes.

What about caution? We treat caution in the same chapter as courage because both virtues are dispositions with respect to fear, though they are differently related to it. If courage is a disposition to mitigate, circumvent, or transcend fears, caution is a disposition to cultivate, refine, and listen to one's fears. It is a disposition of fine-tuning to the hazards in one's environment—social, intellectual, physical—and thus of a *proper* anxiety. To adapt Aristotle's way of thinking about virtues, caution is the disposition to fear the right things, at the right time, for the right reasons, and in the right degree. If this sounds reminiscent of Aristotle's account of courage, it is because Aristotle rolls courage and caution into one virtue and calls them courage (see *Nicomachean Ethics* $1115^a7–1116^a15$). Intellectual caution, like intellectual courage, has its background in the love of knowledge. Intellectually cautious actions are ones that are performed in the course of intellectual practices, and the intellectual practices, when practiced most virtuously, are motivated by the love of knowledge. So the fears most characteristic of intellectual caution are fears that express the love of knowledge—fear of believing falsehoods, of misunderstanding a text or a theory, of failing to see something important, of misleading someone, of damaging our cognitive powers; or fear of one's own dispositions that may undermine epistemic performance—laziness, impatience, boredom, or headlong passionate interest (for example, in making the world safe for atheism, or in showing that virtue epistemology is the wave of the future). But, as we saw in Chapter 6, the virtuous love of knowledge cannot be divorced from a concern for the human well-being to which it contributes and an appreciation of the value of the things that are known; so intellectual caution is expressed also in fears of harms and losses that are connected with intellectual goods without themselves being intellectual harms or losses—fear of injustice or medical disaster that may be occasioned by false judgment or misunderstanding, fear of dangerous and useless military entanglements that may come from bad military intelligence, fear of damaging the environment or experimental subjects in the course of experimentation, fear of creating, by acquired knowledge, threats to human well-being or the well-being of nature, fear of psychological or moral damage that may attend epistemic practice (for example, intimate subjective acquaintance with the mind of a sadist).

One can in a sense be intellectually cautious when one's fear is generated by a concern for goods external to intellectual practices. For example, one might be cautious about the quality of the evidence for one's claims, not out of fear of having insufficiently supported beliefs, but out of fear of getting a bad intellectual reputation or missing the money promised by epistemic success. This is still intellectual caution inasmuch as it is caution with respect to evidence, but it is not the most distinctively intellectual kind of caution. We can acknowledge an analogously secondary kind of intellectual courage: a disposition to master the fears characteristic of intellectual contexts, out of desire not for the intellectual goods, but for goods extrinsic to intellectual practices: reputation, money, power.

Just as the courageous person need not experience fear in every courageous action, so the cautious person need not feel an outright emotion of fear every time he exemplifies caution. When we say that the intellectually cautious person fears making mistakes, we cover cases in which, without actual episodic fear, he is aware or semi-aware of the dangers that would loom if he didn't take sufficient care in his cognitive conduct, and he acts so as to avoid these threats to his and others' intellectual and non-intellectual well-being.

The best sort of intellectual caution and the best sort of intellectual courage are united in their common dependence on the love of knowledge; they can and should be co-present in the personality. Let us now put some flesh on these skeletons. We will conduct our analysis of courage and caution by looking at their three vice counterparts.

Cowardice

In our discussion of self-knowledge in Chapter 4 we cited the case of the brave Nicias who lets Socrates cross-examine him, knowing full well that the examination will be painful. It will be painful because it will expose shortcomings in Nicias's character and actions. To face these shortcomings is humiliating enough in itself, but to do so in the context of a dialogue with five participants is all the more so. Nicias counts the cost and judges the benefit to be worth it: "he who does not fly from reproof will be sure to take more heed of his afterlife" (*Laches* 188b). The benefit of the increased self-knowledge is greater control over one's conduct in the future, the possibility of a self-vigilance by which one may eventually become a better person, a better citizen, a better parent and friend. Nicias is alive to the tendency in himself and others to fly from reproof. Those who regularly fly in obedience to this bad fear are cowards, and they pay the price in deficit of self-knowledge and its consequences for quality of life. This fear needs to be overcome, because it deters one from the good, and because it presents as harmful what is really beneficial. In some comments on self-examination, Robert Nozick agrees with Nicias.

The understanding gained in examining a life itself comes to permeate that life and direct its course. To live an examined life is to make a self-portrait. Staring out at us from his later self-portraits, Rembrandt is not simply someone who looks like that but one who also sees and knows himself as that, with the courage this requires. We see him knowing himself. And he unflinchingly looks out at us too who are seeing him look so unflinchingly at himself, and that look of his not only shows himself to us so knowing, it patiently waits for us too to become with equal honesty knowing of ourselves.[1]

---

[1] Robert Nozick, *The Examined Life* (New York: Simon & Schuster, 1989), pp. 12–13.

Nicias "faces himself" in the Socratic cross-examination. The metaphor suggests a perceptual intimacy, something more than mere justified true belief, something like a confrontation with an emotionally charged object which is himself. And here we have Nozick exploiting the metaphor even more explicitly and illustrating with the literally visual case of the painter who makes a visible image of himself and then faces it, perhaps daily examining himself in the image that he has made of himself. But Nozick also refers here to understanding, and this is especially appropriate to the kind of self-portrait that *he* is making, for his book consists of a series of essays in which he works out and examines his own mind on a variety of topics relating to the meaning and value that living has for him. The whole book will be an (expression of an) understanding of himself, and the exercise will require him to be brave in the interest of honesty, and honest in the interest of knowledge. He wants to know himself, to understand himself, to see himself as he is, and thus to become a somewhat different and better self, by the addition of this disorienting and reorienting self-knowledge. Heinrich Heine is supposed to have said that writers of confessions are *eo ipso* liars, and if this accusation is a bit too harsh, it is testimony at least to the ubiquity of fear and the incidence of cowardice when it comes to this especially touchy kind of knowledge.

In academic circles cowardice often undermines the quality of intellectual life by engendering failures to grasp opportunities for stimulation and growth. Discomfort with being outshone by peers is nearly universal among human beings, for whom status is so important and among whom relative professional performance is such a large determiner of status. Just about the only conditions in which this discomfort is not felt are those in which no intimidating colleagues are in near proximity. In the rare case, this condition is achieved by being so competent oneself that almost no colleague anywhere would outshine one; but usually it is met by not giving the superior much sustained opportunity to be in near proximity—hence the disposition of many academic departments to hire colleagues who will not make them look too bad. Such acquiescence in ignoble fears can cause stagnation in understanding, information, and acquaintance. One might attribute such failure to grasp opportunities to lack of love for knowledge as much as to intellectual cowardice, but the two walk hand in hand down the path of mediocrity. Were I braver, I could express my love of knowledge, thus confirming and deepening it; and if I were more enthusiastic about knowledge, I would be more strongly motivated to overcome my fears. Either virtue might break the cycle of mediocrity and promote the other virtue. Hidden in the history of academic departments that made a transition to greater excellence are, it is plausible to think, virtues such as courage, humility, and the love of knowledge. A related cowardice is that of the philosopher so scrupulous about protecting himself against refutation that he convolutes his formulas with multiple and involved qualifications that render his written and spoken discourse a monstrosity of vacuous and incomprehensible ass-covering.

Another example of cowardice impeding the acquisition of knowledge is the college president discussed in Chapter 5. Out of fear created by a university ethos of political correctness, he fails to put into the public forum all sides of the debate over the strategic value of divestiture in South African industry, thus reducing the probable level of understanding of the issues, university-wide. Often, courage is especially crucial to the acquisition of new knowledge. The reader will remember the example of Jane Goodall, who put herself at considerable risk day after day in the mountain forests of Gombe to learn new things about chimpanzees. In this case, the knowledge that cost the scientist courage is available to us, risk-free, in her books.

Recklessness

Acts of courage are typically goal-oriented. In acting, the courageous person does not overcome fear just for the sake of triumphing over *it*.[2] The courageous department members who hire an intimidating new colleague aim at improving the intellectual life of the department and the quality of the students' education. Goodall wants to know more about the ways of the chimps; the college president wants to promote understanding of the issues that connect South African investment with apartheid; Nozick wants to understand himself better, to become a more mature and wiser person.

Because the goal guides the deliberation or other intelligence going into the action, the really virtuous agent will not run unnecessary risks. We would think something wrong with a department that hired a new candidate

---

[2] Some cases of holding up under torture or facing inevitable death might be exceptions; in such cases perhaps the only goal is to face down fear, to preserve one's own integrity through the ordeal.

just because he was incredibly fearsome and presented a challenge to the department's ability not to self-destruct, or a Goodall who subjected herself indiscriminately to the dangers of the forest. Courage is not recklessness, and the courageous person is typically cautious. Because he is brave, the perceived prospect of harm does not master him, but he does take it intelligently into account. He wants to minimize the potential harm. Before we consider some cases of recklessness, we remind the reader that the love of knowledge is not an indiscriminate enthusiasm for knowledge. Knowledge can be trivial, irrelevant, or unworthy, and the virtuous lover of knowledge seeks knowledge that may have its proper place among the larger range of human goods, both epistemic and non-epistemic. Also, because the value of knowledge is tied up with the value of its objects and the human well-being in which it is involved, there will be no sharp line distinguishing intellectual from non-intellectual harms.

In "The Joker in the Pack"[3] W. H. Auden discusses Iago's treatment of Othello. Analysts of Shakespeare's play confess that it presents an enigma concerning Iago's motives for insinuating Desdemona's treachery and posing questions that so inflame Othello's jealousy that he murders Desdemona. S. T. Coleridge, despairing of an answer, simply refers to Iago's "motiveless malignity". Auden offers the fascinating suggestion that Iago is experimenting on Othello, baiting him to take the measure of his character.

Iago's treatment of Othello conforms to Bacon's definition of scientific enquiry as putting Nature to the Question. If a member of the audience were to interrupt the play and ask him: "What are you doing?" could not Iago answer with a boyish giggle, "Nothing. I'm only trying to find out what Othello is really like." And we must admit that his experiment is highly successful. (p. 271)

Auden points out that we are in no position to criticize Iago for his reckless disregard of the harm to Othello and Desdemona that he risks in his "scientific" inquiry, because we too have "accepted the notion that the right to know is absolute and unlimited. The gossip column is one side of the medal; the cobalt bomb the other" (ibid.). Knowledge needs to be pursued with caution, a restraining survey of possible collateral damage. There is nothing intrinsically wrong with Iago's knowing the

---

[3] W. H. Auden, "The Joker in the Pack", in *The Dyer's Hand* (New York: Vintage International, 1989), pp. 246–72.

counterfactual *If Othello were subjected to stresses x, y, and z, his loyalty to Desdemona would be broken*; if a clinical psychologist has analogous knowledge, it is not to her discredit (though one does wonder what business it is of *Iago's* to know this truth; the psychologist might be justified by her prospects of applying the knowledge in marriage therapy). But it is horribly wrong to risk the destruction of Othello and Desdemona for the sake of learning such a truth. Iago's recklessness in experimentation is a deficit of fear: were he virtuous, he would fear the transparently likely consequences of his experimentation and would be deterred from it. Iago exemplifies not only intellectual recklessness, but also a vicious concern to know (see Chapter 6); for the knowledge he seeks, on Auden's interpretation of the play, is knowledge that can be, for him in his roles and circumstances, nothing but voyeuristic. Even if his research method did not constitute reckless endangerment of the subjects, the research itself would be vicious.

A recent example is an American television program called Temptation Island, which takes engaged couples to a luxurious island setting where beautiful actors and actresses entice the couples to cheat on one another. Everything is engineered to put the couple's fidelity to the test—and for the cameras to be on hand to capture the betrayals and breakups. In one respect this epistemic practice is even more appalling than Auden's example, for these Hollywood Iagos are abetted by couples who recklessly put themselves in harm's way. They will discover truths about themselves that moral and prudential considerations tell us should never have been put into question. Both the couples and the programmers exhibit a lack of proper fear. Of course, some of the couples may go into the experiment with some trepidation for their relationship; perhaps they overcome their fears in the interest of the money or glamour they gain by participating in the show. In such cases it may require something like courage for them to participate. We do want to allow that such cases can qualify as courageous, but the courage in this case would not be intellectual, since the couples themselves are not engaged in a primarily epistemic activity; they are going for the money or glamour. And we would say that, despite their courage, these people show a lack of caution, practical wisdom, and proper fear. They are reckless despite their courage.[4]

---

[4] Since Aristotle does not distinguish caution from courage, he could not allow this combination.

Consider now some remarks by Richard Rorty in which he ironically numbers himself among the heirs of Socrates. (We suspect that in the present case Rorty's irony is unintentional.)

It seems to me that the regulative idea that we heirs of the Enlightenment, we Socratists, most frequently use to criticize the conduct of various conversational partners is that of needing education in order to outgrow their primitive fear, hatreds, and superstitions. ... It is a concept which I, like most Americans who teach humanities or social science in colleges and universities, invoke when we try to arrange things so that students who enter as bigoted, homophobic, religious fundamentalists will leave college with views more like our own. ... The fundamentalist parents of our fundamentalist students think that the entire "American liberal establishment" is engaged in a conspiracy. The parents have a point. Their point is that we liberal teachers no more feel in a symmetrical communication situation when we talk with bigots than do kindergarten teachers talking with their students. ... You have to be educated ... to be ... a participant in our conversation. ... So we are going to go right on trying to discredit you in the eyes of your children, trying to strip your fundamentalist religious community of dignity, trying to make your views seem silly rather than discussable. ... I don't see anything *herrschaftsfrei* [characterized by a reckless use of authority] about my handling of my fundamentalist students. Rather, I think those students are lucky to find themselves under the benevolent *Herrshaft* [domination] of people like me, and to have escaped the grip of their frightening, vicious, dangerous parents. ... I am just as provincial and contextualist as the Nazi teachers who made their students read *Der Stürmer*; the only difference is that I serve a better cause.[5]

Rorty's comments smack of stereotyping, especially if one heeds Alvin Plantinga's suggestion that "fundamentalist" is an indexical expression meaning roughly "a person whose religious views are somewhat to the right of my own". Stereotyping is often one of the poisonous fruits of intellectual recklessness, combined with lack of charity. Rorty's unrestraint seems especially surprising, given his views about the contingency of everybody's final vocabulary and his recommendation that we all take an ironic stance toward our own final vocabulary. Such a view and such a recommendation would surely suggest caution about dismissing out of hand the views of people one disagrees with, labeling people who have reared children capable of being admitted to Stanford or the

---

[5] Richard Rorty, "Universality and Truth", in Robert B. Brandom (ed.), *Rorty and his Critics* (Oxford: Basil Blackwell, 2000), pp. 21–2.

University of Virginia as "frightening, vicious, dangerous parents", and taking towards their children an attitude of undialogical indoctrinating domination. Stereotyping is an activity characteristic of people who are prejudiced against members of minority groups, so it is further surprising to find Rorty engaging in this kind of intellectual recklessness, which of all kinds is perhaps the most universally recognized, in academic circles, as intellectually vicious.

We who teach philosophy know that some of our students will experience cognitive dissonance, maybe even distress, on having their cherished convictions cross-examined philosophically. But truth, intellectual maturity, and self-understanding are more important than their momentary discomfort, and so we counsel courage for them and solicitude, engaged gentleness, and a listening ear for ourselves. Our hope is to help them overcome their intellectual timidity, to get the upper hand of their fears and their preference for the comfortable and convenient. Our recommendations of courage, however, are not just compatible with, but require us to be cautiously concerned for, their intellectual psyches. Throwing them in harm's way unprepared is not the best recipe for fostering intellectual courage. Rather, by being cautious about their fears, we make it more likely that they will develop a wise courage. One can be philosophically rigorous while at the same time an empathetic listener and a constructive rather than a merely iconoclastic critic—overall someone who reassures students that their flourishing is our goal, in terms that connect with their own understandings.

Another of the ironies of Rorty's approach is its variance from his view that cruelty is one of the worst things we do to each other. In his essay "Orwell on Cruelty", Rorty examines how the rupture of self-understanding can result in the disintegration of the self. In George Orwell's 1984, O'Brien's torture of Winston involves systematically breaking Winston by making him believe that two plus two equals five. Rorty notes that the belief's falsity is not crucial to the torture. "If there were a *truth*, belief in which would break Winston, making him believe that *truth* would be just as good for O'Brien's purposes."[6] According to Rorty, the torture renders Winston's world incoherent by shattering his conception of himself. The

---

[6] Richard Rorty, "Orwell on Cruelty", in *Contingency, Solidarity, and Irony* (Cambridge: Cambridge University Press, 1989), p. 178.

worst thing you can do to someone, says Rorty, is to get her to "believe and desire things, think thoughts—which later she will be unable to cope with having done or thought" (ibid.). O'Brien brings Winston to the point where he says of himself,

"Now that I have believed or desired this, I can never be what I hope to be, what I thought I was. The story I have been telling myself about myself—my picture of myself as honest, or loyal, or devout—no longer makes sense. I no longer have a self to make sense of. There is no world in which I can picture myself as living, because there is no vocabulary in which I can tell a coherent story about myself." (ibid.)

Charles Taylor provides insight into how a revision of beliefs can undermine one's psychological well-being by dismantling one's self-understanding.

To know who I am is a species of knowing where I stand. My identity is defined by the commitments and identifications which provide the frame or horizon within which I can try to determine from case to case what is good, or valuable, or what ought to be done, or what I endorse or oppose. In other words, it is the horizon within which I am capable of taking a stand.[7]

Thomas Kuhn mentions numerous examples of disorientation that scientists feel amidst paradigm shifts and quotes Albert Einstein as saying, "It is as though the ground had been pulled out from under one, with no firm foundation to be seen anywhere upon which one could have built."[8] Surprisingly, Rorty seems not to appreciate the identity-constituting, orientation-giving role that religious beliefs often have for people, and thus the harm that may be done to them by changing so rapidly "the coherent story" the student tells about himself.

The kind of caution that is needed in contexts where the beliefs affected by the teacher's discourse provide personal grounding for the student stems from an awareness of the student's fragility, combined with a concern for his or her full education as a person. The goal of full education we contrast with the single-minded, and thus recklessly uncircumspect, pursuit of straightening out the student's beliefs; it treats the student as a developing person, and not just as a seat of beliefs that display one degree or another

---

[7] Charles Taylor, *Sources of the Self: The Making of the Modern Identity* (Cambridge, MA: Harvard University Press, 1989), p. 27.

[8] Albert Einstein, quoted in Thomas Kuhn, *The Structure of Scientific Revolutions*, 2nd edn. (Chicago: University of Chicago Press, 1970), p. 83.

of congruence or incongruence with the teacher's noetic structure. This kind of caution is made of the kind of psychological insight voiced by Taylor, and charity towards the student. Without this concern for the student's deeper, more general well-being, the teacher will not be subject to the fears that constitute caution in this context. Since the teacher too is a whole person, who may be appalled and offended—possibly even threatened—by the student's views, he must be ready to set aside his own perhaps impetuous disgust in the interest of gentle, generous, and respectful dialogue. Socrates' irony, though certainly aimed at the revision of the interlocutor's noetic structure, exemplified this kind of respectful caution.

Here is another area in which philosophy teachers would do well to exemplify caution. The dialectic of many introductory courses in ethics runs the risk that, as Bernard Williams says, "reflection might destroy knowledge".[9] The knowledge we have in mind is a kind of acquaintance, and it is high up on the worthiness scale. A student has received a moral upbringing in which he has not only been taught moral principles (propositional knowledge of ethics), but been nurtured in the associated impressions (a kind of acquaintance with the truth of those principles). He knows that deceiving other people for gain and convenience is wrong, and this knowledge is manifest in his feelings of repugnance for such actions. This student signs up for Ethics 101. A significant portion of the curriculum is the ethical theories that originated in the modern period, theories that attempt to find the conceptual basis for principles like the one about deceiving other people for gain and convenience. The gist of the part of the course that deals with these theories is that none of them succeeds in establishing the basis for the principles. But the "problem" to which the theories were supposed to be answers is treated as a serious problem—one so serious, indeed, that if one does not have an answer to it, the legitimacy of the moral principles is left in doubt. At the end of the course, the student will have been taught two things: (1) the principle that deceiving others for gain and convenience is wrong is in doubt unless we can find a rational basis for it; (2) all the exceedingly smart people who have tried to find a rational basis for it have failed. The result of the

---

[9] Bernard Williams, *Ethics and the Limits of Philosophy* (Cambridge, MA: Harvard University Press, 1985), p. 167.

semester's reflection about "ethics" is a weakened repugnance for actions in which one person deceives another for gain and convenience. Reflection has destroyed (or at least weakened) knowledge. The professor who fears this outcome, and thus the dialectical process that threatens to produce it, exemplifies a virtuous intellectual caution.

Practices of investigation sometimes put the investigator himself in the way of harm, especially from the kind of knowledge that we have called acquaintance. Becoming empathically acquainted with the mind of a serial killer or sadist would risk the investigator's well-being, and not to appreciate the danger or not to know how to guard against it may amount to intellectual recklessness. In his preface to the *Screwtape Letters*, C. S. Lewis comments autobiographically about the strain he experienced from duplicating in imagination the diabolical attitude the text expresses.

Though I had never written anything more easily, I never wrote with less enjoyment. ... though it was easy to twist one's mind into the diabolical attitude, it was not fun, or not for long. The strain produced a sort of spiritual cramp. The world into which I had to project myself while I spoke through Screwtape was all dust, grit, thirst and itch. Every trace of beauty, freshness and geniality had to be excluded. It almost smothered me before I was done.[10]

For this reason, and despite numerous requests, Lewis refused to write a sequel to his highly popular book. His comment shows him to be a stranger to neither intellectual courage nor caution. He was sufficiently aware of himself to see early on the psychic toll the book would exact, but he persisted so that his readers might benefit from his work. Yet he also knew that he should not do so again.

We have sometimes wondered whether Roald Dahl's children's stories, which so often depict sadistic delights in a seductively humorous way that causes the reader, following Dahl, to indulge gratuitously delicious pleasures of empathic vengeance, are not reckless in a way quite foreign to Lewis's wise restraint. The stories do deliver some epistemic goods: in particular, personal acquaintance with the sadistic pleasures of revenge and the *potential* for serious reflections about one's own disposition to take such pleasure. But the serious reflections are not encouraged by the stories, so the artful facilitation of this kind of knowledge in children seems reckless.

---

[10] C. S. Lewis, *The Screwtape Letters* (San Francisco: HarperSanFrancisco, 2000), p. 183.

Scrupulosity

We have been commending intellectual caution, because there really are dangers out there which are best avoided; and we have been saying that a proper fear disposition, in which harms are wisely assessed and carefully circumvented, is a virtue. But another kind of "caution" exaggerates perils or sees harms where there are none. We judge as neurotic people who, after having made the usual efforts to secure their house before leaving on a trip, can't drive down the block before returning, perhaps many times, to check whether the iron is off, the faucets shut, the windows locked. We call this disposition scrupulosity. It is a vice counterpart of caution, because, mimicking caution, it is an acquired disposition to have exaggerated or misplaced fears. It can be a cognitive dysfunction, because it can degrade our ability to acquire and pass on intellectual goods.

A paradigm kind of intellectual scrupulosity is perfectionism. Consider the super-bright philosophy student who as an undergraduate was the best student that many of his professors had taught in their entire careers. He was admitted to the top Ph.D. program in the country. Because of his incisive mind, and because of the nature of philosophy, he found that for anything he wrote, he himself could think of powerful objections. Because he insisted on producing the highest-quality work, he was unable to finish the papers for his courses, and flunked out in the first year. The result: a talented young philosopher was lost to the profession, paralyzed by the fear of imperfection. Scrupulosity here seems to be a failure of practical wisdom, for the young philosopher ought to be able to see clearly that his fastidiousness is undermining his intellectual effectiveness. It is possible, however, that he sees this fairly clearly, but finds himself paralyzed by fear, unable to put his wisdom into practice. His is a dysfunction of the will, and recovery will have to be, in significant part, by way of emotional therapy.

One harm we commonly inflict on ourselves is to form our beliefs without sufficient evidence. W. K. Clifford says that, to attain the goals of our intellectual lives, we must never accept any belief unless we have enough evidence: "it is wrong always, everywhere, for anyone, to believe anything upon insufficient evidence."[11] By accepting beliefs

---

[11] W. K. Clifford, "The Ethics of Belief", in *The Ethics of Belief and Other Essays* (Amherst, NY: Prometheus Books, 1999), p. 77.

without sufficient evidence, we expose ourselves to increased risk of believing falsehoods, and at the same time we form bad belief-forming habits, thus creating for ourselves a dismal epistemic future. Little by little, every time we swallow an unsupported belief, according to Clifford, we weaken our capacity to discern evidence and assess its probative force. Nor are the harms stemming from accepting belief without adequate evidence restricted to the offending agent; they affect his community as well. It can be disastrous if doctors, jurors, and airline pilots form their beliefs incautiously; and who of us does not bear some responsibility for others' well-being, and do so on the basis of our beliefs? Besides such "practical" dependencies, we affect one another's epistemic well-being. Because of our tendency to model for one another and our need for each other to hold us accountable, intellectual carelessness tends to spread through a community. My carelessness propagates itself to my associates, as theirs does to me. Thus Clifford fears the general deterioration of the intellectual practices of an entire society, leading, as he dramatically says, to its sinking back into savagery.

Clifford explains his summary formula with analysis and examples, thereby giving his account of intellectual caution. The essay starts out with dramatic and uncontroversial examples of reckless believing: a shipowner who convinces himself with only the flimsiest evidence that the vessel in which he is sending several families across a wide ocean is seaworthy, and a group who bring public accusations of punishable crime against others with no basis beyond rumor and suspicion. Then he argues that every belief, no matter how trivial it may seem, may bear the load of other beliefs with dire possible consequences like the ones just mentioned; so we must be equally cautious with all our believing. His rules of caution do not rule out believing on the basis of testimony, but testimony can be sufficient evidence only if "there is reasonable ground for supposing that [the informant] knows the matter of which he speaks, and that he is speaking the truth so far as he knows it" (ibid.). Nor does caution rule out believing on the basis of inference from one's own experience, as long as the belief "is inferred from that experience by the assumption that what we do not know is like what we do know" (ibid.).

Still, William James finds Clifford's proscriptions counterproductively restrictive, aimed as they are, almost neurotically, at avoiding mistakes.

For my own part, I have also a horror of being duped; but I can believe that worse things than being duped may happen to a man in this world: so Clifford's exhortation has to my ears a thoroughly fantastic sound. It is like a general informing his soldiers that it is better to keep out of battle forever than to risk a single wound. Not so are victories either over enemies or over nature gained. Our errors are surely not such awfully solemn things. In a world where we are so certain to incur them in spite of all our caution, a certain lightness of heart seems healthier than this excessive nervousness on their behalf.[12]

James's military analogy reminds us that the intellectual life must make room for courage as well as caution, and that the virtuously cautious person realizes that we don't always have the luxury of waiting until we are completely sure that we are not making a mistake. He complicates the picture of caution by pointing out that epistemic goods must be weighed against the value of moral and prudential goods. As a broader-minded empiricist than Clifford, James realizes that human beings have aspirations to know, and a need to believe, regarding questions that are not governed by clear and distinct, universally acceptable canons of evidence. Here James echoes Aristotle, who said, famously, that "it is the mark of an educated man to look for precision in each class of things just so far as the nature of the subject admits; it is evidently equally foolish to accept probable reasoning from a mathematician and to demand from a rhetorician demonstrative proofs".[13] By their nature, religious and philosophical beliefs cannot satisfy the strict standards of caution that Clifford prescribes; and science is an adventure in which any generation will almost inevitably be judged by a succeeding one to have assented to some propositions on the basis of less than adequate evidence. In James's eyes, what Clifford prescribes is not proper caution, but a paralyzing intellectual scrupulosity that would evacuate life of much richness and interest, and cripple us intellectually.

In rejecting Cliffordian scrupulosity, James is not endorsing intellectual recklessness. He is not, for example, commending Clifford's irresponsible shipowner or people who make criminal accusations against others on the

---

[12] William James, "The Will to Believe", in *The Will to Believe and Other Essays* (New York: Dover Publications, 1956), pp. 18–19.

[13] Aristotle, *Nicomachean Ethics*, trans. W. D. Ross, rev. J. O. Urmson and J. L. Ackrill (Oxford: Oxford University Press, 1998), p. 3 (1094^{b}25–7). It is interesting to note that this piece of practical wisdom about the intellectual life comes from a philosopher famous for having distinguished intellectual from practical reason rather strictly.

basis of flimsy evidence. The person who is virtuously cautious in the intellectual sphere has a practical wisdom about what is worth risking for what, and about the degree and kind of evidence that is needed, or can be hoped for, for a certain belief. He knows, for example, that one needs a high degree of certainty for one's belief that the ship is seaworthy if one is going to send people across the ocean in it, and that in such a case no amount of profit justifies avoidable risk of error. And yet he knows that the ship must eventually sail, and that Cartesian certainty is not available in the case. He knows that religious beliefs are not susceptible to the same kind of testing as a ship's seaworthiness, and that if one is to reap the benefits of religious life one must (with courage) venture out with faith.

When I look at the religious question as it really puts itself to concrete men, and when I think of all the possibilities which both practically and theoretically it involves, then this command that we shall put a stopper on our heart, instincts, and courage, and *wait*—acting of course meanwhile more or less as if religion were *not* true—till doomsday, or till such time as our intellect and senses working together may have raked in evidence enough,—this command, I say, seems to me the queerest idol ever manufactured in the philosophic cave. ("The Will to Believe", pp. 29–30)

If the virtuously cautious person is a scientist, he will not risk his time and energy on just any scientific venture, but will select one carefully, asking whether it is the sort of project he is capable of pursuing, how significant the intellectual payoff, if realized, would be, whether the costs, in time and resources, can be met, whether it would be better to pursue the present project rather than some other, and so forth, but all within the awareness that in a generation or two his best scientific claims may well prove to have been inadequate.

Conclusion

Courage and caution are complementary virtues in the life of the mind. Courage is a power to resist or overcome fears that tend to disrupt one's intellectual functioning, and caution is a disposition of proper fear attunement, a disposition to fear what is worthy to be feared, to fear it enough (but not too much) and in the right way, and then to be able to avoid what is feared. Intellectual caution is wise fearing in cognitive matters.

Wise cognitive fears are based on the love of knowledge, and the love of knowledge is a concern for the epistemic goods that situates them among the other goods of human life—a concern for information, understanding, and acquaintance that is significant, relevant, and worthy in the context of a human life. The harms that caution fears are harms relative to these goods. Clifford's conception of caution is not wise, according to James, because it is fanatical; the fears of which it consists are one-dimensional, leaving wider human eudaimonia out of consideration. It is very difficult to lay out, in any more than an indicative way, the structure of a wise fear disposition in the intellectual life. In this chapter we have not got beyond indications by way of a few examples. The learning of proper caution is an emotional training that must be brought about by engagement in concrete complex epistemic activities such as reading, teaching, scholarship, and the sciences, under the tutelage of wise mentors.

Courage is a partner virtue with caution, because not all fears that affect the intellectual life can be dealt with by wisdom. The fears faced down by intellectual courage are adverse to intellectual enterprise, in one way or another. Although many such fears are immature, or even vicious, not all are. For example, Jane Goodall's fear of being beaten up by a chimpanzee is not irrational, immature, or vicious; but the fear of knowing the truth about oneself does seem to be at least immature.

9

Humility

Introduction

Our practice in recent chapters has been to describe virtues in connection with their vice counterparts. Doing so is especially important with humility, which has a negative character. Humility is opposite to a number of vices, including arrogance, vanity, conceit, egotism, hyper-autonomy, grandiosity, pretentiousness, snobbishness, impertinence (presumption), haughtiness, self-righteousness, domination, selfish ambition, and self-complacency. These vices differ from one another in various ways, but all are opposites of humility, and are negatively definitive of it. So a perfectly rich account of humility would explore many of them together. But we think that a fair approximation of the virtue can be achieved by looking primarily at two of its vice counterparts: vanity and arrogance. In this chapter we will explore humility chiefly as the opposite of these two vices, and comment briefly on one other. We will then clarify why humility is an intellectual virtue by tracing the ways in which some epistemic goods accrue to the humble person and his or her associates.

Before we start, however, to get a broader orientation in this field, we'll sketch very briefly some of the other important vices that help to define humility. Conceit is the set of dispositions of thought, action, and emotion that stem from an unwarrantedly high opinion of oneself. Egotism is a disposition to exaggerate the importance of, and focus attention on, oneself and one's own interests, to the neglect of others and their interests. Hyper-autonomy is a disinclination to acknowledge one's dependence on others and to accept help from them. Grandiosity is a disposition, in thought and self-presentation, to exaggerate one's greatness. Pretentiousness is a disposition to claim, in action and demeanor, higher dignity or merit than one possesses. Snobbishness is a disposition to associate oneself, in thought and practice, with persons of high social rank, intellect, or taste, and to shun or contemn persons of lower rank. Impertinence or presumption is a disposition to act without proper respect for the limits of one's powers, competence, or social station. Haughtiness is a disposition to treat others as hardly worthy of one's attention or respect. Self-righteousness is a disposition to ascribe to oneself a greater moral excellence than one possesses, especially in comparison with others. Domination is a disposition to excessive exertion and enjoyment of control over others. Selfish ambition is a disposition to advance one's own long-term interests to the exclusion or detriment of others' interests. Self-complacency is a disposition to approve uncritically of one's own abilities and accomplishments. Many of these vices have intellectual variants.

Humility as Opposed to Vanity

Vanity is an excessive concern to be well regarded by other people, for the social importance their regard confers on oneself. It is thus a hypersensitivity to the view that others take of oneself. Its emotional marks are anxiety about how one appears, joy at making a good appearance, embarrassment or shame at making a bad appearance, resentment of those who criticize or withhold the prescribed admiration, etc. Since part of making a good appearance may be to give the appearance of not caring what sort of appearance one makes, the vain person may cover up these emotions, for others or himself or both. Or he may be so well mannered, and so well situated for his vanity's satisfaction that he hardly shows it, like the Bertram sisters, whose "vanity was in such good order, that they seemed to be quite free from it" (Jane Austen, *Mansfield Park*, ch. 4).

Not just any concern to make a good appearance is vanity. It is no sign of vanity if you are embarrassed upon discovering that you have lectured for an hour with a gaping fly. You are painfully affected by others' viewing you in an unflattering light, but the concern on which your emotion is based is only to meet a minimum standard of propriety of appearance, not to glitter. It seems that, to be vanity, your concern must be to appear in some respect excellent, for only excellence confers social importance; but there is nothing excellent about having your fly closed. Again, you may desire to make a good appearance so as to make money or get promoted, or receive an academic grant or access to a library, or as evidence of some progress in skill that you are interested in monitoring in yourself. Only if you are concerned to make a good appearance for the social importance it seems to entail is the concern vanity.

Thus vanity is typically selective of audience: the vain person may not care to make a good appearance in the eyes of people whose good opinion does not seem to him to confer social importance. A vain philosopher might not mind appearing stupid before an audience of sugar-beet farmers; a woman vain of her beauty might not mind appearing ugly to her children. These vain ones do not mind making a bad appearance before these audiences, because approval by such audiences does not seem to them to confer any social importance on themselves.

Some vanity may seem to want attention for attention's sake, since abusive attention satisfies it. But the vain individual may see even strongly disapproving attention as showing a kind of perverse or reverse excellence, and thus as conferring social importance, in particular as showing at least that the subject is important enough to pay this attention to. Also, a vain person may have other motives than vanity for seeking attention, such as boredom; and such other motives might not be for approval in any sense. But such motives are not the ones that justify the attribution of vanity.

It is hard to say exactly what constitutes an *excessive* concern to put in a good appearance for the sake of social importance. But it is clear that people are not vain simply for having *some* such concern. Just about everyone will feel embarrassed or ashamed upon perceiving that others are shocked by their behavior, and will regret the loss of status if that occurs, and enjoy the status conferred by others' approval. Robustly healthy and virtuous people are a little bothered by others' slighting them in society, not taking them seriously, thinking they are not worth much. But the vain person is very bothered by such things and is hurt by smaller misappearances and elated about successful appearances that the humbler person hardly pauses to note. The vain person is preoccupied with his status-relevant appearances. We are inclined to say that he is enslaved to others' approval of him, or at any rate unduly beholden to it. He demands to be very well thought of, wishes to be adulated, adored, and honored; and feels nervous and unfulfilled unless he is getting this extraordinary sort of attention. Of course the demand may meet frustration and disappointment as well as satisfaction.

Perhaps we have said enough about vanity to start on the humility that is its opposite. The humble person is unvain, but does not merely lack vanity; he veers in the other direction. We have said that vanity is an excessive concern to be well regarded by other people for the sake of social importance, and thus a hypersensitivity to the view that others take of oneself. Humility, as vanity's opposite, is a striking or unusual unconcern for social importance, and thus a kind of emotional *in*sensitivity to the issues of status. Julia Driver takes a line like this, but she talks not about concerns and emotions, but about beliefs. Thus, she says that the virtue of modesty is "a dogmatic disposition" to underestimate one's worth.[1] It is not mere ignorance of one's worth; if the excellent but modest person is presented with all the evidence of her excellences, she refuses to believe it. Thus the moral virtue of modesty is an intellectual vice.

This unhappy conclusion can be avoided while doing justice to the intuition behind Driver's formula. On our analysis, the humble person is not ignorant of her value or status, but in a certain way *unconcerned* about it and therefore *inattentive* to it. She may appear to be ignorant of her excellence or importance, but if she needs to assess herself, she can give as accurate an account as the next person. She is just not very interested in such an assessment, so she is not much inclined to inquire about it, and the evidence for it is not generally salient for her; it does not come easily or automatically to her attention.

We think that in the cases in which humility is clearly a virtue, and not merely the absence of a vice, a certain kind of story can be told about the basis of the unconcern and inattentiveness. We propose that in the best cases the concern for status is swamped or displaced or put on hold by some overriding virtuous concern. In the Christian moral tradition Jesus Christ, the Son of God, is the paradigm of humility. The apostle Paul commends humility to the church at Philippi:

Let the same mind be in you that was in Christ Jesus, who, though he was in the form of God, did not regard equality with God as something to be grasped, but emptied himself, taking the form of a slave, being born in human likeness. (Phil. 2: 5–7)

The Son of God has a very high "social" status, which we might, a priori, expect him to insist on and be preoccupied with. But his love for

[1] Julia Driver, "The Virtues of Ignorance", *Journal of Philosophy* 86 (1989): 373–84, p. 378.

humankind and his concern to accomplish his Father's will overrides the concern for his social importance and moves him to make himself vulnerable to some very unlordly humiliation: "And being found in human form, he humbled himself and became obedient to the point of death—even death on a cross" (Phil. 2: 8). In his status–ignoring love Jesus Christ is at the opposite extreme from the vain person who grasps after recognition and status as though it is the breath of life. So is the Christian disciple who imitates the Lord. As Paul says, "Do nothing from selfishness or conceit, but in humility count others better than yourselves" (Phil. 2: 3). Following our analysis of humility, when the humble person "counts" others as better than herself, she does nothing so foolish as to *believe* that they are better than she—say, better cellists, or of higher social status, or more intelligent or more beautiful—if they are not. Instead, whatever status she possesses or does not possess impresses her little, matters little to her, in comparison with the value of these persons as ones for whom Christ died, whom she therefore honors and respects highly, "forgetting" herself.

Consider now a case of intellectual humility in the same pattern. Alice Ambrose describes G. E. Moore as a teacher:

Moore in his lectures was self-effacing. Criticisms he put forward of claims he himself had made, say in a previous lecture, could as well have been directed to an anonymous philosopher whose mistakes called for correction. For example, in discussing truth, Moore had examined the two propositional forms, "it is true that *p*" and "*p*," maintaining that they meant the same and therefore that "it is true that" has no meaning because "it is true that" is redundant. His comment in the next lecture: "My present view is that so far from its being the case that from the fact that it is redundant it follows that it has no meaning, it follows that if it is redundant *it has got meaning*. No phrase can be redundant in an expression without having a meaning." Some lectures later he notified his class: "I am going to make a jump now because I do not know how to go on."[2]

Is "self-effacing" the right word? Moore does not seem to efface himself, but just to pay little attention to himself because he has more important things to attend to. Self-effacement is a step removed from the kind of humility Moore evinces, in that it involves self-preoccupation, a self that

---

[2] Alice Ambrose, "Moore and Wittgenstein as Teachers", *Teaching Philosophy* 12 (1989): 107–113, pp. 107–8.

invites effacement because it obtrudes. The self-effacing person says, "I am no good," "I am unworthy," "How stupid I am!", thus showing preoccupation with himself. (Wittgenstein often did this.) By contrast, status is not an issue for Moore; to its exclusion, the truth about truth preoccupies him. He has not literally lost track of who he is; nor have we any reason to think that he regards himself as undeserving of his position: without apology he goes to the front of the class and lectures, showing that he knows and accepts that he is the professor. But his lack of concern with status is evinced by the fact that his criticisms "could as well have been directed to an anonymous philosopher whose mistakes called for correction".

So we see in Jesus of Nazareth and Moore of Cambridge a common motivational pattern of humility: an unusually low concern for status coordinated with an intense concern for some apparent[3] good. This pattern may be regarded as virtuous for at least two reasons. First, the concern for status often weakens and confuses more important concerns, with bad behavioral and epistemic consequences; humility as a motivational configuration leaves the more important concern pure and free of such interference. Second, in some moral outlooks—in particular, highly egalitarian ones like Christianity—the concern for status is regarded with moral suspicion. Hierarchical human relations may be necessary to social order, but high status does not motivate the best sort of person.

Another vice opposed to humility, one that involves a strong concern for personal importance but is less oriented than vanity to others' *view* of oneself, is domination. The domineering person is concerned to have power or influence over others. The intellectual variant of this vice is an inordinate concern to be the determiner of other people's opinions, to take special pleasure in shaping others' minds, to be the author of such-and-such an idea that is all the rage, to be the one who convinced so-and-so of such-and-such. Most of us teachers probably have some degree of this concern, but some are very competitive for disciples and feel desolate when disciples defect.

---

[3] We say "apparent" because a person might be unmindful of status, and thus in this sense humble, in the pursuit of some horrendous evil, such as the extermination of a racial group. Thus humility, like courage, is a virtue that can be possessed by otherwise vicious persons. If a humble person is to be fully virtuous, his concern for status must be swamped by virtuous concerns. Humility must stand in a kind of interlocking unity with other virtues (see the final section of this chapter).

Richard Rorty, following Harold Bloom, discusses a particularly grandiose form of intellectual domination (though he does not bill it as a vice)
under the title of "the anxiety of influence", which he attributes to "strong
poets". Philosophers and scientists may be strongly motivated by the desire
to be discussed by future generations, but their claim to fame, if they
have one, will be that they somehow got reality right. The strong poet's
goal is even more ambitious: to *create* reality for himself and personally to
dominate past and future generations by authoring their realities as well.
Rorty comments:

...although strong poets are, like all other animals, causal products of natural
forces, they are products capable of telling the story of their own production in
words never used before. The line between weakness and strength is thus the line
between using language which is familiar and universal and producing language
which, though initially unfamiliar and idiosyncratic, somehow makes tangible the
blind impress all one's behavings bear. With luck—the sort of luck which makes
the difference between genius and eccentricity—that language will also strike the
next generation as inevitable. *Their* behavings will bear that impress.[4]

In other words, the domineering strong poet wants so to impress his
individuality on others that their "individuality" will be not really theirs,
but his. His anxiety is that he will be unable to make his attempted self-
imposition stick, that he will fail in his role of creator of other persons'
worlds. The anxiety of influence stands in the greatest possible contrast to
the self-ignoring humility of Moore and to a whole truth-seeking tradition
of the ethics of intellect. Rorty continues,

The wonder in which Aristotle believed philosophy to begin was wonder at
finding oneself in a world larger, stronger, nobler than oneself. The fear in which
Bloom's poets begin is the fear that one might end one's days in such a world, a
world one never made, an inherited world. The hope of such a poet is that what
the past tried to do to her she will succeed in doing to the past: to make the past
itself, including those very causal processes which blindly impressed all her own
behavings, bear *her* impress. (p. 29)

The domination that would appear to Moore and Aristotle as an intellectual
vice appears to Rorty and his forebear Nietzsche as an inevitable trait of
the most developed human beings.

---

[4] Richard Rorty, *Contingency, Irony, and Solidarity* (Cambridge: Cambridge University Press, 1989),
pp. 28–9.

Intellectual humility as the opposite of intellectual domination would perhaps be exemplified most radically by Socrates, who was contented to regard himself as only a facilitator of his pupils' relation to the truth. The doctrine of recollection (*Meno* 80e−86b) implies that the whole idea of discipleship, in the sense of intellectual dependence, is a big mistake. Intellectual humility, in this connection, would be a disposition to rejoice in the progress of one's students, especially, perhaps, when they advance beyond oneself; and it would be an emotional indifference to the question of the extent of one's *own* influence on them. As the unvain is unconcerned about, and thus inattentive to whether he is making a good impression on others, the undominating is unconcerned, and thus inattentive to his influence on others.

Humility as the Virtue Opposed to Arrogance

Arrogance is a disposition to "infer" some illicit entitlement from a supposition of one's superiority, and to think, act, and feel on the basis of that claim. Examples: the Hollywood star who enters a restaurant unannounced expecting to be given the best table in the house in priority over people who have been waiting for forty-five minutes; the supposed *ius primæ noctis*, the "right" of a feudal nobleman to sleep with the women of his realm on the first night of their marriage; the college president with two doctorates who thinks himself competent to speak with correcting authority in all the fields of his faculty. Typical response to arrogant behavior: Who does he think he is?

Albert Schweitzer was superior to nearly all the people in his social world with respect to his moral character, his learning, and his musicianship, and the detail in his autobiography suggests that he was aware of this (a failure to believe it, given his social world, would evince some weird epistemic defect).[5] This belief concerning his superiority does not by itself make him arrogant. Some "inference" from it, to the effect that it entitles him to treat his inferiors with disrespect (say, neglect, condescension, disdain, or undue suspicion and distrust), or to the effect that he is entitled to special

---

[5] Albert Schweitzer, *Out of My Life and Thought*, trans. C. T. Campion (New York: Henry Holt and Company, 1933).

treatment or exempted from ordinary responsibilities, seems required to qualify him as arrogant.

The inferred entitlement needs to be illicit. Schweitzer might, without exhibiting arrogance, infer from his medical superiority that he is entitled to the best surgical equipment available in Africa and that he is exempt from the tasks ordinarily assigned to men in the village, because this claim to entitlement is justified by his medical superiority, conjoined with the medical needs of the community. (Presumably the supposed inference from *I am superior in X way* to *I am entitled to treat others with disrespect*[6] is always invalid.) Sometimes arrogance is thought to involve by definition an exaggerated self-estimate. But if Schweitzer did infer from his superiority that he was entitled to treat others with disrespect, he would be arrogant even if he did not exaggerate his qualities—say, his musical and medical superiority to others. Thus arrogance does not require a false superiority claim. It is true that one might want to include in the notion of self-estimate the "inference" to the false entitlement claim; the inference shows what the self-estimate "means" to the subject. But we think it is clearer, for purposes of analysis, to keep the premise and the conclusion distinct. The feudal lord who insists on his *ius primæ noctis* is not wrong about being a lord, but he is wrong about what being a lord entitles him to.

One motive for running premise and conclusion together is the fact that no explicit inference is necessary. To indicate this, we have been writing "inference" in scare-quotes from time to time. If asked why he makes the entitlement claims he does, an articulate and self-aware arrogant person would be able to trace the claims to his sense of superiority, but the arrogant person need not be self-aware or articulate; nor does even the articulate arrogant person need to say or think "I am superior, therefore I am entitled...." It may also seem contrary to our analysis that arrogant behavior and attitudes are sometimes strategies to bolster a low self-estimate. In this case, the entitlement claim is not based on a high self-estimate, but a falsely high self-estimate is "based" on the entitlement claim. Yes, but even here, the logic of arrogance goes in the other direction. The arrogant

---

[6] Notice that "treat others with disrespect" is an essentially attitudinal description. Imagine that because of cultural conventions where Schweitzer labors, he will get the community to cooperate with his work only if he treats its members with what in Europe would count as disrespectful (say, condescending, authoritarian) behavior. He may produce this behavior without arrogance, in case *he* does not thereby express disrespect, and therewith a false entitlement claim.

person who bolsters low self-esteem by acting and thinking arrogantly is trading on the supposition that high self-value warrants the behavior in question. The self-estimate (which may not rise to the level of belief) is *psychologically* "based" on the arrogant *behavior*. This is artificial or derivative arrogance (however common it may be as a form of arrogance).

Like us, Valerie Tiberius and John Walker analyze arrogance as involving an inference:

> ... the arrogant person has a high opinion of himself. He differs from the self-confident person [by concluding] ... that he is a better person according to the general standards governing what counts as a successful human specimen.[7]

Thus the inference they detect is not from superiority to entitlement, but from superiority in some respect to superiority as a human being. They point out the kind of overreaching behavior and attitude characteristic of arrogance, but seem to think this automatically included in taking oneself to be superior as a human specimen. We hold that a person can be arrogant without thinking himself superior as a human specimen (the arrogant person's claim to superiority may be more limited), and that one can think oneself a superior human specimen (as presumably Schweitzer and many other virtuous and intelligent people have done) without being arrogant.

Might Schweitzer infer a false entitlement claim from his superiority, without thus showing arrogance? Imagine that, ignorant of a medical missionary compound on the edge of the Gaboon, Schweitzer falsely believes himself to be the best doctor in the region, and so falsely claims entitlement to the best of some scarce medical equipment. Here we want to ask how he is disposed to respond when his premise is corrected. If he gives up his entitlement claim easily when corrected, we are inclined to say that the claim does not show arrogance; but if he insists on it, despite the correction, he gives evidence of being arrogant. This seems to fit our formula: arrogance is a *disposition* to "infer" illicit entitlement claims from a judgment of one's own superiority. If Schweitzer gives up the false entitlement claim easily as soon as the premise on which he bases it is falsified, he does not show the disposition that we have identified as arrogance. This kind of case calls for refinement of our notion of disposition. Arrogance is a disposition of the *heart*; a "disposition" that consists just

---

[7] Valerie Tiberius and John Walker, "Arrogance", *American Philosophical Quarterly* 35 (1998): 379–90, p. 382.

in the falsity of one's premise, plus an ability to make valid inferences to entitlement claims, is not arrogance. Arrogance includes a certain resistance to correction. In the most characteristic cases it is a *motivated* disposition to infer false entitlements. What might the motive be?

It might be sensuality. We can well imagine a feudal lord who is reluctant to give up his *ius* claim even after seeing pretty clearly that being lord does not entitle him to deflower every virgin in his domain. Another motive for drawing the illicit conclusion might be vanity—the preoccupation with the personal importance that is conferred (supposedly) by the special entitlement. Claiming entitlement, especially but not only if one gets away with it, satisfies vanity. The humble person might want the same things that the arrogant person arrogates to himself by entitlement, but does not think of himself as entitled to them; or if he does, entitlement does not have the same ego-expanding meaning for him. Preoccupation with one's entitlements tends to give one a sense of personal importance, but the humble person is not much disposed to that kind of thinking. If his humility is of the most virtuous kind, entangled with other virtues, this inattention is in favor of some noble concern—typically for something outside himself like the health of the community, the excellence of the music, the truth of philosophical claims. Arrogance seldom goes it alone as an anti-humility trait. In the most characteristic cases it is abetted by (and abets?) such other traits as vanity, conceit, snobbery, grandiosity, and pretentiousness, as well as others that are not intrinsically anti-humility, such as sensuality and acquisitiveness. There is something like a unity of the vices, as there is of the virtues.

We said that the humility that is opposed to vanity is not merely the absence of vanity, but goes in the other direction. Shall we say something analogous about the humility that corresponds to arrogance? Is such humility not merely the disposition not to exaggerate one's entitlements based on one's superiorities, but the disposition to *under*rate them? Something about the suggestion seems right, but if we think of humility as a disposition to be *generally* inattentive to entitlements, it would be easy for the opposite of arrogance to become a disabling trait and thus a vice. If, for example, Schweitzer did not notice his entitlements to medical equipment, his work as a doctor might be harmed. But it is not quite right to describe this kind of humility as inattentiveness to one's entitlements. Someone with the humility of unarrogance may be as attentive to particular entitlements as any other alert, rational person. The difference between him and persons who are less humble is that he is relatively inattentive to the ego-exalting potency of his entitlements. Schweitzer may, in humility, insist on his entitlements as an excellent doctor, or as a first-class Bach scholar or theologian, if his interest in those entitlements is "pure", which is to say to the point of medicine, Bach scholarship, or theology, and not to the point of making *him* important.

But it would not be right to make self-exaltation a necessary condition of arrogance. We have allowed that non-anti-humility motives like sensuality and acquisitiveness may be enough to make an overreaching entitlement claim arrogant. The feudal lord who insists on his *ius primæ noctis* is arrogant even if his motivation does not include considering that the exercise of this entitlement shows his personal importance; sheer sensuality is enough. And in a moment we will come to a case in which we may want to ascribe intellectual arrogance to Aristotle where he makes an overreaching entitlement claim in the absence of any vicious motive whatsoever. These considerations lead us to propose a three-tiered analysis of arrogance: (1) in the most characteristic cases, arrogant thought and behavior are motivated by self-exaltation; (2) less characteristic cases have a vicious, but not viciously self-exalting motive; (3) in some cases which are on the outer edges of the class, the "arrogant" behavior is not motivated viciously. So when we say that the difference between a Schweitzer who insists on his entitlements and more arrogant people who insist on their entitlements is his relative inattentiveness to the self-exalting potency of his entitlements, we are assuming that (a) he has no other vicious motive and (b) he is in fact entitled to what he claims to be entitled to.

Let us turn now to an example that will bring us closer to *intellectual* arrogance. Oscar Wilde had undoubtedly an impressive intellect, superior to that of most of his contemporaries, though less so than he claims in *De Profundis*. Wilde details his greatness:

I had genius, a distinguished name, high social position, brilliancy, intellectual daring: I made art a philosophy, and philosophy an art: I altered the minds of men and the colours of things: there was nothing I said or did that did not make people wonder: I took the drama, the most objective form known to art, and made it as personal a mode of expression as the lyric or the sonnet, at the same time that I widened its range and enriched its characterisation: drama, novel, poem in rhyme, poem in prose, subtle or fantastic dialogue, whatever I touched I made beautiful in a new mode of beauty: to truth itself I gave what is false no less than what is true as its rightful province, and showed that the false and the true are merely forms of intellectual existence. I treated Art as the supreme reality, and life as a mere mode of fiction: I awoke the imagination of my century so that it created myth and legend around me: I summed up all systems in a phrase, and all existence in an epigram.[8]

This is not by itself arrogance, though it may be rampant conceit, and we detect not a little of the Nietzschean "virtue" of domination and its auxiliary anxiety of influence. However, Wilde does also exhibit arrogance, ironically in connection with his claim to have learned humility in prison. A biographer comments that the climax of *De Profundis*,

doubtless premeditated from the start, was a section dealing with Wilde's discovery in prison of Christ. This ... is less humble than it seems, since Wilde not only describes Christ without recognizing his divinity, but blends Christianity with aestheticism, as long before he told André Gide he would do. Christ appears here as the supreme individualist, uniting personality and perfection, saying beautiful things, making of his life the most wonderful of poems by creating himself out of his own imagination. He sympathizes with sinners as Wilde in "The Soul of Man Under Socialism" sympathizes with criminals, and recognizes no morality but that of sympathy. Christ is a precursor of the romantic movement, a supreme artist, a master of paradox, a type of Wilde in the ancient world.[9]

It is not simple exaggeration of his importance that signals Wilde's arrogance, but his implicit claim of entitlement to remake Jesus Christ in his own image. And the act of doing so signals arrogance, because Wilde's talents and accomplishments fail to justify his entitlement, because in remaking Jesus he shows colossal disrespect and thus the outrageous extent of his entitlement claim, and because the subsumption of Christ under the categories of his own invention is self-exalting for Wilde. This arrogance is intellectual because the "premise" of the entitlement claim concerns Wilde's intellect (its powers, its achievement, his standing in an intellectual community) and because the entitlement claim is to an intellectual activity (or exemption from some intellectual disciplines that would ordinarily be required of

    [8] Oscar Wilde, *De Profundis* (Mineola, NY: Dover Publications, 1996), pp. 44–5.
    [9] Richard Ellmann, *Oscar Wilde* (New York: Alfred A. Knopf, 1988), pp. 514–15. Arrogance and vanity are often comic, as here. The raillery that Kierkegaard directs at Hegelian philosophers' pretensions to "pure thought", to "starting with nothing", to "making an advance on faith", etc. is a response to these philosophers' pretentiousness.

anyone who undertook to rewrite Jesus Christ);[10] and its viciousness resides in part in the blindness to Christ's nature that Wilde's arrogance works in him.

The Wilde case illustrates the relativity of concepts of arrogance and humility to moral outlooks. We read Wilde as arrogant in his treatment of Jesus as an ancient (albeit somewhat less amusing and artistic) forerunner of Oscar Wilde. But this judgment is morally located. It is a Christian or quasi-Christian judgment. What Christians regard as arrogant, an "aesthete" or a Nietzschean may not, because we have different ideas about what entitlement inferences are sound. A Nietzschean or aesthete believes that a creative genius like Wilde is perfectly entitled to remake Jesus in his own image, because making is what human life is about, and genius carries with it this kind of entitlement. Christians don't think so. Thus what we take to be arrogant behavior, intellectual or otherwise, depends on other contestable beliefs. To take another example, in Aristotle's framework it would not be arrogant for citizens to regard themselves, on the basis of their superiority to natural slaves, as entitled to treat the slaves merely as means to ends and not as beings who have their own ends that must be considered. This entitlement claim would not be arrogant in Aristotle's framework because the inference would be valid; while in Kant's framework the inference would necessarily be false, and would thus qualify as (at least) third-tier arrogance.

Consider, finally, Alasdair MacIntyre's comments on Aristotle's self-limitation of informants for his political dialectic. Unlike Descartes, Aristotle is not an epistemic Lone Ranger. His approach to knowledge is highly collegial, and to this extent humble. As part of his investigation he is careful to consult the opinions of those who are most likely to know about a subject-matter. But some of his beliefs about human nature lead him to limit his informants and discussion partners in a way that we would be a little less likely to do.

For while Aristotle understood very well the importance of the relevant kinds of experience for rational practice—"we see," he wrote, "that the experienced

---

[10] It seems that both premise and conclusion must be "intellectual" for the arrogance to be so. It does not seem to be *intellectual* arrogance when the president of Mensa presumes that his position entitles him to be given the best table in priority over guests who have been waiting for forty-five minutes; or when Madonna regards herself as entitled by her status as popular entertainer to make public pronouncements about the meaning of life.

are more effective than those who have reason, but lack experience" (*Metaphysics* A 981ª14–15)—in neither ethics nor politics did he give any weight to the experience of those for whom the facts of affliction and dependence are most likely to be undeniable: women, slaves, and servants, those engaged in the productive labor of farmers, fishing crews, and manufacture.[11]

Aristotle's intellectual conduct assumes that slaves and women need not be consulted when asking ethical and political questions, because they have no important insight or information to contribute. For someone who occupies a Christian or other non-elitist perspective, this intellectual policy involves a false "inference" along the following lines: slaves and workers are inferior human beings, compared to us investigators, so we are entitled to ignore their testimony as a source of ethical and political information. MacIntyre's point is that this policy is a blinding or information-impeding one. And our point is that the policy expresses something like the vice of intellectual arrogance. Here the conclusion is not obviously self-exalting, or motivated by sensuality, greed, or any other vice; so it is only third-tier arrogance.

Humility and Epistemic Goods

What, then, is intellectual humility? The foregoing analysis suggests that it is an unusually low dispositional concern for the kind of self-importance that accrues to persons who are viewed by their intellectual communities as talented, accomplished, and skilled, especially where such concern is muted or sidelined by intrinsic intellectual concerns—in particular, the concern for knowledge with its various attributes of truth, justification, warrant, coherence, precision, load-bearing significance, and worthiness. Intellectual humility is also a very low concern for intellectual domination in the form of leaving the stamp of one's mind on disciples, one's field, and future intellectual generations. As the opposite of intellectual arrogance, humility is a disposition not to make unwarranted intellectual entitlement claims on the basis of one's (supposed) superiority or excellence, out of

[11] Alasdair MacIntyre, *Dependent Rational Animals* (Chicago and La Salle, IL: Open Court, 1999), p. 6.

either a concern for self-exaltation, or some other vicious concern, or no vicious concern at all.

Our thesis is that intellectual humility fosters certain intellectual ends when it is conjoined, in a personality, with other epistemic virtues. Our claim is not that all people who lack humility will be in all respects epistemic failures; we even think that vanity, arrogance, and other anti-humility vices can on occasion contribute to the acquisition, refinement, and communication of knowledge. Rather, we claim that in the long run, just about everybody will be epistemically better off for having, and having associates who have, epistemic humility. We have been doing conceptual analysis, but now our thesis is empirical. One can imagine a study in which investigators of various sorts are tested for their intellectual humility and this trait measure is correlated with accomplishments such as discoveries of new knowledge and purveyance of knowledge to others. If it turned out that epistemic humility was predictive of more of these epistemic goods than intellectual vices like vanity and arrogance, our hypothesis would be confirmed.

If not, it would be disconfirmed. But the disconfirmation of that hypothesis would not, on our account, imply that intellectual humility was not a virtue, and that intellectual vanity and arrogance were virtues. The reason is that epistemic humility does not get all of its claim to virtue status from the narrowly intellectual advantages that we believe it affords. It is a virtue because the acquisition, maintenance, transmission, and application of knowledge are integral generic parts of human life, and a life characterized by humility with respect to these activities, as well as many other activities, is a more excellent life than one that lacks it. It is an intellectual virtue because it is exemplified in the context of intellectual practices. If the empirical study showed that humility led to a slightly lower output of epistemic goods, other traits being equal, than vanity and arrogance, we would be less than elated, but would not give up our claim that humility is an intellectual virtue and arrogance an intellectual vice. "Reliability" is not the only intellectual desideratum. Moore's humility about his ideas would be intellectual humility even if it did not afford him any more epistemic payoff than the professor down the hall gets from his vanity and arrogance. Intellectual virtues, like their moral counterparts, are dispositions to proper human functioning, and what counts as proper human functioning is determined by basic human nature. Virtues are traits of the person who is functioning as persons are supposed to function.

If it did turn out that intellectual vanity and arrogance delivered, on average, more of the epistemic goods than intellectual humility, we would try to explain this disturbing result by reference to some other fault in the individual or some corruption in the epistemic environment. Perhaps individuals need vanity as a motivation, because their upbringing does not instill in them an enthusiasm for knowledge as such. Or we might locate the pathology socially—say, in the fact that the whole intellectual community is warped by vanity and arrogance, hyper-autonomy and unhealthy competitiveness, so that in that fallen community some vices actually become more "functional" than their counterpart virtues.

Let us now try to make plausible the thesis that humility is intellectually advantageous to most of us in most of our actual intellectual environments. The humility that is the opposite of intellectual vanity and arrogance has the primarily negative role of preventing or circumventing certain obstacles to acquiring, refining, and transmitting knowledge. Vanity and arrogance are epistemic liabilities that beset many people, so the intellectually humble person stands out in his or her freedom from these impediments.

Much acquisition, refinement, and communication of knowledge occurs in a live social setting whose mood and interpersonal dynamics strongly affect these intellectual processes. Research is often pursued by collaborative teams, and even scholars who spend most of their working days alone consult from time to time with colleagues and come together in professional meetings to share and test their findings. Classrooms are obviously social settings. Humility promotes these processes in two dimensions: in the functioning of the individual who possesses the virtue, and in the functioning of the social context with which he or she is interacting—colleagues, teachers, and pupils.

The intellectually vain person is overly concerned with how she "looks" to the people who count; she wants to impress, and is very concerned not to look silly at conferences and in front of her bright students. She may be genuinely concerned to accomplish intrinsic epistemic ends: to figure out what's what and to give her students a good education. But she *also* has the extrinsic concern to look good intellectually, and this is often a liability. By contrast, the lack of concern to look good frees the intellectually humble person to pursue intellectual goods simply and undistractedly (think of

G. E. Moore). He has one obstacle less to the correction of his views, especially in public and "competitive" contexts like philosophy colloquia. The humble person will be free to test his ideas against the strongest objections. His humility may also make for intellectual adventure: he will not be afraid to try out ideas that others may ridicule (here if one lacks humility, courage may be a substitute).

The intellectually arrogant person is inclined to act on a supposed entitlement to dismiss without consideration the views of persons he regards as his intellectual inferiors. Young "analytic" philosophers sometimes exemplify this vice vis-à-vis Continental or informal philosophy, just as young Continental philosophers sometimes suppose the profundity of their school to warrant dismissing the work of their analytic counterparts as superficial technical gamesmanship. Highly reputed older scientists may dismiss out of hand the unorthodox proposals of their graduate students or younger colleagues. Subramanyan Chandrasekhar was once asked why he was able to do innovative work in physics well past the age at which most people retire, while most physicists do their innovative work only when young. He said:

For a lack of a better word, there seems to be a certain arrogance toward nature that people develop. These people have had great insights and made profound discoveries. They imagine afterwards that the fact that they succeeded so triumphantly in one area means they have a special way of looking at science which must be right. But science doesn't permit that. Nature has shown over and over again that the kinds of truth which underlie nature transcend the most powerful minds.[12]

In face of reality's capacity to surprise even the smartest of us, a certain skepticism about one's entitlement to disregard the views of minorities, of the unorthodox, and of the young may be a significant asset. As MacIntyre's comments on Aristotle suggest, the humble inquirer has more potential teachers than his less humble counterparts. And this is due not just to numbers, but also to permeability of noetic structure: in interacting with persons whose minds are somewhat alien to his own, the strongly unarrogant person is better able, in the words of James Sterba, "to achieve the sympathetic understanding of [their] views necessary for recognizing

---

[12] Quoted in Allan L. Hammond (ed.), *A Passion to Know: Twenty Profiles in Science* (New York: Charles Scribner's Sons, 1984), p. 5.

what is valuable in those views and what, therefore, needs to be incorporated into [his] own views".[13]

As brilliant and productive a scientist as Galileo Galilei was, his work was impeded by his arrogance. He was in many ways an admirable man, and no doubt the social conditions of the dissemination of his views were horrific enough to elicit a bad reaction from many a person of pretty good character. Still, more humility would have been a boon to him. His sense of intellectual superiority led him to disregard the work of other scientists who disagreed with him, and the incorporation of which could have improved his own work. He overestimated the probative force of his arguments for heliocentrism, and thus underestimated the justification of those who hesitated to accept the hypothesis.[14] In fact, his favorite argument—that the earth's motion accounts for the tides—was unsound (p. 78).

To the end of his life, Galileo held to a simplified version of the Copernican system in which all the planets move in perfect circles. Although he preached open-mindedness, he never lent an ear to Kepler's arguments about elliptical paths. (ibid., p. 26)

This despite the fact that, only by allowing the orbits to be elliptical could one make sense of the planets' orbiting around the sun. Galileo's superiority also gave him a sense of entitlement to treat others with contempt and a disposition to underestimate those others' ability to detect the contempt, thus making the social conditions of his scientific work more problematic than they needed to be. In 1611, Galileo enjoyed an affectionate friendship with Maffeo Barberini (elected Pope as Urban VIII in 1623), but in his *Dialogue on the Two Chief World Systems* he put the Pope's favorite argument for a stationary earth—that God can do anything that is not self-contradictory—in the mouth of Simplicius, a simpleton character, on the assumption that his critics in the Vatican would not be smart enough to notice (pp. 141–2). They did notice, and their resentment worked ill for Galileo at his trial in 1633. As one contemporary commented, "Galileo caused his own ruin by thinking too highly of himself and despising others. You should not be surprised if everybody plots against him" (Orazio Grassi, as quoted on p. 172). Even a great scientist like Galileo can learn

---

[13] James Sterba, *Justice for Here and Now* (Cambridge: Cambridge University Press, 1998), p. 4.

[14] William R. Shea and Mariano Artigas, *Galileo in Rome* (New York: Oxford University Press, 2003), pp. 73–4.

from fellow scientists, and needs to make some kind of social life with his contemporaries, especially ones who can affect his opportunities to do his work and disseminate its results; for both of these reasons, more humility would have served Galileo well.

Conclusion

We have construed humility negatively—as a relative lack of concern to appear excellent to others, as a disposition not to make illegitimate entitlement claims on the basis of one's superiority, as a relative weakness of desire to be the author of other people's minds, as a disposition not to ascribe to oneself a greater moral excellence than one possesses, especially in acts of comparing oneself with others. And so forth. But by itself, none of these lacks and negations amounts to a virtue. A person with a certain kind of damage to the frontal lobes of his brain lacks completely both the concern to appear excellent to others and the desire to be the author of other people's minds,[15] but this does not give him any kind of virtuous humility. In describing the humility of Jesus and that of G. E. Moore, we said that the lack of concern for status is coordinated with another virtue, in Jesus *agapē* for humanity, in Moore a passion for philosophical insight. And we think this fact represents a general feature of humility—that it is internally connected, in the personality of the virtuous person, with other virtues. We cannot induce virtue by damaging frontal lobes, because such damage undermines concern across the board, while virtue consists in *selective differentiation* of concern: intense concern for what is worthy of it and relatively little concern for what is less worthy.

The virtues most likely to come to mind on reading our litany of intellectual humility's probable epistemic advantages are intellectual daring and self-confidence. People can be debilitated not only by intellectual vanity and arrogance, but also by timidity and diffidence. To be the most advancing of knowers, people need to be willing to think outside the presuppositions of their communities, to doubt authorities, and to imagine unheard-of possibilities. And it seems intuitively clear that intellectual timidity and diffidence hinder such activities. We might worry that an inquirer who

---

[15] See Antonio Damasio, *Descartes' Error* (New York: Avon Books, 1994), ch. 3.

markedly lacks vanity, arrogance, domination, and grandiosity is not very likely to be daring and self-confident.

These vices can sometimes substitute for virtues. The terror of appearing foolish before members of her profession may prompt a scholar to extreme care and thoroughness. Brash claiming of intellectual entitlement by bright graduate students is sometimes a crucial stage on the road to epistemic success. Given the pervasiveness of human vice, such biographies of knowledge may even be the norm, in a statistical sense. But intellectual daring and self-confidence are not tied by any necessity to these vices. Moore was an unusually energetic and venturesome epistemic agent who seems not to have depended on vanity and arrogance. To stand up before an audience of Cambridge intellectuals and prove the existence of the external world by reference to one's own two hands takes intellectual pluck. It is true that the same act might be motivated by vanity and arrogance, but in this case it wasn't. Other notable individuals in whom these traits combined were Barbara McClintock, the Nobel prize-winning geneticist, and Rosalind Franklin, both of whom we will look at in Chapter 11. Galileo, like many prominent scientists, was arrogant, but it seems that the love of knowledge was a still more prominent motive for him; and he would have been a more effective scientist had he been more humble. In all these people, the love of knowledge was a more important explanation of their intellectual success than arrogance or vanity.

10

Autonomy

Introduction

A number of the intellectual virtues reflect the social nature of intellectual practices. These practices are prey to social dysfunctions typical of human beings and may be promoted by salutary patterns of interaction for which we have the potential. The virtue of intellectual autonomy reflects certain facts about the social nature of human *agency*—in particular, that to be effective (or to exist at all) human actions must be prepared for by an education at the hands of the human community; that actions are often concerted and coordinated; that people depend on their contemporaries for information, stimulation, and critical correction; that the intelligence with which an action is performed belongs to a tradition of practical intelligence that may be centuries or millennia old but that intelligent action is never determined algorithmically by such an education or tradition; that ultimately, actions are always performed by individuals; that human beings often disagree about what should be done, and that disagreements can often be settled by discussion in which each party shows an independent spirit. These and other facts about human agency all bear on the analysis of autonomy, and they are evident no less in intellectual than in other practices. Indeed, the notion of practices "other than intellectual" is fishy; any activity that warrants the name of "practice" will perforce be shot through with knowledge. To be autonomous in those contexts that we call political or moral, or in pursuit of productions of various kinds, is to *think* autonomously.

In this chapter we will develop a concept of intellectual autonomy according to which one becomes an integrated, independent thinker by fittingly appropriating one's vast intellectual debts and dependencies. The resources of an intellectual tradition—the propositional knowledge it embodies, its understandings of things, its logic, its great creative thinkers, the world views it contains, its controversies, its ways of testing claims and understandings, etc.—far from limiting the autonomy of the tradition's heirs, are the heirs' resources for developing their own autonomy. Autonomy is a cultural achievement passed from generation to generation. This autonomy is exemplified in the student or researcher who is able to work on his own, where working on his own involves a wise dependence, a willingness and ability to tap the intelligence and knowledge of others as needed; but it also means an intelligent ability to stand one's own ground against bullying, as well as gentler forms of pressure to conform.

The word "autonomy" will be associated, in some readers' minds, with the philosophical controversy over the metaphysics of freedom—the issue of freedom versus determinism. That is not the topic of this chapter. We will treat autonomy here somewhat as we treated self-knowledge in Chapter 4. There we noted that philosophers like David Hume and Derek Parfit present arguments to the conclusion that *no one* has *any* knowledge of himself as a continuing center of consciousness. Our brief account of self-knowledge assumed, with common sense, that we do have such knowledge, and then moved on to discuss the richer kind of knowledge that mature and virtuous people have of themselves. Similarly here, we will assume that people have varying degrees of freedom of choice—perhaps this can be conceived in either a libertarian or a compatibilist way—and will spend the chapter exploring the virtue that may or may not be built on this basic feature of human nature.

Regulation by Self and Others

In the period of the Enlightenment, intellectual autonomy was highly touted, and Immanuel Kant virtually identified it with enlightenment:

Enlightenment is man's release from his self-incurred tutelage. Tutelage is man's inability to make use of his understanding without direction from another. Self-incurred is this tutelage when its cause lies not in lack of reason but in lack of resolution and courage to use it without direction from another. *Saper aude!* "Have courage to use your own reason!"—that is the motto of enlightenment.[1]

---

[1] Immanuel Kant, "An Answer to the Question, What is Enlightenment?", in *Practical Philosophy*, trans. Mary J. Gregor, in *The Cambridge Edition of the Works of Immanuel Kant*, (Cambridge: Cambridge University Press, 1996), p. 17.

The autonomy in question would be a disposition to use one's reason "without direction from another". Which other? *Any* others? Under what conditions? What is "direction"? And what is the disposition made of (so to speak)? We must answer these questions if we are to understand the virtue of autonomy, and they were not answered clearly either by Kant or by those who more recently have thought autonomy to be a vice—of arrogant and extravagant claims to self-sufficiency or self-creation, of solipsism, ingratitude, and a sense of entitlement to make texts mean whatever one fancies. However the virtue of autonomy was interpreted, it was conceived of as some *proper* ability to think for oneself and not to be *improperly* dependent on or influenced by others; and however the vice of autonomy was interpreted, it was some denial or underrating of one's real and legitimate and salutary intellectual dependencies. Here we are looking for the virtue of autonomy and will need to keep one eye on the vice that sometimes goes by the same name.

Autonomy may be defined, very abstractly, as "self-regulation" ("autonomy" comes from Greek words for "self" and "rule"). Its lexical contrary is heteronomy, or "regulation by others". So intellectual autonomy is the virtue of proper self-regulation, but always with regard to other-regulation or the possibility thereof. (Autonomy is, after all, a *social* virtue.) If we try to imagine the extremes of self-regulation and regulation by others, the absurdity of both is manifest. The virtue in this area of life must partake of both self- and other-regulation, and the task of the virtue epistemologist is to delineate the interactions of these in the trait.

Imagine first the person who is self-ruled "all the way down". He is the single unaided author (or at any rate original discoverer) of all the logical rules he uses, all the experimental standards, all the vocabulary of inquiry, all the guiding questions he addresses—that is, of everything that regulates his intellectual practices. No such standard is an inheritance. He has discovered for himself all the factual background that regulates any present inquiry, and has by himself contrived all the explanations that any present inquiry presupposes. He is the complete autodidact, never having had a teacher other than himself, with literally no one to thank for his intellectual powers and accomplishments. He has never darkened the door of a university or any other school. He works entirely alone, never consulting colleagues, never listening to criticism from others, never reading what others have written. This is not the autonomy that Kant calls enlightenment; it cannot be what it means for an individual to "make use of his understanding without direction from another". The prospects of such an "autonomous" individual having any light on anything are dim indeed.

Next imagine the heteronomous extreme. He is a "thinker" who cannot regulate himself in any way whatever. When he follows a rule of inference, he must not only have the rule dictated to him by some authority (a teacher or a logic textbook), but he must have guidance in how to apply the rule to the present case (that is, the teacher must tell him that he got it right, or somehow the book must show this, perhaps by an example). When he does an experiment, he must be guided at every step by his research director. He never "plays" with vocabulary, but must be able to find exactly the required meaning in a dictionary, and regularly needs confirmation by a teacher that the meaning he thinks he has found is indeed the required meaning. He writes down nothing that has not been warranted by some authority, either a teacher or an authoritative book. He takes course after course in the university, collecting notebooks full of lecture dictation that he duly memorizes, but never ventures to put any of the ideas together in his own way. He does not even rearrange the ideas he finds in these notes, but tries to reproduce strictly the order in which they were delivered by the authoritative lecturer. This character does not represent the ideal that the critics of autonomy have in mind.

Clearly, an intellectual agent is wanted who has been, and continues to be, *properly* regulated by others, but has at the same time a mind of his own, being an independent and creative thinker and inquirer. If autonomy is to be a virtue, it must incorporate elements of intellectual heteronomy—not the vice, of course, but the phenomenon of being regulated by others. Perhaps we can get a bit clearer about this trait by putting before our minds some of the chief ways in which people regulate one another's intellectual practices. Such an exercise will enable us get a more perspicuous view of the proprieties and improprieties in this connection. We will see that some kinds of hetero-regulation, at the appropriate moment and as accepted in the appropriate way, are intellectually beneficial and even indispensable, while the same hetero-regulation, at a different moment or as accepted in a different way, would be unvirtuous; while other kinds of hetero-regulation are always or almost always inappropriate, and others are always or almost always appropriate. Consider then the following possible ways of being intellectually regulated by one or more other persons. Such persons may supply us with knowledge (information, training, understanding); guide us with their questions, critical and otherwise; model intellectual discipline for us, providing us intellectual "ideals" or "heroes" (inspiring us); reward or punish us for doing well or badly; create a social ethos of expectations, proprieties, and proscriptions; encourage us (support us emotionally in our more difficult epistemic efforts) or, as it may be, discourage us; compete with us, intimidate us, "threaten" us; and they may function as authorities. In each case some ways of receiving direction from another are compatible with, or even essential to, autonomy, and some ways are unvirtuous. The virtue of autonomy is largely a disposition actively to exhibit the former and shun the latter kinds of dependence. Accordingly, it is enhanced by a dispositional awareness of the extent to which one's epistemic life is regulated by others, and a disposition to orient one's epistemic practices intelligently to the facts of this dependence. In all the intentional undertakings of the intellectual life—the expressions of full and mature intellectual agency—one or several of the hetero-regulators are operating, and fully intelligent intellectual agency takes them into account. People become *less* autonomous, not more so, by refusing to acknowledge and understand hetero-regulation, and as a consequence fail to be at their epistemic best.

The other as imparting knowledge Knowledge builds on knowledge; information and deeper understanding raise more questions, the pursuit of which uncovers more information and deepens our understanding. All the knowledge we have has been mediated to us by others, since acquisition of knowledge is always regulated by knowledge already acquired, and a significant portion of the knowledge we already have is inherited. For even the most creative person, then, the intellectual life is a network of deep dependencies.

Consider the potential for seeds of autonomy in a case that looks like extreme intellectual heteronomy. We hear of schools in the Islamic world where the education consists almost exclusively of memorizing the Qu'ran in Arabic. This transmission process tends in the direction of the sheerest heteronomy; but still, if the child is an Arabic speaker, it would be extreme to say that this education gives the child merely the intellectual status of a tape-recorder or a filing cabinet, because the child very likely understands a bit of what he has memorized, and understanding is a seed of autonomy. Having understood something, he has a way to distinguish the sentences he understands from the ones he doesn't, and this allows him to ask his teacher about the meaning of the ones he doesn't understand. The asking and listening for an answer is an act of his own, an act of incipient autonomy, and if the teacher answers him intelligently, he gets more understanding and thus more intellectual agency. And so he is put in a position to ask more questions. As he does so, he sees more connections between Qu'ranic passages and begins to have more questions, and so gains more intellectual control in his study of the Qu'ran. So sparks of autonomy are possible in even a very oppressive education. In similar schools in countries like Pakistan, where the language is not Arabic, children who spend their days memorizing the Qu'ran do seem to be reduced to the status of tape-recorder.

Autonomy is fostered more by insight and understanding than by propositional knowledge, though, as we have pointed out (Chapter 2), even the simplest kinds of propositional knowledge presuppose a bit of understanding, and so harbor at least a tiny seed of autonomy. Since the teacher may or may not encourage such questioning, it is in his power to stifle or promote the autonomy of the pupil. He could promote it by encouraging the questioning and rewarding proffered insights with approval; he might even give special approval to the more "independent" judgments of the pupil. Thus the child may owe his self-regulation to regulation by the teacher.

To turn to a rather different kind of education, a good Ph.D. program aims to turn out scholars who are independent thinkers, and as a way of achieving this end, students are given lectures, reading courses, and supervision, though ideally less and less as they progress through the program. And, at the end of a forty-year career in the academy, a properly autonomous scholar will still be able to detect in her work and orientation the fingerprints of her mentors. Indeed, the best education always aims at stage-appropriate autonomy; as a child moves through grade school and high school to college, the idea is to make her, in certain ways, independent of supervision. Many colleges advertise their curriculum with mottos like "creating life-long learners", suggesting both a determining influence and that that influence promotes intellectual independence. At every level, we praise the student who is a self-starter, who can work on her own, who does not require to be instructed in every little detail, yet this outcome is supposed to result from instruction.

We want to emphasize how autonomy, like most of the virtues we discuss in this book, is a modification of the individual's will. But this is the place to note the importance of sheer content-specific learning to the exercise of this virtue. One reason why people gain in autonomy as their education proceeds is that they increasingly know their way about the "field", and naturally enough are able to navigate with less present and explicit guidance. They understand things that are said, they know what they need to find out, and they know how to find it out. The more expert they are, the rarer and more specialized will be the occasions when they need to call in the consultants. But note that even where an expert's knowledge is most extensive, she will often call on help (provided she does not have a character defect that makes her unwilling), and that autonomy involves knowing when to call on help, what kind of help to call on, and being humble enough to do so. Autonomy here is part expertise and part character trait.

John Benson has pointed out that whether the need for information is a sign of immature heteronomy can depend on what kind of knowledge the agent needs help with.

The belief that whales are viviparous is none the worse for being taken from a reliable textbook. I may not know what the reasons are for this proposition; but it is enough that I know that there are some. But it is doubtful whether I know what I am saying if I say that torture is wicked, if my only reason is that I am confident that someone else has good reasons, though I do not know what they are.[2]

In effect, Benson is suggesting that understanding is a kind of autonomy; to "know what I am saying" when I say that whales are viviparous, despite having learned it from a reliable textbook, is just to understand it adequately; and not to know what I am saying when I say that torture is wicked, in case I take it on somebody else's authority, is just *not* to understand *that* adequately. To understand is to stand, to that extent, on one's own intellectual feet. But Benson also points out, in effect, that "adequately" always has an implicit index to some context or purpose, and so, thus, does autonomy. He says:

---

[2] John Benson, "Who Is the Autonomous Man?", *Philosophy* 58 (1983): 5–17, p. 13.

It may be consistent with the role of critical enquirer to ask a competent authority whether smoking will damage my health, but it is not consistent with the role of critical moral agent to ask anyone whether I ought to be a conscientious objector, practice contraceptive intercourse, or approve of abortion. ... To be autonomous in morality involves a greater degree of self-sufficiency than to be intellectually autonomous. (ibid., p. 211)

I can take it on authority that smoking is unhealthy or that whales are viviparous without prejudice to my intellectual autonomy, because it is not my business to understand such things deeply; but I can't take it on authority that torture is wicked and still be thought an autonomous moral thinker, because it is everybody's business to understand this much. But Benson seems to err in thinking that it is essentially morality that makes the difference in these cases. If I am a marine zoologist and I take it on authority that whales are viviparous, then I *am* short of intellectual autonomy; and in some areas of moral reasoning (say, where the issues are too technical for the layperson), it may be acceptable to base a moral judgment on authority. Intellectual and moral autonomy are not different in kind, because moral autonomy is a kind of intellectual autonomy—that is, it is autonomy as a moral *thinker*. The difference is that, generally speaking, moral understanding is required of everybody, but zoological understanding isn't. Once we specify narrowly enough the context or role, we see that just as much self-sufficiency is required in the "intellectual" sphere as in the "moral".

What makes, then, for autonomy with respect to knowledge gained from another? First, we would note that in one sense, the autonomy of the individual will vary from area to area of knowledge. No one is equally autonomous across all fields of knowledge. I may be rather autonomous within my specialty, but as soon as I get out of my depth, whether with respect to plumbing or microbiology, I become much more dependent on testimony and advice that I have only a rough ability to assess. So in this respect, autonomy is a matter of area-specific knowledge—certainly of propositional knowledge and of acquaintance, but above all of understanding as mediated by these and by reflection. Such understanding gives one a vantage point from which to assess evidence, organize and make use of new information, and thus have a certain ownership of the contents of one's mind. It makes one less likely either to be swayed by contrary opinions, new information, intellectual fads, and social pressures to conform intellectually; or to dismiss such inputs out of hand—that is, without giving oneself adequate opportunity to see what merit they may harbor. Instead, one is in a position to process such inputs actively from one's own point of view, to think for oneself.

But autonomy vis-à-vis knowledge that comes from others is not *just* a matter of area-specific learning. Even in this limited (though very important) area, autonomy is more like a character trait than area-specific learning. It is a kind of wisdom about knowledge, a large-perspectival self-understanding with respect to the fields of learning. It is a practical wisdom such that the agent knows what she knows and knows the limits thereof, but also has enough general grasp of what is on the outer edge of her knowledge that she can figure out how to assess proposals there as an intelligent layperson. Such assessment will often involve consulting people who have more information and deeper understanding than herself, as well as books. Autonomy here is provided by having a feel for who these people and books are, enough humility not to mind seeking help from others, a bit of skill in putting the questions, enough understanding to grasp and assess what they say, and the self-confidence to venture judgments on the basis of these sources. So here autonomy is proper heteronomy. Specialized knowledge is no doubt an *entrée* to this more generalized ability to size up and assimilate knowledge on the periphery of one's expertise. It gives one insight into what it is *really* to know something, an insight that may beget both proper humility and a kind of generalized competence, both of which are aspects of intellectual autonomy.

A person will not have developed this understanding, skill, self-confidence, and humility without loving the epistemic goods. And she will love them in two ways. First, she will love them in the way that seeks confirmation and resolution and the holding of an understanding. Her will will have a teleology, and its aim will be knowledge; and this concern will tend to make her an independent thinker. But autonomy is also served by a sheer love of ideas, of reasoning, of thinking up schemata, of trying on ways of thinking. The dialectical versatility nurtured by such playfulness will serve the thinker well in thinking for herself, in making her own the knowledge that she gets from others—provided that her will is oriented by the more serious epistemic goal of truth. The individual who *just* enjoys being "creative" may seem even more autonomous than the one whose creativity is subordinated to a concern for truth; but this is an illusory and fantastic sort of autonomy, not the autonomy of the intellectually most virtuous agent.

The other as critic   Criticism is another way in which one person may guide another's intellectual practice. A teacher comments on a student's paper, pointing up faults and offering suggestions for the next draft. A professional literature colloquium consists, in part, in the members' offering criticisms of one another's comments and suggestions on how to extend an argument. In contexts of receiving criticism, autonomy sometimes involves resisting the criticism, sometimes accepting it; but in either case the agent may owe his increase of knowledge to the critic—and this happens at *every* level of sophistication and expertise, from the kindergarten to the professional physics or philosophy colloquium. The autonomous person has the presence of mind to judge evenly and rationally here. He is ready to assert himself, rather than accept criticism obsequiously; he is tenacious enough in his intellectual commitments to make the critic work hard, if that is warranted. But he is not defensive or proud to the point of rejecting criticism when he shouldn't; he is open to criticism, and this is as much a mark of autonomy as proper tenacity is.

   Thus again we see that autonomy is not a matter of sheer independence, but of what one *does* with one's dependence. Recently a student of one of us declined an honors project on a topic in which the professor was doing research, out of fear that his own "originality" would be swamped or stifled by the teacher's greater expertise. He chose to do his project, instead, in an area where the professor had little expertise or interest. This choice, by an undergraduate (even a very bright one, as in the present case), is not an expression of intellectual autonomy, though the student may have thought of it in that way. Instead, the choice was made out of the undergraduate equivalent of what Harold Bloom calls "the anxiety of influence", an intellectual pathology that belongs in the general area of intellectual heteronomy (see Chapter 9 for more discussion). Practical wisdom, motivated by love of knowledge and freed by humility or supported by a bit of courage in the face of criticism, would more likely enjoin intellectual symbiosis with the professor and self-subordination to the professor's interests and direction; and this would be an impressive age-appropriate autonomy in the undergraduate's case. Autonomy for the student may involve more acquiescence in what the teacher says than autonomy in the professional philosopher involves acquiescence in what his critics say. But in both cases, autonomy involves a reasonable, active use of guidance from another.

The other as model Modeling occurs at all levels of sophistication and character development. The child models himself on his parents, teachers, and peers; the doctoral student models herself on her mentors and peers; colleagues model themselves on one another; scholars model themselves on respected figures in their field. Modeling often has an unconscious aspect. I may just "find" myself speaking, writing, or behaving like someone I admire. I may not even realize I admire somebody until I notice myself imitating him. This is a kind of heteronomy. To the extent that we are unaware of somebody's control over our epistemic life, we are less in a position to conduct ourselves autonomously toward that other's influence. Consciousness and self-knowledge are important elements of autonomy.

Modeling is a natural part of human development and interaction, and is crucial for our epistemic performance. But for optimal development, we need to control it and channel it rationally. In colleges, we hire faculty with a view to whether they will be salutary models for the students. And in deciding which job offer to take, a young professor who is wise will factor into his decision the potential of his new colleagues to provide him with good models. ("Good model" here does not necessarily mean "razzle-dazzle intellectual superstar". It means someone with intellectual virtues.) So in this dimension autonomy implies a conception of what a good model is like and an active practical wisdom about human development and about one's own development. It implies being self-aware enough to notice, pretty reliably, if one is being led down the wrong path. The autonomous individual is constantly alert to intellectual deficits in herself and her associates, but without cynicism or despair. She is reflective about the intellectual life—does not just pursue it, but thinks about what it is to pursue it and what kind of persons best pursue it; and this makes her a constant evaluator of herself and others. Clearly, the reflectiveness described in this paragraph is not characteristic of all autonomy, but of its higher degrees.

The model can be incorporated authentically or inauthentically. The authentic incorporation of an excellent model will be an incorporation of the virtues of that model, rather than of incidental traits and peculiarities—catch phrases, facial expressions, and other mannerisms, or even vices such as the disposition to mistreat students and selfish, defensive hording of data. The model may encourage worshipful discipleship rather than critical modeling. The most authentic incorporation will itself be characterized by autonomy, by intelligent, conscious assessment of the model. The best relationship is one in which both model and modeler are autonomous, neither having a pathological need for the other, and both committed to an intellectual ideal beyond the relationship.

Another permutation of the anxiety of influence is the fear of modeling, a fear of compromising one's autonomy by being like one's elders or one's peers—or worse, one's juniors. We spoke of courage as an aspect of autonomy in facing one's critics, but it seems odd to speak of courageously modeling oneself on another. Often modeling, even when quite conscious, is less an act and more a letting-happen, with the actions of autonomy being more a matter of checking the happening. But if so, then it may be possible to express autonomy here in a courageous letting-happen of modeling, against the anxiety of influence. Envy is another emotional impediment to modeling. Envy is unhappy admiration, as Kierkegaard says, and it can motivate a rebellion against the envied one—a desire to be as little like her as possible. But envy is a kind of bondage, a disposition not to see the good in the envied one, or to see it through a filter of invidious qualifications. The more autonomous the individual, the less will he have this envy; he will be glad to model himself on aspects of these others, grateful to have associates worthy to be modeled on, and confident of his independence. Or if he has the envy, he will have an inclination and ability to dominate it in the interest of the truth.

The other as sanctioner   The critic and model, as well as others, often mete out rewards and penalties for epistemic behavior. Parents and mentors express approval and disapproval, teachers give grades and class rankings, honorary societies invite membership, readers pay money for books, students write evaluations of their professors, colleagues give or withhold tenure, review boards accept and reject manuscripts, and Nobel prizes reward the highest levels of scientific research. Such sanctions powerfully guide our intellectual feet along the paths of conformity; they would not exist in such abundance or so pervade the world of learning if they didn't.

Nor is it obvious that the world of the intellect would be better off without such sanctions. One can guess that without the rewards and penalties, a lot less excellent intellectual work would get done. Some very virtuous epistemic agents might never have become such had they not been molded early by extrinsic rewards and penalties.

But the sanctions are not an unmixed blessing. In the best case, good behavior is rewarded and bad penalized; but sometimes people are rewarded for compromising, or they compromise to get the reward; and are penalized for good behavior or compromise excellence to avoid penalty.[3] In the best case, sanctions rule epistemic behavior primarily at the earlier stages of development or provide a minor extra stimulus to excellent performance; but in reality often the sanctions determine epistemic behavior in a major way both early and late. Intellectual autonomy involves a dispositional orientation of the will to the parameters of reward and penalty in all their forms. In general, autonomy is a freedom from domination by sanctions, but this freedom is no more absolute than that from informers, critics, and models. This last claim might be doubted. Are not sanctions more capable, in principle, of being shunned altogether than informers, critics, and models, these last three being more nearly essential to the intellectual life of human beings than sanctions? We are of two minds about this. Sanctions are ingredients in the very business of critics and models. Critics, by their nature as critics, are approvers and disapprovers; and models, by their nature, function as indirect critics. If so, then sanctions are as natural to human epistemic enterprises as are critics and models. Yet we do think that in the most mature intellectual characters the hope of reward and fear of penalties can subside to something quite negligible; whereas one never outgrows one's need for critics, and one's most important models live on in one's mind and will.

Autonomy is the ability to keep money and fame in perspective when these are tied to epistemic performance. But what is the required perspective? Rare individuals may be completely indifferent to some of the kinds of sanctions, and this will certainly count as autonomy (assuming

---

[3] Brian C. Martinson, Melissa S. Anderson, and Raymond de Vries, "Scientists Behaving Badly", *Nature* 435 (9 June 2005): 737–8) document the disturbingly high number of scientists funded by the National Institutes of Health who engage in behaviors that conform to the US Office of Science and Technology Policy definition of research misconduct as "fabrication, falsification, or plagiarism". For example, 6 percent admitted failing to present data that contradict their research, and 15.5 percent admitted changing the design, methodology, or results of a study due to pressure from a funding source.

the individual is not indifferent to the epistemic goods). But we think it very rare indeed that anyone be indifferent to all and sundry intellectual sanctions, and we do not make indifference to them a requirement for autonomy. Rather, autonomy is the ability to enjoy rewards or suffer penalties for one's ideas without the sanction affecting one's assessment of the value of the ideas; it is the ability to keep the value of the sanction in a different category from the value of the goods. And it is more than this. It is also the ability and inclination to let the value of the epistemic goods appropriately dominate that of the sanctions, so that when one must choose between, on the one hand, the enjoyment or avoidance of the sanction and, on the other, the acquisition, maintenance, application, or transmission of the good, the agent can give the latter their full due. Intellectual autonomy's dependence on the love of knowledge should be obvious.

As we have indicated, the freedom of autonomy has a historical and developmental character as well. Autonomy is freedom from the push and pull of sanctions in the same way in which Wittgenstein's Tractarian philosopher is free from the ladder of referential language—not absolutely free, because had the philosopher not climbed up on reference, he would not be where he is today, floating on his wise nonsense. But *now* he does not need the ladder.

The other as authority   Authority is the kind of hetero-regulator that people first think of in connection with the virtue of autonomy. It is certainly prominent in Kant's mind. To be gullible or credulous is to be disposed to accept others' testimony "on authority", and in the more extreme versions of modern thought, autonomy is never accepting testimony without independently verifying it. In earlier chapters we have agreed with Thomas Reid's general point that the tendency to believe testimony without testing it for oneself is not intellectually substandard as such (though it is of course also not autonomy as such). Throughout the preceding discussion we have construed autonomy not as an immunity from hetero-regulation, but as a disposition to respond virtuously to hetero-regulation—variously and appropriately and actively. Not all circumstances call equally or in the same way for caution about testimony, and the autonomous individual is disposed to be cautious about testimony in whatever way is right for the circumstances—sometimes very cautious, sometimes implicitly trusting. In this discussion of autonomy in relation to authority we will consider not just credulity and gullibility (lack of autonomy with respect to testimony) but also servility (lack of autonomy with respect to directives). Both involve a deficit of independent critical thinking, and in that way are intellectual deficits.

An authority is a source of testimony or command such that, in virtue of its status relative to its subjects and within its domain, its testimony or command is *prima facie* to be accepted or obeyed.[4] Authorities gain their status in a variety of ways. Some authorities have this status by virtue of *knowledge*—for example, the expert and the eyewitness. Some have their authority by *office*—for example, presidents and police officers. Some have their authority by virtue of their relationship to subjects—for example, parents to their children and God to his creatures. Subjects of such authorities can express autonomy vis-à-vis the authority if they accept the authority's testimony or command intelligently—that is, with an understanding of the authority's status as authority. To understand an authority's status is to understand the authority's limits. An authority can be limited in two ways: in its domain and in its competence.

To accept the authority of an eyewitness is to credit the witness with a competence, the competence to report what he saw. It is thus to understand how eyewitnesses get to occupy their position of authority. But it is to understand also that the domain of the eyewitness's authority is just what he saw, and to be ready, thus, to withdraw one's trust in case the eyewitness exceeds the bounds of his authority by claiming things he didn't witness. It is also to understand that eyewitnesses are fallible (subject to faulty seeing, imperfect understanding of what they saw, and possibly even lying about what they saw) and thus to recognize the propriety of cross-examining them as a way of upgrading the evidential status of what they report. Analogous things can be said about autonomy vis-à-vis experts such as scientists, lawyers, and historians. To accept the authority of a police officer is to accept intelligently the officer's authority to command certain things—say, to see your driver's license—and it is no compromise of your autonomy, but rather an expression of it, that you obey such a command with this understanding. Out of such understanding it is part of your autonomy that you ascertain (if at all in doubt) that the officer is a legitimate member of the

---

[4] See Mark Murphy, *An Essay on Divine Authority* (Ithaca, NY: Cornell University Press, 2002).

police force, and that you know and insist that while he has the authority to see your driver's license, he does not have the authority to set your standards of theological orthodoxy or strip-search you by the side of the road or command you to shoot out the tires of the next car that drives by. A child is autonomous in accepting her parents' authority to the extent that she understands their authority to be ordained for her good and the proper order of society. Of course she is not autonomous in her acceptance of their authority when she is very young, but if they exercise it benevolently and wisely, she grows in her autonomy as she grows in understanding of their authority. This will also be an understanding of the limits of their authority—that, say, they do not have the authority to command her to act immorally—and of their fallibility in the exercise of it (that what they do justifiably and benevolently command may not always be for the best). We propose, then, that an important element of autonomy vis-à-vis an authority is the subject's understanding of the authority and its limitations: the authority's fallibility and the limits of its domain. The entire tradition of civil disobedience depends on this conception of authority.

Perhaps we can gain some insight into autonomy as a virtue by considering the disturbing results of Stanley Milgram's experiments concerning obedience to authority.[5] Three fictional characters make up the scene: the "experimenter", the "teacher", and the "learner". The "experimenter" is dressed as a technician and gives instructions. The "teacher" is the unsuspecting subject of the experiment. He is told that the experiment is to test the effects of punishment on learning, and that he will be dispensing electric shocks of increasing severity to the learner. The "learner" is strapped into a chair with electrodes on his wrists. The experimenter and learner are party to the deception; the learner will not be shocked as the teacher believes. The learner's task is to pair words: he reads the first word of a pair and four terms, one of which is the correctly paired word, and chooses a word by working one of four switches. The experimenter tells the teacher to administer shocks of gradually increasing intensity each time the learner gives a wrong answer; the first level is 15 volts, and the levels increase in 15-volt increments up to a maximum of 450 volts. The teacher administers the "shock" by moving a lever on a control panel with the

---

[5] Reported in Stanley Milgram, *Obedience to Authority: An Experimental View* (New York: Harper and Row, 1974).

voltages marked, together with descriptive phrases "slight shock" up to 60 volts, "danger: severe shock" up to 420 volts, and then "XXX" for 435 and 450 volts. By pre-arrangement, the learner gives incorrect answers about three out of every four times. If the teacher expresses unwillingness to keep shocking the learner, the experimenter gives him pre-arranged prods starting with "Please continue" up to "You have no other choice, you *must* go on." If the teacher protests that the learner does not want to go on, the experimenter says to the teacher: "Whether he likes it or not, you must go on until he has learned all the word pairs correctly. So please go on."

Of the forty subjects in Milgram's original 1963 study, none stopped before reaching 300 volts, and twenty-six subjects, 65 percent of the total, went all the way to 450. The experiment seems to show that in certain circumstances, of which the experiment is one, otherwise autonomous people are prone to be inappropriately compliant—to do, in response to authoritative orders, things they oughtn't to do. In particular, in this circumstance the vast majority of normally autonomous people make bad judgments about the domain of an authority's authority. What can we learn from this about the nature of virtues, and of autonomy in particular?

Virtues in general have two "contrary" properties: circumstance indexicality and circumstance independence. We have seen, especially in Chapter 4, that some virtue epistemologists think of virtues as properly functioning faculties. We have not adopted their concept of a virtue, but circumstance indexicality is a property that faculties share with virtues as we understand them. Faculties are adapted to a special range of circumstances, beyond which even the healthiest faculty cannot be expected to function as it should. Human eyesight, for example, is adapted to work in a certain range of lighting, on objects of a certain range of size, at a certain range of distance, in a body that is neither too stationary nor too rapidly moving relative to the objects of sight. If the lighting is too intense or too dim, or the objects too small or too far away or too close up, or if the eye is absolutely stationary or whirling rapidly around, even the person with 20–20 vision cannot be expected to see much.

Similarly, circumstance indexicality is virtues' adaptation to circumstance types. For example, anybody's courage will be somewhat specialized. It fits him to perform well in situations whose threatening features are of certain determinate physical and social types that fall within a certain range of degrees of severity. A person might be quite courageous in most social situations but easily overwhelmed by physical heights or a storm at sea, where another courageous person might have the opposite "specialization". Or someone might have courage fitting him for situations of a certain degree of social threat, but be undone by ones exceeding this. Similarly, a person's autonomy fits him to behave well in situations of actual or potential regulation by others as knowledge-imparters, critics, models, sanctioners, and authorities, where these hetero-regulators fall within a certain normal range and belong to recognizable subspecies. But it seems that the situation of the Milgram experiments was such that almost nobody's virtue of autonomy was up to coping with it. Certainly it was not an everyday situation for any of the unsuspecting subjects; nor is it likely that many of the subjects had ever been burned in a situation in which a mad experimenter was asking people to do such outrageous things under the cloak of science in a respectable university (Yale). And Peter Goldie is certainly right to point to "the insidious incremental nature of the required shock levels to be administered"[6] as part of the explanation of why these normally mature people performed so abysmally. If situations calling for autonomy more typically had this incremental feature, normally autonomous people would, presumably, be better prepared for the experimental situation.

The complement of circumstance indexicality is circumstance independence. While no one can be expected to exhibit a virtue if the circumstances calling for it are sufficiently eccentric, still it is a mark of greater virtue to be more adaptable, to have a wider range of circumstances to which one's virtue is adequate. Few compassionate people are inclined to exhibit compassion in as wide a range of difficult circumstances as Mother Teresa; few forgiving people exhibit forgiveness in as wide a range of circumstances as Nelson Mandela; few persons of integrity maintain their integrity as consistently in tempting circumstances as Billy Graham has done.[7] These people are exemplars of extraordinary virtue at least in part because they are somewhat independent of the narrower, more typical range of circumstances for which the virtue fits most of the people who exhibit it.

---

[6] Peter Goldie, *The Emotions: A Philosophical Exploration* (Oxford: Oxford University Press, 2000), p. 174.

[7] See the stories of these and other "great souls" in David Aikman, *Great Souls: Six Who Changed the Century* (Nashville: W. Publishing Group, 1998).

So it is not beyond possibility that a person of extraordinary autonomy should come along, and be a subject in Milgram's experiment, and because of the independence of his intellect and heart see pretty quickly that he is under no obligation to continue shocking his "learner" and have the presence of mind to exit the procedure—perhaps even to challenge the "experimenter" to stop his cruel experimenting. We will examine such a case—one of Milgram's—in Chapter 12. Milgram's experiment seems to show that people who have this kind of circumstance independence will be rare. Perhaps they are almost as rare as Mother Teresa, Nelson Mandela, and Billy Graham. (Given some of the stories of Mother Teresa standing up to US presidents and other authority figures to plead compassion for the unborn, one can imagine that she would have passed Milgram's autonomy test with flying colors.)

Some of the "teachers" who were found so disturbingly compliant in the Milgram experiments were presumably, at each stage of "torturing" the victim, making judgments about the propriety of following the orders. According to Milgram, indications of nervousness and tension "were characteristic rather than exceptional responses to the experiment".[8] One of the subjects, Morris Braverman (a pseudonym), who administered "shocks" all the way to 450 volts, showed signs of conflict and emotional stress while doing so, and in a follow-up interview he expressed regret and dismay at his behavior. "There was I. I'm a nice person, I think, hurting someone, and caught up in what seemed a mad situation...and in the interest of science, one goes through with it." He giggled during the ordeal and tried to stifle laughter. He said, "This isn't the way I usually am. This was a sheer reaction to a totally impossible situation. And my reaction was to the situation of having to hurt somebody. And being totally helpless and caught up in a set of circumstances where I just couldn't deviate and I couldn't try to help. That is what got me" (Milgram, *Obedience to Authority*, p. 71). Braverman feels himself to be in bondage because it doesn't occur to him that he is in control. The situation imposes such limits on what he can seriously imagine himself doing that it does not occur to him that he could just refuse to go on; *in situ*, his realistic imagination of options of resisting putative authority doesn't extend to this kind of situation. The

[8] Stanley Milgram, "Behavioural Study of Obedience", *Journal of Abnormal and Social Psychology* 67: (1963): 371–8, p. 375; see pp. 376–7.

more autonomous individual will be one whose repertoire of imaginable responsible actions transcends the impositions engineered by Milgram. The more autonomous a person is, the greater the repertoire of rational actions that can occur to him as genuine options—things he genuinely *could do*—in the face of authority.

But also, the more autonomous a person is, the more discriminating he will be among his options in the face of authority. Braverman has (let us say) generally good discrimination about which authorities to obey when, but he is caught unprepared for the scenario in the psychology laboratory at Yale. He hasn't thought through this type of situation; he certainly has not previously thought out what to do if a Yale experimenter with whom he has agreed to cooperate asks him to send 450 volts through a person's body for incorrectly pairing one word with another. Autonomy, we said earlier, is a kind of understanding of authorities, in particular of the rationale for their authority and thus of their fallibility and the limits of their domain. It looks as though Braverman's deficit of autonomy in the special circumstances of Milgram's experiment is an unclarity about the domain of the experimenter's authority. He rightly attributes to the experimenter a kind of intellectual authority, assuming justifiably that a Yale psychologist will know what he's doing and can be trusted not to be doing stupid or cruel things to subjects. When this experimenter then commands him to send high-voltage electricity through the body of a violently protesting subject for having paired words wrongly, he does not see (clearly enough) that the experimenter has vastly exceeded the boundaries of his authority or (alternatively) doubt with sufficient confidence the authority's competence. Perhaps he does see it, in a way, as indicated by his emotional reaction to the situation; but if so, he does not have enough confidence in his own perception to act on the disparity between the experimenter's authority and the experimenter's implicit authority claim. Autonomy is not a merely "intellectual" knowledge of the domains and fallibilities of authorities, but one that is integrated into more or less spontaneous perception and thus action.

An intellectual authority is a source of regulation to which we accord *prima facie* exemption from criticism. Thus Christians accord such an exemption to the Bible or the teachings of the Church; some Freudians accord one to the writings and doctrines of Freud; good children treat their parents as having such an exemption; and this is how Mr Braverman treated the experimenter (he would presumably not have obeyed just anybody who ordered him to behave so shockingly). In the case of legitimate authorities the exemption will not be without rationale. As Gadamer comments,

> But the authority of persons is ultimately based not on the subjection and abdication of reason but on an act of acknowledgment and knowledge—the knowledge, namely, that the other is superior to oneself in judgment and insight and that for this reason his judgment takes precedence—i.e., it has priority over one's own. [9]

People are sometimes quite reflective about their commitment to an intellectual authority. A child who thinks through the authority of his parents might support the exemption by the consideration that they are older and wiser than he. Christians treat the Bible or the Church as authoritative because they believe these to be divinely inspired and appointed. Such rationales can be part of the proper use of the hetero-regulator that we associated with autonomy in the preceding discussion. Thus it would be part of the autonomy of a Christian who treats the Bible or the Church as an intellectual authority that he can articulate well why the authority is a legitimate authority for him.

Christian autonomy, like any intellectual autonomy, is an inclination and ability to think for oneself, and thus to resist conflicting hetero-regulators. But, as we have argued generally for autonomy, it cannot be the inclination or ability to resist all possible hetero-regulators. So it is a disposition and ability to resist *some* hetero-regulators by virtue of obedience to *another* hetero-regulator. For example, a Catholic layman might exhibit intellectual autonomy in resisting the teachings about sexuality or material consumption that are patent in the secular culture in which she lives. The firmer and more articulate and nuanced she is in her resistance to the secular teachings, the more intellectual autonomy she displays, but of course she gets her "position" from a hetero-regulator, the Roman Catholic Church. The secularist's resistance to the Catholic teachings on the same issues may also exhibit autonomy. Both parties will have greater intellectual autonomy the more the behavior is a matter of standing on one's own two feet with respect to the issues. Thus if the pressure of the secular culture is very great, so that secularism is the default position, so to speak, the position into which most people unthinkingly fall, it will take more autonomy on

---

[9] Hans-Georg Gadamer, *Truth and Method*, 2nd rev. edn, trans. by Joel Weinsheimer and Donald G. Marshall (New York: Continuum: 1989), p. 279.

the part of the Catholic to resist the secularist doctrines than it takes the secularist to resist the Catholic doctrines. But if the culture is predominantly Catholic, then it may take more autonomy to be secular in one's thinking. In both cases, autonomy is a matter of resisting one hetero-regulator by virtue of adherence to another.

But how can adherence to a *hetero*-regulator be *auto*nomy? The answer that we have been developing in this chapter is that the hetero-regulator must be assimilated or appropriated to some extent by the epistemic agent; it must become part of the *autos* (self) of the agent. How does the agent appropriate the hetero-regulator? Three modes or features of appropriation can be distinguished.

First, he does so by *understanding* in terms of the hetero-regulator. A person who has mere propositional knowledge of the regulator—say, a list of believed catechetical propositions, warranted in some externalist way—cannot be said to have appropriated the regulator in the way required for autonomy. If these propositions regulate the individual's intellectual life at all, it will be in some way that could hardly be called autonomy. Understanding is the ability to "go on" (on one's own), to make creative or at least intelligent use of, say, an inherited scientific or scholarly procedure, the doctrines of Marxism, the testimonies of scientists, or Scripture. Special indicators of autonomy are invention, improvisation on the basis of the hetero-regulator, wisdom in its terms, and application to new cases; and the more of this an agent has, the greater will be his autonomy with respect to the hetero-regulator. It is important to autonomy that the agent not only understand his own hetero-regulator and understand the matter at hand in terms of it, but also understand the hetero-regulator he is resisting. Otherwise, his resistance can hardly be intelligent, and without intelligence it cannot be autonomous. He will understand the resisted hetero-regulator both on its own terms and in terms of his own hetero-regulator. The former will be a case of having an understanding; the latter of holding one as well. For example, our autonomous adherent to a Catholic view of sexuality will have an articulate understanding of that view, but also a deep enough understanding of the secular viewpoint to make her resistance to the latter intelligent.

We are saying only that a fairly articulate understanding of the resisted view is *characteristic* of autonomous resistance, and characteristically represents an *increase* in autonomy. To make such understanding a necessary condition of autonomous rejection would be too strong. For example, Mother Teresa might pass the Milgram autonomy test with flying colors without being at all clear where Milgram is "coming from", other than understanding that he is asking her to torture another human being without a good enough reason. But Mother Teresa could not be an autonomous adherent of the Christian moral tradition without understanding *it*. Not that she must understand it as well as God understands it; autonomy must be compatible with accepting particular things the rationale for which one does not grasp. One scientist can, without prejudice to her autonomy, accept the testimony of another scientist in an area where the first scientist is not an expert. And the Catholic can autonomously accept the teachings of the Church on sexuality without understanding the rationale for everything in those teachings; but she will be heteronomous with respect to those teachings if she can say nothing about why the Church is authoritative or about how the teachings work and are good; and the more she can say, other things being equal (see the next two points), the more autonomous she will be.

A second aspect of appropriation of a hetero–regulator is the habitual or spontaneous character of its use by the intellectual agent—for example, thinking without need for prompting in terms of the Catholic understanding of sexuality and material acquisitions. The thinking pattern of the hetero–regulator is more deeply appropriated the more it occupies the cross-situational default position with regard to an agent's ways of thinking, the more it is ingrained in the agent, not just something she can muster. A person who thinks well in terms of the Catholic understanding of sexuality and material acquisitions during discussions in church, but who has to remind herself to think in its terms when on a date or walking through the mall, is for that reason less autonomous with respect to that hetero–regulator.

A third mode of appropriation is incorporation by the will. The human self is formed according to the saying of Jesus, "For where your treasure is, there will your heart be also" (Matt. 6: 21). The heart, here, is the inmost self, the *autos* itself. To think autonomously in terms of a hetero–regulator is to love in terms of the hetero–regulator, to care, to be concerned, to be emotionally involved in those terms; it is to be intrinsically motivated to think in those terms. For example, when the autonomous Catholic thinker thinks through the issue of homosexual "marriage" in terms of the

Catholic tradition, she not only understands the tradition and understands the issues in terms of it, and thinks spontaneously in these terms; she also cares about the institution of marriage, and cares about God as the source of the tradition. Were the issue merely "academic" for her, her thinking would be less autonomously *in terms of the tradition*, since her own (*autos*) self would be less involved in the thinking. Sometimes autonomy has been thought of as disinterested, and here the threatening hetero–regulator is not another human being or tradition, but the non–rational part of the self, its emotions and desires, which are thought to impede the autonomous functioning of the intellect. But on the present analysis, autonomy is not a property of the intellect as a faculty or part of a person, but a property of the thinker, the epistemic agent. The importance of the emotions and desires as an integrating factor in the intellectual life is perhaps more obvious in the case of the moral knowledge that has illustrated much of the present subsection, but the same is true in such "objective" areas as scholarship, history, philosophy, and science. A scientist will not have thoroughly appropriated a way of thinking or proceeding scientifically until he has become attached to it, committed to it, self–involved in it.

The Autonomous Will

Near the beginning of this chapter we said that one of the questions that epistemologists need to ask about intellectual autonomy is *What is the disposition made of?* We have said that it is made of knowledge (competence in a field) and especially the kind or aspect of knowledge that we call understanding, and we have stressed the inherited or derived character of most of that knowledge. We have touched again and again on structures of motivation in connection with autonomy. Let us finish this chapter with further reflections on motivation. We can distinguish two questions here. First, what is the value of autonomy? That is, what properly motivates a person to seek the trait of autonomy in himself and others? Second, what are the motives characteristic of autonomy as a virtue? What moves the intellectually autonomous person, insofar as he is autonomous? We begin with the first question.

In his *Discourse on Method*, Part 2, René Descartes likens knowledge to a city. It is a structure with many interrelated parts, and the more elegantly that structure can be set up, the more beautiful and functional it will be. A city that is haphazardly put together, with crooked streets, dead-ends, redundant functions, poorly organized neighborhoods, and so forth, is confusing and hard to get around in. The same is true of a structure of knowledge. The greater its elegant systematicity, the more it fosters clarity of understanding. Descartes concludes that the best structure of knowledge is achieved not through the pooled contributions of numerous investigators, but by a single individual such as himself. Thus the desire for clarity of understanding is his motive for seeking something like intellectual autonomy. The motive is laudable, but the idea that a single person could be the architect of all knowledge is spectacularly unrealistic, and does not consider the ways in which a community of investigators gradually evolves something like the more elegant structure that Descartes envisions. Furthermore, the idea of intellectual autonomy operative in this argument—the idea of a single investigator working alone to create a structure of knowledge—bears little resemblance to the concept of autonomy that we have developed in this chapter.

Virtues are fulfillments (completions, mature states) of human nature, and as such may be aimed at, as a more or less blurry target, by a more or less specific natural desire. Autonomy belongs to this case. It is mature competence, an ability to perform well without the kind of regulation or direction that is needed in early stages of development. We see the desire for independent action even in small children, who want to tie their *own* shoes, put on their clothes *themselves*, find out various things for themselves, and so forth, and we can all remember the satisfaction of finally being able to do something well without our parents' or teacher's guidance. At the beginning of Chapter 6 we quoted Aristotle on the natural human desire to know. Perhaps the natural desire to know autonomously is a variant of that desire, and also of the general desire to be a competent independent agent. This fact about natural human motivation would entail that the value of intellectual autonomy is not entirely instrumental, not merely a matter of improved epistemic output. It is also a basic satisfaction of life, as the acquisition of knowledge is. As such, intellectual autonomy will be rationally desired or valued by a normal human being.

However, when teachers desire to foster intellectual autonomy in their students, they also desire them to have the virtue for the more instrumental kinds of reasons. Dialectical exchange is more likely to produce understanding, propositional knowledge, and insights if the interlocutors are autonomous thinkers—because autonomous people are often better listeners, freer to accept correction and advice from colleagues, and more likely to give credit to their intellectual opponents. Scientists and other scholars seem more likely to make discoveries and achieve deep understanding if they have assimilated the traditions of science and the regulations of their teachers, predecessors, and colleagues in a mature, autonomous way. It is perfectly legitimate, then, to desire autonomy as likely to foster the delivery of epistemic goods. Our answer to the first question, then, is that autonomy is properly desired both as an intrinsic good of human life and as tending to increase the harvest of intellectual goods for the individual and the community. Our second question is, What are the motives characteristic of autonomy as a virtue?

Autonomy is an ability to resist improper hetero-regulators. This formulation leaves open the question as to which hetero-regulators are improper and, correlatively, which ones properly regulate thought. So maybe we should see the motivational structure of autonomy on the model that we have suggested for courage: as having no characteristic motivation of its own, but as deriving whatever motivation it has, in a given person, from other virtues or other motivations (maybe even vices). Just as courage is an ability to act with aplomb in the face of perceived threats, intellectual autonomy is (in part) the ability to think with aplomb under pressure from alien hetero-regulators. And just as a nasty Nazi or thief might have the ability to act with aplomb in the face of perceived threats, so someone with less than virtuous motives might think autonomously.

Richard Feynman offers some rules/examples of what a person must do to display what he calls "a kind of scientific integrity, a principle of scientific thought that corresponds to a kind of utter honesty—a kind of leaning over backwards".[10] On Feynman's description, integrity is very similar to autonomy, as involving resistance to intellectual hetero-regulators. He is thinking especially about influences from the worlds of commerce and politics that often threaten to regulate the practices of scientists. He says that, regardless of such pressures, the scientist should report all the results of his experiment, not just the ones that support

---

[10] Richard Feynman, *You Must Be Joking, Mr. Feynman*, as told to Ralph Leighton, ed. Edward Hutchings (New York: W. W. Norton, 1985), p. 341.

a commercially or politically favored outcome. He mentions an ad for Wesson Oil that claims, correctly, that Wesson Oil does not soak into food (at a certain temperature). But scientific integrity requires that the company point out also that *no* oil soaks into food (at that temperature), and that all oils, including Wesson, soak into food at higher temperatures. A Wesson staff research scientist or company executive who insisted on disclosing all this information would exemplify scientific autonomy; that is, his assertions would not be driven by truth–irrelevant concerns about how his results are taken by others. Feynman disapproves of a friend who goes on the radio to explain the "applications" of his cosmological research, when in fact he knows there aren't any, but also knows that laypeople will be less interested in funding research that has no applications. "If you're representing yourself as a scientist, then you should explain to the laymen what you're doing—and if they don't want to support you under those circumstances, then that's their decision" (p. 343). When a scientist is hired by a politician to determine whether an expensive hole should be drilled in his state, and the scientist determines that the hole should be drilled in somebody else's state, she should publish the results anyway; otherwise, science is simply being used as a way of getting political advantage. Truthfulness is thus autonomy, independence, integrity. It is autonomy from the rule of pressures from persons who want a certain result, regardless of truth.

Feynman says that he is not giving advice about full disclosure to your wife or girlfriend about "cheating": "I'm talking about a specific, extra type of integrity that ... you ought to have *when acting as a scientist*" (ibid., p. 343; italics added). But why limit this bending–over–backwards truthfulness to matters of science? Is it less important for your wife to know that you've been messing around with the secretary than for laymen to know that so-and-so's research has no applications? Isn't the reason why you wouldn't bend over backwards to let your wife know what you've been doing with the secretary just that it would inconvenience you for her to know this? Is this relevantly different from the inconvenience it will cause the politician to pay all that money to the scientist only to have him go blabbing that the expensive hole really needs to be drilled in another senator's state? Clearly, Feynman thinks that intellectual honesty bears on communication with others; why does the wife or girlfriend get excluded from the strictures of honesty?

For that matter, why bring in honesty at all? If the business executive is fundamentally committed to making money for the company, surely that motive can be the basis of his intellectual autonomy. He is to be pure in heart in intellectual matters—that is, to make only those claims that are in the interest of making money. For him, honesty is an alien hetero-regulator, something he has no commitment to, something extraneous to his purposes; and when it conflicts with what he is committed to, it is a matter of *his* integrity that he resist *that* hetero-regulator, stopping his ears to the siren beckonings of truth. If autonomy is simply a reliable disposition of resistance to alien hetero-regulators, then *which* hetero-regulators are alien is a matter of outlook, and *which* motivation orients a person in this resistance is indifferent to this virtue as such.

Of course, such a character as we have just described has *intellectual* autonomy only in a very attenuated sense of "intellectual". The word here ranges only over claims, whereas for most people it ranges also, all-importantly, over truth. And that is how we construe it in this book, for we have placed the chapter on the love of knowledge (truth) at the very head of Part II, to signal its encompassing and fundamental relation to the other virtues. Still, if we are to distinguish the virtues at all, we need to assign them particular roles in the psychological economy of the intellectual life, and the role of autonomy as such is not to desire truth but to resist alien hetero-regulators. And so we want to affirm, in our somewhat abstract way, that autonomy does not as such contain a motivation; it derives its motivation from other parts of the array of virtues. The lover of knowledge, you will remember, is a lover of all important kinds of knowledge. If so, there is something deeply wrong, intellectually, with the person whose intellectual autonomy applies when he is doing science but not when he is talking to his wife.

Conclusion

Finally, let us mention gratitude as one more aspect of the motivational disposition of the autonomous person. For us, autonomy is a genuinely intellectual virtue only when it is supported by the love of knowledge, because knowledge is the chief and central intellectual good. Against the current of interpreting autonomy as some kind of hyper-individualism or quasi-solipsism, we have analyzed the virtue as incorporating proper hetero-regulators. The autonomous intellectual is such, not because he is an intellectually self-made man, but because he has actively and intelligently appropriated the regulators in his noetic structure. The reflective lover of knowledge incorporates proper hetero-regulators in the interest of knowledge. Autonomy is not only a negatively social virtue (sheer *in*dependence of others) but a positively social virtue (a dependent independence). In the ideal case, then, there should be some motivational indicator of the positivity of autonomy, and it seems to us to be gratitude. The autonomous individual's positive relationship to his proper hetero-regulators—his intellectual tradition, his teachers, his peers and colleagues, his critics, his models, his sanctioners, and his authorities—is one of happy acknowledgment. Thus he has not only integrated these hetero-regulators, but has done so with some awareness of his debt, and willingly. He sees his indebtedness as a good and fitting thing, not at all second-rate or to be regretted. This too is a way in which he has made the hetero-regulators his "own", and is thus an enhancement of his autonomy.

11

Generosity

Introduction

Generosity is a disposition to give valuable things—material goods, time, attention, energy, concessions, credit, the benefit of a doubt, know-ledge—to other persons. It is associated with the idea of freedom and is sometimes called liberality (*liberalitas*). It is a disposition to give "freely", gladly, and without calculation of repayment. But this freedom is not mere prodigality; generosity is a disposition to give for the good of the recipient—*his* well-being, *his* pleasure, the fulfillment of *his* purposes; this "altruism" is the kind of motivation characteristic of generosity. The man who sets the contents of his overstuffed garage on the street for anonymous neighborhood scavengers may have a partially generous motivation, but if he does so primarily to clear space in his garage, his act is not a paradigm of generosity.

The recipient of the gift may be unknown, but the giver must have a definite enough idea of the recipient to believe that she will receive some benefit from the gift; and he must have at least a vague conception of how the gift will serve her. These required bits of belief or knowledge serve a rationality requirement of generosity. Since the generous person wants his gift to benefit the beneficiary for her own sake, he will be interested in giving appropriate gifts to appropriate people in appropriate ways (for example, anonymously or not, at the right time, and so forth). A person who gives "freely" but is not interested in such questions of benefit and propriety is not generous but prodigal. The giver must aim to make his gifts into real benefits by considering appropriate beneficiaries, gifts, times of giving, and so forth. But a person whose efforts were woefully inadequate in particular cases, through no lack of effort and calculation, would still count as generous. Of course, if human efforts to do one another good through free giving *generally* failed to benefit people, then the disposition to make such effort would not count as a virtue. In this social–dispositional sense, generosity has a "success component".

The vices opposite generosity are *stinginess* and *greed*. The stingy person holds on inordinately to her own valuable things. She is disposed to reserve them for her own use and protect them from use by others, while the generous person is open and sharing. The greedy person takes valuable things inordinately and does so without sufficient regard for the good of others, while the generous person takes ordinately, or (even more characteristically) less than ordinately, because of a concern for others. If ordinate taking is justice, then at times the generous person does herself an "injustice" out of regard for others.

Stinginess and greed are different but related kinds of unfreedom. We can think of these vices as at one extreme of a continuum with generosity at the other extreme. Ordinary people, who are a little bit generous but also a bit stingy and greedy, will fall somewhere between the extremes. The stingy person is in a kind of bondage to her goods, subject to anxiety and distress and sorrow should they be lost, while the greedy one is in bondage to anxiety about the threat of competition and vulnerable to disappointment at not winning the desired good. (Greed goes with envy, stinginess with fear or anxiety.) The generous person is relatively free of this bondage, though he has his own characteristic anxieties, potential distresses, and disappointments.

The generous person is "free" *with* valuable things because he is "free" *from* them; he is not obsessed with them, does not cleave to them desperately. Yet he does value them. A person who gives freely of things that have no value at all to him is not generous. So the freedom of the generous person is not merely stoical detachment from valuables. His freedom from the valuables is partially a consequence of a concern for others that can override his concern for the valuables. In the greedy and the stingy the balance of concerns tilts toward the valuables and away from others' interests, while in the generous the balance of concerns tilts the other way. One valuable that the generous person is free with is personal credit. By praise and recognition he credits others freely for the good they have done, but he is relatively insouciant about receiving credit for what he has given, achieved, or produced. Again, he is not indifferent to this good; the peculiar balance is what makes for generosity. The generosity that we have just described is covertly Christian—that is, it is the Christian virtue of generosity minus its theological connections. Let us now make the Christian connections explicit, and then compare this virtue with counterparts in other world views.

The Christian vocabulary for this freedom and this kind of motivation is "grace"; generosity is "gracious"; it is an important division of the great Christian virtue of love, and thus is one of the traits that are trained for in Christian sanctification. In the same way in which courage is a characteristic virtue for honor moralities like that of the Homeric epics because of the prominence of battle in that way of thinking about life, so generosity is a characteristic virtue for Christianity because of its basis in the generosity of God. Christians worship a God who is from the human point of view above all a Giver—of life, of provisions for life, of forgiving merciful redemption in Jesus Christ. As recipients of God's gifts, our first virtue is gratitude, but its mirror image is a generosity in which we reflect back, however faintly, in our own attitudes and actions, God's extravagant altruism. Christianity has affected the character of many who are not confessional Christians; this is shown in their genuine concern for the well-being of others for the others' sake, and their willingness to give freely of valuable things for the benefit of others. (We are not saying that such generosity cannot arise apart from Christianity, but only that much of the secular generosity that we see is in fact derived historically from Christianity.) But the most distinctively Christian kind of generosity takes as explicit point of departure the grace of God in Christ. In it the concern for others' well-being and the disposition to give freely of valuable things is connected, in the individual personality, with gratitude to God for the valuable things he has given us, and above all for our redemption. It arises, in part, from this happy acknowledgment of dependence, and the more articulate Christian will, when pressed for the reasons for his generosity, cite God's generosity.

Generosity is not unreflectively spontaneous. We have noted that because of his interest in doing recipients real good with his giving, the generous person is careful to give appropriately in a variety of ways, and this takes reflection, or if not always explicit deliberation, at least good judgment. But in the most generous persons, generous actions are spontaneous in the sense that the agent does not have to struggle with himself motivationally. He does not have to force himself to part with his valuables; he does not typically struggle against contrary selfish inclinations. Few people are generous to this degree. Those who are only approximately generous will find they need the sense of duty and the power of self-discipline as supplements to whatever generosity they have. The sense of duty with respect to generosity is a knowledge of what the ideal requires in the way of generous actions and a desire to satisfy the ideal in one's own case. Self-discipline (or self-control) in this connection is the ability to manage one's ungenerous urges in the interest of generous actions and motivations. A person who is skilled in self-discipline may be able to bring himself, despite ungenerous urges, to a better view and feeling about the situation that confronts him. It is true that a person who brings himself to act generously from a sense of duty does not fully exemplify the virtue of generosity; but if the sense of duty refers to a duty *to be generous* (rather than, say, conceiving the action as a requirement of justice), then the motivation is enough like that of generosity to warrant calling the action generous.

We have expounded Christian generosity in both a theological and a de-theologized version. Other variants of generosity are possible. Such traits resemble the generosity that we have elucidated in some respect or respects that justify calling them generosity, while significantly differing from Christian generosity. Let us illustrate this point by considering Friedrich Nietzsche's proposed counterpart of generosity, as well as Aristotle's.

Nietzsche's Zarathustra preaches a little sermon on *die schenkende Tugend* ("the bestowing virtue") in *Thus Spake Zarathustra*.[1] He distinguishes two kinds of selfishness, a "free" and healthy selfishness and a bound and sickly one. Sickly selfishness involves a needy, obsessive, and anxious acquisitiveness, a boundless desire to take goods to oneself, a unidirectional accumulating that seems to suppose that what is accumulated makes one what one is, gives one "substance". We might call this bondage "the grasping vice". Readers of J. R. R. Tolkien's *Lord of the Rings* will be reminded of Gollum as a paradigm case. By contrast, *die schenkende Tugend* is a disposition to give to others. But it too is selfishness, according to Zarathustra: "heil und heilig heiße ich diese Selbstsucht." This selfishness is healthy and holy because it is secure in itself and free. When the giver acquires what he is to give, he does so not anxiously and obsessively, but as part of the project of becoming and being a great soul. His soul's greatness

---

[1] Friedrich Nietzsche, *Also Sprach Zarathustra*, Part I, §22 (Munich: Wilhelm Goldmann's Verlag, n. d.).

is measured not by what he has accumulated, but by the attitude with which he accumulates: the accumulated goods are not his substance, but an adornment, and they adorn him most effectively when he bestows them on others. He gives out of his abundance—not so much a material abundance as an attitude of abounding—a sense of himself as a self-sufficient plenitude, an overflowing. This is the "liberality" of Zarathustran generosity.

Christian generosity differs markedly from Zarathustra's. In the Nietzschean version the greatness of the giver is the central and salient feature; the giving is an "expression" of this self-overflowing abundance. The recipient's need of the gift, or pleasure in it, is incidental. The concern is not to help the other, but to express one's great self. Thus Nietzsche calls this generosity a *Selbstsucht*. By contrast, the Christian takes the interest of the recipient to heart and thus, in successful giving, takes satisfaction in the other's satisfaction for the other's sake. Yet abundance is in the Christian picture of generosity, and Nietzsche's analysis reminds us of this. The Christian, like Zarathustra, gives out of her abundance, even if she, like the widow of Mark 12: 41−4, gives all that she has in her poverty. Just as Zarathustra's abundance is spiritual, far more a sense of the fullness of his self than of his bank account, so the Christian's abundance too is spiritual. But it is not a sense of the fullness of her *self* exactly (or directly), but of the fullness and greatness and abundance of God. " 'My grace is sufficient for you, for my power is made perfect in weakness.' " To which the apostle Paul comments, "when I am weak, then I am strong" (2 Cor. 12: 9a,10b). The strength, the overflowing, is God's, and the disciple's by association: "For all things are yours, whether Paul or Apollos or Cephas or the world or life or death or the present or the future, all are yours; and you are Christ's; and Christ is God's" (1 Cor. 3: 21−3). "What have you that you did not receive? If then you received it, why do you boast as if it were not a gift?" (1 Cor. 4: 7). Thus, Christian generosity is connected with gratitude and humility in a way that *die schenkende Tugend* is not.

In this respect, Aristotelian generosity is closer to Nietzschean generosity. Aristotle says that liberality or generosity is a disposition to use wealth well.[2] Since spending is more properly the "use" of wealth than acquiring is, generosity has especially to do with spending. Generous spending differs from virtuous (just) spending in commerce, in which one pays the right

---

[2] Aristotle, *Nicomachean Ethics*, 1120^{a}6−8.

price for goods received. Generous spending is not buying, but giving. The generous person "will give for the sake of the noble, and rightly; for he will give to the right people, the right amounts, and at the right time, with all the other qualifications that accompany right giving; and that too with pleasure or without pain" ($1120^{a}23-7$). The generous person takes pleasure in giving because he desires wealth largely as something he can give to others and is relatively indifferent to it for other purposes. Because generosity is in this way an attitude, it is not measured by amounts given: nothing prevents "the man who gives less from being the more liberal man, if he has less to give" ($1120^{b}10$). The "freedom" of generosity differs from that of prodigality in its being shaped by rationality: this is a free giving for the sake of the noble, to the right people in the right amounts, and so forth. This kind of giving is thoughtful or intelligent—bounded by considerations—even when it is spontaneous in being done without deliberation.

At first sight, the well-being of the other seems less incidental for Aristotle than for Nietzsche. He tells us that the generous person does not "neglect his own property, since he wishes by means of this to help others" ($1120^{b}2$), and "it is the nature of a liberal man not to look to himself" ($1120^{b}6$). But he also says, "it is not characteristic of a man who confers benefits to accept them lightly" ($1120^{a}33$). Like the magnanimous man (Book IV, 3), the generous person likes the position of giver and dislikes the position of receiver, which strikes him as lowering his status. So the desire to help others is really the generous person's desire for his own characteristic means of self-promotion, and when Aristotle says that the generous man does not "look to himself", he must mean that he does not look to money as something to spend on himself; for he *does* look to money as something that will build up or maintain his status by his giving it away. So for Aristotle, as for Nietzsche, the generous person's greatness as giver seems to be uppermost in his mind, and in this way their conceptions are distant from the Christian concept of generosity. The Christian can second Aristotle's stress on the rationality of generosity: like the Christian's, Aristotle's kind of generosity is thoughtful, seeking to give to the right person, in the right amount, at the right time, and in the right way. Christian generosity adds another qualification of this sort—"the right thing"—for as we have said, the range of things that can be given generously includes far more than material wealth. Giving a person one's time, attention, credit for a job well done, the benefit of a doubt, knowledge, or other valuables may be "rightly" generous in cases where it would be quite wrong to give him money or material goods.

Virtues are beneficial dispositions, ones that make life good for the virtues' possessor and for persons affected by him or her. It is not hard to think of some benefits of generosity. Sharing tends to beget sharing, with the result that generosity will often increase the number and quality of resources for everyone. In addition to resources, the friendly relations that are fostered by well-considered generosity are a very great good in themselves, a source of well-being that stands in starkest contrast with the anxieties of cut-throat competition and the envy, resentment, and frustration that are so closely associated with stinginess and greed. And it seems to us that the Christian version of generosity is more fit to yield these benefits than the Aristotelian and Nietzschean generosities, which are competitive and invidious in their own subtle ways.

Intellectual Pursuits

The word "intellectual" rings natural as a qualifier of some virtue terms. Thus, intellectual humility, intellectual integrity, intellectual courage. But intellectual temperance, intellectual self-control, intellectual justice? To our ears "intellectual generosity" has the second, somewhat less plausible, ring. It would certainly have sounded odd to Aristotle. Yet generosity, like most of the virtues that have been classified traditionally as "moral" rather than intellectual, bears enormously on the life of the mind. It is possible to be generous in the conduct of intellectual practices, or stingy and greedy, just as in the handling of material and other goods. The reason is that the intellectual life has its own set of goods, and these can be shared with others and given to others, or grasped and hoarded for oneself.

We noted in Chapter 5 that some goods are internal, and others external, to intellectual practices. Among internal goods are understanding, acquaintance, and true, justified or warranted beliefs. By contrast, fame, adulation, power, position, money, Nobel prizes, and suchlike are external goods that sometimes come with intellectual achievement. Another fact bearing on the importance of generosity to the intellectual life is that the acquisition and development of the goods internal to intellectual practices always depend, in some way or other, on the transfer of such goods from one person to another. Philosophical dialogue, without which ideas do not emerge or deepen, depends on give-and-take among the interlocutors. The partners contribute and receive good things from one another—proposals, refinements, criticisms, objections—and such contributions beget yet more and better goods of the same kind. Science, too, is an essentially communal enterprise. No single person can collect all the data necessary to a significant scientific discovery, and conversation about ideas is as important in science as in philosophy. So scientific work is always collaborative—usually in a direct and literal way but, at a minimum, scientists always depend on the work of their predecessors, even when they reject large amounts of that work. And, of course, the institution of teaching, of passing intellectual goods on from the less ignorant to the more ignorant so that the more ignorant can become less so, is in the very warp and woof of human life. Without teaching our life could not be human. To some extent, virtually every even semi-mature person is both pupil and teacher, receiving intellectual goods from others and passing them on to still others, and some of us are professional teachers, our chief and special business being to convey intellectual goods to others.

These two facts—that the intellectual life has its transferable goods and a take-and-give character—suggest that generosity can be an intellectual virtue. Following our general analysis of generosity, we might say that the intellectually generous person is someone who gives the intellectual goods freely to others, for their own sake, and takes pleasure in doing so. The intellectually stingy person reserves for himself what intellectual goods he has acquired, and is disinclined to share them with others. The intellectually greedy person has an inordinate concern to acquire the intellectual goods, in disregard for others' acquisition of them. But the distinction between internal and external intellectual goods requires the analysis of intellectual generosity to diverge in some respects from the paradigm case.

Some Exemplars

This is so because generosity applies ordinarily to ownable goods, goods such that, if one person has them, others do not. Paradigmatically, generosity is a disposition to give *property*. But only the extrinsic intellectual goods have the property of being potential property. Thus when James Watson and Francis Crick published their initial note on the structure of the DNA molecule, they shared the intrinsic intellectual good of that discovery, and it became equally available to anyone who could understand it. Once it was published, they gave up all possibility of hoarding it *as an intrinsic intellectual good*. They put it into the public domain, where all other scientists could acquire it, appreciate it, and use it for their own scientific purposes. In a purely performative sense (that is, disregarding the motivation), such giving over to others may look like an act of generosity. But it is clear from Watson's own account of that discovery in *The Double Helix*[3] that in publishing their discovery, he and Crick were staking a property claim. This claim was not to the exclusive ownership of the knowledge of the DNA structure, but to exclusive ownership of the *position*, in history, of discoverers of the DNA structure, with all the other extrinsic intellectual goods entailed by that position: fame, prestige, the Nobel prize, professional positions, money, and so forth.

While it is clear from Watson's account that he and Crick were very interested in intellectual problems and were interested in the structure of DNA because of its status as a key to many other biological discoveries, it is also clear that a very large part of their motivation to pursue DNA was the extraordinary set of ownable, extrinsic goods that would accrue to its discoverers, including, in all likelihood, the Nobel prize. The terms in which Watson describes Linus Pauling, a chemist at Cal Tech with whom he and Crick conceived themselves to be in the fiercest competition for these extrinsic goods, are terms of a violent sport, if not war. They take comfort from Pauling's being in California, far from the Cambridge–London axis of their own work, where it is unlikely that he will get to see the X-ray crystallographic photographs of DNA that Rosalind Franklin is making at King's College, University of London, which are in the end a crucial key to their own success. Pauling writes to Maurice Wilkens, who later shares the Nobel prize with Watson and Crick, asking for copies of the X-ray photographs, and Wilkens responds with a lame excuse for not sending them. Watson and Crick become anxious when they hear that Pauling is coming to London for a meeting, and Watson comments, "One could never

---

[3] James Watson, *The Double Helix: A Personal Account of the Discovery of the Structure of DNA* (London: Weidenfeld & Nicolson, 1968).

be sure where [Pauling] would strike next. Particularly chilling was the prospect that he would ask to visit King's" (p. 116). They become anxious again when they discover that Pauling has sketched a structure for DNA, and then greatly relieved when they realize that Pauling's sketch involves a mistake in chemistry. Watson warns Crick of the possible "fatal[ity]" of "smiling too long over [Pauling's] mistake" (p. 159). They talk about the possibility of Pauling's finding the structure in terms of "threat" (p. 145) and "all was lost" (p. 159) and "danger" (p. 170) and their own success as a "defeat" for Pauling. Even after they have the solution, Watson, having described it in a letter to Max Delbrück, asks "At the bottom of the letter that broke the news of the complementary chains [of bases], ... that he not tell Linus [Pauling]. I was still slightly afraid something could go wrong and did not want Pauling to think about hydrogen-bonded base pairs until we had a few more days to digest our position" (p. 217).

This is a fairly extreme case of stinginess with intrinsic intellectual goods motivated by an intense desire for extrinsic intellectual goods. We can only think that the motivation was the extrinsic goods, since it seems clear that anyone whose overriding desire was to know the structure of DNA would gladly have shared information with somebody as able as Linus Pauling, with a view to hastening the discovery, and perhaps improving on it. Sharing the intrinsic intellectual goods is very likely to promote more goods and of higher quality, and withholding the goods one has from fellow inquirers is likely to slow up and weaken intellectual progress. Nobody would fail to notice this unless blinded by ambition. We draw a tentative conclusion here: namely, that intellectual generosity is likely to be found in a personality in which concern for the intrinsic intellectual goods is strong relative to the interest in extrinsic intellectual goods. Since stinginess and greed apply much more to the ownable intellectual goods, stinginess and greed about the intrinsic intellectual goods (such as information relevant to discovering the structure of DNA) must derive from a concern for the ownable ones. Thus, someone who cared very little about fame and money but a great deal about knowing important truths would be more likely to be intellectually generous than somebody who cared equally about both kinds of goods, or more about the external rewards than about the truths.

One might think that the kind of competitiveness we see in Watson and Crick, with the greed and stinginess that attend a passion for the goods external to intellectual practices, are just a fact of the intellectual life, perhaps a necessary evil, but still necessary, as the motivation that drives inquiry. Is ambition for extrinsic rewards the indispensable fuel of inquiry? If so, then what looks very much like moral vice is in one way an intellectual virtue.

We can't deny that selfish ambition sometimes propels intellectual excellence. Watson and Crick did good work, and Watson attributes not just his secrecy, but his care and precision, to his ambition. Still, we do not think that vicious ambition is the necessary fuel of inquiry. In Chapter 6 we followed Aristotle's suggestion that it is natural for human beings to want to know. Children are naturally exploratory, interested in explanations and in understanding the shape and character and workings of their world. Adults listen to PBS science shows because explanations of the natural world interest them intrinsically; we like to resolve puzzles and explain mysteries. That is, we have a natural appetite for the goods internal to intellectual practices. (It is true that we sometimes do *not* like to have our beliefs corrected, but this discomfort itself often stems from our love of settled explanation.) So we have no reason to think that scientists couldn't get their work done if they were not given money and honors as rewards. We are not saying that some scientists are completely indifferent to money and honors, but rather that in some scientists—and these tend to be the intellectually generous ones—the love of the goods external to intellectual practices is minimal, incidental, and these goods are something they can do without. Not all scientists are like the Watson and Crick of the early 1950s.

Take Linus Pauling. If Pauling had construed the possible success of Watson and Crick as a "danger" and a "threat" which, if it eventuated, would be a "defeat" in which "all was lost", then we would expect that, upon finding out that they had solved DNA, Pauling would be devastated with disappointment. But Watson reports that when Pauling saw the solution, "[his] reaction was one of genuine thrill". In other words, the concern that operated in his spontaneous emotional response to the solution was a concern for the chief good internal to the practices of searching for the structure of DNA—namely, the understanding of that structure. If he was also concerned to have the position of the discoverer of that structure (we have no doubt that he would have liked to have that position), it was relegated to a quiet background in the spontaneity of his response.

Another scientist who was close to figuring out the structure of DNA, but whom Watson and Crick didn't regard as a serious "threat" since they didn't realize that she was onto its helical structure, was Rosalind Franklin, who was making X-ray photographs of the molecules. It was Franklin who first distinguished the A from the B form of DNA, and her data suggested a two-chain model and the diameter of the helix; it was rather late in the game when Watson saw that she had been right about the bases being in the center and the backbone on the outside. About the place of competition for goods external to scientific practice, Franklin's biographer, Anne Sayre, comments:

To know that other people are scrambling after the same prize can be something of a spur, but only within limits. Rosalind, for example, was so much in the habit of pushing herself to the full extent of her energy and application that competition could not have elicited a great deal more than was already forthcoming.[4]

Furthermore, according to Sayre, the intrinsic intellectual goods were far more important to Franklin than the extrinsic:

... a lack of prospects of rising in terms of the organization [in the Centre National de la Recherche Scientifique in Paris] would not have troubled Rosalind in the least—her ambitions were never for status or power, and on later occasions she voluntarily avoided the sort of promotion that gratified only with power or status and otherwise distracted from what she had in mind to do. (p. 80; see also p. 170)

What was her reaction to the discovery by Watson and Crick?

Whether she was disappointed when news of the Crick–Watson triumph at Cambridge finally filtered through to King's no one knows. If she was, she gave no indication of it, and her disappointment cannot have been very acute. She sat down to redraft her paper for *Nature* in the new form of a supporting document for the Watson–Crick structure with every sign of pleasure, none of bitterness or chagrin. To begin with, the structure they proposed genuinely delighted her, as it did everyone capable of grasping its simple beauty. ... That their smashing success converted much of what was in Rosalind's draft paper into secondary material, that her discoveries were abruptly swallowed up by their larger discovery, seems not to have troubled her at all; or if it did, nothing she wrote or said testified to it. The paper which had represented, while she and Gosling were working on it in the first weeks of March, a new high-water mark in research into the structure of DNA, was promptly redrafted into a supporting paper. It reads serenely in the second version, as one might expect; there is no hint in it of "yes, but I saw that first". (pp. 169–71)

[4] Anne Sayre, *Rosalind Franklin and DNA* (New York: W. W. Norton, 1975), p. 116.

This is a picture of an intellectually generous person, and all the more impressive when we consider that at the time Franklin did not like Watson and Crick. The gladness and freedom with which she lets the credit go to them, and the lack of insistence on even the credit that was minimally owed to herself, is due in large part to Franklin's consuming focus on the goods internal to her intellectual practice. This generosity differs significantly from the "moral" generosity that we expounded in the first part of this chapter. There, the well-being of the recipient is a primary and necessary concern of the generous person, while here the well-being of Watson and Crick is at most a side consideration. There, concern for the well-being of the recipient tends to override the giver's personal attachment to the goods he gives, while here it is interest in the goods internal to intellectual practice that overrides attachment to its external goods. We might call this "impersonal" generosity.

The generous person does not characteristically insist minutely on her own rights, but this does not exclude her caring about her rights when the issue is momentous or the violation of them gross. Anne Sayre highlights the way in which Watson and Crick used Rosalind Franklin's data, acquired without her knowledge, without crediting her. To the end of her life Franklin did not know the extent to which their triumph depended on her work. Sayre, who knew Franklin personally, speculates about how she would have reacted had she discovered their reliance on her:

She seems to have taken the Cambridge structure as it was presented, as a work of perception, insight, and inspiration, and though she was pleased that it confirmed her work precisely as her work confirmed it, she did not know that, indeed, it incorporated her work. Whether she would have been pleased by the use to which her findings had been put, or resentful at both the way in which they were obtained and the way in which they were left unacknowledged, is a nice question to speculate about. My own guess—freely disputable—is that Rosalind might well have risen like a goddess in her wrath, and that the thunderbolts might have been memorable. (p. 172)

Such a reaction is compatible with remarkable generosity. The generous person is indifferent neither to the goods with which she is free, nor to her rights with respect to them.

Another outstanding geneticist with a remarkable intellectual character is Barbara McClintock. As a research scientist at Cornell University, the young McClintock was exploring the morphology of corn chromosomes, correlating features of the chromosomes with genetic features. In her late twenties, around 1930, she saw her way clear to provide, for the first time, conclusive evidence of the chromosomal basis of genetics, and she produced some corn seed with properties that would allow the correlation of cytological markers on their chromosomes with genetic markers. In 1929, Harriet Creighton, a promising 20-year-old, came to Cornell as a graduate student. McClintock took the younger woman under her wing and gave Creighton this important research as a project. McClintock's biographer reports:

Harriet Creighton describes Barbara McClintock's generosity in giving the seeds for this important project to such a novice as herself as fitting a tradition established by [Rollins] Emerson [a senior geneticist at Cornell with whom McClintock worked]. It was his policy, she recalls, to give a new student "the best and most promising problem you have." Young Creighton herself hardly realized its significance and, by [Marcus] Rhoades's recollection, required constant prodding from McClintock to get it done.[5]

Eventually it dawned on Creighton what she had been handed, and in 1931 she gained worldwide recognition as coauthor with McClintock of the article resulting from her research.

Behind the Emersonian policy is a concern for the well-being of one's students and a willingness to give them some of the best things the profession has to offer, both internal and external to its practices. Such altruism is a mark of generosity generally, but we have seen that another mark, which is perhaps even more salient in intellectual generosity, is a kind of detachment from the goods external to intellectual practices. It is not a complete indifference to them, but a higher valuing of the internal goods. When Barbara McClintock spoke of her work and the plants whose cells she investigated, she often used words like "joy" and "affection". Evelyn Fox Keller reports McClintock's reflection on the years 1931−3:

"I was just so interested in what I was doing I could hardly wait to get up in the morning and get at it. One of my friends, a geneticist, said I was a child, because only children can't wait to get up in the morning to get at what they want to do." She tells a story about driving back from Cal Tech to Missouri. It was a time when news of a number of automobile accidents was fresh in people's minds,

⁵ Evelyn Fox Keller, *A Feeling for the Organism* (New York: W. H. Freeman and Company, 1983), p. 58.

and she had been cautioned about driving. "My only concern was that if I were killed I'd never get the answer to that problem!" she remembers. Foremost in her mind was "purely the subject matter. I don't remember having any [professional] aspirations." Later, when she was in her mid-thirties, she remembers waking up and saying "Oh, my goodness, this is what they call a career for women!" (p. 70)

Keller records her comments about her relationship with the chromosomes she was studying, after an experience of breakthrough:

"I found that the more I worked with them the bigger and bigger [they] got, and when I was really working with them I wasn't outside, I was down there. I was part of the system. I was right down there with them, and everything got big. I even was able to see the internal parts of the chromosomes—actually everything was there. It surprised me because I actually felt as if I were right down there and these were my friends."

In telling this story McClintock sat poised on the edge of her chair, eager to explain her experience, to make herself understood; equally eager to avoid being misunderstood. She was talking about the deepest and most personal dimension of her experience as a scientist. A little later she spoke of the "real affection" one gets for the pieces that "go together": "As you look at these things, they become part of you. And you forget yourself. The main thing about it is you forget yourself." (p. 117)

In a comment that suggests the place that acquaintance can occupy in the development and experience of a lover of knowledge, McClintock said,

"No two plants are exactly alike. They're all different, and as a consequence, you have to know that difference," she explains. "I start with the seedling, and I don't want to leave it. I don't feel I really know the story if I don't watch the plant all the way along. So I know every plant in the field. I know them intimately, and I find it a great pleasure to know them." (p. 198)

Evelyn Witkin once asked McClintock how she had managed to persevere in her research during a period when its outcome was uncertain. She said,

"It never occurred to me that there was going to be any stumbling block. Not that I had the answer, but [I had] the joy of going at it. When you have that joy, you do the right experiments. You let the material tell you where to go, and it tells you at every step what the next has to be because you're integrating with an overall brand new pattern in mind." (p. 125)

Starting in the early 1950s McClintock experienced a period of professional isolation. Because her work was at odds with some broadly shared assumptions, because it was very complicated, and because genetics had taken a molecular turn, away from McClintock's organism-oriented kind of research, she found that her colleagues were not much interested in what she had to say. In her characteristic alignment and tilt, concerned with the intrinsic goods and unconcerned with the extrinsic, she took the situation not as a crisis but as an opportunity.

"It was fortunate, because people love to talk about themselves and their work, and I had an opportunity to listen. And I listened very carefully." One reason she found it worthwhile was that so much was going on in genetics during those years. "I was being educated, and it was an opportunity for me I do not regret; in fact, I think it was a great opportunity not to be listened to, but to listen. Difficult as it may seem." (pp. 142–3)

When, later in life, McClintock's work came to be understood and appreciated, she was showered with honors and other goods external to her intellectual practices, including a Nobel prize. Clearly, the appreciation gratified her, though not as an unmixed blessing, because it often distracted her from her work.

Conclusion

Several pages ago we voiced the concern that the kind of stinginess and greed begotten of a consuming passion for goods external to intellectual practices might be a necessary fuel of scientific and other intellectual activity. But the examples of Franklin and McClintock should lay this fear to rest. A major motive of their work was the love of knowledge; it appears to have included a relatively small concern for the goods external to their practices (though they were not indifferent to such goods), yet the quality of their scientific work was in the same league as that of Watson and Crick, if not superior in some respects.

It is a mark of virtues that they are advantageous in some way or other. They are fulfilling in themselves, or the episodic attitudes and behaviors in which they issue yield good things for their possessor and/or her associates. We can expect that some of the advantages of intellectual generosity will be intellectual ones, in particular a yield of intrinsic intellectual goods. In the stories of Franklin and McClintock we see that their focus on the intrinsic goods gave them perseverance in the face of the indifference of their colleagues. Someone less intrinsically motivated might not have had that perseverance. The result was a yield of new, high-caliber scientific knowledge. The kind of generosity that McClintock showed to Harriet Creighton enabled the particular project she gave to Harriet to move ahead (if she had kept it for herself alone, it might have been slower coming to fruition) and freed McClintock for other activities that were also, no doubt, intellectually productive. It also had the educational advantage of initiating a bright young woman into creative scientific endeavor, thus promoting biological knowledge.

Something *like* generosity is an important condition for the transfer of intellectual competence from one generation to another. Intellectual practices would develop more slowly and less well if senior practitioners did not invest time and energy and encouragement in younger ones and share projects with them. Such "generous" behavior may be encouraged by teaching loads, compulsory office hours, and the like; and sometimes senior inquirers selfishly exploit their juniors, even unjustly. But where the generosity is genuine, a significant portion of the motivation is a concern for the well-being of the younger person and for the goods internal to intellectual practices.

Generosity can also be exemplified in collegial relations, where the colleague gives freely of his time and expertise to the criticism of a colleague's work. In philosophy it is important to have colleagues who will give one deep and detailed critical readings of one's work. Sometimes such gifts take considerable time and energy, and the exercise may or may not advance the giver's own work. The more sacrificial of the giver's private interests the exercise is, the more likely it is to exemplify real generosity; but joy in the giving is also a mark of generosity, so sacrifice need not entail pain.

Generosity also comes out in the tone and character of the criticisms. Criticisms can be meanly competitive in spirit, or they can be generous. Generous criticisms are no less critical, but they are marked by a charitable interpretation of the work, one whose tone credits the philosopher with intelligence and, wherever possible, with having something to say even if it is not said clearly or precisely. The generous interpreter, when confused by the discourse, looks for plausibilities and intelligent intentions. He does so by keeping in mind that the author is a human being with something like parental affection for what he has come up with, which therefore ought to be treated with respect. This humane kind of intellectual interaction tends to bear the fruit of good collegial relations, which in turn tend to beget fruitful cooperation and mutual helpfulness. And these, in turn, are likely to result in an increased yield of intrinsic intellectual goods. Such generosity must of course be tempered with intellectual rigor; a misguided generosity runs the risk of being insufficiently helpful because insufficiently critical.

We noted earlier that the behavior of Watson and Crick resembled that of people playing a competitive game. The goal of such a game is to win, and all players assume that the other players are aiming to win, and trying to prevent the other team from winning. As it turned out, not all the players in the DNA "game" regarded what they were doing as a competitive game. Some of them were oriented by a more intrinsically scientific kind of goal. In the context of a competitive game, generous behavior is out of place—for example, teaming up with the opponents to help them make a goal. Such "generous" behavior would be inconsistent with the spirit of the game, which is frankly competitive. Because virtues are context-specific (for any virtue, not every context calls for the exemplification of that virtue), it is possible both to play such a game and to be a generous person. So, if Watson and Crick indeed thought of the search for DNA's structure as a game, it is not an automatic indictment of their character that they were not generous in the context of the search. In that case their mistake was a sort of category confusion in which they treated scientific work as a game. But it seems that if one were really serious about science *as science*, one would not confuse it with a competitive game. To do so is to impede inquiry, precisely because in inquiry generosity is advantageous.

Robert M. Adams has pointed out how virtues are supported by social-environmental factors. It is easier to exemplify generosity if one's environment is generous; it is easier to remain chaste if one is not in close social contact with people one likes who ridicule chastity and live licentiously. It is easier to be honest if we live in an open and truthful community that prizes honesty and would be disappointed in us if we shaved the truth. We see this phenomenon at work in the contrast between Watson and Crick, on the one side, and Franklin and McClintock, on the other. It appears that the social milieu in the laboratories at Cambridge and King's College, London, was pretty competitive. It would have taken a very mature and well-formed personality to resist the influence of this social atmosphere. Furthermore, Watson and Crick were young men, really little more than graduate students, in a field in which it was expected that bright young men would advance professionally and the failure to do so would be something of a disgrace.

By contrast, in virtue of their being women in the first half of the twentieth century, both McClintock and Franklin were in a significant sense outsiders to their profession. Both of their biographers point out that, professionally, they didn't have much to aspire to. Such "hopelessness" is arguably a psychological advantage in the promotion of intellectual virtues like generosity. A person who *can* have little by way of professional aspirations will tend to have fewer of them, and will enter less readily into the spirit of the game. And if she already has intrinsic scientific interest (and any young scientist surely has *some* such), it will be easier for that kind of interest to dominate in her character.

In this chapter we have expounded a kind of generosity that is most at home in Christianity, but none of the historical exemplars central to our exposition were Christians, so any influence of Christianity on them must have been from cultural osmosis. It is not hard to see how Christian character, in a scientist or other intellectual, would constitute intellectual generosity. We have seen that this virtue is a glad willingness to give intellectual goods, both intrinsic and extrinsic, to others, and that this willingness is based on a dominance of two kinds of concerns: an interest in the intrinsic intellectual goods of knowledge, information, confirmation (or disconfirmation) of hypotheses, understanding, and other such goods; and an interest in the intellectual well-being of other people. In particular, these two kinds of concerns dominate over the concern to have, for oneself, such extrinsic intellectual goods as position, honors, and wealth. We have said that generosity belongs, stylistically, to Christianity, and it does so because of the centrality of the Christian virtue of love (*agapē*). The centrality of love is a consequence of God's generous love as revealed and embodied in Jesus Christ. But the other concern that is an ingredient in intellectual generosity is also encouraged by Christian nurture: namely, an intrinsic interest in important truths about history, nature, and human beings. Nature, including human beings, is God's creation and reflects his intelligence and beauty; and he is the Lord of history. It is a natural extension of the worship of God to have reverence for and interest in the things he has made and rules.

12

Practical Wisdom

Introduction

We end our book with a discussion of a virtue that the nature of our topic has forced us to mention in just about every previous chapter. Practical wisdom has a privileged place in the array of intellectual virtues, one that corresponds to the special place occupied by the love of knowledge, with which we began Part II. Both of these virtues pervade the intellectually excellent life, showing up as a presupposition or necessary background of all the other virtues. The love of knowledge provides the intellectual motive for exemplifications of such virtues as humility and courage which don't have a motive of their own, and it provides the distinctively intellectual part of the motive for intellectual generosity. Practical wisdom, too, is involved in every virtue, as constituting the good judgment without which no human virtue could be exemplified in action, emotion, or judgment. Insofar as virtues are human, they are infused with and qualified by reason, as the ancients would say; they are dispositions of intelligence.

Elements of Practical Wisdom

Aristotle includes practical wisdom (*phronēsis*) among the intellectual virtues, but conceives it as a hybrid, the only intellectual virtue that is also a moral virtue. It is the intellectual dimension of the moral virtues. It is "practical", as its name implies. Practice or action (*praxis*) belongs where we humans can make a difference—where things do not have to be as they are, where we can change the world by our actions. Aristotle thinks that the fully intellectual virtues, by contrast, take objects that cannot be otherwise than they are (think of mathematics and physics), aspects of the world that we cannot change but can only contemplate.

As practical, practical wisdom is an "aiming" virtue: it posits ends or an end to be achieved through the actions that it guides. It is akin to cleverness, but unlike cleverness, which can be used with bad aims as well as good, practical wisdom implies good aims. In Aristotle's construction it aims at real human well-being, or eudaimonia, not what merely appears to somebody to be good. Thus if an observer of an agent were mistaken about the good, he might attribute practical wisdom falsely to someone who was merely clever and using his cleverness to achieve goals that were only apparently good.

Since actions are always particulars, performed in particular situations with particular features that distinguish them from similar situations, practical wisdom is a power to judge of particulars. Rules of practice are always general, and thus never tailored perfectly to any particular situation. The particularity of actions and the situations that call for them implies an element of improvisation in the exercise of practical wisdom. Because of the great variability of situations in their details, even the best rule formulas do not by themselves determine what is to be done. Instead, the determiner is the person of practical wisdom, the agent who interprets and applies the formulas (if such there be) and judges what is particularly to be done in these situations.

Aristotle allows at least two different kinds of "cognition" as exemplifying practical wisdom. It is a power of *deliberation* (*bouleusis*; see *Nicomachean Ethics* 1139ª12–15), but also a power of *perception* (*aisthēsis*; see 1142ª25–30). Deliberation is an activity, but perception involves an element of passivity. This mixture of activity and passivity is typical of virtue exemplifications. For example, the compassionate person deliberates how best to help somebody in trouble, and then acts intentionally on the result of his deliberation; but also, spontaneously and involuntarily, he notices people's troubles where less compassionate people do not notice, and spontaneously and involuntarily wants to help. Both kinds of processes are intelligent and require judgment or quasi-judgment, and thus display practical wisdom. A perception exemplifying practical wisdom can always be converted into a proposition, and the virtuous person will assent to the proposition if it is put to him; so a perception in this sense is an incipient judgment. (This formula is approximate. In the less than perfect constitution, it may happen that a wise perception is not recognized as such, in which case it is possible that when the perception is put in propositional form, the subject would not assent to it; obviously, such a case will occur only where practical wisdom is imperfect.)

In our account of intellectual virtues, we have taken over part of this classical conception of practical wisdom. We have stressed that the intellectual life is characterized through and through by practices, and that the intellectual virtues fit us well to pursue these. We are not claiming, *contra* Aristotle, that we always affect the objects of our investigations, as constructivists in the sociology of knowledge do. We assume something like a realist view of mathematics, for example, according to which mathematicians do not create, but discover, mathematical truths. Often we must take special care to *minimize* the influence our investigations have on what we are investigating (for example, subjects of psychological experiments and populations of animals). But investigations are obviously practices, richly various voluntary activities in which we make a difference, by our actions, in what we and others know.

Furthermore, intellectual practices aim at goods, just as Aristotle's moral practices do, in this case the goods that constitute knowledge: propositional knowledge, understanding, and acquaintance. The love of knowledge is the trait in which the agent personally aims at genuine intellectual goods. If a person cannot be practically wise, in Aristotle's conception, without pursuing genuine eudaimonia, so a person cannot be intellectually practically wise, in our conception, without the love of knowledge. So intellectual practical wisdom is oriented on action and presupposes a love for genuine intellectual goods.

The last clause needs to be qualified in two ways. First, the notion of *genuine* needs to be relativized to outlook. Within limits we want to be able to attribute intellectual virtue to a person with a systematically distorted conception of the intellectual goods. Consider our attitude to an orthodox Marxist—one who treats Marx's writings as authoritative with regard to economic and political questions. Perhaps we regard Marx's writings as not worthy to be attributed such a status because we think the conception of human nature in them is seriously flawed. Yet we might attribute to such a Marxist the virtue of love of knowledge, if she cares deeply and seriously about understanding the social world ever better through the interpretation and application of Marx's writings. In the central teleology of her investigations she is not in fact pursuing genuine knowledge, but because she thinks she is, and shows the requisite seriousness about knowledge as she conceives it, we are willing, with these provisos, to attribute to her the virtue of love of knowledge, and thus the kind of goal orientation required for intellectual practical wisdom. Similarly, the Christian with the love of knowledge will care deeply about knowing God ever better, but if God does not exist or is very different from what Christians conceive him to be, then what the Christian loves in loving knowledge virtuously is not really knowledge, but only knowledge as it is conceived in the Christian outlook. The second qualification of the statement that practical wisdom involves a pursuit of knowledge correctly conceived is that the conception need be only roughly correct, inasmuch as the very notion of *pursuing* knowledge implies not yet possessing it, and thus being not entirely clear what it is like.

Aristotle thinks that while everybody naturally loves the end of practical wisdom, very few people love it as it *is*. We all seek eudaimonia, but he thinks that it takes a great deal of reflection and education to get a clear enough conception of it really to aim at it in our practice. Many foolish things people are motivated to do—say, pursue self-destructive riotous living, or devote themselves headlong to money making—aim at eudaimonia, but with a misconception of what is aimed at. It is a business of philosophers to help people get a clearer view of it, but deft conceptual analysis can help only those who have been brought up in a way that predisposes them to make proper use of such analysis. We are claiming that what is true of eudaimonia is true also of knowledge—that everybody already and automatically desires it, but most people don't know very well how to conceive this object of their desires. We aim at it in less than virtuous ways, through lack of reflection about it, as well as through lack of proper education and epistemic maturity. If *Nicomachean Ethics* is a book of practical wisdom—a book designed to help people aim more precisely at what they already aim at—it is such largely by offering a conception of eudaimonia, which for Aristotle is the life of virtue lived in a well constituted city-state. In Chapter 6 we offered a conception of knowledge as a genuine good; we intend this too as an exercise in helping ourselves aim better at what we already aim at, since everyone has a natural urge to know, but the urge does not always constitute the virtue of loving knowledge. Throughout our book we have offered a conception of the good intellectual life, just as Aristotle offers a conception of the good civic life. As an exercise in regulative epistemology, our whole book has been intended as a guide to the virtue of intellectual practical wisdom.

Some of the virtues we have treated in this book do not carry with them their own motivation, so to speak. Notable here are courage and humility, in their different ways. Other virtues do have their own motive: we attribute the love of knowledge to a person only if he is routinely moved by the good of knowledge; we attribute generosity to a person only if he cares about the well-being of other persons for their sake. But if a person acts with aplomb in a situation of significant perceived threat, we may attribute courage to him even if we find out that he was motivated by hatred, desire for unjust gain, or a theological delusion. Thus we may attribute courage to the terrorists of September 11, 2001. If a person controls his anger in an impressive way but out of a desire to escape detection in a crime he has committed, we still attribute self-control to him, and may regard this as a virtue. But we think that the *action* performed with courage or self-control is *fully* virtuous only if it is virtuously motivated. So the actions we have described here are both virtuous (exemplifying courage and self-control) and vicious (exemplifying cruelty or injustice).

What about practical wisdom? Is it a motivational virtue, like generosity, or does it, like courage, borrow any virtuous motivation it may utilize from other virtues? How does practical wisdom differ from courage? One test is this: Does it make sense to say that practical wisdom motivates one to seek something genuinely good? Yes. Does it make sense to say that courage motivates one to seek something good? No. However, if instead of speaking of courage *simpliciter* we speak of *intellectual* courage, then we have specified the motive; one cannot have intellectual courage without loving the intellectual goods. So intellectual courage does supply a motive.[1] Aristotle distinguishes practical wisdom (*phronēsis*) from cleverness (*deinotēs*).

Cleverness is an ability to succeed in accomplishing one's goals. This ability is praiseworthy if the goal is good, but if the goal is bad it is knavery. Thus we say that both practically wise people and knaves are clever. Practical wisdom is not

---

[1] By the same token we could speak of just courage or compassionate courage, and these specifications of virtue would specify the motive. These will qualify, by the standard of Chapter 3, as distinct virtues, since situations of justice and compassion are generically human and important in a way that ice hockey situations are not.

identical with this ability, but presupposes it. (*Nicomachean Ethics*, 1144ª23–9, trans Roberts)

So our vocabulary (like Aristotle's) differentiates the trait that lacks the virtuous motive from the one that entails it. Had we lacked the lexical distinction, as we do in the case of courage, we might have called practical wisdom "moral cleverness" on the model of "intellectual courage". Intellectual practical wisdom is just practical wisdom narrowed toward the intellectual goods.

Practical wisdom, however, has special claim to be an intrinsically motivating virtue because of its status as a general virtue, like love of knowledge and unlike courage, generosity, and humility. Intellectual practical wisdom is in a sense the whole of intellectual virtue—not a specialized part, like courage. As ranging over all the practices of the intellectual life, it is strictly symbiotic with the love of knowledge, which ranges similarly. Without the motivation to seek, distribute, maintain, and apply intellectual goods, intellectual practices cannot go on, and without excellent motivation they cannot go on excellently. Conversely, without good concrete judgment, exercised throughout the intellectual practices, the love of knowledge could not be brought to fruition in those practices. We map the terrain of intellectual excellence by an articulated and diversified vocabulary, but the most exemplary cases approximate a unity of the virtues, of the intellectual personality of which the various virtues are really aspects rather than separable units. It stands to reason that the two general virtues of the intellectual life should depend so strictly on one another that they might as well be just two sides of a single virtue. But because of the enormous importance of the two elements—proper orientation of the will and correct practical thinking—it is helpful to distinguish these virtues.

The intrinsically motivational character of practical wisdom is also secured by the fact that aiming is essential to it in a way that it is not to courage. It is true that all actions, including courageous ones, have aims; but because wisdom is a power of deliberation—of figuring out how to accomplish what is good—the aiming belongs to the virtue itself and not just to the actions in which it is exemplified.

Let us now think about how practical wisdom relates to the special virtues that we discussed in Chapters 7–11. We will assume these virtues to be unified by the love of knowledge: that is, to be genuinely intellectual virtues. On this assumption each of the virtues has its own department of practical wisdom: firmness, courage, humility, autonomy, and generosity each has its own patterns of deliberation (non-deliberation) and perception (non-perception)—terms in which the agent thinks about and sees the situations of his epistemic life, and all this cognition is aimed at the epistemic goods. The intellectually firm agent thinks in terms of the new and the old in his own intellectual life, making judgments about, and seeing, how to adjust to the new by adjusting the old. The intellectually courageous or cautious agent thinks in terms of risks and potential harms, with an eye to the goods that risky acts may garner and the harms that cautious acts may avoid. The humble individual is such by *failing* to think in terms of status, prestige, and domination over others, and by *not* thinking about entitlements in the ways characteristic of arrogance; and is thus freed in various ways to think more clearly in terms intrinsic to the intellectual practices. The autonomous individual thinks about and sees epistemic situations in terms of actual and potential hetero-regulators of his thought and practice. The generous agent thinks in terms of the intellectual well-being of others and ways in which he can contribute to that well-being. Each of these departments of practical intellectual thought picks up on aspects of the situations—psychological, social, and epistemic—that confront, nearly daily, anyone who is intellectually active.

Many epistemic situations lend themselves to thinking in patterns deriving from more than one of these departments. It is not hard to see that full excellence of intellectual practice over a long stretch of one's life requires excellent practical thought in all these areas. Practical wisdom consists in both the patterns of thought and perception characteristic of the specific virtues (each of these having its own brand of practical wisdom) and also the unification of all these patterns, a facility for switching from one to another as occasion requires, for blending the considerations characteristic of one virtue with those of others, and for adjudicating between the different appeals of virtues when they seem to conflict. While the special virtues are keyed to kinds of situations or aspects of epistemic situations, practical wisdom and love of knowledge are general virtues, having situational universality. In Chapter 6 we stressed that the virtuous lover of knowledge discriminates in favor of worthy knowledge and discriminates the worthiness of knowledge, in part, by its connection to human well-being more broadly conceived. An analogous thought with respect to our current topic is that completely general practical wisdom is a disposition to adjudicate well, in the concrete circumstances of life, between the concerns characteristic of intellectual practices and more broadly human concerns. For example, the practically wise person would judge excellently of situations in which the demands of research compete with those of family life.

Because of practical wisdom's participation in all the virtues, the following discussion will serve as a review of Part II, in a somewhat new key.

Practical Wisdom in the Virtues

Let us now look at some examples from earlier chapters, freely improvising on the examples to consider how practical wisdom figures in and among the virtues.

Philip Rightmire is a palaeoanthropologist working on the site in Dmanisi, the Republic of Georgia, where a recently discovered hominid skull about 1.75 million years old has invited deep revisions in the current account of human origins. Scientists like Rightmire previously thought that a large brain and symmetrically shaped, standardized stone tools were necessary for hominid migration out of Africa into Eurasia. They also thought that such migration did not occur until about 500,000 years later than the age of the Dmanisi skull. The hominid discovered there had a brain smaller (600 cc as compared with about 1,200 cc for modern humans) than was thought needed to sustain exploration, and was surrounded by simple stone tools characteristic of more primitive hominids previously found only in Africa. So it looks as though stupider, smaller, and less well equipped people accomplished the feat of migration and did so earlier than scientists previously thought, calling into question several of the earlier scientific explanations of migration. This epistemic situation calls on the resources of firmness, that is, on wise response in terms of holding fast or loose to established beliefs, understandings, and perceptual dispositions.

The reader may remember that in Chapter 7 we compared Rightmire, who seemed "almost gleeful" about his theoretical world's having been turned upside down, with another scientist, who commented, with anything but glee, that "They ought to put [the skull] back in the ground."

And we noted that the spirit of intellectual adventure suggested by Rightmire's glee is intellectually healthy and an aspect of the virtue that we call firmness. But it would not reflect practical epistemic wisdom if Rightmire had no conservative streak at all in his scientific thinking—if he *simply* sought and took delight in the destruction of his own latest constructs. And Rightmire has been quoted as saying, "It's nice that everything's been shaken up, but frustrating that some of the ideas that seemed so promising eight to 10 years ago don't hold up anymore."[2] So Rightmire's love of knowledge moves him not only to be excited about new possibilities of knowledge, but to want to settle some questions, and to feel disappointment when promising avenues dead-end. This motivation will lead him to deliberate ways to revise his construction of the early history of human beings so as rightly to preserve what was excellent in it while taking full account of the new, anomalous information. If he has good powers of deliberation between these complementary poles of the old and the new, then he has, with respect to the domain of firmness, the virtue that we call intellectual practical wisdom. Generally good judgment about hold will not be enough to make an excellent palaeoanthropologist. Intellectual skill specific to his field and subfield—its standards of error and accuracy, of sufficiency of evidence, etc., as well as a great deal of information assimilated into a scheme of understanding—will need to be incorporated; the virtue emerges only in the context of discipline-specific skills. Rightmire's practical wisdom will also have a perceptual dimension, which we judge to be very important where the work involves looking at what are often very degraded pieces of things so as to picture them filled out with their other parts. The perceptual wisdom characteristic of firmness will be a flexible capacity of vision enabling the clear perception of anomalies but also an imaginative and intelligent integration of the anomalous feature into the older construct when possible, and good sense for when such integration is not really working. Firmness is a kind of strategy for getting and keeping intellectual goods, and its own wisdom is the rationality or rule of that strategy as embodied in the character of an individual.

Now consider the university president imagined by Glenn Loury, discussed in Chapter 5. This president wants to know, and wants his

---

[2] Quoted in Kate Wong, "Stranger in a New Land", *Scientific American*, Nov. 2003: 74–83, p. 82.

community to know, whether withdrawing investments from South African businesses is a good way for the university to advance the struggle
against apartheid, and he thinks that understanding the issues requires open
public debate. This judgment is a deliverance of intellectual practical wisdom, expressing the virtue of epistemic caution. From long experience in
intellectual practices, this president knows that unanticipated insights can
emerge from intense, learned debate of issues, insights that are very unlikely
to be gained in any other way; and because he loves knowledge, he wants
debate. But he also wants to stay on the good side of the students (both
for personal reasons and to keep the lines of pedagogic communication
open), and he knows that the strictures of political correctness among
the students make it probable that his reputation as a good liberal will
be compromised if he invites to campus strong and intelligent dissenters
from divestiture to join the debate. This judgment too expresses wisdom, a
practical acquaintance with the spirit of the campus and an understanding of
the immature student mind, as well as an intuitive or explicit understanding
of the principles governing what Loury calls "meaning-in-effect". (We
commented in Chapter 5 that Loury's essay can serve as a primer in this
area of intellectual practical wisdom.)

This president also knows himself: namely, that he has too strong a
repugnance to being in disfavor with the students, and one that has led him
to judge poorly and act weakly in the past. Another factor in his practical
wisdom is that he cares about the students and believes them to be not foes
or masters but young persons in process of formation and need of guidance.
He knows how to act with gentleness regarding their foibles and excesses,
and knows too that such behavior tends to keep communication with
them open, though sometimes his defensiveness submerges this gentleness
and he sees them as foes. He knows this and struggles to keep the gentle
attitude in his thought and action, and to control his defensiveness. He has
learned some strategies of self-management that enable him to do this, and
his knowledge of these strategies is also part of his practical wisdom in the
interest of epistemic goods. This president's practical wisdom, as applied
to intellectual contexts, trades on, balances, and blends the considerations
characteristic of a diversity of particular virtues—courage, caution, self-
control, gentleness, friendliness, love of truth and understanding, generous
concern for the students—making for nuanced judgments and perceptions
in the developing circumstances of the day's work.

Think next about G. E. Moore, whom we discussed as exemplifying a certain kind of intellectual humility in Chapter 9. We said that Moore's humility consisted in his being quite a bit less concerned than most people are about the social standing that philosophical competence, brilliance, or success brings to a person when others recognize it. Moore cared so little about standing, accumulated in this way, that he employed none of the usual strategies for securing recognition: parading successes, enhancing the impression of competence, camouflaging weaknesses, failures, and changes of mind, and so forth. This selective insouciance freed him to focus his attention on pursuing the epistemic goods, made him more receptive to correction, and widened the population of his potential teachers. Humility would not be recognized as a virtue (or any kind of trait at all) if human beings were not so widely susceptible to vanity, arrogance, domination, and other anti-humility vices. It is a quite "negative" virtue, consisting in the absence of certain dysfunctional patterns of concern, thought, and action. So we might be inclined to think that it does not, like the other virtues we have been examining, have its own department of practical wisdom, its own patterns of judgment, deliberation, and perception. But by the same token that we think of humility as a virtue, despite its negativity, we can think of it as having its department of wisdom. In the context of the general run of philosophers and professors, Moore is striking for his *not* deliberating on how to enhance his standing, and for his *not* seeing retracting a statement he made yesterday as a cause for embarrassment. This not-deliberating and not-seeing surely is a cognitive pattern, and an excellent one. It is true that this pattern was not hard-won in Moore's case, if his contemporaries are to be believed,[3] and so does not have the voluntariness that some people regard as a necessary condition for a trait's being a virtue. But this pattern might be voluntary. A person might, on seeing vanity and arrogance in himself, undertake certain disciplines not to think and act in those patterns, and thus come, by degrees, not to think in them. (There is a paradox about willing not-to-think and not-to-see in specified ways, if we think of the context as temporally short, but if we stretch it out over a developmental period, the paradox disappears.) If such a person's lack of vain and arrogant deliberation and perception is wisdom,

---

[3] See Norman Malcolm, *Ludwig Wittgenstein: A Memoir*, with a biographical sketch by Georg Henrik von Wright (New York: Oxford University Press, 1958), p. 80.

then Moore's more naïve exemplification of this lack may also count as a kind of practical wisdom. This is all the more a genuine practical wisdom because Moore's humble "thinking" is in the service of his explicit and concerted thought and perceptions involved in the pursuit of intellectual goods such as the truth about truth.

In Chapter 10 we met Morris Braverman, one of the numerous "normally" autonomous individuals who miserably failed to show the practical wisdom characteristic of autonomy in the context of Stanley Milgram's obedience experiments. A few of Milgram's subjects performed well, however. Particularly interesting is the one Milgram designates as "Professor of Old Testament". He was a subject in the Proximity condition—that is, with the "learner" present in the same room as the "teacher". This arrangement offered him a way to keep himself well informed of the state of the learner during the procedure, and the professor availed himself of this advantage: "he adjusted his seat to look at the learner while administering shocks."[4] This is in strong contrast with several other subjects, who seemed inattentive to the learner's state because they were so preoccupied with asking the questions and administering the shocks in accord with the experimenter's instructions. In his desire to keep relevantly informed, in his judgment about what information is relevant, and in his knowledge of how to keep so informed, the professor shows practical epistemic wisdom.

By pre-arrangement the "learner" shows signs of increasing discomfort at shock levels between 75 and 150 volts, but at 150 volts he cries out "Experimenter, get me out of here! I won't be in the experiment any more! I refuse to go on!" (ibid., p. 23). This is the point at which the Professor refused to go on. The experimenter then told him to disregard the learner's protests, and the following dialogue ensued:

EXPERIMENTER: It's absolutely essential to the experiment that we continue.
SUBJECT: I understand that statement, but I don't understand why the experiment is placed above this person's life.
EXPERIMENTER: There is no permanent tissue damage.
SUBJECT: Well, that's your opinion. If he doesn't want to continue, I'm taking orders from him.

---

[4] Stanley Milgram, *Obedience to Authority: An Experimental View* (New York: Harper and Row, 1974), p. 47.

EXPERIMENTER: You have no other choice, sir, you must go on.
SUBJECT: If this were Russia maybe, but not in America. (ibid., p. 48)

In further discussion with the experimenter the Professor is emotionally agitated, but "seems in no way intimidated by the experimenter's status but rather treats him as a dull technician who does not see the full implications of what he is doing" (ibid.)

SUBJECT (*spontaneously*): Surely you've considered the ethics of this thing. (*extremely agitated*) Here he doesn't want to go on, and you think that the experiment is more important? Have you examined him? Do you know what his physical state is? Say this man had a weak heart (quivering voice).
EXPERIMENTER: We know the machine, sir.
SUBJECT: But you don't know the man you're experimenting on. ... That's very risky (*gulping and tremulous*). What about the fear that man had? It's impossible for you to determine what effect that has on him. ...

The Professor's emotions are appropriate. They are mostly anxiety about the well-being of the learner, though we suspect that remorse and anxiety about his own complicity in the evil scenario are involved too. These emotions are all expressions of virtues, especially compassion and conscientiousness. They are strong evaluative perceptions of their respective objects: the learner as harmed and/or subject to harm, himself as having been complicit in evil and in danger of further and deeper involvement in it. As such, the emotions are themselves wise "cognitions", exemplifications of the practical wisdom characteristic of each of these virtues.

The reader will remember that Morris Braverman, who "shocked" the learner all the way to 450 volts, had similar emotions, which were expressed in giggling but had no other consequence in his behavior. The difference is that the Professor is less impressed with the experimenter's authority. If he is initially disposed to feel respect for the experimenter as a scientist in a great university, he pretty quickly puts this emotion in the perspective of the whole situation, so that it fades. He is aided in this by his critical disposition to subject ostensible authorities to evaluation. He asks, as it were, whether this person, who at first blush appears to be competent and operating within the bounds of his authority, is actually competent and authoritative in what he is demanding. Braverman, by contrast, remains confused by his conflicting emotions and is carried along "helplessly" by the inertia of the situation. He seems not to have a strong practical sense of the limits of authorities—or at least, of *this* authority. The difference between Braverman and the Professor may be, in part, that the Professor, being a colleague at Yale, is more aware of the fallibility of Yale professors than Braverman, who is a social worker.

Milgram appears to want to minimize the Professor's autonomy and practical wisdom. He describes him as "officious" and "fastidious" and makes him out, paradoxically enough, to be too concerned with obeying orders. He points out that "he initially justified his breaking off the experiment not by asserting disobedience but by asserting that he would then take orders from the victim" (ibid., p. 49). The Professor was asked what he thought to be the best way to strengthen a person's resistance to inhumane authority, and he answered that a person whose ultimate authority is God is less impressed with human authorities. And Milgram comments, "Again, the answer for this man lies not in the repudiation of authority but in the substitution of good—that is, divine—authority for bad" (ibid.). But on the analysis of autonomy that we offered in Chapter 10, the correction for servility is not a disposition to repudiate authority, but a disposition to respect authorities in and only in their proper domains—thus to make wise judgments, *in situ*, concerning such domains. And the Professor's point is that a person who respects God as the final moral authority will be freer to see when human authorities have overstepped their domains, and freer also to act on that perception or judgment.[5] As we have pointed out repeatedly in this book, virtues must be indexed to world views. In a theistic world view it makes perfectly good sense to think that autonomy of judgment is compatible with taking God to be the ultimate moral authority.

What, then, are the ingredients in the Professor's practical wisdom, as shown in this exemplification of autonomy? First, he showed epistemic wisdom in positioning himself for maximal relevant information: he did this with skill, with good judgment about which information was important for him to have, and was motivated by the desire to know and to act on good information. Second, he showed good judgment about competing values. As soon as he saw that the experimental subject was in serious distress, he saw that the value of the experiment did not match the value of

---

[5] John Benson cites Bruno Bettelheim as reporting that, in the Nazi concentration camps, the Jehovah's Witnesses were one of the two groups best able to keep their integrity in the face of Nazi "authority". See "Who Is the Autonomous Man?", *Philosophy* 58 (1983): 5–17, pp. 16–17.

the subject's well-being, and disobeyed the authority who was expressing an opposing priority. Third, he showed a proper epistemic caution about the ostensible authority's claims to know what he was doing and offered arguments against them. Such arguments are often an epistemically wise course even if the one who proposes them is not convinced by them, since they elicit further information about how competent the alleged authority is. Fourth, the Professor's virtues of compassion and conscientiousness make him perceive clearly, via his emotions, features of the situation that he needs to perceive to make an all-things-considered judgment about the purported authority's legitimacy. And fifth, the Professor's respect for a moral authority that transcends all human authority appears to free him from being overly impressed with any human authority, and thus frees him to judge and perceive accurately the value of the human authority's pronouncements and directives. These, then, are the ingredients of the case, and give us some idea of the elements of the practical wisdom that goes with the virtue of intellectual autonomy.

Jane Goodall, the ethologist discussed briefly at the end of Chapter 5, provides our final case. She illustrates some features of practical wisdom as it connects with the virtue of intellectual generosity. Before we turn to generosity, however, we note that Goodall was from early on a sort of "philosopher", a person with an impulse to put the most important things she knew into an overall perspective. Yet the perspective that she gradually worked out was not merely theoretical, but action- and passion-guiding, designed to determine her conduct and make emotional sense of her experiences. In her book *Reason for Hope*,[6] she gives an account of the development and character of this outlook to which her scientific activities contributed and from which they made a kind of eudaimonistic sense to her. The "practicality" of this perspective is suggested by her account of its origins:

Looking back, I see clearly that my own personal philosophy was gradually molded during those first two decades by my family, my schooling, my living through the war, my years of listening to extremely powerful sermons; also by the books I read, the hours I spent outside in the natural world, and by the animals who shared our house. Now the *Kenya Castle* [the ship she took to Africa at age 26] was carrying

---

[6] Jane Goodall, with Phillip Berman, *Reason for Hope: A Spiritual Journey* (New York: Warner Books, 1999).

me forward into a new world, where the lessons would be taught by life itself in all its wonderful, sometimes tragic, often harsh, inconsistencies and surprises. And I could move into this new era without fear, for I was equipped, by my family and by my education, with sound moral values and an independent, free-thinking mind. (p. 40)

As is typical of practical wisdom, this rich moral–intellectual–emotional formation oriented Goodall to action in ways that were often intuitive— spontaneous situational expressions of her nature, rather than deliberations guided by formulas.

Louis Leakey was a palaeoanthropologist who seems also to have had a good deal of intellectual practical wisdom. Goodall so impressed him by her love of Africa and animals that he took her on as his private secretary and then surprised her by offering to make her—who had no formal training in ethology or in science—to undertake long-term field research on chimpanzees that was to inform his understanding of human origins.

I'm sure I stared at him open-mouthed. How could I possibly be considered suitable for such an important study? I had no training, no degree. But Louis didn't care about academic credentials. In fact, he told me, he preferred that his chosen researcher should go into the field with a mind unbiased by scientific theory. What he had been looking for was someone with an open mind, with a passion for knowledge, with a love of animals, and with monumental patience. Someone, moreover, who was hardworking and would be able to stay long periods away from civilization, for he believed the study would take several years. (ibid., p. 55)

Here is a case of intellectual autonomy—rational judgment concerning the value of credentials standards and intellectual tradition as hetero–regulators in the particular context of choosing a research captain. Leakey's judgment seems to be based on a discernment of just the personal qualities that Goodall mentions, plus an appreciation of their value in the pursuit of this partic- ular research. Here was another person whose judgments concerning the practice of science were based in a broader set of intuitive and deliberative dispositions.

From early on in her life, Goodall felt an affection for animals that impelled her to close observational acquaintance with individual members of species. This judgment, at first intuitive and then ever more justi- fied by accumulated acquaintance, of the complexity, intelligence, and beauty of animal behavior served her well in generating new knowledge of chimpanzees. In a period when ethologists tended stingily, human-chauvinistically, to exaggerate the intelligence gap between us and our fellow mammals, Goodall's liberality with the credit she gave other animals supported a patience in observation that yielded much propositional knowledge and understanding.

As I got to know [the chimpanzees] as individuals I named them. I had no idea that this, according to the ethological discipline of the early 1960s, was inappropriate—I should have given them more objective numbers. I also described their vivid personalities—another sin: only humans had personalities. It was an even worse crime to attribute humanlike emotions to the chimpanzees. And in those days it was held (at least by many scientists, philosophers, and theologians) that only humans had minds, only humans were capable of rational thought. Fortunately I had not been to university, and I did not know these things. And when I did find out, I just thought it was silly and paid no attention. ... How right Louis had been to send someone to the field with a mind uncluttered by the theory of reductionist, oversimplistic, mechanistic science. (ibid., p. 74)

Her generosity of spirit towards the chimpanzees also supported an unorthodox but epistemically fruitful empathy.

In order to collect good, scientific data, one is told, it is necessary to be coldly objective. You record accurately what you see and, above all, you do not permit yourself to have any empathy with your subjects. Fortunately I did not know that during the early months at Gombe. A great deal of my understanding of these intelligent beings was built up just *because* I felt such empathy with them. (ibid., p. 77; italics original)

This empathy, begotten of generosity, not only earned Goodall the trust of the animals she was studying, but brought still other virtues, such as humility and gratitude, with their constitutive practical wisdom, into play:

A sudden shower of twigs and the thud of an overripe fig close to my head shattered the magic. David [David Greybeard, one of her favorites] was swinging down through the branches. Slowly I sat up, reluctant to return to the everyday world. David reached the ground, moved a few paces toward me, and sat. For a while he groomed himself, then lay back, one hand under his head, utterly relaxed, and gazed up toward the green ceiling above our heads. The gentle breeze rustled the leaves so that the shining stars of light gleamed and winked. And as I sat there, keeping vigil, I thought, as I have thought so often since, what an amazing privilege it was—to be utterly accepted thus by a wild, free animal. It is a privilege I shall never take for granted. ... Most primates interpret a direct gaze as a threat; it is not so with chimpanzees. David had taught me that so long as I looked into his eyes without arrogance, without any request, he did not mind. And sometimes he gazed back at me as he did that afternoon. His eyes seemed almost like windows through which, if only I had the skill, I could look into his mind. How many times since that far-off day I have wished that I could, even if just for a few short moments, look out onto the world through the eyes, with the mind, of a chimpanzee. One such minute would be worth a lifetime of research. For we are human-bound, imprisoned within our human perspective, our human view of the world. Indeed, it is even hard for us to see the world from the perspective of cultures other than our own, or from the point of view of a member of the opposite sex. (ibid., pp. 79–81)

Goodall goes on to tell of the insights into the developmental psychology of mother–child attachment that she garnered from observing, comparing, and recording generations of chimpanzee mothering behavior and its differential consequences in the personalities of the offspring. She includes a chimpanzee in the list of her tutors in mothering: "In the end I raised my own son on a mixture of wisdom gleaned from Vanne [Goodall's mother], Flo [a particularly wise chimpanzee mother], Dr. Spock—and mother nature" (p. 89). And she talks about how having a child of her own gave her insights into the anger of a chimpanzee whose little one was threatened.

As we noted at the end of Chapter 5, Goodall saw that only if her research team freely pooled their data and insights could the enormous project of documenting and understanding the Gombe chimpanzees approximate completion. Thus the impulse to have these intellectual goods, along with the practical judgment that the task could not be accomplished by any single individual and that it would be accomplished only slowly and inefficiently if individuals took a stingy or greedy competitive attitude with one another, implied the practice of generosity that Goodall inspired in the young people on her research team, and the happy spirit of generous sharing that she describes in *Through a Window*. For Goodall, the students who worked for her were not just sources of information. She cultivated them as independent researchers. She trained Tanzanians so that they could carry on the work without her. Where a more dominating mentor would be anxious to nurture disciples, Goodall trained scholars to autonomy. Her goal was to bring the knowledge of the chimpanzees into the world, for all to have. And she saw that this end was best accomplished by making others intellectually independent.

Goodall wanted knowledge of the chimps not only to be created; she wanted it to be widely distributed. Another wise choice she made, expressive of her intellectual generosity, was to spend a portion of every year writing, lecturing, and making film and television presentations of her work whereby she shared it with the larger world. Towards these three parties, then—the chimpanzees, her fellow scientists, and the interested world at large—Jane Goodall directed her intellectual generosity, and in each case her choices were governed by practical intelligence.

Conclusion: Epistemology as Practical Wisdom

We began this book with reflections about the nature of epistemology. In the interest that some epistemologists have recently shown in the intellectual virtues, we saw an opportunity to think of and practice epistemology in a new way. Whereas the founders of the recent movement have used the concept of a virtue to answer the routine late twentieth-century questions about justification and warrant, we have made the virtue concepts themselves the focus of our study, digging down into their interior to see what we could find. Focusing on the nature of the traits that make a person an excellent epistemic agent, we have adopted a different teleology of epistemological reflection. We aim not to produce a theory of justification, warrant, knowledge, or rationality; nor are we trying to answer the skeptic. Instead, we have aimed to use the virtues as the focus of reflections to increase our practical understanding of the inner workings of the intellectual life. Like earlier epistemologists, we have analyzed concepts; but, unlike most of the recent ones, our purpose in this has been less to produce an epistemological theory than to generate understanding of the epistemic agent and thereby to guide practice. Clearly, such guidance is not a set of action rules: do this and that, and don't do that and this. It is more in the nature of a map of a personality ideal whereby one might come to see where one stands, relative to one or another set of coordinates of the ideal.

The guidance that this trait analysis provides is not of the sort that any particular science or course of study provides for its practitioners. If you are a chemist or an ethologist or an interpreter of Victorian literature, clearly our epistemology is no substitute for apprenticeship in your particular discipline. Yet we think that it is relevant to any discipline, and ought to be of interest to anyone who seriously seeks to acquire or transmit knowledge. Epistemology, as it has been done in a variety of ways across the ages, has almost always aspired to be meta-disciplinary, and ours is no exception. The virtues we have explored—love of knowledge, firmness, courage and caution, humility, autonomy, generosity, and practical wisdom—are excellences across the disciplines.

In the present chapter we have argued that intellectual practical wisdom is the power of good perception and judgment that an agent needs to exemplify the particular intellectual virtues in the contexts of intellectual practices. If this is correct, then one might see the function of this book as an attempt to *formulate* intellectual practical wisdom. As we saw in the second section of this chapter, the situational and improvisatory character of practical wisdom prevents its capture in any formula. So any formula will be at best imprecise and suggestive. Yet articulating formulas is what analysis consists in. The reader will also notice that the analyses of the virtues in Part II, as well as a sizable portion of Part I, supplement the more abstract formulas with narrative examples, often employing such examples as loci for the analyses themselves. And we think that this combination of abstract analysis and narrative fragments is exactly the kind of discourse that is best suited to formulate practical wisdom.

Index

44409977R00189

Made in the USA
Lexington, KY
29 August 2015